CZECHS AND GERMANS

A STUDY OF THE
STRUGGLE IN THE HISTORIC
PROVINCES OF BOHEMIA
AND MORAVIA

BY

ELIZABETH WISKEMANN

OXFORD UNIVERSITY PRESS
LONDON : NEW YORK : TORONTO

*Issued under the auspices of the Royal Institute
of International Affairs*

1938

Printed in the United States of America

PREFACE

THIS book was undertaken at the invitation of the Royal Institute of International Affairs as the third in a series of studies initiated by the Institute on the practical results of the territorial provisions of the Peace Settlement in problematical areas. The previous volumes in the series were *The Peace Settlement in the German-Polish Borderlands*, by Ian F. D. Morrow, and *Hungary and Her Successors*, by C. A. Macartney. The present study has been precipitately overtaken by the rushing course of events; the German annexation of Austria in March 1938 transformed the Central European situation just as the book was going to press, and must, I fear, help to account for statements which may become suddenly obsolete. It is impossible for me to attempt to cover developments since March 1938. I can only hope that my work will help to provide some explanatory background to the eight Henleinist demands made at Carlsbad on April 24th and to any consequences which these demands may precede.

A word of explanation seems necessary as to my use of place-names. Here the need to hasten publication has prevented consistent revision. I intended always to use the language of the majority in any town or district at the period about which I was writing, with the alternative name in brackets. In the historical chapters, however, the German names alone have often been used, not as indicative of the majority in such and such a century, but rather on account of their naturally greater familiarity to an English public. No political implication whatever is intended. I have only had the opportunity to acquire a distant familiarity with Czech, and am only too well aware that this lays me open to criticism.

It would be difficult to find an adequate way to thank every one who has helped me to gather the material for this book. From officials and laymen, from Czechs and Germans throughout the Historic Provinces, I have encountered unwearying kindness. I want also to use this opportunity to thank every one concerned at Chatham House, and, in addition, one or two personal friends without whose sympathy it would have been very much more difficult to have written the book to its end.

It should perhaps be repeated that only I am responsible for the statements made and the opinions expressed.

April, 1938.   ELIZABETH WISKEMANN.

CONTENTS

MAPS

CHAPTER I

BEFORE THE WHITE MOUNTAIN

BOHEMIA and Moravia, with Southern Silesia, the Historic Provinces of the Bohemian Crown, lie at the very heart of Europe, on the road from Vienna to Dresden, or from Munich to Breslau or Cracow. Mountains and forests hem in their richness and their beauty. For Nature wished well by Bohemia; if she could not make real Shakespeare's sea-coast, she nevertheless enriched her with variety and fertility, with mineral wealth and water-power. This lavishness has, however, been constantly counteracted by the destructive forces of racial passion, forces which have become more conscious and therewith more aggressive as the centuries have passed. For Bohemia long ago became the battle-ground *par excellence* between the Germans and the Slavs. In the Historic Provinces they came to find themselves living within common frontiers, yet often engaged in the bitterest struggles as to whose authority was to be accepted as supreme in the land. The political problems of the twentieth century are so much complicated by the chauvinistic distortion of history that it becomes important not only to study the strange disguises poor Clio must wear, but also to try somehow to catch a glimpse of her features beneath all the masks, and perhaps to feel for a moment her own steady gaze.

The problems of Central and Eastern Europe are proverbially unintelligible in the west, because various races live there in an odd mosaic pattern, in medieval disregard of the territorial conventions which, since the days of the Renaissance, have prevailed in the west. German settlers have everywhere created a political complication, because, arriving whether in the twelfth or the sixteenth or the eighteenth century, they have—unlike the Flemish weavers or the French Protestants who came to England—refused to be assimilated, on the general grounds that they were socially more advanced. To the Slavs, among whom they mostly settled, they appeared as invaders and robbers, though rigid frontiers were perhaps only erected long after the German colonists had appeared.

In Bohemia[1] the Slav-German conflict has, all through history, been particularly intense. This is not to be explained simply by the wealth of the country, nor by the importance of its position, which is said to have provoked most great men into classic utter-

---

[1] Bohemia is the most important of the Historic Provinces, and is often used in a loose way to stand for all three, all the more since they came to be united under the Bohemian Crown. Silesia was only added later (see below).

ances to the effect that the master of Bohemia will be master of Europe. The explanations lie rather in the dual qualities with which geography and history have endowed it. Bohemia has a striking geographical unity of its own, which draws its unwilling inhabitants into some kind of inevitable unity too. On the other hand, a country so shut away from the sea is immensely dependent upon its neighbours, if only because its rivers must cross the domains of other states before they can reach the sea. The Czechs, the Slav majority living in Bohemia, heirs, as they feel, to the Slavonic heritage of the medieval kingdom of the Přemyslids, are proud to appear as a Slavonic vanguard in central Europe. To the German Bohemians Bohemia is an ancient German land, one with the German lands of Saxony, Bavaria, and Austria. The Bohemian king was chief among the German Electors and Prague one of the greatest cities of the Holy Roman Empire of the German Nation. Indeed, to German minds the Czechs of Bohemia, in so far as they may have preserved their racial integrity, should themselves be regarded as a small minority tolerated in the midst of the wide territories where German is spoken. In its most popular form the German view of the Bohemian question is that Bohemia geographically belongs to the Germans, and that it is only unfortunate that German colonists, coming into Bohemia at different periods, did not bring with them sufficient peasants to settle in the interior of the land.[1] The popular view among the Czechs regards the whole of Bohemia, Moravia, and Silesia as an integral and historic Slav unity; the frontier districts should therefore be recaptured from the German invaders who have unjustly absorbed them. These romantic theories, repudiated though they are by diplomats or scholars on both sides, are held by many a village schoolmaster —be he Czech or German—and are eagerly accepted by his pupils.

The writer does not feel called upon to examine the early history of the Historic Provinces in detail, but it is clear that the reader, in view of such fiery controversy, will require some indication of the facts which may be regarded as fairly established. The earliest inhabitants of Bohemia and Moravia about whom anything is definitely known appear to have been Celts called Boii, and the name Bohemia (Tacitus refers to Boiohaemum) is of undisputed Celtic origin. Germanic tribes are said by Pfitzner[2] to have pushed up the Elbe across the frontier of to-day as far as Bodenbach between 300 and 100 B.C. The important change, however, came towards the end of the last pre-Christian century with the conquest and settlement of Bohemia by the German Marcomanni; a

[1] See lecture by Studienleiter Helmut Lüpke at the National Socialist History Teachers' Conference at Bremen, 1935; also J. Pfitzner, *Sudetendeutsche Geschichte* (Reichenberg, 1937), p. 26, or R. Jung, *Die Tschechen* (Berlin, 1937).

[2] Pfitzner, op. cit.

few years later the Germanic Quadi subdued Moravia and much of Slovakia. To what extent Celts and Celtic influences survived is very much disputed among historians; the Historic must at any rate be regarded as Germanic Provinces for the following four or five centuries. During the fifth century A.D. both the Marcomanni and Quadi gradually moved into Bavaria, taking the old Celtic name with them, for the word Boii had apparently developed into 'Baiowari'. After a brief Lombard interval Slavonic tribes, pushed westwards by the pressure of the Avars, appear to have settled in Bohemia and Moravia fairly extensively; Slav place-names dating from this period are even found in the Eger country in the north-west, where the population has since the twelfth century been almost exclusively German.

It is probably correct to regard the period from the sixth to the twelfth century as a period when the inhabitants of Bohemia and Moravia were almost entirely Slav, although the geography of the activities of a famous ruler named Samo in the seventh or eighth century is disputed. Towards the end of the ninth century Svatopluk (870–94) was the greatest of the rulers of a Great Moravian Empire which included Western Slovakia and very probably Bohemia,[1] and is thought to have extended into Silesia, Galicia, and Pannonia. But early in the tenth century Great Moravia was destroyed by the Hungarians, who overran Slovakia and held it from the eleventh to the twentieth century. This Moravian realm had constituted the very cross-roads of Europe, for in the ninth century it seemed for a time as if it would be absorbed into the Byzantine world with the arrival in 863 of the Greek missionaries, Cyril and Methodius.[2] It is difficult to estimate their actual success, since the only historians of the time were later supplied by their adversaries of the Roman Catholic Church. At all events Cyril and Methodius died relatively soon, and the Magyars cut off the Moravians from the East. Proximity and organization had already favoured western competition, and as early as 845, fourteen Czech nobles were baptized at the court of King Louis the German in Bavaria. Early in the tenth century the holy St. Wenceslas, as King of Bohemia and Moravia, was the ardent supporter of the German representatives of the Roman Church, and in 973 Prague became a bishopric under the archbishopric of Mainz.

[1] According to C. A. Macartney, *Hungary and Her Successors* (London, 1937), it has never been actually proved that Great Moravia extended west of the river Morava; Professor Bretholz produced evidence, however, that it did—see *Geschichte Böhmens und Mährens bis zum Aussterben der Přemysliden* (Reichenberg, 1921–5), p. 48.

[2] Cyril and Methodius were in touch with Rome as well as Byzantium. See Wostry (*Zeitschrift für Sudetendeutsche Geschichte*, May 1937, p. 24) and other authorities.

It was through the success of the Roman Church that German influences—but not yet anything much more—now extended over the lands of the crown of St. Wenceslas. The clergy, both regular and secular, were mostly German immigrants, though it can never be too often emphasized that the language and attitude of the Roman Church and of the medieval world were Latin and cosmopolitan, and are misinterpreted and distorted out of recognition when modern national criteria are applied to them. More admittedly German were the many princesses who married kings or princes of Bohemia in the medieval period, and who brought what they could from their German homes. In quite early days, moreover, Prague, by virtue of its position, became a flourishing market which attracted the interest of German merchants; Pfitzner puts this in the tenth or at the latest in the eleventh century, when he believes that Brünn, Troppau, and Olmütz had also become commercial centres of note. In the twelfth, and increasingly in the thirteenth, century a real immigration from the neighbouring lands set in, and many Germans settled in the *Rand-Gebieten* of Bohemia which they inhabit to-day. This German movement is generally regarded by historians as part of the great eastward expansion of the Germans during the earlier medieval period. Meanwhile the Kingdom of Bohemia had been consolidated by the Přemyslid dynasty, of whom Vratislav actually received the title of king from the Emperor Henry IV in 1086. The Přemyslids welcomed German immigration, especially Ottakar II, the greatest representative of the dynasty, who ruled in the second half of the thirteenth century, and who systematically encouraged skilled craftsmen from abroad to settle in his kingdom. In the thirteenth century, moreover, the transition to a money economy brought great social changes, an interest in the copper and silver deposits in the Bohemian lands and the rapid development of life in towns. German miners were in demand, German burghers, with German civic rights guaranteed to them, were attracted by widening prospects.

Historical controversy poisons the relations of the Germans and Czechs of to-day, and one of its favourite disputes centres around the German immigrants of the thirteenth century. In 1912 Professor Bretholz of Brünn published his view to the effect that the Germans of the pre-Christian era never really left the frontier districts and that the appearance of German activities there in the twelfth and thirteenth centuries was not to be explained by immigration but rather by an indigenous development, in fact a renaissance among the direct descendants of the Marcomanni. In 1922 the Bretholz theory was effectively destroyed by Professor Wostry, History Professor at the German University of Prague, in his book

Das Kolonisationsproblem, in which he established that any German continuity between the sixth and twelfth centuries must be regarded as too trifling to matter. Though the Bretholz theory is destroyed for scholars, it continues a little to pervade the popular consciousness of the Bohemian and Moravian Germans; to the foreign observer it seems of singularly little importance to-day whether they can trace their descent six hundred or nearly two thousand years back. Academic controversy still exists as to the extent to which the *Rand-Gebieten* were settled by Slavs in the period after the Marcomanni and Quadi withdrew. Professors Hassinger[1] and Pfitzner suggest that the Slav population lived only in the rich lands of the interior and never penetrated into the hills and mountains of the frontier districts. Professor Wostry, on the other hand, while emphasizing that the population was sparse, points to all sorts of earlier Slavonic traces, and Professor Hassinger seems aware of the Slavonic inscriptions in Egerland, subsequently the most exclusively and aggressively German corner of Bohemia, if indeed Bohemia it be.[2] To the inexpert traveller the number of obviously Slavonic village names in the German districts of to-day is certainly striking, and clearly suggests German incursions into territory previously settled by Slavs, whether these incursions occurred in the thirteenth century or in the later Habsburg period.

The powerful Přemyslid dynasty died out in 1306 and was soon succeeded by the House of Luxembourg. Before his death Ottakar II, once the lord of wide dominions stretching right down into Styria, had lost all but Bohemia and Moravia. In 1335, however, Poland finally confirmed the cession of Silesia to the crown of Bohemia, so that Silesia became part of the mystical unity[3] of the lands of St. Wenceslas's crown. At this time Silesia had become strongly German, and after the great Tatar invasion which culminated in the Battle of Liegnitz in 1241, Breslau was refounded by Germans. Thus in 1335 the German element in the Historic Provinces, now grown to three, was noticeably augmented. These, moreover, were the days of remarkable German literary activity within the Kingdom of Bohemia, of which the *Ackermann aus Böhmen* by Johann of Saaz was the greatest achievement. It is sometimes asked how it was that the Germans did not at this time overwhelm and absorb the Czechs. To this the distinguished Czech historian, Jaroslav Goll, replied that the partial Germanization of the Czechs in fact saved them from complete Germanization.

[1] H. Hassinger, *Die Tschechoslowakei* (Vienna, 1925).
[2] See below Chapter XI (i) *d*.
[3] I use this phrase in no misapprehension of the fact that the Crown of Bohemia was never marked out by special gestures from the Pope as in the case of the Crown of St. Stephen. But in the minds of the Czechs the mystical unity of the Wenceslas lands became a psychological fact.

But there is more to be said than this. A few years after the acquisition of Silesia the great Charles of Luxembourg succeeded to the crown of Bohemia, and the very glorious reign which was thereby inaugurated was less Germanizing than it appeared. Since the days of Charlemagne the Czechs had acknowledged the suzerainty of the lord of the west, and in the twelfth century the King of Bohemia became the hereditary cup-bearer of the Empire with the rights of an Elector. In 1346 Charles of Bohemia became Holy Roman Emperor of the German Nation, and Prague the capital city of the Empire; the golden days of Charles IV are the happiest tradition of Bohemians, be they German or Czech. For Charles was the finest type of medieval man. Though he was brought up in France and studied at the Sorbonne, he knew and spoke Czech—he refers, incidentally, to having forgotten it during his absence in France, but Wostry speaks of the 'incontestably slavonic Bohemian (i.e. Czech) patriotism' of 'this most responsible of all Emperors'.[1] In 1348 Charles founded the first University of the Empire at Prague, with Latin, of course, as the language of instruction; students from every land were welcomed and divided up into four great sections (fortuitously referred to as nations) according to the group of countries from which they came. Meanwhile the Empire had to be administered, and the imperial chancery of Charles IV in Prague proved to be the laboratory from which High German emerged in its final form. While, on the one hand, Charles cherished the cult of the Slav Apostles, Cyril and Methodius, on the other, he called the West German, Peter Parler, from Swabia, to ennoble Prague with his architectural genius. In this loveliest period of Bohemian history, painting, too, could boast of exquisite achievement. While Parler's buildings displayed their German inspiration, the works of the Master of Třeboň and his contemporaries were strikingly French in character, with traces of Italy and Flanders about them, and yet a Czech individuality of their own. Czech fourteenth-century writers, too, were the fitting contemporaries of Johann of Saaz, such men, for instance, as Tomaš of Štítné whose exhortations (in Czech) to his children have become famous.

In the days of Charles IV Bohemia and Moravia seemed to be moving towards a very remarkable synthesis where Latin, German, and Slav influences might have blended into a unique nationality. 'Why did the Czechs and the Germans not merge into a new national formation with a new common language as occurred in similar circumstances (in England or France) in the West?', Professor Rádl asks. 'This problem has not yet been solved although it is of fundamental importance for the understanding of European

[1] Wostry, in *Zeitschrift für Sudetendeutsche Geschichte*, May 1937, p. 28 n.

history.'[1] As it was, the subjects of Charles IV seemed to be bound together only by the personality of a strong king; when this was taken from them, they fell apart. In Rádl's view Czechs and Germans failed to find a common political conception which, as he believes, constitutes the keystone to the arch of any stable nationality. And so Charles IV, too, has become the plaything of paltry chauvinists, on the one side those who declare that the *Kultur* of his Bohemia was purely German and his university German because most of its students undoubtedly spoke German in private; on the other, those who regard his reign as a time when the Empire was subjected to a Slav, and who claim the University of Prague as an inheritance for Czechs alone.

Not only posterity but also his immediate heirs were unable to appreciate the potential fertility of Charles's cosmopolitanism, and the Hussite Revolution followed within some thirty years of his death. That the foundation of the University of Prague should have stimulated theological controversy was only to be expected, but that theological differences should have split the Bohemians along racial lines provides an anachronism which is not at first sight easy to explain. All along the German immigrants of the thirteenth and fourteenth centuries had been frowned upon by the Czech nobility, who naturally disliked the wealth and strength they brought to the Crown. The celebrated example of Dalimil's chronicle,[2] written in about 1320, by a priest probably of noble family gives voice to the native Czech resentment against the incoming foreigners; frequent irritation is expressed that the Germans make no attempt to learn the language of the country they have chosen to adopt. In the university much resentment was felt that the Germans from abroad who predominated in three out of the four 'nations' could always outvote the Bohemians, until in 1409, by the famous Kutna Horá decree, the Bohemians received three votes and the foreign Germans only one. Even more virulent, perhaps, was the feeling cherished against the Germans, both Bohemian and foreign—it was often difficult to distinguish between them—by those who ranked as their social inferiors. As the towns developed the Germans remained as wealthy and privileged, the clergy still predominantly German had been further enriched by Charles IV, and the poorer Czech-speaking townspeople were ready to express their indignation against the arrogant foreigners whenever an opportunity should occur. It was the time of the

[1] E. Rádl, *Der Kampf zwischen Tschechen und Deutschen* (*Boj Čechů s Němci*) (Reichenberg, 1928).
[2] Cf. *Mitteilungen des Vereines für Geschichte der Deutschen in Böhmen*, Heft 3–4, 1915, containing 'Ein deutschfeindliches Pamphlet aus Böhmen aus dem 14ten Jahrhundert', von Dr. W. Wostry, with thirteenth- and fourteenth-century examples of the Czech feeling that as Slavs they must resist the Germans.

Papal Schism. It was a period of Papal greed and priestly corruption. A wave of protest passed across Europe. Idealists longed for a great purification. From Wyclif[1] the impulse spread to the Czech Jan Hus, yet there were Germans in Bohemia who were at first as eager for reform as the Czechs. Gradually, however, the Reform Movement became a Czech revolt against German priest and burgher, and when the Emperor Sigismund pronounced, as he was sure to do, the imperial authority to be the enemy of the rebels, Hussitism became Czech national defiance of the world. Though the Hussites were themselves divided into moderates and extremists, they successfully resisted the German crusades sent by the Empire against them, and towards the middle of the fifteenth century set up the Utraquist or moderate Hussite, George of Poděbrad, as Bohemian King.

The extraordinary achievements of the Hussites have, in their turn, become the occasion of bitterest controversy. In the eyes of the Czechs the movement represents a heroic uprising in the interests of religious truth, and a return to simplicity and social equality.[2] A devoted fanaticism enabled them to defy the whole world. To the Germans, on the other hand, whose forefathers were driven out or driven back, the Hussite Movement represents an outburst of destructive brutality, typical of the Slav races.[3] No reasonable person will deny that a great deal of destruction occurred, nor that the Czech nobility took advantage of the situation, gradually reducing the peasants to serfdom. It is, nevertheless, impossible to agree with the popular German view that Hussitism inaugurated an entirely retrograde period, when Bohemia, robbed of its German leadership, fell back into something like barbarism; Czech painting in the fifteenth century is only one of the arguments which demolish this case.

The Hussite wars brought a noticeable change in the position of the Germans in Bohemia. The tendency for German influence to expand and for the German settlements to extend was abruptly

[1] See O. Odložilík, 'Wycliffe's Influence upon Central and Eastern Europe', in *Slavonic Review*, March 1929.

[2] The sect of the Bohemian and Moravian Brethren, which grew out of Hussitism, has clung to these standards from those days to these.

[3] While German historians usually harp upon Hussite excesses, there is plenty of evidence that the Germans gave the Hussites as good as they got. The following description of events in 1419 may deserve to be quoted:

(Translated from the Latin.) In their eagerness for the aforesaid truth, they (the Germans) hunted down and handed over to the hill-dwellers, in various places within the kingdom, those priests and laymen who were zealous for the communion of the cup (i.e. the Hussites), and sold some of them for money. The German hill-dwellers (*montani Theutonici*), and especially those of them who were cruel persecutors and enemies of the lovers of Christ's truth, exposed them to various blasphemies and different kinds of punishment, and used to throw them, especially at night time, in an inhuman way into the deepest trenches ..., some alive, others decapitated. ... So great was the outburst of cruelty and ruthlessness on the part of the hill-dwellers against the faithful in Christ, that in a short time 1,600 of those who favoured the most holy cup were killed by them in pitiful fashion ..., and the tormentors were often worn out with fatigue from their butchery. (Mag. Laurentius de Březina, *De gestis et variis accidentibus regni Bohemiae, 1414–1422*, quoted in Konstantin Höfler, *Geschichtsschreiber der hussitischen Bewegung*, vol. i, p. 346.)

reversed. Towns such as Saaz, Aussig, Leitmeritz, Komotau, Budweis, Prachatitz, in Dr. Krofta's opinion,[1] from being German became predominantly Czech. The break, however, was astonishingly
short. Even before the end of the fifteenth century fresh German
immigrants were settling in towns and villages which had been
depopulated through the wars. In the sixteenth century the German element in the Historic Provinces was inevitably strengthened.
Within a century of Hus, and indeed consciously inspired by him[2]
Luther had begun to tread the same path. The Germans in Bohemia became Protestant, and with this the old bitterness between
the Czechs and the Germans for a while faded away. In 1526,
moreover, with the death of King Louis of Bohemia and Hungary
at Mohács, the Bohemian Diet elected Ferdinand of Habsburg to
be King; it insisted, of course, that Bohemia's connexion with
Austria and Hungary should consist of nothing but the fortuitous
identity of the head of each State. Thus the Czechs were drawn
towards the Northern Germans as they had never been before at
the moment when their three-century association with Austria
began, a moment when the Turkish advance created the need for
the Habsburg Empire in more or less the form in which it endured
for four centuries.

Now while the Germans as a whole cried out against Charles V
as a Spaniard, the Czechs distrusted his brother, Ferdinand, as a
German—not without substantial justification. A Habsburg King
automatically Germanized in the sixteenth century when dynastic
influences developed so much strength. Purely Czech nobles were
influenced into Germanisms by their desire to stand well at court;
the royal administration became partly German in language; land
already tended to fall into German or at any rate foreign hands.
At the beginning of the seventeenth century the Bohemian nobility,
aware of these tendencies, was determined to check them. In 1611,
when Count Dohna was delivering a message from the Emperor
to the Bohemian Diet, he was shouted down with the words: 'Let
German be spoken in Germany, but Czech in our country.'[3] In
1615 the Diet forbade the acquisition of land in Bohemia by any
one who could not speak Czech. In 1618, after a forced election
of the notoriously intolerant Habsburg heir[4] to the throne, the Diet
recanted, and thus precipitated the Thirty Years War, which
began with the catastrophic defeat of the Bohemian nobility in
1620 on the famous White Mountain outside Prague. Nineteenth-

[1] K. Krofta, *Das Deutschtum in der tschechoslowakischen Geschichte* (Prague,
1934), p. 56.   [2] Ibid., p. 64.
[3] Fischel, *Österreichisches Sprachenrecht* (Brünn, 1910), p. xv.
[4] In 1609 a guarantee of religious toleration (the so-called Letter of Majesty)
had been extracted from the Emperor Rudolf, but it was notorious that Ferdinand of Styria, his heir, would repudiate all promises of the kind.

century historians of the Gothic Revival mentality have encouraged
the Czechs to regard 1620 as the year of their national martyrdom,
and to believe in the theory of a brutal German tyrant who stamped
out parliamentary government together with religious freedom,
and distributed the land of the nation among German plunderers.
In fact the conflict was one between a Catholic absolutism and a
Protestant oligarchy.[1] The Bohemians had rejected the cosmopolitan Habsburg in order to place on their throne the German,
Frederick of the Palatinate, in 1618; in 1620 the Habsburg victor
executed German, along with Czech, Bohemian rebels. In 1627
an Imperial Decree[2] only put German upon the same footing as
Czech for all official purposes, and the integrity of the administration of the Historic Provinces was not destroyed until 1749.[3]

And yet much in the anti-German White Mountain legend is
true. The Czech nobility was so sternly dealt with that the nation
was left without leaders, and, as the result of large-scale emigration, Czech became a language spoken only by peasants and workmen. The confiscated estates were distributed among people of
any nationality provided the Emperor regarded them as his reliable
servants; in fact these foreigners, who depended upon a German
court, were easily Germanized and Germanizing. And right up
to the collapse of Austria-Hungary in 1918, Bohemia and Moravia
presented a remarkably feudal face to the world, with their vast
noble properties dating largely from this time, and their land-
hungry peasants. Although after the end of the Thirty Years War
more German peasants and workmen were brought in from Austria,
from Bavaria, and from Swabia to settle in the desperately depopulated areas, the general effect of the upheavals of the seventeenth century was to create a state of affairs in which the upper
social strata were German and the lower were Czech. Thus, the
outlines of the social question of the nineteenth century were beginning to appear. In the view of Dr. Krofta and other authorities,
the territory inhabited by Germans in Bohemia and Moravia increased during the seventeenth century so that by 1700 the language
frontiers were drawn for some two hundred years. Saaz, Prachatitz,
Krumau became mainly German again in the seventeenth century;
in 1650 the first German names appeared in the records of the
district of Pilsen, and it was after 1700 that Mies and Leitmeritz
were Germanized.

[1] Professor Šusta has pointed out that it had much in common with that
between Philip II and the Netherlands.
[2] The famous *Verneuerte Landesordnung*.
[3] Cf. Kramář, *Poznámky o české politice* (*Anmerkungen zur böhmischen
Politik*) (Prague, 1906).

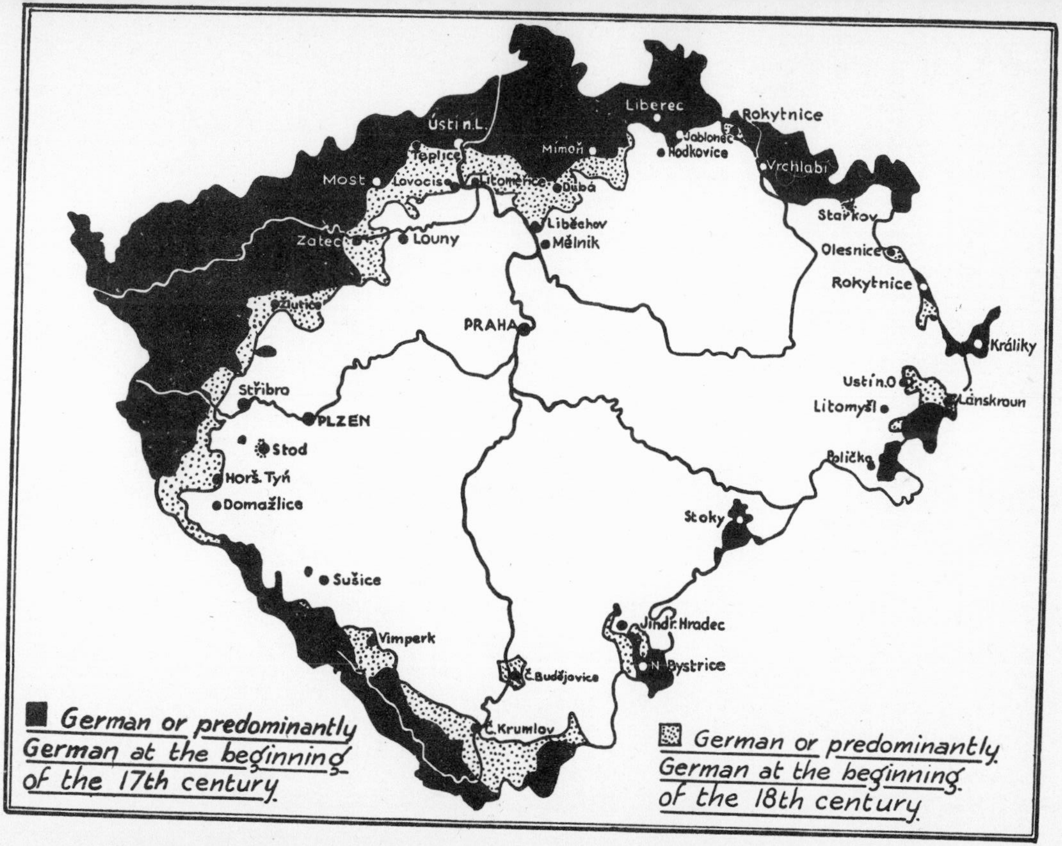
Ústi n.L.
Liberec
Rokytnice
Jablonec
Hodkovice
Mimoň
Teplice
Most
Lovocis
Litoměřice
Dubá
Vrchlabí
Starkov
Libĕchov
Mělnik
Zatec
Louny
Olesnice
Rokytnice
Žlutice
PRAHA
Králiky
Ustí n.O
Lanskroun
Litomyšl
Stříbro
PLZEN
Stod
Polička
Horš. Tyn
Domažlice
Stoky
Sušice
Jindr. Hradec
Vimperk
N. Bystrice
Č. Budějovice
Č. Krumlov
German or predominantly German at the beginning of the 17th century
German or predominantly German at the beginning of the 18th century

DEVELOPMENT OF GERMAN SETTLEMENTS IN BOHEMIA, 1700–1800

CHAPTER II

'AUFKLÄRUNG' AND ROMANTIC REVIVAL

WITH the installation of an alien aristocracy the Jesuits sprang into the saddle and the Counter-Reformation, which had driven out the Bohemian Brethren and their great educationist, Komenský, endeavoured to stamp out the last traces of Hus. John of Nepomuk was canonized in 1729 to be made into Bohemia's local saint. Meanwhile magnificent baroque buildings enriched the land, culminating perhaps in the glories of the Dientzenhofer church of St. Nicolas, completed by the younger Dientzenhofer, whose family had come in from Franconia, but who was himself born in Prague. To Dr. Krofta, Bohemian baroque is a clearly Czechified baroque and therefore illustrates the vitality of the Czech spirit in adversity, but many critics[1] will question this view and find in the eighteenth-century buildings of Bohemia little essentially different from the work of Fischer von Erlach, Hildebrand, and the rest.

The eighteenth century now brought enlightened despotism with it, that is to say Viennese centralization, Government interest in education and economic development; it brought also a further series of wars, and, incidentally, the loss of part of the St. Wenceslas heritage to Frederick the Great, to whom Glatz and the major part of Silesia were ceded. All these things contributed, posthumously rather than immediately, to Czech hostility towards the Habsburg dynasty. The Empress Maria Theresa (1740–80) and her eldest son, Joseph II, who reigned with and after her (dying in 1790), were perhaps the two most admirable examples of the *prince eclairé* of the century, and strove unceasingly and intelligently to improve the conditions in which their subjects—of whatever race —had to live. In the effort to simplify and speed up the cumbrous administrative machine of her various principalities Maria Theresa united the administration of Austria and Bohemia. In 1749 the Bohemian Chancery was removed from Prague and absorbed in the Viennese government offices, and this constituted the first frank invasion of the guaranteed rights of the crown of St. Wenceslas. Inspired by the new French notions of the potential equality of every human being, the Habsburg Government now sponsored the beginnings of public education. The claims of administrative efficiency, and the need to compete with Frederick's Prussia, combined with a rationalistic inclination to underestimate primitive emotional forces; a unilingual policy was therefore adopted for the

[1] Cf. Professor J. Pekař, *Smysl Českých Dějin* (1936).

new schools, and if a living language must be chosen, it could but
be German. Maria Theresa was far too practically shrewd to try
to eliminate the non-German languages spoken in her various
dominions; after all, the Bohemian Diet still issued some patents
in Czech[1] and the new bureaucracy must in Bohemia and Moravia
know something of Czech if it wished to be understood by the
poorer people. The Empress therefore introduced the study of
Czech at the University of Vienna in 1775; the celebrated schools
law of the previous year, which made German more and more into
the language of instruction in most of the elementary schools,[2] and
the law abolishing Czech in the grammar schools in 1780,[3] were
intended as measures of general practical advantage. But public
education thus created, in its modern form, that language question
which was to embitter the political life of the nineteenth, and
indeed of the twentieth, century. Joseph II, who believed that
half-measures were a betrayal of mankind, in 1784 decreed German
as the official language of all his Empire but Galicia and the
Italian-speaking provinces; all lectures at the University of Prague
must now be delivered no longer in Latin but in German. But
Joseph, lover of the peasants, was no deliberate denationalizer.
Mankind or the State were the conceptions of his time, for
modern nationalistic principles had scarcely been formulated—to
Joseph they would have seemed to represent only a provincial
obscurantism.

Just as centralization and public education in practice meant
Germanization, so Government interest in economic development
brought an active encouragement to the further immigration of
Germans into Bohemia and Moravia, if they were prepared to
found industries. German textile manufacturers had been encouraged under Charles VI (1711–40), and the concerns established at Eger, Rumburg, Reichenberg, Trautenau were reinforcing
a non-Czech patriciate and already creating a divergence of interest between the German industrial fringes and the Czech agricul-

---

[1] Kerner, *Bohemia in the Eighteenth Century* (New York, 1932).

[2] The wording of this great piece of legislation is ill defined, but it speaks
always of the provisions to be made for the German schools as if there were
no others. The whole inference is that German shall gradually be introduced
in the elementary schools (*Trivialschulen*) as extensively as is practicable. While
Czech was usually retained in the lower classes the rapid extension of the use
of German in the Bohemian elementary schools is shown in *Geschichte der
Theresianischen Schulreform in Böhmen*, compiled from the reports from the
schools between 1777 and 1792 by Anton Weiss (1906). Cf. also Šafránek,
Školy České (1913).

The Bohemian schools developed with exceptional rapidity in the later eighteenth century, thanks to the zeal of the priest Ferdinand Kindermann, who
was put in charge of Bohemian education by Maria Theresa.

[3] In 1770 it was decreed that German was to replace Latin in the grammar
or secondary schools.

tural interior of Bohemia.[1] Meanwhile the German language frontier was pushing steadily forward, especially around Mies and Leitmeritz. Apart from many years of war, the loss of so much of Silesia was a heavy blow to the Historic Provinces, not only because of the Silesian industry which passed to Prussia, but because Silesia had been something of the middleman for Bohemia and Moravia, and now the Oder traffic was cut. Maria Theresa and Joseph, into the bargain, tried to ruin Prussian Silesia by means of a tariff war,[2] and Joseph, in spite of his physiocratic interests, was altogether too mercantilist. As for the agricultural interior, the plight of the peasants since the influx of alien landlords in the previous century was such as to fill both Maria Theresa and her son with distress. Joseph toured the country and was well aware of the state of affairs. Early in the seventies there was a serious peasant rising in Bohemia, and it is interesting that old Hussite songs were to be heard.[3] The Patent of 1775 brought about a regulation of services, and private landowners were encouraged to follow the royal example and commute them. Though Joseph afterwards went farther,[4] the obstruction of the Estates restricted his efforts. It is nevertheless true that the Czech peasantry had much for which to be grateful to Maria Theresa and Joseph, and the land of Hus, one might have thought, would have blessed the monarchs who drove out the Jesuits, and above all the Emperor who relaxed the censorship and in 1781 proclaimed the religious freedom of his subjects. But Joseph lacked the time and the means to carry out his policy, and what little he could do was partially destroyed or perverted by twenty-five years of European war. And so he not only died prematurely with the tragic conviction that he had failed in all he had undertaken, but in 1918 Czech demonstrators rejoiced in destroying the statues which had been set up to his memory. There was, indeed, a brief two years' interlude before the storms of war really descended, the interlude provided by Leopold II's reign (1790-2). Leopold, who had ruled Tuscany, was Joseph's brother, and apparently as tactful as Joseph was rash. He reversed Joseph's most provocative measures, summoned all the Estates of the Empire and asked to have their grievances laid before him. In 1791, at the time of his coronation in Prague, Leopold was addressed by the Czech savant, Dobrovský, who made much of a theme which is always associated with 1848, the importance of the Slavs in Austria. Leopold even went so far as to attend theatrical performances in Czech. Administratively

[1] E. Denis, *La Bohême depuis la Montagne Blanche* (Paris, 1903), vol. i, p. 444.
[2] Kerner, op. cit.
[3] Grünberg, *Die Bauernbefreiung und die Auflösung des gutsherrlich bauerlichen Verhältnisses in Böhmen, und Mähren und Schlesien.*
[4] See below.

he prepared for educational improvements to include some possibilities of Czech secondary and higher education,[1] and he alleviated the rigour of Joseph's commercial policy. But war and Metternich soon obliterated the little mirage of Leopold's reign.

Out of the Age of Enlightenment, in the later years of the eighteenth century, was born the Romantic Revival and the spirit of modern nationalism and the Czech-German problem as we know it to-day. Romanticism was partly, of course, an emotional reaction against the rationalists, a reaction expressed by Rousseau in the person of his *vicaire savoyard*; but the romantics also took over from the *philosophes* a sense of the value and dignity of man *qua* man. While agreeing with Denis that Czech nationalism owes much directly to Joseph II, it would be inaccurate not to observe with Kerner that the Czech literary revival was already alive[2] before Joseph had made himself felt, and in conflicting with the consequences of his administration also gained strength. In the conflicts and impacts of the years around 1800 the modern consciousness of both the Germans and the Czechs was born. The French revolutionaries swept across Europe and the reaction of the Germans as a whole is familiar to every one who concerns himself with the problems of the Continent. But in the Historic Provinces, now all but entirely German in outward aspect, a tremendous transformation took place. Slav consciousness was stirred afresh by the Russian defeat of Napoleon, but it was also nurtured by the German romantic writers, by the Bohemian Germans and even by the German-speaking aristocracy. The attitude of Germans like Herder[3] to the Slavs was something like that of Rousseau to the noble savage. The Slavs, it was held, had been rudely interrupted by brutal conquerors from an ideal community life in which peace and social equality prevailed. What is known to-day of early Slavonic societies does not, incidentally, destroy this supposition entirely. Meanwhile, from an entirely opposite position, the racial consciousness of the Czechs was fostered by the local aristocracy, who, in their resistance to the absolutism of the dynasty, took up the Czech language as against the laws in favour of German, and

---

[1] In consequence a Czech course, directed by Pelcl, was inaugurated at the University of Prague in 1791.

[2] The Bohemian Society of Learning was publicly founded in 1784. It had existed in private since 1769.

[3] Herder lived from 1744 to 1803. His most important work was written between 1784 and 1791. Typical of his attitude is the following extract in which he addresses the Slavs:

The wheel of changing times turns relentlessly, and since these nations mostly inhabit the most beautiful piece of Europe—should it be built over and trade opened up there—and since one cannot but suppose that legislation and statesmanship rather than a warlike spirit must and will more and more further quiet work and trade among the peoples, so will you too, once industrious and happy peoples, at last awake from your long sleep, shake off your slavish chains and use your beautiful districts from the Adriatic to the Carpathians and from the Don to the Mulda [sic] and there be able to celebrate your ancient festivals of quiet industry and trade.

encouraged all provincialisms in order to strengthen their claim to control the administration through the local Estates.

'L'aristocratie de Bohême', wrote Louis Eisenmann[1] in 1904, when speaking of the first half of the nineteenth century, 'était comme elle l'est encore, la plus riche et la plus orgueilleuse de l'Autriche.' This aristocracy was certainly innocent of any sympathy with the revolutionary ideas of the time. Its members hoped to deflect contemporary political passions away from racial into territorial channels. They wished to foster a Bohemian patriotism (*Bohemismus*) which would be less disruptive than Germanic or Slavonic notions. Neither Czechs nor Germans, but Bohemians was their motto, 'parole intraduisible même en tchèque, où les mots Bohême et Tchèque se confondent'. This confusion, big with future conflict, immediately bore fruit, for the Bohemian nobles gave financial encouragement to the leaders of the Czech literary revival of the period, the period of Dobrovský, Jungmann, and a little later of Havliček and Palacký. With a tremendous energy the medieval literature of the Czechs was unearthed and studied, and the language thus revived by people who, it must be remembered, most naturally spoke German even among themselves, since Czech was the spoken language only of peasant and artisan. It is interesting that Mozart's *Don Giovanni*, the very first performance of which was in Prague in 1787, was first played in Czech on April 9th, 1825, for a charitable purpose; even then the programme was more than half in German. Along with the reinstallation of their ancient literature, the Czechs became increasingly aware that Bohemia had a great Czech history. In the schools which Maria Theresa and Joseph II had founded, simpler people, though they learnt in German, were made aware of the existence of literature and history, and were afterwards able to take a rough, but none the less intense, interest in the activities of the patriot *littérateurs*. In the *Telegraph* of 1838 a German writer named Rebenstein, who belonged to the Karl Gutzkov circle, once described the extraordinary historic consciousness of the Czechs in Prague.

Full of character as these people are [he wrote] yet they are only a pale reflection of the history of the past which lives in them. . . . When did the battle of the White Mountain take place?—they do not know, but that it did they not only know but they feel and even see it still, how the brave fighters were overcome and how they were enslaved. In all the wild merriment of this people the keynote is that of elegy, just as all their song is a charming mixture of defiance and of sorrow.

In the eagerness of those days it is not altogether surprising that not every one of the historic documents now revealed to the nation

[1] L. Eisenmann, *Le Compromis austro-hongrois* (Paris, 1904), p. 58.

was genuine. The case of Hanka's famous Königinhofer (Králové dvur) Forgery (1817) is frequently quoted by the enemies of the Czechs as if its exposure had discredited the whole of Czech history. 'Just one big forgery', such opponents will say, with a knowing smile. It is true that the Moravian historian, František Palacký, along with his contemporaries, accepted the Hanka forgery; to that extent he is vulnerable. It was in 1836 that Palacký, under the patronage of Count Sternberg and other members of the aristocracy, brought out in German the first volume of his famous *History of Bohemia*; the second volume followed in two instalments in 1839 and 1841 respectively and carried him down to the end of Charles IV's reign. Difficulties with the Metternich censorship now became acute, for Palacký was a Protestant and the Catholic authorities, in spite of aristocratic intervention, were loath to see him justify the heretic, Hus. Among the many points to which the censors took exception was Palacký's reference to an authority who described the Emperor Sigismund as having blushed when Hus claimed the protection of the safe-conduct promised to him.[1] Thus between 1841 and 1848, only the first part of the third volume could be published in 1845. Even so much of the history, which was now brought down to the outbreak of the Hussite wars, was eagerly read, and a stern censorship had accustomed the public to read between the lines.

No one who has studied his writings or his career can fail to recognize in Palacký a fine intelligence and a very genuine idealism, and in forming the nineteenth-century Czech mind this man was the most powerful influence. To Palacký the history of the Czechs acquired a meaning of its own which depended upon the age-long clash between Czech and German. As Professor Pekař put it:[2] 'Palacký, of course, regarded our history as a clash and a conflict between two worlds, the one a world of Freedom, of Peace and Goodness, i.e. a democratic Slavonic world, and the other a world of domination, force and oppression, that is the feudal Germanic world.' Thus Palacký, himself a member of the Brotherhood, glorified Hussitism as the expression of the simple Slavonic virtues, and its champions as the men who tried to distribute these blessings in an unappreciative world; the battle of the White Mountain, which he only described in a much later volume, was to him the final defeat of the original civilization of the Czechs. This kind of romanticism was typical of the nineteenth century, not of the Czechs in particular. But because the nineteenth century lifted them out of oblivion into consciousness, its ideology

---

[1] 'als Huss mit Berufung auf den Geleitsbrief ihn in der Sitzung anblickte.' See 'Palacký und die Censur', von K. Köpl in *Památník na oslavu stých narozenin Františka Palackého*, 1898, xlii, p. 59.   [2] Pekař, op. cit.

impressed itself with particular force upon the mentality of what may be only inaccurately regarded as an adolescent nation. And while one must reject these wholesale interpretations one cannot reject them wholesale. Egalitarian principles, nurtured perhaps by the subjection to which the Slav nations have often been condemned, are undoubtedly less popular among the Germans and Hungarians as a whole, in whom historical circumstances appear to have fertilized the notion that some races are born to rule others, i.e. of a racial caste-hierarchy. Even in the earlier years of the nineteenth century aggressive ideologies pervaded the German universities. In Europe east of the Rhine, where national states on the French or the English model had not emerged, the phrases of the west were subject to the strangest distortion before they could be applied. The nationalistic conception was linked far too narrowly, first with language and then with race, though in the west it obviously meant some kind of territorial unity with a much broader political base than either language or race could provide. It was particularly disastrous that in the Habsburg lands, for instance, where race and language were so immensely mixed, they should have been chosen as ultimate criteria, for this meant that each race began—if only subconsciously—to believe that the denationalization of its rivals would justify the ambitious territorial claims dictated by its maximum historical extent. And with this impulse the invisible boundary between assimilation and denationalization would be easily overstepped, as soon as the weaker races consciously wished to remain intact. Thus the problems of the last period of Austro-Hungarian history were born, and already in Bohemia, of all the lands of the Habsburg Crown, they developed most quickly, and rapidly assumed the most critical proportions.

In the years leading up to 1848 some of the Germans of Bohemia, men like Ebert and Meissner, enthusiastically joined in the excavation of the history of the Czechs, but they and the Bohemian nobles were but digging their own graves. That synthesis which might have been achieved if Charles IV's successors had been greater men again proved to be still-born. It was impossible to achieve 'Bohemianism' against the growing popularity of Arndt's language theories, even if the importance of race had not yet been so radically emphasized as it was to be after 1866. In 1837 the German-Bohemian, Rudolf Glaser, founded a German-Czech literary review which was to draw Germany and the Slavonic East together and so contribute to a new world literature.[1] But one of the collaborators afterwards wrote: 'no god could still have united the politically and nationally disparate elements of "East and West", of Pan-German and Pan-Slav. . . .' To those who clung to other

[1] Wostry, as above.

values—for whom perhaps the human values of the eighteenth century remained greater than those of speech or blood—how strange the conflict in Bohemia already must have seemed. Why, such people must have asked themselves, should Bohemians exert themselves to create linguistic rivalries when German has the convenience of being generally understood, but why again should German claim a particular virtue rather than to be of general use? Still more ludicrous must racial distinctions have seemed where, except among the peasants, so much Slav-German mixing had occurred. The number of Slavs with German names or vice versa[1] was striking, while the German qualities of the Bohemian Czech or the Slavonic qualities of the Germans of Vienna have certainly been evident for the last hundred years. And yet the Revolution of 1848 was quickly to show that only the Metternich System had formed any real bond between the Germans and the Czechs of Bohemia in the 'pre-March' days.

[1] Cf. Pekař, op. cit., where it is pointed out that the many Czechs in Bohemia with German names show to what extent Germans have been Czechified.

CHAPTER III

1848

DURING the years of the rebirth of Czech national feeling economic developments of the greatest significance for the future of Bohemia, Moravia, and Silesia were also taking place. Even before 1815 the Continental System had provided a great stimulus to the sugar industry of the Historic Provinces, an industry which was to become a political factor of importance; protection against England had also helped textiles, in Moravia, for instance. In 1817 coal-mining began in earnest, and in 1828 the Habsburg Archbishop of Olmütz founded the ironworks of Vitkovice. Meanwhile Liebig's textile concern had appeared at Reichenberg, and a little later Rothschild capital began to construct a skeleton railway system in the Habsburg lands; the first railway line actually to be used was that connecting Budweis with Linz. In the forties political revolution was heralded by economic disturbance. In 1844 textile machines were wrecked in Prague and in Reichenberg; in 1846 serious rioting occurred among the mainly Czech working-men of Prague and Pilsen, as among the German artisans of Eger and Komotau.

Politically, too, the atmosphere had been changing, and a faintly abdicatory attitude on the part of authority encouraged the hopes of reformers. In spite of Metternich's contempt for the Slavs, the Emperor Ferdinand had been crowned King of Bohemia in 1836, and in the forties the censorship slightly relaxed its vigour and the Bohemian Estates became more active than the earlier years of the century had allowed. Finally in 1846 the Galician insurrection brought to the forefront two intimately associated Austrian problems, that of the peasants and that of the Slavs. Galicia was nearly half Ruthene (Ukrainian), but the Polish as well as the Ruthene peasantry was whole-heartedly on the side of the Austrian Government in resisting the Polish aristocrats. The struggle died down; the Emperor Ferdinand annexed the Free City of Cracow, once capital of Poland, and issued a Rural Edict in favour of voluntary settlements between the nobles and peasants; but the social and national questions involved, far from being solved, were aggravated. Thus in 1848, when the news of the February Revolution in France spread to Austria, behind the academic claims of the opponents of absolutism were ranged the passionate indignation of the now restless nationalities, that of the peasants, and that of the new and as yet small industrial working-class. The year of revolution provided, however, the stock example of how the political and social aspirations created by circumstances in France were overshadowed or distorted by the racialistic rivalries stirred up in Central Europe by the notion that the Voice of the People is the Voice of God. In Central Europe the question had arisen, which people? And from that day to this German, Slav, and Magyar have battled for the right to speak for Heaven. Wise men in every camp have pointed out that God has many voices, but each people is loath to abandon its claim.

The one great positive achievement in the Austrian lands in 1848 was the emancipation of the peasants. Joseph II had given them personal freedom, the right to move, to marry, to study without the permission of their lords, and he had sought unsuccessfully to free them from forced services. Further, the centralization of the administration had to some extent provided them with bureaucratic protection, but that which Joseph had most desired, that the peasants' land should be their own, he had not been able to achieve. In the Parliament which met in Vienna in 1848 —it was about 25 per cent. peasant, and less than half the deputies could speak German—the German Silesian Hans Kudlich on July 10th demanded the complete emancipation of the peasants, and on September 7th all the peasants of Austria were freed from the *Robot*, i.e. forced, services. Still more important, it was enacted that tenant farmers should become the free masters of the land they tilled; more precisely, they either undertook to pay a free money-rent or give up a portion of the area concerned. The big proprietors were compensated over a period of years, the provincial authorities guaranteeing a proportion of the payment, which was all cleared off by 1857. Like the emancipation laws in other countries, this measure mainly helped the better-off peasants and, often depriving the poorer labourers of patriarchal protection, encouraged them to leave the land and look for work in industry. The reform, however, was another great step in the revelation of the nineteenth century that—leaving Hungary aside—Austria was largely a Slavonic land. In the eighteenth century it had appeared to be a German country with, if you liked, a wealth of local dialect. Now there had come not only an intellectual movement which refused to regard itself as merely sentimentally folklorist, but a reform which, beside the big landowners and the town patriciate, placed on the political map a numerically impressive array of peasant proprietors. And whereas the landowner and the *bourgeois* —taking Austria (without Hungary) as a whole—were German or at least 'Austrian',[1] a very high proportion of these peasant proprietors were Slav. And the farther down that social and political recognition descended between 1848 and 1914, the more the

[1] See below.

numerical balance tilted in favour of the Slavs and against the Germans of Austria.

In the earliest days of the March Revolution the finest idealism, whether German or Slav, believed that Liberty and Equality could cement the fraternity of the Austrian peoples; men like the German Bohemian leader, von Löhner, wished for the Germans to conduct the other nationalities along such paths. Alas, 1848 was but to provide one of the many examples of the destruction of Humanity's noblest hopes through the envious greed of nationalism. At this time Austria was still the presiding member of the German Confederation created in 1815. In a Germany which included Confederate Austria with its Czechs and Slovenes, the democratic centralization advocated by most Germans would automatically give their nation the lead. While democracy within the frontiers of Austria alone would mean a Slavonic majority, inclusion in any form of Greater Germany would reduce the Slavs to a small minority. Threatened with submergence so soon again, some of them listened to voices like those of the Slovak poet Kollár and began to dream of over-trumping the German unificators by insisting upon the unity of all Slavs. Bohemia, Moravia, Silesia became in the most literal sense the crux of the whole situation, for their Germans and Slavs were most intermingled and aware of each other. The Germans of the Historic Lands soon became eagerly *Grossdeutsch* or Pan-German, while most of the Czechs developed the idea of a federalized Austria and their extremists began to think in Pan-Slav terms, applying the ideas they had learnt in the west to the Great Empire of the east.[1] Since the Tsar was just about as terrible an ogre in the eyes of the German Liberals of 1848 as Stalin appears to be to the German National Socialists of 1938, the optimism of men like Löhner had to be speedily revised.

If the Revolution of 1848 revealed the complexity of the Slav-German problem in the Historic Provinces, it also offered a solution to which central Europe has in a sense been trying to grope its way back for the last ninety years. The major events of 1848 are, therefore, of capital importance to this study. At first both Czechs and Germans in Bohemia were at one in demanding a moderate democratic constitution with guarantees for personal freedom and for the autonomy of the Historic Provinces as a whole. On March 11th the famous meeting at the Baths of St. Wenceslas occurred, at which a joint committee to frame a petition to the Emperor was set up; on April 8th the Imperial Government acceded to the wishes expressed, thus implicitly accepting the integrity of the lands of St. Wenceslas's crown. Thereupon difficulties sprang up like armed men born of dragons' teeth. In spite

[1] Wostry, op. cit.

of Palacký's appeal to his province, the Moravians were suspicious of the Bohemians. Though the Moravian Czechs heavily out-numbered the Germans, the Diet at Brünn contained 123 Germans to 124 Slavs, most of the latter being very Catholic peasants with no strong political views of their own. The Moravian diet there-fore protested against the imperial grant of April 8th, to which the Silesian Diet was unanimously opposed.[1] Meanwhile, the Slav and German ways were parting on the grand scale. When they found, not only that democratic principles would give the Slavs a majority, but also that this majority would refuse to be led by the German minority, the Bohemian Germans very soon began to turn against the Czechs. Since the censorship had gone, journalism had become tremendously active, and the greatest of the Czech journalists in Bohemia was Havliček, who had started the news-paper *Narodni Noviny* on April 5th. His for all time characteristic attacks on the Germans deserve to be quoted.

By equality [he wrote] we certainly do not mean that the Germans should have one half and we the other; we should consider such a division as iniquitous, since the Czechs constitute three-quarters of the population and the Germans only one quarter. . . . You repeat inces-santly [he said to the Germans] that liberty must not be sacrificed to nationality, but in fact the liberty you claim is liberty to oppress us. Liberty without the guarantee of nationality is nothing but a poisoned morass for us, beautified suicide . . .[2]

The Germans as a whole had decided to summon an all-German Parliament to Frankfurt-on-the-Main, and it was taken for granted that Bohemia would participate without consideration for its dual nationality. In reply to this presumption Havliček wrote:

The point was not whether Bohemia would send to Frankfurt the 68 Deputies allotted to her—the question was a bigger one. What was at stake was the very existence of the country; would it be a free kingdom in a free Austria or a province lost within a Germanic empire constructed on the ruins of the Habsburg monarchy.

This became the platform of the Czechs, to work for a democratic federalized Austria, in which the Slavs would automatically have plenty of scope, as against a *Gross-Deutschland* which, since the Slavs would not accept that beautified suicide, would necessitate the break-up of the Danubian Empire with its immense and splendid possibilities. On April 6th Palacký had been invited by letter to Frankfurt to co-operate in the preparatory work, and on April 11th he wrote his famous letter of reply in which he, too, became the champion of the Austrian idea. Palacký refused to go.

---

[1] K. G. Hugelmann, *Das Nationalitätenrecht des alten Österreichs* (Vienna, 1934), p. 45.   [2] See Denis, op. cit., vol. ii, p. 264.

to Frankfurt, first because he was not a German, nor, as he explained, had his country ever accepted incorporation in Germany.

The second reason [he wrote] which forbids me to take part in your deliberations is the circumstance that . . . you necessarily intend to weaken Austria as an independent Empire beyond recovery, indeed to make Austria impossible—a State whose preservation, integrity and the strengthening of which is and must be a great and important matter not only for my people but for all Europe, indeed for humanity and for civilization.

He then went on to consider the development of Russia which, he said, he observed with interest and satisfaction.

As, however, for all my profound love for my own people, I have always put the interests of Humanity and of Learning above those of nationality, the mere possibility of a Russian world domination[1] has no more decisive enemy than myself—not because it would be Russian but because it would be world domination.

The Danube, to Palacký's mind, was the main artery of the society of nations which must be formed in order to guard against the Russian danger. And here comes the much-quoted sentence: 'In truth, if the Austrian Empire had not long been in existence, in the interest of Europe, in the interest of Humanity itself, one would hasten to create it.'

It has seemed worth while to quote both Havliček and Palacký at some length for several reasons. These two were the true leaders of the Czech nation not only in 1848 but over a very long period; Havliček died early, but Palacký lived until 1876, and his disciple and son-in-law, Rieger, led the Czechs until almost the end of the century. In Havliček one finds some of the most vigorous, in Palacký some of the most magnificent expressions of their people, and much of what they wrote has a curiously direct application, *mutatis mutandis*, to the conditions of to-day. By these two men was expressed that Austrian idea of a mainly Slavonic federation which should be bound together by free institutions and should fully enjoy that economic unity which the valley of the Danube seems to create. It is easy to say that Palacký was only out for Czech domination; after all, the more advanced Czechs were bound to be the leaders of the Austrian Slavs.

Bohemia amidst the Poles, Moravians, Slovaks, Illyrians, Dalmatians and Croats, makes with them the glorious constellation of the Austrian Slavs, the oriflamme which lights the Western and Southern Slavs on to Progress as to Victory.[2]

---

[1] Literally 'universal monarchy'.
[2] Quoted in P. Geist Lányi, *Das Nationalitätenproblem auf dem Reichstag zu Kremsier.*

It is easy, too, to say with Fischel[1] that the Czechs were for Austria when she seemed likely to give them what they wanted, and when not, for Russia; to some extent such an indictment is true of every political opponent. The fact remains that Palacký worked during many years for his Austrian idea, and that 'Austro-slawismus' had much to be said for it.

There were, of course, Germans like von Löhner who had their own Austrian idea and wished for *Deutschtum* to be in the modern world the civilizing and mediating factor which its pre-national forerunner had been in medieval days; the Austrian Liberal Party cherished this conception to the end of the century. And there was yet another Austrianism which in spite of all its weaknesses was inestimably precious, for it was genuinely cosmopolitan and often struggled bravely for human interests when they were threatened by national ones. This Austrianism, though it too was descended from Joseph II and lived on in the bureaucracy created in the eighteenth century, was also nurtured by the aristocracy and the Catholic Church, and was later to play a big part at the court of Francis Joseph when the centralism of the Liberals should have played itself out.

In the nationalistic whirlpool of 1848 most of the Czechs supported Palacký and found themselves in the role of uneasy champions of the Habsburg dynasty; though Palacký refused the ministerial portfolio which was offered to him, the Germans denounced the Czechs as the allies of reaction. Frankfurt sent delegates to inquire into the 'separatism' of Bohemia. Schilling, one of the men who was sent, explained to the Czechs that Austria must be German or she must cease to exist, a pretty illustration of the justice of Palacký's assumptions. Hartmann, originally a Czechophile Bohemian German, who had then gone to Frankfurt, recommended that Bohemia should be forced by military means to come in with Germany, and a society for the protection of German interests in the eastern frontier lands was canvassed among the Germans of Bohemia and Austrian Silesia. Meanwhile Vienna had glowed with *Schwarz-Rot-Gold*, the colours of German unity, when the Frankfurt Parliament assembled. While official Russia looked for a French alliance[2] if a Greater Germany was about to be born, the direct answer to Frankfurt came in the first Pan-Slav Congress which significantly assembled in Prague on June 2nd, 1848, and declared among other things for the resurrection of Poland and for the national rights of Slovaks, Croats, Ruthenes, Serbs. Although this congress was far too revolutionary to be anything but bitterly hostile to their bugbear, the

[1] A. Fischel, *Der Panslawismus bis zum Weltkrieg* (Stuttgart, 1919), p. 308.
[2] Ibid., p. 259.

Tsar, the Frankfurt deputies were impressed and alarmed. A Styrian representative, Marek, proposed a constitutional clause in favour of equality of rights for non-Germans, but Palacký complained to the Governor of Bohemia, Count Leo Thun, 'of the lies and calumnies . . . with which the almost entirely unscrupulous journalism of the Germans overflows everywhere nowadays, whenever Slavs in general or Czechs in particular are mentioned'.[1]

Young Czech radicals now impatiently staged a revolutionary demonstration in Prague, and Windischgrätz with his troops soon afterwards occupied the city. This put an end to the April concessions according to which the political unity of Bohemia, Moravia, and Silesia was to be recognized. The Czechs, if they could not have their own Parliament at Prague, agreed to attend the Constituent Assembly which met in Vienna in July. Apart from the freeing of the peasants, little work had been done by October, when, after a fresh Viennese rising, directed against Jelačić and the Slav campaign against the Hungarians, Windischgrätz occupied the capital of the Empire; owing to their support of Jelačić the Czech deputies had already withdrawn from the pro-Magyar disturbances in Vienna.

In November the Emperor summoned his Parliament to meet in the calmer air of Moravia, and the deputies assembled at the little episcopal town of Kremsier. Before they were dispersed in March 1849 they worked out a constitution for the Austrian lands the admirable sanity of which could never again be attained. In refusing to put the Kremsier constitution into practice, the Habsburgs, it is not fantastic to suppose, may there and then have condemned their Empire to destruction. And that part of the work of Kremsier which handled the problem of the two nationalities in Bohemia might have forestalled ninety years of bitterest conflict; indeed, the proposals of Kremsier are still regarded by serious people as desirable, if it were possible to apply them in the altered circumstances of to-day.

The work of Kremsier was facilitated by a friendlier feeling between the Germans who were present and the Czechs. The most aggressive Germans were in Frankfurt; of those who remained the Moravian Mayer was conciliatory; the Czechs were by now disappointed in the court and determined not to be used by it. Palacký and Mayer presented not altogether dissimilar proposals—both of them aimed at transforming Austria into a democratic and at the same time federal state, for with the nationalities the one depended for realization upon the other. Palacký actually suggested that the administrative frontiers should be drawn along national lines, and it is noteworthy that he proposed that the Slovaks should

[1] Palacký, *Gedenkblätter* (Prague, 1874), p. 169.

be included in the same *arrondissement* with the Czechs. Mayer's plan was the one which was finally adopted. According to this the boundaries of the Imperial Provinces (*Kronländer*) were left undisturbed, but within the larger provinces there was to be an administrative division according to the 'national settlements'; thus Czechs and Germans in Bohemia were to be separated into 'circles' for local government purposes. In addition, paragraph 113 provided that for the provinces of mixed nationality there should be special arbitration courts to deal with questions of a purely national kind. For the constitution of a central parliament, the Kremsier plan decided for a bicameral system. A people's chamber of 360 deputies was to be directly elected by every one who paid 5 gulden a year in taxes, while a chamber representing the *Länder* was to contain six deputies sent by each provincial diet together with one sent by each circle.

Eisenmann[1] wrote of the work done at Kremsier:

C'était néanmoins une idée heureuse que de créer dans le cadre provincial des circonscriptions nationalement homogènes, pour diminuer dans les irritantes questions de langues les surfaces de friction, et concilier ces deux forces également puissantes, la nationalité provinciale ou historique et la nationalité ethnique ou linguistique. . . . Au fond [he wrote in a footnote dated April 1904] la division en cercles n'est pas autre chose qu'une forme atténuée, plus modérée et moins provocante, de la division nationale en Bohême, que les Allemands réclament complète, et dans laquelle, en principe et toutes réserves faites sur le détail, ceux qui restent des réalistes de Bohême, M. Masaryk et son parti, voient la solution de l'avenir.

'Measured either by moral or intellectual standards', in the opinion of Redlich, 'it [the Kremsier constitution] remained as the one great political monument of common goodwill towards the State which the nations, through their representatives, achieved in imperial Austria.'[2]

The Kremsier deputies were dispersed by the military on March 7th. The Government then published a pale version of their work, with a few emasculated phrases about the rights of the peoples, but even this declaration was immediately suspended, and abrogated on December 31st, 1851. Political night, as it were, descended upon the peoples of Austria and Hungary, and the military advisers of the young Francis Joseph blotted out the year of revolution as completely as they could.

[1] Op. cit., p. 131.
[2] J. Redlich, *Das österreichische Staats- und Reichsproblem* (Leipzig, 1920), Bd. I, p. 323.

CHAPTER IV

DUALISM

ABOUT the fifties, thanks to the completeness of the political reaction under the régime of the renegade democrat Alexander Bach, there is actually little to say. In spite of an acquittal at Kutná Hora the immensely popular Havliček was in 1851 taken off to a Tyrolese prison; he was not released until 1855 and then only to die. The Czechs, like the other subjects of the Habsburgs at the time, were not allowed to concern themselves with the present; with Palacký now publishing volume after volume of his *History* in Czech[1] they took refuge more than ever in the past. The most epoch-making volume, that which dealt with the period of the Hussite wars, appeared in 1851. It has often been said that the Czechs are essentially Hussites whatever the Counter-Reformation may have done. With Palacký's exposition, pride in John Hus became eagerly conscious and pride in the mission of his people to struggle for truth and light against the obscurantism and greed of popes and emperors. Just at the time came the Concordat of 1855 between Francis Joseph and Pius IX, by which the religious freedom created by Joseph II was surrendered to Pius, the betrayer of Italian liberty in the eyes of the men of 1848; the Concordat was, of course, as bitterly hated by many Germans as it was by the Czechs.

The fifties were, however, a period of remarkable economic development to be largely attributed to Bruck's liberal tariff policy, and, above all, to his abolition of the tariff frontier between Cisleithan Austria and Hungary on July 1st, 1851. From this day on, until the disintegration of Austria-Hungary in the World War, a great Danubian free-trade area, in which industry and agriculture were happily balanced, was materially to bless the warring nationalities ruled by the Habsburgs. Territorial adjustments occurred on the Italian and Balkan frontiers between 1851 and 1914, but, although the Hungarians periodically played with the idea of repudiation, as they did before the Compromise of 1907, the Customs Union endured to the end.

The Hungarian market provided a very great stimulus to the industries of Bohemia, Moravia, and Silesia, and the economic development which followed directly affected the relations of the Germans and Czechs in the Historic Provinces. In the second

---

[1] From 1848 the early volumes began to appear in Czech, and the later part of the work was written in Czech to begin with. In the fifties, owing to the attitude of men like Count Leo Thun, the censorship was never restored to a troublesome rigour.

half of the century a Czech *bourgeoisie* developed apace to compete
with the German employers and financiers who had hitherto
extended their power and activities without challenge. Thus the
Czech national movement soon ceased to depend on a student's
dream or a pedant's whim, it was backed by free peasant farmers
and a growing middle class. The development of industry, moreover, created a new demand for labour, and this the more prolific
Slav populations were readier to satisfy than were the Germans.
The effect of industrialization upon the relations of the nationalities
was to prove tremendous, but it was not until the seventies or
eighties that it was to be fully felt.

Meanwhile the Hungarians were enraged by the annulment of
their ancient constitution, and the Germans, though in general
agreement with a Germanizing centralism, chafed at Bach coercion
and the Concordat. They themselves, as a matter of fact, were
already regarded as oppressors without being aware of it, and on
the other hand now became accustomed to regard themselves, as
Eisenmann wrote, as the *ciment de l'État* and *le peuple élu*. When
Napoleon III had beaten the Austrian armies at Magenta and
Solferino and Francis Joseph had been forced to surrender an
eager Lombardy to Piedmont, it became clear to the Imperial
Government at Vienna that the shaken foundations of the Habsburg throne must be reinforced. There followed a period of some
seven years of constitutional fumbling and tergiversation, which
envenomed the relations of the Czechs with the Germans of
Bohemia at a time when Prussia was thrusting dangerously in all
directions to clear the ground for the foundation of a new German
Empire to the north.

Five constitutional steps were taken between March 1860 and
December 1867, but never in the same direction. The Patent of
March 5th, 1860, pronounced for a stronger Reichsrat with extensive functions, whereas seven months later the October Diploma
set up a federal system by which the provincial diets were largely
to control the administration. Now the Czech-Austrian idea was
a federal one, and it had been becoming increasingly clear that the
centralist-federalist issue hardened German-Slav differences, since
the Germans in many of the mixed Crownlands (and of the 17 only
4 were unchallengedly German)[1] were in a minority and could
scarcely hope to maintain the leadership which they regarded as
their unquestionable right except through the maintenance of
centralism. Centralism imposing a superficial German uniformity
had been, in the eyes of the Germans, the redeeming feature of the

[1] The Crownlands were the accumulated provinces united in Austria
(without Hungary); the four purely German ones were Upper Austria, Lower
Austria, Salzburg, and Vorarlberg.

Bach régime. The strongest political tendency among the Germans was the so-called liberalism[1] of the upper middle class, the liberalism in particular of the German politicians of the Historic Provinces. They uncompromisingly condemned the October Diploma; not only was it federal in character, but its federalism was feudal in the way it was to work; against this gift to the landed aristocracy the Czech *bourgeois* even saw eye to eye with the German. The Goluchowski Cabinet bowed before the storm and Anton von Schmerling came into power.

As Redlich has said, to Schmerling and the German Liberals Germany without Austria playing a leading role in it, and on the other hand, Austria as a State without *deutscher Charakter*, were unthinkable. They were completely *Grossdeutsch*. They ignored the aspirations of the Slavs, which they neither understood nor wished to understand. Inspired by Hans von Perthaler, Schmerling therefore enacted the Patent of February 26th, 1861. Coming, as it did, on top of the federal hopes aroused in the previous October, nothing could have been more exactly calculated to create Slav indignation than the centralism and the so-called 'elective geometry' introduced by Schmerling. 'Faire une majorité allemande artificielle c'est le but du système électoral de Schmerling.'[2] Government was to be recentralized and controlled by two houses, the Staatsrat and Reichsrat. The provincial diets were now to do very little but elect the members of the Reichsrat. They themselves were to be elected and constituted after a fashion grotesque not only in modern eyes but also in those of a generation which had by no means forgotten the hopes of '48. For the tax-paying population[3] was divided into four *curiae*, those of the big landowners, the chambers of commerce, the towns, and the country districts. To the Bohemian Diet, for instance, the big landowners (a mere handful of people) could elect 70 representatives, the chambers of commerce 15, the towns 72, the country 79. Thus the towns which were German or had a high proportion of Germans had a deputy to 11,666 inhabitants, while the country districts—predominantly Czech—had a deputy to 49,081 inhabitants.[4] Another good example of the Schmerling system was the voting arrangement for the city of Prague. The city was divided into five districts each represented by two deputies. But

---

[1] Continental liberalism was primarily anti-clerical; on an anti-clerical and centralist basis, a Liberal Party was then built up.
[2] Eisenmann, op. cit., p. 282.   [3] There was a 10-gulden census.
[4] Charmatz, *Österreichs innere Geschichte* (Leipzig, 1911), Bd. I, p. 51), puts the situation in a different way, pointing out that the town districts where German had a deputy to about 10,000 voters, where Czech to about 12,000, while the country districts where German had a deputy to about 40,000 and where Czech to about 53,000.

in a district largely inhabited by German officials one deputy actually represented only 54 people qualified by their wealth to act as electors, while 2,800 people lived in the area concerned and 4,850 gulden were annually paid from it in taxes. In another district which happened to be almost entirely Czech, one deputy was elected by 885 people and represented 32,416 inhabitants and a tax-paying capacity of 131,579 gulden a year.[1]

By the Schmerling constitution the Crown agreed to share its absolute powers with a German oligarchy which depended for the preservation of its authority upon a centralized system far less applicable to the Austrian lands than in the days of Maria Theresa and her son. The principle of Schmerling's *Wahlgeometrie*, moreover, was maintained for nearly half a century until the introduction of universal suffrage in 1907: indeed, in municipal elections it continued up to the last hour of Habsburg rule. The Schmerling system became increasingly provocative as it became increasingly unjustifiable. It was based upon the assumption that their more advanced civilization made the Germans more valuable than the members of the other races ruled by the monarchy. As the years passed, the Czechs in particular were steadily catching up in education of all kinds, the theatre, and so on, but their constitutional privilege induced in the Germans a conviction of permanent superiority, an actual caste consciousness, which was strengthened by the fact that their language and habits were the language and habits of good society. It is still with considerable difficulty that Germans of really good will adapt themselves to the post-War assumption in central Europe that one German is no better than one Slav.

More and more the importance of the German-Czech rivalry in the Historic Provinces—and notably of course in Bohemia—became clear. It was here that the most active and competent Slavs protested against the inferior status allotted to them; it was here that the Germans, becoming aware that their artificial supremacy was increasingly precarious, fought most uncompromisingly to maintain it; without it they would be reduced to minority status. The Czechs were the obvious leaders of all the Slavs in the Empire, the Sudeten Germans[2] were the most aggressive supporters of the

---

[1] These figures are based on Palacký's calculations—see his speech on the revision of the electoral system delivered in the Bohemian Diet on Jan. 29th, 1863, in Palacký, *Spisy drobné* (Prague, 1898–1903), vol. i. Altogether the speech contains a remarkable number of striking constrasts, e.g. that in the German town of Reichenberg there were 6,288 voters to a deputy while in the Czech town of Pardubice there were 14,359 voters to a deputy, or that in the German country district around Joachimsthal in the Erzgebirge there were 15,898, while in the Czech district around Smichov there were 93,740, voters to a deputy.

[2] The phrase 'Sudeten German', early in the twentieth century, began to be used to cover all the German inhabitants of the Historic Provinces—see below. It is, strictly speaking, an anachronism to use it here.

Schmerling system which had particularly and deliberately over-weighted their influence. As Eisenmann wrote, 'C'est en Bohême, d'ailleurs, qu'est la clef de voûte de tout l'édifice; c'est la députa-tion de la Bohême qui, dans le systéme de Schmerling, fait la majorité au Reichsrat, et toute la loi électorale est combinée pour que la députation de la Bohême soit favorable au gouvernment.' This arrangement was made, partly because of its immediate advantages from the Government point of view, but also because it was increasingly realized that any solution of the Slav-German question must begin with a tranquillization of the fierce rivalries of Bohemia. Moreover, with the Czechs and the Germans at each other's throats, Cisleithan[1] Austria was at a growing disadvantage in dealing with the Hungarians, who would certainly have to be dealt with—they would not accept Schmerling centralization a moment longer than they were compelled.

In the view of the Czechs the lands of the crown of St. Wenceslas, like those of the crown of St. Stephen, had legally maintained their integrity as guaranteed by Ferdinand I in 1526, and wrong would only be righted when the autonomy of both was restored. In dealing with Vienna the Hungarians did better than the Czechs because their nobility was eagerly nationalist and could bring its social weight to bear at court. The Bohemian nobility reflected the Janus-like character of Bohemia which differed from Hungary in having a highly developed and politically articulate minority nationally similar with the people of the Alpine Crownlands and the rest of Germany. Palacký and his celebrated son-in-law, Rieger, who had already been prominent in 1848, decided to remedy their weakness by drawing the Bohemian nobility definitely into the Czech camp. The nobles, among whom Clam Martinic was then the most prominent, were still, inevitably, territorialists. They wished for the integrity of the Wenceslas provinces in order that they themselves should have more scope. In January 1861 Palacký and Rieger made an agreement with them by which the Czech cause was to take its stand upon the rights of the Wenceslas crown, or, as it came to be called, upon *Böhmisches Staatsrecht*. This agreement hardened Czech opposition to any attempt at an administrative division such as the Kremsier constitution had envisaged, and *Böhmisches Staatsrecht* played a decisive part in the days which saw the setting up of the Czechoslovak Republic of to-day.

At first the Czech deputies led by Rieger attended the sittings of the Schmerling Reichsrat and Palacký[2] took his seat in the

---

[1] The River Leitha separated Austria from Hungary, and Austria without Hungary was therefore referred to as Cisleithan, or as Cisleithania.
[2] Palacký was the only Czech among 39 nominated members.

Staatsrat. Their reception by the most energetic German deputies, among whom the German Bohemian, Herbst, and the German Moravian, Giskra, were two of the most prominent, was anything but encouraging. Eisenmann gives, in a footnote, a description of an incident on June 19th, 1861, which appears to have been typical of the atmosphere in the Reichsrat and which is sufficiently illuminating to deserve to be recounted almost in full. Giskra had attacked *Böhmisches Staatsrecht* as a slogan with which its adherents were trying to intoxicate the masses. Rieger in answering said, 'We know that it is as difficult for nations as for individuals to be as just towards others as towards themselves. We have certainly found it to be so with the Germans and we still repeat this sad experience every day.' At this point the President of the Chamber, Hein, a Silesian German, called him to order and requested him to resume his seat. Rieger, protesting, said, 'I appeal to the House—have I said anything insulting?' whereupon Hein told him that what he had said was certainly insulting to the German nation, and was cheered from the left where the German Liberals sat. Rieger declared at once that he had had no such intention and was allowed to speak again. 'I will say no more about the national question,' he continued, 'since I see that freedom of speech is fettered here.'[1] Hein immediately broke in again requesting him to sit down since he had accused the President of suppressing freedom of speech. Rieger, in a voice of thunder, cried out, 'Long live the freedom of speech which prevails in the Austrian Reichsrat!' and was finally compelled to sit down. In such circumstances it is not altogether surprising that the Czechs withdrew from the Parliament in Vienna in 1863, and did not reappear until in 1879[2] a new era had evidently dawned.

In the summer of 1865 occurred the fourth constitutional change-over since March 1860; before the fifth could take place in December 1867 the momentous Prussian War and the Compromise with Hungary had intervened. In 1865 the Belcredi Government suspended the constitution, and at the same time press control was relaxed and many Slav journalists released from prison. All other developments were, however, dwarfed by the Six Weeks' War in the summer of 1866 when the Austrian armies were overwhelmingly defeated by the Prussians upon the Bohemian battle-field of Königgrätz.[3] With the expulsion of Austria from the German Confederation and with the establishment of a new German unity

---

[1] Rieger afterwards claimed a slight modification of this sentence in the parliamentary journal. See Eisenmann, op. cit., p. 341, n. 1.
[2] During the 1870–1 negotiations they actually put in a fleeting appearance.
[3] The Czechs were very definitely pro-Austrian and anti-Prussian in 1866; they traditionally disliked the Prussians as the destroyers of the Slavs of the Elbe and as the perpetrators of the rape of Silesia.

entirely dominated by Prussia a revolution had occurred, from the results of which many of the Germans of Styria, Bohemia, and Salzburg are still smarting to-day. For the Germans of Austria, who had believed themselves to be the leaders, above all the spiritual leaders, of Germany, found their homes put out of German bounds for the first time in history, and found themselves degraded to the status of *Auslandsdeutsche*. The extremer nationalists declared that the Austrian Germans had become 'children of pain cast out helpless into the world';[1] phrases like this were current, and pessimists prophesied that the Danube would become a tributary of the Moldau,[2] the river of the Czechs. The Slavs of the Empire, led as ever by the Czechs, naturally, and to some extent correctly, believed that the idea of a mainly Slav Austria had come much nearer to realization. In 1866 Austria had also lost Venetia to Italy; she was blocked to north and to south; she could only expand in influence and territory south-eastwards, farther into Slav or Roumanian (i.e. Slavophile) territory.

For the moment, at any rate, the importance of Hungary had greatly increased and rumours began to circulate of impending 'Dualism', i.e. a division of the Empire between Vienna and Budapest by which Francis Joseph would indeed recognize the claims of the crown of St. Stephen and give the Magyars *carte blanche* to do as they would with the non-Magyar populations involved. That the historic claims of the Hungarians should be admitted and the equivalent claims of the Czechs be ignored was an unbearable thought to the Czechs, and that their brothers, the Slovaks, should be handed over without any safeguards to Magyar mercies they could never accept as a final solution. In 1865[3] Palacký launched a last and powerful appeal against dualism; it was entitled *Österreichs Staatsidee*, and it expressed all that was best in the aspirations of the Austrian Slavs of that day. Dualism, he declared, would be twice as bad as centralism, for it would indeed mean centralism twice over. A free hand to the Magyars who oppressed and divided the Slavs would hasten the end of the Austrian Empire, which, federalized, he still regarded as an essential and desirable factor in European civilization. To-day one seldom meets a German who does not justify Palacký and declare that the free hand of 1867 to the Magyars to denationalize was a free hand to stab Austria in the back, since the Slavs and Roumanians of one half of the Empire would never remain tranquil while those of the other appeared to them to be persecuted. He warned any statesman who might be flirting with the dualist idea that one could only be guilty of this if one's national sympathies and antipathies were

---

[1] Quoted by Charmatz, op. cit., vol. 1, p. 69.   [2] Quoted by Charmatz, ibid.
[3] Appeared in 1865 in Czech and in 1866 in German.

stronger than one's desire for the maintenance of the Austrian Empire. For dualism meant the handing-over of the Slavs to the mercies of the Germans on this side of the Leitha and of the Hungarians on the other. Palacký here drew attention to the fact that 'in the great and speculative German nation peculiar philosophers are always forthcoming who . . . seem able to prove *a priori* that the principle of equal rights for nationalities is nonsense. . . . The Germans, who are by nature more gifted, stronger, nobler than the Slavs, can therefore by no means be put in the same category.' Now Palacký willingly admitted that the Germans of the day, owing to the advantages they had enjoyed, were more educated than the Slavs, but he utterly rejected the theory of permanently superior and inferior races. 'If the Slavs', he wrote, 'are really to be declared to be a lower race . . . and fit only to be the stuff for two other people to rule' terrible consequences may follow and Pan-Slavism will inevitably emerge in its most alarming forms. 'We Slavs are peaceful people, but we warn you; do not sow wind lest you reap storm. . . . Is that man free to whom it is said, "Thou shalt be free, but not as thou willst, only as I dictate to you."?' And finally Palacký uttered his famous dictum, 'Wir waren vor Österreich da, wir werden es auch nach ihm sein.'

Palacký had uttered a magnificent warning, but it fell on deaf ears both in that century and this. Dualism triumphed; the compromise with Hungary was made and Francis Joseph crowned King in Budapest. The frontier of the Leitha divided Germans from Germans, Czechs from Slovaks, and so on; only the Magyars remained whole.[1]

There remained the task of at last coming to a constitutional conclusion in Cisleithania, and on December 21st, 1867, the Austrian constitution was finally enacted. The electoral system remained as it had been and the Diets continued to elect the Reichsrat until 1873; the balance of power was shifted a little away from the extreme centralism of Schmerling towards greater competence for the Diets. The most interesting clause was the famous Article 19 which declared the equality of the nationalities and of all *landesüblich* (i.e. in provincial use) languages[2] in the schools and in the administration. This declaration, though not juridically binding and not necessarily put into practice,[3] satisfied the dominant

[1] Renner wrote: 'Die Leitha als Grenze ist so unsinnig, dass sie die natürliche Verschiedenheit künstlich in Gleichheit verwandelt, dass sie die Einheit erst zu Bewusstsein bringt: sie macht erst recht sichtbar, dass drüben genau dasselbe Völkerkonglomerat lebt und also ethnisch nichts gewonnen ist.' *Grundlagen- und Entwicklungsziele der öst-ungarischen Monarchie* (Vienna, 1906), p. 173.

[2] Confusion arose between the *landesübliche Sprache* and the *Landessprache*, i.e. the language of the province, confusion which the nationalities exploited as far as they could.

[3] Cf. R. Sieghart, *Die letzten Jahrzehnte einer Grossmacht* (Berlin, 1932), p. 88.

legislators of their own generosity, and could always be quoted as the law of the land. From that day to this, unfortunately—and no doubt ever since laws have been tabled—legislators have been satisfied that laws should be recorded, but subjects have complained that they are not therefore carried out.

For another decade Austria was to be ruled by the German Liberals with spasmodic pro-Slav interruptions on the part of the dynasty. Liberal rule was to a large extent Sudetendeutsch rule; the Auersperg Ministry of 1867, for instance, contained Hasner, Giskra, and Herbst, of whom Charmatz says that he always saw Austria's problems in terms of Germans retreating before a Czech offensive. Later that distinguished Egerlander, Ernst von Plener, became the mind of German Liberalism. In justice to a political party which nowadays finds no defenders, it should not be forgotten that the Liberals had a fine conception of that German civilization which they prized so highly, and further that it was thanks to them that police rule gave way to the reign of law and the recognition of individual rights, including those of the Jews.[1] They introduced public education provided by the state in 1868, two years before the corresponding measure in England.

In the first years following the dualist arrangement with Hungary the Czechs still struggled to be recognized as the equals of the Magyars, whose connexion with the Habsburgs dated from 1526 like their own. In 1870, indeed, under Potocki, *Böhmisches Staatsrecht* was accepted in principle, and the coronation of Francis Joseph was positively promised again.[2] Under the Hohenwart-Schäffle Ministry in 1871 a general settlement[3] with the Czechs seemed finally to have been reached. Officials and judges in the Historic Provinces were to speak both languages, though administrative divisions were to follow the language frontier as far as was possible. Germans and Czechs were to be divided into national *curiae* in the Diet in Prague which was to enjoy an authority in the lands of St. Wenceslas's crown not altogether inferior to that of the Budapest Parliament in the lands of the crown of St. Stephen. Immediately Andrássy protested vehemently on behalf of the Magyars. As for the Germans they were outraged. Austria would be reduced to chaos if every nationality were to have home rule—and there was a monster demonstration at Teplitz against the throwing of the Germans of Bohemia and Moravia to the Czech lion. On October 20th an Imperial Rescript, therefore, withdrew all that the Czechs believed they had won, and the appointment

[1] The Liberals thus carried on the tradition of Joseph II. They succeeded in getting rid of the Concordat in 1870, and they strongly sympathized with Bismarck in his anti-Catholic campaign.
[2] This was the third time this promise was made, and broken.
[3] Generally known as the Fundamental Articles.

of a new Auersperg Ministry, with the German Bohemians and Moravians strongly represented, resubjected them, as they felt, to the German yoke. The special rights granted to the Poles in Galicia (at the expense of the Ruthenes) in 1868 had helped to whet the appetite of the Czechs who were numerically nearly 2 million stronger than the Austrian Poles. The profound and bitter disappointment experienced by the Czechs in the years from 1867 to 1871 made a permanent impression upon them. From that time onward the mass of the nation—and very genuine idealists among them—developed a certain chauvinistic intransigence, which ruined many subsequent negotiations. They had known that the Sudeten Germans were their uncompromising enemies, but from 1871 they never again trusted the dynasty which had, as they saw things, so treacherously surrendered to the most aggressive of the Germans; the nation as a whole decided that dogged obstinacy was the only thing that paid.

CHAPTER V

FROM TAAFFE TO BADENI ('ÄRA TAAFFE'), 1879–1897

AS the seventies passed the Russo-Turkish War stimulated Slav enthusiasms, and it became impossible for the German *verfassungstreu*[1] Liberals to maintain their rigid objections to making concessions to the other nationalities. In 1878 the Emperor dismissed them, and in August 1879 his childhood's playmate, Count Taaffe, became Minister-President. A new era had opened indeed, for Taaffe was to rule for the next fourteen years in alliance with the Clericals, the aristocracy, and from 1882—when the franchise was lowered from 10 gulden to 5—the *petite bourgeoisie*; the spirit of his administration was Austrian in the sense that he believed that Austria could only be preserved if she took more account of her Slav majority, and he created a precedent by appointing Pražak, a prominent Czech, to a seat in the Cabinet. The Taaffe coalition, or, as it came to be called, the 'Iron Ring', reduced the Germans to something like impotence in the Reichsrat, to which the Czechs, on the other hand, in 1879 consented to return. The reform of the franchise and the language question became the crux of political controversy, but it was not until 1896 that the Slavs, in alliance with the German Social Democrats, could gain more than the 5-gulden law referred to above.[2] The elective system which Schmerling had invented had, incidentally, given rise to a curious scuffle before an election with the object of buying up land in order to count in the big landed proprietors' *curia*. So long as the German Liberals had ruled, they facilitated purchase by their own supporters. But the Czechs organized the buying up of land on their side, and after 1879 they ceased to encounter systematic opposition from the Government.

The language conflict was, if possible, even more envenomed than the electoral tussles, and it more directly affected everyday life. It had two main aspects, one administrative, the other educational. As ever the fight raged most fiercely in the Historic Provinces because, as Eisenmann says, they were more and more the middle-class provinces, and it was the smaller *bourgeois* who wanted State jobs for his sons and felt most strongly about the languages used in the schools. The Czechs always demanded that officials and judges should be bilingual in Bohemia, and they wished to break down the rule, strictly enforced in German Liberal days,

---

[1] 'True to the constitution', which they had every interest to preserve.
[2] From 1873 the Diets no longer elected the Reichsrat, but it was elected directly by the various *curiae*, a further move towards centralization.

that the so-called 'inner' civil service (*Innere Dienst*) should use only German. The Germans, of whom many regarded it as a degradation to speak Czech, had in 1868, in the absence of the Czechs from the Bohemian Diet, passed a law by which pupils at a German secondary school might not be compelled to learn Czech.[1] Thus the Germans were afraid that they would be driven out of the administration by the Czechs who were forced by circumstances to be bilingual; as for the question of the *Innere Dienst*, they regarded the use of German alone as a piece of indispensable uniformity.[2] The first expression of the new Taaffe tone was provided by the Language Decrees of 1880 by which both Czech and German might be used in courts of law and administrative offices, i.e. for the 'outer service' only. The Germans of Eger, Karlsbad, and Reichenberg were outraged by this concession, but the Czechs could ask them in reply why they should feel so very much concerned. For at the time German young men preferred to go into the army, and more and more, in those booming days,[3] into commerce, and the little bureaucratic jobs were automatically left to the Czechs.

Since about 1860 elementary schools in admittedly non-German districts had more and more been conducted in the local language. In the secondary schools, however, the teaching in the higher classes was solely in German. This state of affairs remained more or less the same until 1859. Thus the Czech *bourgeoisie* were unable to complete even their school education in their own language; as for the universities, the Germans regarded any suggestion that a non-German university could exist in Austria as an insult to German civilization. On July 20th, 1859, the Emperor had declared that in the secondary schools in predominantly non-German districts the education need not be completed in German, provided the pupils had a thorough knowledge of the German language.[4] This, of course, led to endless disputes as to which districts were predominantly non-German. In Moravia, moreover, no change was necessitated, since though the population was 70 per cent. Czech,[5] the Germans were concentrated in the towns where the secondary schools were bound to be, so that the Czechs had gained practically nothing.

The quick and intensive industrialization of the sixties and seventies created an elementary school conflict where none had existed before. For it involved a great population movement, a

---

[1] This was the law of Oct. 5th, 1868; see Sieghart, op. cit., p. 405.
[2] See Plener, *Reden*. Speech of Jan. 28th, 1884.
[3] There was, of course, a big financial crash in Vienna in 1873, but the general trend was a steeply rising one.
[4] Hugelmann, op. cit., p. 135.
[5] 70·34 per cent. according to the census of 1880. See Hugelmann, op. cit., p. 99.

Czech immigration into the frontier districts which was economically just as natural as the German immigration in earlier centuries
as a consequence of which the Germans regarded those regions as
German. From about 1860 German employers, especially in the
great lignite area of Northern Bohemia, were glad to take on Czech
labour from the interior, not only because it was cheaper but also
because it was more virile and therefore more satisfactory for unskilled work. The German working population lived on much
poorer soil and was to some degree decadent. The rapid development and high birth-rate of the Czechs and their propensity for
cobbling and tailoring now brought an increasing number of small
Czech craftsmen and shopkeepers into the German towns. These
changes were the more dangerous because they emphasized the
tendency for the German-Czech struggle to identify itself with
the social question of the day: German employer *versus* Czech
working-man.[1] Meanwhile the tendency for Czechs to take jobs as
small officials brought little Czech bureaucrats into the German
districts too. The reaction of the Germans to these things was
inconsistent. They expected to set up their factories or do what
they would, *qua* Germans, in the territory they admitted to be
Czech, e.g. in the towns surrounded by a Czech peasant population, but they regarded the German territories of Northern Bohemia as sacrosanct German soil. If Czechs chose to settle there
they must be willing to be completely Germanized; after all, as
the Germans were never tired of pointing out, German was a
world language which the Czechs should be thankful to learn.
The Czechs, therefore, encountered the most determined opposition to the building of any schools at all for Czech working-class
children. The administrative practice had developed of interpret-
ing Article 19 of the constitution so as to necessitate the building
of a State elementary school for any nationality if forty children of
school age and of that nationality lived within a radius of half a
mile.[2] In the North Bohemian lignite districts the Germans would
hear of no such thing; they even objected to the private schools
which the Czech School Union[3] soon tried to set up.

In the eighties, thanks to the Taaffe régime, the Czechs were put
into a position where they could fight about on equal terms, and
from that day to this the school struggle has raged between Germans and Czechs in the Historic Provinces with unabating fury.
National societies of various kinds multiplied on both sides in
these years. For the Czechs the foundation in 1868 of their first
big bank—the famous *Živnostenská Banka*—not controlled by
Vienna, had been perhaps as important in the fight as the fall of

[1] A good many of the employers were German-speaking Jews. See below.
[2] Hugelmann, op. cit., p. 134.   [3] See below, Chapter VII, p. 55.

the German centralist ministers from power. The Živno (as it is habitually called) financed the Czech national societies. It enormously facilitated the expansion of Czech industry, which brought with it growing strength in the Chambers of Commerce *curiae*. In 1883 the Budweis Chamber of Commerce began to send only Czechs to the Reichsrat, and there were tremendous tussles among the business men both of Pilsen and Prague. The two proudest achievements of the Czechs were the opening of their first national theatre in Prague in 1881,[1] and the division in 1882 of Prague University into separate German and Czech institutions; with the establishment of the first Czech University, Thomas Masaryk was summoned from Vienna to Prague as Professor of Philosophy. Musical developments were also the cause for justifiable gratification in view of the tradition which Smetana and Dvořák were building up; it was an opera by Smetana which was chosen for the first performance at the new national theatre in 1881.

With the beginning of the 'Iron Ring' period, the noisiest sections of German opinion in Austria became much more radical and began to find its expression in the Pan-Germanism of Georg von Schönerer, the mouthpiece of the students, who had originally found his way into the Reichsrat in 1873. Schönerer reacted first of all against the German Liberals, who had, as he taught his followers, betrayed the German cause. He criticized them as the tools of Big Industry, but above all he discovered their treachery to the German race to be due to the fact that Jews were prominent in their party; pure race became one of his slogans. This linked up with his violent condemnation of the political division, since 1866, of the Germans in Austria from those in what in 1871 became the Hohenzollern Empire. In the new Germany he saw his ideal state, and he longed for the Germans of Austria to be liberated from the racial impurities of the Habsburg Empire in order that they might become the happy subjects of the glorious Hohenzollerns. The *Anschluss* which he desired to see would have brought to Germany all those Austrian lands which had been included in the German Confederation; he must therefore have anticipated the total Germanization of the Czechs and the Slovenes. To the Habsburg dynasty he was soon frankly disloyal; he condemned it for its associations with Rothschild capital and above all for its friendliness with the Holy See, which in its supernationalism he regarded as hostile to the German race. 'Versunken im Wotanskult', as Sieghart writes, he was a precursor of General Ludendorff. Schönerer, further, denounced the dynasty and the

---

[1] The foundation-stone was laid in 1868; actually the theatre was burnt down before the end of 1881 and only reopened in 1883. Before that Czech performances were occasionally allowed at the German *Ständetheater* in Prague.

Catholic Church as, for instance in the person of Taaffe, the allies of the Slavs, who were also catalogued among the deadly enemies of Germanism. It was a fact that in the second half of the nineteenth century the lower clergy in Austria were mostly Slavs for the simple reason that the Germans did not wish to be priests. Nationalist Germans therefore accused the Church of trying to de-Germanize, but there is very little evidence that Slav priests in general did more than bring Slav maidservants with them into German districts; this they certainly did.

Schönerer began his political life on the Left,[1] and co-operated with future Socialists like Viktor Adler and Pernerstorfer in working out the Linz Programme of September 1st, 1882. According to this, the 1879 alliance with Germany was to be strengthened and developed into a grand *Mittel-Europa* customs unity. Within the monarchy, Dalmatia (together with Bosnia and Hercegovina), Galicia, and Bukovina were to be cut away from Austria (and possibly, Dalmatia certainly, incorporated with Hungary); in the Austria which remained, the German State language was to be definitely enforced. Upon this basis Schönerer founded his *Deutschnationaler Verein*. The indignation against Schönerer of the Czechs and the Slovenes, who were thus to be cut off from their fellow Slavs, to become a minority, and lose everything they had gained, can easily be imagined. To Schönerer, of course, the Germans in Austria were cut off and kept at a disadvantage in just the same way by the state of affairs which actually existed. It is the tragedy of Central Europe that every administrative demarcation appears arbitrary to those whom it reduces to be a minority. And in old Austria—it was the same with every school law or new language regulation—it seemed impossible to legislate so that one nation's gain was not the other's loss.

Georg von Schönerer was turbulent and quarrelsome. To the tune of his slogan *Durch Reinheit zur Einheit*, he was always purging his party, and his enemies whispered *Durch Reinheit zur Kleinheit*. His movement became increasingly aggressive, yet it had much more historical significance than the votes he ever polled would suggest. For one thing he formulated the expansionist views of a great many Germans with a crude frankness which has lasted from that day to this. This discredited the German case while stiffening the attitude of the anxious races who lived among or next door to the Germans. Schönerer was the author of the anti-Semitic phrase, 'In der Rasse liegt die Schweinerei', yet his wife turned out to have a Jewish great-grandfather. Nor was the

---

[1] It should not be forgotten that the 'Left' on the Continent has often been particularly nationalistic, and quite divorced from a British 'Lib.-Lab.' attitude towards international relations.

famous incident of 1888 reassuring. In this year the Emperor William I of Germany was lying on his deathbed, and the *Neues Wiener Tageblatt*, deceived by a telegram from Berlin, prematurely announced his death. On reading the *démenti* published a little later, Schönerer, with twenty-seven friends, broke into the editorial office of the *Tageblatt* and abused, insulted, and threatened the Jews on its staff for having trifled with Germany's Majesty—they were told to apologize on their knees, that the Day of Revenge was come, &c.[1] Schönerer was subsequently condemned to four months' prison for this, and it was said that the Emperor Francis Joseph insisted upon the punishment.

And here again lies the importance of Schönerer, that he alienated many Austrian Germans from the monarchy, which increasingly tended to become, instead of the mouthpiece of one dominant race, an impartial arbiter between the races. In the period from 1878 to 1908 the Habsburg dynasty approached fulfilment of the Austrian conception of the Danubian mediator. It was, unfortunately, too late for Francis Joseph to persuade the Czechs of his sincerity; after all, they were not quite wrong when they declared he was but bowing to the necessity which their strength had created. Democratic ideology, industrial development, and the higher birth-rate of the Slavs made it inevitable that the Germans in the Historic Provinces should steadily lose in power, influence, and wealth in the second half of the nineteenth century. The worst crime of Schönerer was that he queered the pitch for successful political adjustments to the new conditions. In order not to surrender to the logic of events, he and his friends vociferously took up the claim, which Palacký had criticized, and which Schmerling and Plener had tacitly made in more justifiable circumstances, that the Germans are a *Herrenvolk* born to rule and guide others.

German Bohemia had been a stronghold of the Liberals and did not immediately respond to the call of Schönerer. Later the German Bohemians, especially the vigorous *Egerländer*, became the pillars of Pan-Germanism, and Schönerer was for many years deputy of the district around Eger Town. Signs of Czech discontent with the moderate tone of Rieger's leadership had already appeared in Gregr's Young Czech revolt; it is easy to imagine how the Schönerianer stimulated the Young Czech movement which despised the Old Czechs as feudal, clerical, and ineffectual. Since about 1876 Gregr had been agitating against the Rieger abstinence policy, and after the Czechs returned to the Bohemian Diet and the Reichsrat itself, his following still continued to grow; it was

---

[1] See *Process Georg Ritter von Schönerer—Neues Wiener Tageblatt* (1888), especially p. 173.

not, however, until 1889, seven years after the Linz Programme, that the Young Czechs actually outnumbered the Old Czechs in the Bohemian Diet elections of that year.

The appearance of an intransigent younger generation on both sides did much to wreck a series of attempts at reasonable compromise which were undertaken by moderately minded Germans and Czechs in the eighties and nineties, and, indeed, at frequent intervals up to 1916. In 1883, in the Bohemian Diet, the big estate *curia* was won for the Czechs, and the Germans in their turn refused to attend from 1886 to 1890. Before their departure they roundly demanded the administrative demarcation of the German territory from the Czech for Bohemia, Moravia, and Silesia, and the withdrawal of the 1880 Language Decrees which this would imply. As Herbst said at the time, the Germans would never again drop this demand.

It was in January 1890 that the most important of all pre-War Czech-German negotiations took place between Rieger and the Germans, Schmeykal and Plener. The German negotiators gave way on minority schools, and the 40-children-in-a-district condition was accepted, provided the families of the children had been settled in the place for five years.[1] But Rieger not only accepted the administrative division principle, but actually agreed to go back on the 1880 laws, and he consented to the plan that 15 out of the 41 judges of the Bohemian Supreme Court need only speak German while the remaining 26 must know both German and Czech. When it came to putting this agreement[2] into practice it was the Czech turn to make difficulties. The Young Czechs created an uproar against Rieger, and the elections of 1891 gave them 37 seats in the Reichsrat as against a mere 12 Old Czechs. In the end nothing very much can be said to have remained of the 1890 plan except the division of the *Landesschulrat*—what we should call the Education Committee—into separate Czech and German sections, a division which has survived to the present time.

It would be tedious to examine every abortive negotiation between 1890 and 1916. The nineties became increasingly turbulent and the turbulence culminated in the troubles which followed the famous Badeni Language Decrees of 1897. In 1896 a fifth *curia* was added to the central government electoral system, a *curia* in which universal suffrage prevailed, those who voted elsewhere being able to vote here as well.[3] In consequence the elections of March 1897 further strengthened the Czechs, and on April 5th their long-fought-for wish was conceded by the Badeni Cabinet

[1] The Germans, as they still do to-day, complained that the Czech population was a merely visiting one. See below, Chapter VII, p. 56.

[2] Always referred to as the *Punktationen*.

[3] This reform did not apply to the election of the Diets.

that in Bohemia and Moravia, not only in dealing with ordinary people but as between officials, German and Czech should be on the same footing. Years of bitterest turmoil followed. While the Czechs demanded the extension of the decrees to Silesia as well, the extremist German Nationals multiplied their supporters. The Egerlander, Karl Hermann Wolf, the 'Dauphin'[1] of the Schönerer Movement, had been elected a deputy in March 1897, and he led the commotion in the Reichsrat, protesting against legislation by decree, and declaring on May 6th that 'the Germans would not stand everything from the Czechs, Slovenes, and other inferior nationalities'. The Pan-Germans frankly sang irredentist songs in those days. On July 11th the most memorable of all anti-Badeni demonstrations[2] occurred at Eger in spite of an official ban; consignments of Prague police (mixed German and Czech) were brought in, but the demonstrators crossed the frontier into Germany. Rioting between the Czech and German students in Prague after the Badeni Decrees was so frequent and so violent that the Germans for the first time mooted the transfer of the German University to a town in Sudetic German territory. In the notorious 'Badeni times' (*Badeni Zeiten*) civil war was perhaps only narrowly averted.

[1] Sieghart, op. cit., p. 309.
[2] R. Jung in his *Die Tschechen* (Berlin, 1937) gives an interesting indication of the Pan-German excitement in 1897 in Iglau.

CHAPTER VI

FOREIGN INTERLUDE, 1897–1899

THE struggle between the Germans and the Czechs in the Historic Provinces was not merely concerned with jobs and schools. Once the Czechs had arrived at the point at which, in 1879, owing of course to many extraneous circumstances, the Emperor preferred to rule with rather than against them, their interest in foreign policy made itself felt, and the vague background of Pan-Slav and Pan-German aspirations more directly affected diplomacy. As a matter of fact, Bismarck had only tolerated the Taaffe Ministry in Vienna on condition that Austria-Hungary was bound to Germany by the Dual Alliance of 1879. It was not, however, until the Badeni times that German diplomacy began to reckon seriously with the Czechs and the other Slav nationalities who, except for the Poles, followed their leadership. Palacký and Rieger had been to the Slav Congress in Moscow in 1867, and, as Masaryk[1] wrote, Palacký returned with his old formula 'Austria against Russia' changed into 'Austria beside Russia'. Nevertheless, the despotism which had prevailed since the assassination of Alexander II in 1881 reduced Czech enthusiasm until the time of the Revolution of 1905. It was rather from France that many of the Czechs of the nineties felt that they had learnt the most precious lessons of life, whether through Charles IV's studies at the Sorbonne or through the pioneers of European liberty who appealed to the peoples in the days of the first great French Revolution.

Many a traveller will feel that the Czechs are in several ways more western than the Germans and will breathe a sigh of understanding when he discovers that they know Dostoievski best via French translation. Just as the Sudetendeutschen of to-day reject silencing claims upon their loyalty and strive to make their fate into a European question, so did the Czechs, justifying their action upon the never legally abrogated independence of Bohemia and Moravia, work in pre-War days to bring their case before Europe. It was natural, therefore, that Rieger should have presented Napoleon III with a memorandum in 1868. In 1871 the Czechs expressed their distress at the conquest of Alsace and Lorraine by Germany. It was at this point, perhaps, that the clash between Prague and the nationalist Germans at home or abroad became most strikingly clear; from that day to this it has never ceased to be in only too great evidence. Many of the Germans in Austria had felt deeply

[1] T. G. Masaryk, *Palackýs Idee des böhmischen Volkes* (Prague, 1898), p. 47.

gratified by the German military successes of 1870, and to future followers of Schönerer the restoration of Alsace and Lorraine to their racial homeland, newly united by Prussia, was a very glorious event. To the Czechs it spelt the acquisitive greed of Pan-Germanism, which, given the power, would wish to swallow all bi- or multi-lingual provinces where German happened to be spoken, and would justify itself by belittling the extent to which any other language prevailed. With the growing strength of Hohenzollern Germany, Czech eagerness to insist that Bohemia and Moravia should be regarded, not as mixed, but as Czech, is easily explained, quite apart from *Böhmisches Staatsrecht* or Czech economic expansion. It was in this spirit that, when the Czech gymnasts of the *Sokol*[1] visited Nancy in 1892, their leader declared to their hosts, 'Our enemies are yours, and yours ours.'

The western orientation of the Czechs had been emphasized by the Realist movement. Though Rieger had started the Little-Mother-Moscow phrase in 1867, the Young Czechs were the keenest Pan-Slavs at the time of the Russo-Turkish War. They combined hostility to the Roman Church at home with a sentimental religious leaning towards Russia; some of them, regarding Orthodoxy as akin to Hussitism in its primitive simplicity, believed that the Czechs should support those Russians who wished to identify Pan-Slavism with the Orthodox Church. Three men of personal and academic distinction, Masaryk, Kramář, and Kaizl, had, however, formed an alliance in the name of realism. The Realists were, in very truth, protestants against all kinds of romantic excess. They called upon the Czechs to face things as they are. Against the violent opposition of Gregr Masaryk had exposed for all time the Königinhofer forgery—Czech patriotism, in Masaryk's view, could find its best justification in the scrupulous emphasis of truth. The Realists also questioned the value of Pan-Slavism, but while Masaryk came out for the greater advantage for the Czechs of the inspiration and friendship of France and the Anglo-Saxon west, Kramář gradually evolved his Neo-Slav idea and, from being a Realist, in 1897 himself became the Young Czech leader.

With the Dual Alliance between France and Russia in the early nineties, the ground was cleared for Czech aspirations which were bound to sympathize whole-heartedly with the new constellation. Count Taaffe, and later Count Badeni or Count Thun, were an admission of the fact that Austria had been forced to face numbers and admit herself to be predominantly Slav. Foreign affairs, it is true, were the joint affair of Austria with Hungary, and the Magyars were always pro-German in order to be anti-Slav. Never-

[1] See below, Chapter VII, p. 55.

theless, there were a great many Slavs in Hungary itself, vigorous Magyarization notwithstanding, and it seemed increasingly worth while, in the eyes of Czech leaders such as Dr. Kramář, to try to push Vienna out of the Triple Alliance of 1882 into line with France and Russia. The irritation of the Emperor Francis Joseph with the Schönerianer[1] drew him away from his alliance with the Hohenzollern Empire to which they so loudly longed to belong. Indeed, in the years immediately following 1897 Berlin was seriously alarmed by the diplomatic infidelity of Vienna, while the Austrian Government suspected Germany of positively encouraging irredentists in Austria.

Pan-German enthusiasts had increasingly been gathering together in Germany itself ever since 1870, and to heal the 1866 wound was perhaps the chief point on the programme; in its final form the Pan-German Union had been established in 1894 under the presidency of a certain Dr. Hasse.[2] It was closely connected with the German Navy League (which had conspicuous friends at court), and Reichstag deputies of nearly every complexion other than Socialist belonged to the Union. It controlled various newspapers, the chief ones being *Heimdall* and the *Alldeutsche Blätter*. Further, it patronized a network of educational societies both within Hohenzollern frontiers and beyond them.[3] The Pan-German Union regarded national fights in Austria as of general German concern; 'Schönerianer and members of the Austrian People's and Progressive Parties[4] repeatedly addressed meetings of the Pan-German Union which at that time took a lively interest in the excitements in Austria and which was in touch with the German nationalist societies there.'[5] Before the Badeni Decrees ferment had subsided, Schönerer and Wolf began their *Los von Rom* campaign, urging their followers to leave the Roman Catholic for the Protestant Church, to which Wolf already belonged. Schönerer announced that he was prepared to be converted to Protestantism when 20,000 persons had preceded him, and he

[1] See Eulenburg's dispatch to Hohenlohe, March 5th, 1898; in Germany: Auswärtiges Amt, *Die grosse Politik der europäischen Kabinette*, 1871–1914 (subsequently referred to as *Die grosse Politik*), vol. xiii, no. 3472.

[2] It is usually considered to have come into existence in 1893 under Peters. For an illuminating account of Pan-German activities in Germany proper see a dispatch from the British Consul-General at Munich to Sir E. Grey sent off on Jan. 24th, 1906 (F.O. 371/76, no. 14); in Great Britain: Foreign Office, *British Documents on the Origins of the War*, edited by G. P. Gooch and H. W. V. Temperley, vol. iii, chap. xxii.

[3] It is interesting that in 1902 it is stated in Dr. Zemmrich's *Sprachgrenze und Deutschtum in Böhmen* that the Saxon branch of the Reich German School Society provided a third of the money (40,000 marks) spent on German schools and kindergartens on the Bohemian language frontier.

[4] See below.

[5] Quoted from P. Molisch, *Geschichte der deutsch-nationalen Bewegung in Österreich* (Jena, 1926), p. 193.

actually accepted conversion on September 2nd, 1900. The *Los von Rom* offensive was enthusiastically received by Protestant pastors in Germany, though the Protestant authorities in Austria looked askance at this flow of political conversions. The Emperor Francis Joseph, who with advancing years—at least in the opinion of the German Embassy in Vienna—was drawing closer to the Catholic Church, himself expressed annoyance[1] when the signature of Faber, General Superintendant and *Probst* of Berlin (i.e a State official), appeared among others on an appeal in support of the Protestant movement in Austria. Although Bülow sent correct instructions from Berlin, the German diplomats in Vienna clearly sympathized with the Schönerianer. The Chargé d'Affaires, Prince Lichnowsky, regarded Wolf as the true 'spiritual leader of the German people in Austria',[2] which incidentally he believed the Emperor's Slavophile policy was utterly destroying, a good Wolf-Schönerer view.

The Czechs, in the eyes of the Ambassador, Eulenburg, as of Lichnowsky, were playing the sinister role of pushing Austria away from Germany into the arms of Russia and France.[3] It happened that in 1897 a *détente* between Vienna and St. Petersburg had materialized in a Balkan Agreement between them, Russia's Far-Eastern preoccupations making their relations relatively simple. It was natural that the Czechs should seek to use all these circumstances in order to ease that feeling of being caught between millstones which the alliance with Germany increasingly gave them as Pan-German activities grew; it was just as natural that the out-and-out Germans, whether of the German Embassy at Vienna or of the Austrian Parliament, should resent Czech excursions into foreign policy, more especially since in the days of the Thun Ministry (1898–9), with Kaizl as Minister of Finance, the Czechs had some chance of success. The future of Central Europe was, after all, at stake—whether or not it should be a German *Mittel-Europa*, which the Germans regarded as decreed by the laws of nature, and the Linz Programme. The possibility of Russian domination of the Danube Valley was not, I believe it would be generally agreed, a serious alternative, but a genuinely nervous condition had been induced in many Germans by the idea of Russia in their midst and they started the habit of referring to Prague as the 'Western Moscow'.

During this period the Prussian Government was engaged in a

---

[1] Eulenburg to Hohenlohe, March 31st, 1899 (*Die grosse Politik*, vol. xiii, no. 3506). The Emperor Francis Joseph pointed out that Austria had never interfered with Germany in *Kulturkampf* days.

[2] Lichnowsky to Hohenlohe, June 13th, 1898 (ibid., no. 3474).

[3] Eulenberg to Hohenlohe, April 13th, 1899 (ibid., no. 3509) describes Germany's request that the Slavs in Austria shall be kept in their place.

severe anti-Polish policy and welcomed opportunities for the expulsion of Slavs in order to bring German settlers into its Polish provinces. The question was in so far as Austrian subjects were concerned brought up by Slav deputies at Vienna in November and the answer of the Prime Minister, Count Thun, was considered by the German Government to have been provocative to Berlin. Before this incident was finished with, Prince Eulenburg heard on December 16th that the distinguished Young Czech leader, Kramář, whose relations with the French Ambassador Eulenburg described as notorious,[1] was about to publish an article in the *Revue de Paris*, advocating a French-Russian-Austrian alignment. The article did not actually appear until February 1st, 1899,[2] and had by then been considerably watered down; even so, Francis Joseph appears not to have been best pleased, and when Count Clary succeeded Count Thun in the autumn, Vienna had swung back to a moderate pro-Germanism.

The feelings aroused by the Kramář article were characteristic of the general situation at the time. William II, of course, peppered the dispatches from Vienna with indignant comments. But the Czechs persisted, and Kramář provided Delcassé with a memorandum on the Bohemian question in 1902. He and his countrymen watched Germany's power in Turkey and her interest in Bagdad, and they knew that Prussia had pressed the other German states into the Hohenzollern Empire by economic means. To stem the German stream—as yet only economic—Kramář wrote in 1905 'is the life interest of the Czech people—and of the Habsburg dynasty'.[3] As he pointed out, the victories of Japan had by then cut down the possibilities of Far Eastern expansion and emphasized Germany's interest in the Near Danubian lands and the Middle East. He believed that but for the Czechs she might sweep Austria entirely away.

It is true that Kramář was married to a Russian and was strongly Russophile. But round about the turn of the century he had begun to advocate what he called Neo-Slavism. This he distinguished from Pan-Slavism in that, while it emphasized the cultural links between the Slavonic peoples, Neo-Slavism abandoned all thought of political union. The different Slav groups each had its own task to fulfil. 'For the future as for the past', he wrote, 'it will remain true that the Czech people performs an invaluable service to the Slav cause by the very fact of its existence, in that it drives a living wedge between the Germans. It is thus its first duty to be so strong and healthy that not the smallest anxiety need exist lest it

[1] Eulenburg to Hohenlohe, Dec. 16th, 1898 (*Die grosse Politik*, vol. xiii, no. 3488).
[2] Count Münster to the German Foreign Office, Feb. 1st, 1899 (ibid., no. 3499).
[3] Kramář, op. cit.

give way to German pressure.' Kramář was just as sincere in this belief as the nationalist Germans of Prussia or Bohemia who regarded him as the evil genius of Central Europe. It was of the essence of the whole situation that the various brands of enthusiastic Slavs or Germans invariably believed that the others disguised sinister political ambitions beneath cultural-unity claims, and threatened to encircle and choke their helpless victims who only desired to live.

CHAPTER VII

THE GENERAL POSITION AT THE BEGINNING OF THE TWENTIETH CENTURY

COUNT CLARY'S Government finally withdrew the Badeni Decrees in 1899, but the atmosphere continued to be electric for some years. Of the parties mentioned above[1] in relation to the *Reichsdeutsch* Pan-German Union, the Progressive Party was the heir to the now *passé* Liberals, while the German People's Party, founded in 1894, was intensely nationalistic but in practice prepared to make compromises. The Progressives and the People's parties had in May drawn up their so-called Whitsun Programme, in which they of course insisted upon the German alliance as indispensable. The other points on this programme were clearly inacceptable to the Czechs—for instance a German State language, administrative division in Bohemia, Moravia, and Tyrol, and German to be on the same footing with Czech in the city of Prague, which was only about 5 per cent. German. Meanwhile Schönerer was becoming more extreme. He condemned the Whitsun Programme because it conceded the division of Bohemia. He now insisted upon calling his party Pan-Germans, and in April 1901, for instance, he spoke in public of the dissolution of Austria as a step towards the salvation of the German people.[2] The Young Czechs also continued their violence, and in the stormy elections of 1901 the extremist groups were strengthened in the Reichsrat, the Pan-Germans increasing from 8 to 21. The constructive proposals of the Prime Minister, Körber, advocating a triple partition of Bohemia into a German, a Czech, and a mixed territory, were now foolishly ruled out by both nations.

In the early years of the new century passion gradually gave way to an evident fatigue; but the Russian Revolution then had a tremendously stimulating effect upon the Slavs and the German Social Democrats of Austria. Two notable reforms were in consequence made possible, one the Moravian Compromise of November 1905, the other the introduction of universal suffrage early in 1907. These remarkable achievements disposed of the theory that nothing positive could be achieved in pre-War Austria; they created the conditions in which the last stage of pre-War Austrian life was lived. Briefly, the Moravian Compromise stabilized the

---

[1] See Chapter VI, p. 47.
[2] See Molisch, op. cit., p. 210. On June 16th, 1900, Schönerer sent a telegram to a meeting at Olmütz as follows: 'Auf! Los von Juda! Los von Rom! Lasst Heimdalls Horn erschallen! Lasst deutsche Banner wallen! Heil allen Gleichgesinnten!'

relations between Germans and Czechs by fixing the proportions in which they were to be represented in the Diet at Brünn (Brno). The population of Moravia at the time was over 70 per cent. Czech. In the urban *curia* there were to be 20 Germans to 20 Czechs, in the country one 14 Germans to 39 Czechs, in the general one 6 to 14; only the big property *curia* was not nationally divided. Voting was no longer to be on a purely territorial but partly on a personal basis, for voters had to be inscribed in the lists according to their nationality. The language or languages in official use were, as far as possible, to be locally decided; in a town with at least a 20 per cent. minority, its members could legally claim to be officially dealt with in their own language.

The most enlightened, perhaps, of all Francis Joseph's prime ministers, Freiherr von Beck, was appointed in 1906 soon after the Moravian Compromise had been reached. The pressure from the Slav nationalities, and especially from the German Social Democrats, who had been able to make themselves felt (if quite disproportionately to their numerical strength) in the Reichsrat since the half-measure of 1896, had been bound to increase in favour of a logical conclusion; if the fifth *curia* men had a right to vote at all they were certain to urge the One-Man-One-Vote claim. But in a nationality state like Cisleithania, universal suffrage was a much more tricky affair than the Englishman easily imagines. The Germans, even while many of them had come to accept the inevitability of every man voting, were mostly unable to face the prospect of a non-German voter becoming politically equivalent to a German one. They regarded their willingness to consider the reform as in itself a magnanimous sacrifice to the inferior or backward nations, but they tried—the Social Democrats excepted—to ensure that together with the Italian deputies, who were on bad terms with the Adriatic Slavs, they could never be out-voted in the Reichsrat. They therefore proposed that the 10 million Germans should be represented by 241 deputies, and 6½ million Czechs by 97 in a house of 516 deputies. This suggestion was finally modified so that the Germans had 233 deputies to 109 Czechs; even so the Czechs agreed that there should be 55 German to 75 Czech deputies for Bohemia, although the population was as about 1 to 2.[1] For Moravia the compromise arrangements were incorporated. At last the law was completed, and elections immediately followed. Though national differentiation was far from being obliterated, with the enfranchisement of every man over 24 Austria had achieved a more democratic electoral system than Great Britain for its central Parliament, though its Diet and other local elections remained unaffected. Beck did not rest on his laurels. The labours

[1] Hugelmann, op. cit., p. 365.

he had performed in working out the new parliamentary constituencies had involved an agreed delimitation of national frontiers,
since the constituencies were territorial and nationally more or less
homogeneous. Having thus in effect achieved a preliminary agreement in Bohemia, he hoped to crown his work by even reaching
the elusive goal of a final Bohemian settlement, since the Bohemian
question was, as every one knew, the most difficult and also the
most dangerous among all the problems of Austria. Every one
was tired of it and yet often enough, as the phrase went, only 'a
wall as thin as paper' separated the German and Czech negotiators.
Unfortunately differences of opinion over the Austrian annexation
of Bosnia and Hercegovina led in 1908 to Beck's fall. During the
last six years of peace no outstanding event with regard to Bohemia,
Moravia, or Silesia took place; the new Reichsrat, unhappily,
proved as unworkable as the old.

At this point, therefore, a general review of the conditions of
life in the Historic Provinces in the last decade or so before Sara-
jevo may be usefully attempted. All along the language frontiers
in Bohemia and Silesia a bitter struggle raged. Every town-council
election was a national test in the mixed and frontier districts. It
should be remembered that the electoral reform of 1907 had left
municipal and other local elections untouched, i.e. all of them
weighted in favour of the rich. How much the more maddening
for the poor Czech workman to have an independent vote for a
parliamentary candidate, but to be helplessly silenced in his own
locality. (Of course the number of rich Czechs was increasing, but
in general wealth remained out of all proportion in German hands.)
If the Czechs could gain a majority in only one *curia* in the towns,
they then began to be able to express opinions with regard, say, to
elementary schooling, which was primarily the concern of the
municipal authorities. The process of winning so many votes
developed into a canvassing match between the national societies
on both sides. Earlier, the most painful decisions among the intelli-
gentsia had occurred when often enough one brother would decide
for his father's nationality and the other for his mother's, or one for
the nationality to which he owed his education, the other for the one
into which he was born. 'National renegade' is one of the bitterest
terms of abuse which the Central European knows, and yet other
people have the most casual way of announcing a man's nationality.
'X a Czech, why, that's absurd', a German will say to one, 'why, he
was born or bred as a German' (i.e. in territory claimed as German).
'X a German, why, that's ludicrous,' a Czech will say, 'every one
knows his father was a Czech', and X himself is scarcely asked.

Working-people had often ignored the whole business, but after
the turn of the century it became increasingly difficult for them to

do so. Some of the Czechs were certainly glad to be Germanized and to enjoy the advantages of being 'in' with the dominant German groups, and of talking a language familiar to tens of millions of people in the world. On the whole the Czech societies had much the more difficult job, for their members had to go round persuading people to risk dismissal by the German employers, many of whom frankly used economic terrorization to attain national ends.[1] Whenever the census was taken in pre-War Austria, people were registered according to their *Umgangssprache*, i.e. their language of everyday use. This meant that a good many Czechs could be entered as German, because they worked in a German concern where one spoke German; if they reported as Czechs they might lose their job. Pre-War statistics were thus biased against the Czechs and the other Slavs. Further, the economic structure of northern Bohemia, partly on account of the age of its industries, was such as to facilitate intimidation, for the working-people tended to live in villages outside the towns; it was easier, therefore, for the authorities to know how people had voted[2] or what nationality they had registered, and it was more difficult to build up trade-union organizations. The working-people, also, were nearly always housed by their employers or by the local authorities, who in the lignite area were all Germans, and often more or less the same Germans.

The most important national societies on the German side were the *Schulverein*, founded in 1880, and the *Bund der Deutschen*, founded in 1894; the first covered all Austria, the second only all Bohemia; the smaller localities each had their local *Schutzvereine*, of which the *Böhmerwaldbund*, founded in 1884, was one of the most vigorous. Some twenty years older than the *Schulverein* was the *Turnverband*, a great gathering-place for youths and young men. These societies were either founded by Pan-Germans or rapidly dominated by the Schönerer spirit, and they did all they could to instil Pan-German views. Most of them excluded Jews from membership, and loudly abused Jews and Slavs in the same breath. The *Bund der Deutschen* was, as it is to-day, the economic backbone of the nationalists, and interested itself, for instance, in keeping land in German hands as against Czech acquisition. The *Schulverein* was concerned to make certain that no hypothetically German child should lack a German education; in pre-War days it had relatively little to do in the way of providing schools since the *curia* system of election overweighted German influence in the towns

---

[1] See quotations from Cajthaml's book below.
[2] The ballot had been nominally secret in Cisleithania since the beginning of the constitutional era in 1860, but in practice it worked out with much local variety; Galicia and Dalmatia were notorious for frankly incorrect elections; in the Historic Provinces one hears only of indirect pressure.

which were responsible for elementary education, while the State was sufficiently *deutsch geführt* to ensure that plenty of German secondary schools were kept going. The *Schulverein* exerted, however, a very great influence upon the education of German children, for it endeavoured to enrol all schoolmasters as its members; the tone of teaching in the German schools in pre-War Austria was outstandingly nationalistic and even Pan-German in tone, and there was very little effort made to educate in the spirit of a conciliating and mediating Austria. Only the Catholic Church and the Socialists did something to work in this direction, and the *Schulverein* was, of course, their eager opponent. The high proportion of Sudetendeutsch university professors and schoolmasters all over Austria was striking, and their views were predominantly Pan-German.

Most of these 'Defence' organizations were duplicated on the Czech side. The *Sokol* was founded in 1862 in answer to the German *Turnverband*. The Czechs had their own School Union, the *Ustřední Matice Školská*, also founded in 1880, and they had founded a number of regional unions in the eighties of which that in north Bohemia (*Národní jednota severočeská*) and in the *Böhmerwald* (*N. j. pošumovská*) were the largest and best known. At that time the Czechs had had a vital interest in buying up land or industrial shares through the possession of which alone they could compete with Germans in the elections to the privileged *curiae* of the big landed proprietors and the chambers of commerce. Equally important to them was the ability to offer to a Czech workman some kind of compensation or temporary maintenance if he had been turned out of his cottage or had lost his job because his German employer believed him to be voting for a Czech party, entering as Czech in the census returns, or showing other signs of revolt. The provision of their own schools for Czech children living in predominantly German districts was a matter of perhaps more vital importance to the Czechs than anything the German societies had to do. There was, after all, a fairly steady flow of Czechs to the lignite mines of Northern Bohemia, and, in general, from the overcrowded Czech peasant centre of the country, where, owing to the enormous extent of aristocratic holdings, land was short, to the German or mixed towns where small shops had plenty of chance to make good. Though the Czech birth-rate began to fall down to the German level before 1900[1] and the flow slowed

[1] According to the Austrian census figures taken every ten years, the Czech birth-rate in Bohemia fell slightly behind that of the Germans between 1890 and 1900, but after 1900 overstepped it again. (Cf. Rauchberg, *Nationaler Besitzstand in Böhmen.*) In contrast with these figures, the Czech population in the lignite district (Brüx, Dux, Teplitz) rose from 8 per cent. in 1880 to 12·5 per cent. in 1890 and to 18·5 per cent. in 1900, reaching 21·5 per cent. in 1910. See E. Strauss, *Die Entstehung der Tschechoslowakischen Republik*, p. 38.

down, it was bound to continue for a time. The children concerned, if they went to German schools, would find it more convenient to accept Germanization, and would be permanently lost to the Czechs—they would have no occasion to re-learn Czech if the Germans could successfully block legislation like that of Badeni. The *Matice*, therefore, worked first to get permission from the local authorities to start a private school, and then to find the funds to keep it going, apart from *Živnostenská* Bank credits. Getting permission was, however, not easy. A Czech miner called Cajthaml has published a book called *Sketches from German-Bohemia* in which he gives many instances of the state of affairs as he knew it in pre-War days. He describes, for example, how at a mining village called Seestadtl (Ervěnice) (between Brüx (Most) and Komotau (Chomutov)) the Czechs had asked for a school in 1897, whereupon 35 out of 55 applicants were evicted from their homes. In 1907 62 parents representing 305 children petitioned again, and 2 Czech engineers, Vybulka and Brabec, were consequently dismissed from the local mines as 'ringleaders'. An inquiry was held.

The Germans objected that the applicants were not working at Seestadtl but in neighbouring pits. Many of them at the census, so it was alleged, had been registered as Germans (although they themselves were not aware of it). The Czechs of Seestadtl, it was further alleged, were a shifting element and were not ratepayers and therefore they had no right to a Czech school. Moreover, there was no need for a Czech school for the children of Czech parents who also knew German, nor for those who had already been admitted to German schools.

Herold, the German Radical deputy for Brüx, was very active in exposing 'those persons who are trying to undermine the German character of our town', and 30 more evictions occurred. Cajthaml refers to the whole first generation of Czech children in another mining village, Mariaschein (Bohosudov), north of Teplitz (Teplice), as having been Germanized.

Of course if the attendance at a *Matice* school could be got up to forty children who could be proved to belong to fairly permanently settled families, the local authorities were legally compelled to take over the school. Indeed a German, Dr. Zemmrich, writing in 1902,[1] complains of the *Matice*: 'Once such a school is foisted on to a German commune, the means thus freed are immediately used to found another school in a German locality. Up to the present, and including Moravia and Silesia, about 100 such schools[2] have been built and a large number of these must now be supported by German communes.' On the other hand, German complaints were not lacking against Czech children attending

[1] Zemmrich, op. cit.   [2] In German '*solcher Kampfschulen*'.

German schools on account of the German children then picking up Czech instead of learning other things.[1] The official statistics of 1902 showed that the Czech minority schools, i.e. public elementary schools in predominantly German districts, were at a disadvantage in that the classes were bigger than those in the German elementary schools. The figures for fairly typical predominantly German towns were as follows:[2]

				Average number of German children per class	Average number of Czech children per class
In Northern Bohemia in Reichenberg				52	62
,,	,,	,,	Trautenau	61	74
,,	,,	,,	Teplitz	54	70
,,	,,	,,	Dux	46	68
,,	,,	,,	Brüx	58	63
,,	,,	,,	Bruch	49	156
In Southern Bohemia in Budweis				52	75
,,	,,	,,	Rudolfstadt	53	69
,,	,,	,,	Krumau	40	88
,,	,,	,,	Prachatitz	37	82

According to Hugelmann, for the school year 1913–14, there were in Bohemia taken alone:

	German	Czech
Elementary schools	2,334 (plus 73 private schools)	3,359 (plus 94 private schools)
Upper elementary schools	242 (plus 16 private schools)	382 (plus 2 private schools)
Secondary schools	59	86

Though the proportions were numerically unjust to the Czechs, the injustice was markedly smaller than thirty or forty years earlier, but, as we have seen, it was in its turn augmented by the greater size of the classes in the Czech schools.

A typical case of the disputes and misunderstandings which arose in this period is provided by the school situation in Prague. The nationalist Germans complained that the proportion of German to Czech schoolchildren in the capital was much higher than that of German to Czech population as a whole.[3] This was explained by the assumption that the municipal authorities, when the census was taken, used means to reduce the figure for the Germans, and of course that German-speaking Jews had registered as Czech. The Czechs, on the other hand, pointed to the number of Czech

[1] The *Čechische Revue* of 1907 (p. 671) had an article quoting and discussing such complaints. The *Čechische Revue* was an admirable Czech periodical published in German by academic people, some of them friends of Professor Masaryk.   [2] *Čechische Revue*, 1910, p. 17.
[3] Zemmrich, op. cit.

children attending German schools because their parents wanted them to have the advantages of being bilingual and who were therefore registered on the German schools list.[1] As a matter of fact the number of German elementary school children fell in Prague between 1880 and 1907 by 48·2 per cent., and the Czechs complained that for the reduced numbers there were far too many schools.

All these school quarrels were only acute in Bohemia and Silesia,[2] because in Moravia, at the time of the Compromise of 1905, the *Lex Perek* had been passed, which forbade that German children should go to Czech schools or Czech children to German ones; even after this, practical difficulties sometimes arose, and one hears in 1910 of the—in the Czech view illegal—closing of a Czech school at Poštorná (Unter Themenau) near Břeclav (Lundenburg) in southern Moravia. The increasing flow of Czechs to Vienna in these years presented the school problem in Viennese form.

The influence of the Czech nationalist societies was just about as uncompromisingly and romantically chauvinist as that of their German competitors. While the Germans fondled the idea of putting history right by a new and thorough Germanization of all Bohemia, the Czechs through their school-teachers instilled the reconquest theory into their pupils. This derived indirectly from Palacký's theory of history and the *Staatsrecht* idea. Czech children were brought up to believe that all Bohemia and Moravia had once been unadulteratedly Czech—so far so good, perhaps—and that it was their duty to reconquer the German districts from the usurping German invader by crowding into the German towns, winning majorities on councils, setting up factories, and making the land once more their own.

One of the most foolish chauvinist practices which arose presumably in the eighties[3] and has never subsided was that of buying from tradespeople of one's own nationality and boycotting the rest. It would not be possible to establish with certainty when this habit began. The Czech minorities in the German districts would naturally go to Czech shops, perhaps, and some of the Germans who resented the appearance of these minorities would naturally try to avoid them. These tendencies developed, in the small towns especially, into economic battles with 'Buy only Czech' as war-cry against 'Buy only German'. It was characteristic of K. H. Wolf that in a speech at Olmütz (Olomouc) in June 1900, when he was perhaps at the height of his popularity, he said, 'The women too must bring up their children to be rigidly national and when they go shopping they must go only to German shops even if these

[1] *Čechische Revue*, 1910, p. 17.
[2] The struggle for a Czech grammar school in Troppau (Opava) went on for years; it was finally successful.
[3] Referred to in a speech of Plener's in the Reichsrat on Jan. 28th, 1884.

should be more expensive.' Since the same sort of thing was urged by the Pan-Germans against both Czechs and Jews, not only did shopping become complicated, but the Czechs, who were spasmodically anti-Semitic themselves, became more indignant than ever. The chauvinist Germans had a habit of describing as parasites the Slavs as well as the Jews, and in Eger (Cheb) in 1897, for instance, one hears of hotels and cafés which used to show notices, 'Czechs, Jews, dogs, not allowed here'. This sort of thing was often seriously meant from the one side and always bitterly resented on the other.

Of course between students and schoolboys mutual insults did not necessarily matter very much. It was not very nice of Czech students to throw rotten eggs at the German street inscriptions in Prague until they were finally removed, and it was not very nice of Germans always to make fun of 'Wenzel' and the queer way he spoke German. But these things in themselves need not have had unhappy consequences. In fact they led to lamentable misunderstanding. For instance, a student coming to the German University in Prague would be told that it was impossible to know Czechs, for they would be certain to behave provocatively towards him. Only through some fortunate accident would the barriers occasionally break down and German-Czech friendships of great value be formed.

As men like the deputy, Dr. Franz Jesser, or the university lecturer, Dr. Spina, pointed out at the time,[1] the Germans in Eger (Cheb), Karlsbad (Karlovy Vary), or Reichenberg (Liberec) judged the Czechs entirely by a few workmen or struggling little tradespeople who lived in considerable isolation among them. They had absolutely no idea of what, for instance, the Czech intellectual world in Prague was like, where the Czech University had all along an array of really distinguished scholars to show. Both Germans and Czechs were to blame for the gulf that yawned between them. The frequent obstinacy of the Czech professors in publishing their work only in Czech cut them off from the intellectual life of France and England as much as it did from Germany, while Czech was not sufficiently close to the other Slav languages to be useful to scholars in other Slav universities, though Slav men-in-the-street might be able to read each others' newspapers.

Most educated Germans, on the other hand, could never bring themselves to regard Czech as anything but a servants' language

[1] Dr. Jesser belonged to the German People's Party and in 1912 published an extremely valuable pamphlet called *Das Wesen des nationalen Kampfes in den Sudetenländern*. Dr. Spina lectured in Czech literature at the German University in Prague; he wrote a particularly illuminating article in *Deutsche Arbeit*, vol. vii, pp. 433–9, in 1910.

which they despised, or, if they came from Vienna, they ridiculed. It is not an exaggeration that many of them considered it not fit to learn. They never could believe that a Czech had any difficulty in speaking the great World-Language German, which would bring him all the delights of German literature and obvious practical convenience. German was the language of Society, the language of the Court, the Army, and the Higher Civil Service. Some Czechs, therefore, spoke German because of its social prestige, but most of them would not, as a protest against snobs, although in the towns nearly all Czechs could speak German when necessary. The following incident is characteristic. The historian, Professor Bachmann, another Egerlander, was elected to the Reichsrat in 1907. Soon afterwards the Czech politician Herold addressed an open letter to him in the Czech newspaper *Národní Listí*, expecting an answer in German. Dr. Bachmann, who knew Czech well, refused to answer on the grounds that he had no time for Czech and begged Dr. Herold in future to address him in German 'nach dem Gebote guten Tones'.[1] . . . Czech country people, of course, were quite often genuinely unable to manage German, and it should not be forgotten that most Czechs over 30 remember painful incidents in their childhood caused by this fact. One could cite an unending number of examples. I need only refer to A. B., who came from the country near Brünn (Brno). As a child he tried to buy a ticket at Brünn station; he could only speak Czech so they refused to serve him, though even the inner city was by then about 40 per cent. Czech. His father, a forester, spoke both languages, his mother only Czech; he has never forgotten a German colleague of his father who on one occasion shouted at his mother (in German), 'It is a scandal that you still don't speak German.'

It should quickly be added that many Germans had no conception of how much offence they gave through incidents of this kind. Sudeten Germans have often said to me, 'The Czechs, it is certain, felt themselves to be oppressed or humiliated by the Germans under the *ancien régime*, but we had no idea of it.' For the Germans could only see that the Czechs had a powerful delegation in the new democratic Reichsrat and a majority in the Bohemian and Moravian Diets. They had their schools, their university, their theatres, they had their officials and even their Ministers since Pražak and Kaizl. Indeed, in many German eyes, the Czechs, as we have seen, were favoured out of all proportion by the Emperor, and were greedily absorbing far more than their due in the civil service and in the railways. Hugelmann states that just about at the time when the Great War began the Germans had 421 pro-

[1] = as good tone requires. See *Čechische Revue*, 1908, p. 480.

vincial officials and 4,817 (Imperial) State officials less than their
numbers would justify in Bohemia. Dr. Zemmrich (in 1902) complains that, since Kaizl, Czechs to Germans serving under the
Ministry of Finance in Bohemia are about 3 to 1.[1] Among administrative officials, judges, and other legal officials he estimates the
proportion to be 4 to 1. He complains that the Badeni Decrees
might as well not have been withdrawn because, for instance, the
Czech text is still unlawfully allowed to precede the German one in
the official journal of a town called Schüttenhofen (Sušice) which is
the capital town of a *Bezirk*[2] (or county) containing both German
and Czech territory. He particularly blames the State Railway
Control for systematically sending Czechs into German territory
and cites, among other examples, the case of Komotau (Chomutov),
where in 1900 the Germans numbered 15,528 and the Czechs 397,
of whom 203 were railway officials; on the line from Komotau to
Bodenbach (Podmokly), which crosses mixed, but in his view
purely German, territory, he reports 28 Germans at work to 84
Czechs. German is supposed to be the language of the railway
service, but one hears only Czech spoken among the railway
personnel.[3] These Czech railwaymen, he writes, are 'mostly
married and their families draw Czech craftsmen and tradespeople
after them. In this way the whole German territory [in Bohemia]
is Czechified by the Imperial and Royal State Railway.'

This account of the preference shown for Czechs and for Czech
by the Ministry of Finance, the Ministry of Justice, and the Prague
head office of the State railway sounds so exactly like the German
complaints which one hears thirty-five years later that one sometimes wonders how much of all this is in the nature of things. I
have already referred to reasons which led to a high proportion of
Czechs among unskilled workmen such as a railway service can to
a large extent employ, and to reasons which caused Czechs rather
than Germans to hold small bureaucratic posts; in addition, the
fact that the Czech candidate for these posts was more or less
bilingual was of obvious practical advantage. On the other hand,
reconquest ardour undoubtedly caused particular favour to be
shown to Czechs by Czech authorities, who regarded the Historic
Provinces as Czech, whether they contained a large German population or not. It is interesting, however, to read Dr. Zemmrich's
account of how the Czechs were being steadily driven back by the
Germans in the district around Mies (Stříbo),[4] where in his

[1] Zemmrich, op. cit. ·
[2] Within the provincial frontiers there were *Bezirke* and within those *Kreise*
(circles) for local government purposes in Bohemia. Moravian and Silesian
administration varied slightly.
[3] Though they were compelled to pass a German language test.
[4] See below, Chapter XI.

opinion no German had even set foot before 1650; on the rarer occasions when movement is in this direction he is perfectly content. For he also describes with obvious satisfaction the 'winning back' of the town of Trebnitz (Třebenice) since the arrival there in 1889 of a certain Dr. Titta who became the local German *Führer*.[1] No satisfactory explanation of the German-Czech question in the fifty years which preceded the War can be found unless it includes and emphasizes the view held by men as different as Jesser and Renner, that a period of great economic expansion was creating conflicts in which the competitors eagerly seized upon chauvinist slogans to further their interests. As for the matter of the Gazette of Schüttenhofen, it deserves notice as an illustration of the German reaction whenever the position of German as the State language was challenged.

In the Czech view, as a matter of fact, the Germans kept the higher posts in the civil service for themselves, leaving only the inferior ones to the Slavs. The *Čechische Revue* examined this question in commenting upon an article which appeared in *Naše Doba* in 1910. The writer began by defending the Kaizl tradition in the Imperial Ministry of Finance in Vienna, a tradition, that is, of favouring candidates with a knowledge of more than one language. He proceeded to analyse the higher personnel at the Ministry itself at the time:

Of the 6 Principals (*Sektionschefs*)	5	were German,		1 Polish.		
„ 18 *Ministerialräte*	13	„ „		3 Polish,	1 Czech	
					1 Italian	
„ 18 *Sektionsräte*	14	„ „		3	„	1 Czech
„ 35 *Ministerialsekretäre*	30	„ „		3	„	2 Czech
„ 35 *Ministerialvizesekretäre*	28	„ „		4	„	3 Czech
„ 35 *Ministerialkonzipisten*	29	„ „		4	„	2 Czech

In the next ranks, in the *Rechnungskanzleien*, the proportions were very much the same; it should be remembered that the German, Polish, and Czech populations were, roughly, 10, 5, and 6½ millions respectively. In inferior jobs in Galicia or other remote provinces, the writer concluded, few Germans would be

[1] Trebnitz was very near Lobositz (Lovosice), and the language-frontier district from there to Leitmeritz (Litoměřice) was contested with the greatest heat. Though Leitmeritz itself was founded by Germans in 1225, the Hussites had changed its character; only in the eighteenth century must it be considered German again, and the neighbouring villages remained Czech until nearly 1800. In the second half of the nineteenth century the Czech counter-offensive began, but was eagerly resisted by the Germans. Although there were officially only fourteen Czechs in Werbitz, a village near by, Dr. Zemmrich himself writes that Werbitz was actually bilingual, for most of the women were Czech, so that the children began by only speaking Czech. Until about 1880 the Werbitzers had been educated in a neighbouring Czech parish, but since then a German school and kindergarten had appeared. In many ways this Lobositz-Leitmeritz area was fairly typical, and shows to what extent the Germans may be regarded as taking the offensive from the eighties onward.

found, but many Czechs condemned to long years of exile. These figures have particular interest because the Ministry of Finance was always regarded as the most Czechified of the Imperial Government offices. Hugelmann's figures for January 1st, 1914, give 71 non-German officials at the Ministry of Finance, out of a total of 295; of the 71 only 24 were Czech. In general, and allowing for a more anti-Slav policy in Vienna from 1908, it seems true to say that if the Bohemian authorities favoured the Czechs, the imperial ministries preserved the predominantly German character of the higher civil service, in the interests no doubt of imperial coherence and at the dictation perhaps of the social code of the Habsburg Empire.

The presumption of social and cultural superiority made by the Germans led to serious Czech grievances with regard to university life, and, on a smaller scale, with regard to the theatres. At the time of the separation of the Prague University in 1882, the Germans and Czechs had remained together in the same buildings for the time being, though the Czechs had been promised that new buildings should follow. The Germans complained that the Czechs wished to drive the German University out of the town, and they claimed that the Government again favoured the Czechs in university questions as a whole. As a matter of fact in 1910 the Government proposed to provide 1,763,600 crowns for the Czech University with 4,128 students and 1,612,000 crowns for the German University with 1,733 students.[1] The greatest inequity was envisaged with regard to the medical faculties; the German one with 344 students was to receive 769,300 crowns and the Czech one with 631 students 724,400 crowns. Conditions in both universities were none too good and the students accused the Government of an obscurantist attitude; a Czech publicist complained that 'our students are brought up to cherish learning and to love the Imperial State in underground holes . . .'.

The Germans were opposed in principle to the foundation of any further non-German universities in Austria.[2] About this time, however, the necessity for a second Czech university had been accepted 'in principle', though German obstruction was sufficiently effective to prevent the principle ever developing into practice. The Czechs had had a technical college in Brünn (Brno) since 1899, but it was natural that they should feel no shadow of doubt that Moravia, with 72·4 per cent. Czech inhabitants to 27·6 per cent. German ones, should see the new university in its capital town. Brünn at the time had about 140,000 inhabitants, of whom 40 to 50 per cent. were Czech, and it was surrounded by Czech

[1] In university expenditure, again, the Poles were favoured above the Czechs.
[2] Molisch, op. cit., p. 229.

suburbs. There was, however, not a single Czech on the city council, street names were put up solely in German, and Brünn society was determined to preserve the German veneer intact. While there was talk of establishing a new German university in Brünn, it was suggested that the Czechs should set up their new university in a small town like Olmütz (Olomouc) or Kremsier (Kroměříž), but it is not surprising that the Czechs held out for a great centre like Brünn, nor yet that they refused to accept Königsfeld (Královo Pole), one of its Czech suburbs, for the site. As for the theatre question, the Czechs pointed out that whereas the Germans had had theirs built for them by princes or directly by the State, they themselves had collected four-fifths of the total cost (nearly 7 million crowns) of their National Theatre in Prague privately among themselves, while the remainder was paid out of the taxes by the Kingdom of Bohemia.

Party developments in the early years of the century are not without an important bearing on the German-Czech problem. After their successes at the 1901 elections Wolf's private entanglements were the occasion for a final break between Schönerer and himself. Schönerer remained almost alone in complete Pan-German intransigence; he continued until 1907 to represent Egerland together with his colleague Iro. Karl Hermann Wolf with his *Frei-alldeutsch* followers became and remained the heart and soul of the movement on a less frankly irredentist basis than Schönerer required. He remained indiscreet on the grand scale, was involved in the notorious Brüx libel case,[1] and allowed the Sugar Cartel to finance his paper, the *Ostdeutsche Rundschau*, a tactical error which naturally became a favourite theme among the cartoonists of those days. His supporters were, on the whole, the small middle-class shopkeeper type, and the 1907 elections had therefore cost him politically less than they had cost the more propertied German parties. As time went on, however, and the Germans realized how much weaker universal suffrage had made them, Wolf increasingly advocated dictatorial methods.[2] He was naturally a great enthusiast for the *Schutzvereine*, of which the *Ostdeutsche Rundschau* was therefore a fervent advocate; so early as 1893 he had written there: 'One characteristic of the *Ostdeutsche Rundschau* is to work for our defence against the Slavs . . . to arouse all Germans in Austria, and to help to finance the legitimate national *Schutzvereine*.' In 1903 Dr. Titta founded the German National Council of Bohemia (*Deutscher Volksrat in Böhmen*) at Trebnitz (Třebenice), in order to link all the national organizations together; councils of this kind

---

[1] Wolf prosecuted a certain Dr. Schalk for commenting upon his (Wolf's) private life, but was unable to insist upon very much satisfaction.

[2] Sieghart, op. cit., p. 310.

had already been formed in Moravia and Silesia, but it is interesting that no one at this time thought of uniting the three. In 1910 a German National Parliamentary Union was formed to which, it was hoped, all German non-Social Democrat deputies would belong; the *Volksräte*, incidentally, always found nearly all deputies other than the followers of Schönerer and Wolf far too cautious and moderate. Meanwhile the strongly nationalist movement had given birth to two new political parties: the German Working-men's Party, built up from various nationalist working-men's groups which had grown up since the eighties, was founded in 1904, and the German Agrarians in 1905. The latter drew the Bohemian peasantry into the political arena on the one side of Wolf and the former brought a few working-men on to the other; the *Deutsche Arbeiter-Partei* (German Working-men's Party) developed by stages into the *Deutsche Nationalsozialistische Arbeiter-Partei* or Nazi Party in the Czechoslovak Republic. With its Agrarian and Working-men collaborators, Wolf's party, now rechristened German Radicals, became more and more identified with the Germans of Bohemia, Moravia, and Silesia; in the elections of 1911 the German Radicals returned 22 deputies, all in the Historic Provinces, the German Agrarians 26 deputies, 15 from Bohemia, 5 for Moravia, and 2 from Silesia. Of the 4 Schönerianer, 3 represented Bohemian constituencies; of the 3 German Working-men's deputies, 2 were Bohemian and 1 Silesian. The much bigger Clerical Party, strong in its turn in the central provinces of the post-War Austria to be, was extraordinarily weak in Bohemia (one deputy), where of course it was damned as Slavophile. The Social Democrats, who in 1907 had become the biggest party in the Reichsrat, and who in 1911 had 81 deputies to 76 Clericals, had 23 deputies representing industrial Bohemia in 1911. It is interesting that only Bohemia and Silesia produced any German working-class opposition to the Social Democrats, who were denounced by Pan-Germans as racial renegades because they included international aims in their programme. Among the Czechs, meanwhile, the intransigent Young Czechs lost in importance, and two great parties of the future emerged into prominence, the Czech Agrarians and the Czech National Socialists.[1] With the growth of the Czech Agrarians a short-sighted protectionism appeared among the Czechs[2] in favour of that customs frontier between Austria and Hungary, the absence of which was the least questioned blessing provided by the Danubian Monarchy.

[1] This party, founded in 1897, wished to combine socialism with nationalism, but along strictly democratic lines; it must therefore never be confused with German National Socialism. The most distinguished person later associated with the Czech National Socialists was Dr. Edvard Beneš.

[2] Renner, op. cit., p. 219.

It was unfortunate that the Bohemian Germans should thus have identified themselves with national intransigence in which German public opinion in the other provinces did not support them. It is intelligible that the loss of wealth and prestige which economic development, and especially the movement of the population, had necessitated, should make them hypersensitive and aggressive, but it is equally intelligible that moderate Czech opinion felt convinced that the Germans in the Wenceslas lands were 'hopeless' people who would never attempt to give the Czechs a fair deal because they were eaten up with *Herrenvolk* notions. Indeed, the Czechs not unnaturally tended to presume that all Germans were as aggressive as the ones they knew best. Many an Austrian laments that first of all the aggressive Magyarization carried on in post-*Ausgleich* Hungary kept the whole monarchy disturbed with Slav reverberations, and second that the arrogance of the Germans who shared the Historic Provinces with the Czechs stimulated undying distrust and caricatured the immense contribution to Danubian civilization which Germans had indeed made. What sort of civilization was it, the Slav races asked, which spoke with the greedy and boastful and, as we shall see, sometimes brutal voice of the Egerlander, Karl Hermann Wolf? The German Radicals and their allies were more positively dangerous to the peace of Austria than the most opinionated Czech chauvinists because there was no escaping them. As Kaizl said to Eulenburg in 1899, 'The difficulty of the general political situation lay in the brutality of this party.'[1] The average German did not know Czech and was unaware of foolish Czech utterances, but average Czechs. mostly understood German. 'Budweis is, then, in spite of its Czech majority still a German town and will, let us hope, remain so.'[2] This sentence is typical of the mentality of the Bohemian Germans; the reaction of any Czech is easily imagined. The Pan-German groups were, of course, all in favour of joining Germany at the first favourable moment. Many of them stuck to the Schönerer plan of attaching all the provinces once in the German Confederation (1815–66) to the Hohenzollern Reich. The Germanization of the Czech interior of Bohemia was a favourite theme of discussion.[3] Some of the Germans believed it could be done through consistent pressure exerted by German officials, employers, and schools; others believed that only systematic peasant settlements, such as

[1] *Die grosse Politik*, vol. xiii, no. 3504, Eulenburg, March 26th, 1899.
[2] Zemmrich, op. cit.
[3] *A propos* Germanization, at the time of the elections to the Bohemian Diet in 1901, the Pan-Germans issued an appeal to the electors as follows: 'Our motto can be nothing but purely German, Pan-German and undivided! The Germans in Bohemia must decide whether they wish to become Slavs, or whether, in accordance with their destiny, they will Germanize. A third possibility does not exist.'

the Prussian Government was sending into Polish territory, could succeed, and these would presuppose the disappearance of the Habsburgs or of Francis Joseph at the least. The Czechs could read these discussions all around them and reacted angrily to the suggestions made.

More practical conversations were going on all the time as to what solution could really be found between Sudeten German and Czech; although the Körber plan had failed, negotiations intermittently continued. His triple division proposal had been rejected because neither Czechs nor Germans were willing to admit that the mixed districts were mixed. The Czechs continued to stick to *Staatsrecht* and their claims to have the Badeni regulations restored. Kramář, though his party lost ground after 1907, on these points was still their most representative spokesman.

The Germans [he wrote] will finally be compelled to admit that the political pre-eminence which they have so long possessed in Bohemia and Moravia cannot be preserved. In Moravia they have partially admitted this. . . . On the other hand we must realize that the theory of the reconquest of the Germanized territories is a childish fantasy, since the Germans are so economically powerful that they can easily resist every attack upon their property. We shall be able to be content, when, through the raising of the political and cultural standing of our people, we have got so far that isolated German concerns scattered in Czech districts do not make so much of German superiority and busy themselves with that modesty and reserve which they expect from our minorities in German areas. Further it is superfluous that it should be the duty of those who belong to the other nationality to learn the other language to more than the absolutely necessary extent, and this should apply to us as it does to the Germans. . . .[1]

The Germans insisted, as they still do to-day, that the Czechs in the lignite areas were only temporary settlers for whom the Czech interior of the country remained their real home. They regarded the Czech attitude towards *Böhmisches Staatsrecht* as hysterical,[2] indeed, Sieghart admits that they never understood it.[3] Dr. von Medinger, a nationalist but by no means an extremist, advocated a territorial partition between the two nationalities 'together with a national veto so that the Germans are liberated from political violation, the soil on which they live safeguarded and they themselves changed from desperate oppositionals into contented citizens'.[4] Among the Germans opinion divided into two sections, one for *Zweiteilung*, i.e. territorial partition between the two nationalities (to this demand the Radicals later also adhered), and the other for the extension of the personal classification which had been

---

[1] Kramář, *Poznámky o české politice.*
[2] See an article by von Medinger, Aug. 9th, 1912.
[3] Sieghart, op. cit., p. 325.
[4] von Medinger, op. cit.

introduced into Moravia in 1905. The objection to the first plan
was that German minorities in towns, and especially in Prague,
would be handed over to the mercies of the Czechs; owing to the
prevalence of big German groups in the Moravian towns, territorial
division there had all along been out of the question. As Molisch[1]
writes, 'While some of the Bohemian Germans inclined to it
[personal classification] on account of the German minorities in
Czech territory, the majority were more influenced by the fact
that it would have made the Czech minorities in the German
country more felt.' In addition the group influenced by Reichenberg, and also many German Radicals, held the view that a people
'can only be considered in relation to the land on which it lives
and cannot be divorced from the soil, and that the question of the
Czech towns, especially of Prague, was largely one of German-
speaking Jews', i.e. people whose claim to German nationality
should not be recognized. The Reichenberg people actually spoke
in 1912 of leaving the Bohemian Diet (where the Germans mostly
obstructed) and setting up a *de facto Deutsch-Böhmen* (German
Bohemia); in their indifference to the Czech miners in their midst
they displayed exactly the equivalent territorial state of mind as
the Czech adherents of *Böhmisches Staatsrecht*. Outside Bohemia
nationalist Germans were not so much in favour of *Zweiteilung*
because they feared that German influence over the non-German
minorities, for instance in Silesia or Styria, would be lost, but the
Bohemian Germans worked out a best-of-both-worlds plan by
which they hoped to preserve German predominance (*Übergewicht*)
in the non-German territories cut away by territorial demarcations.

Altogether the state of affairs from 1908 to 1914 was dis-
appointingly unsatisfactory. The Czechs were exasperated by the
more German aspect of the Government in Vienna, and while the
Germans obstructed in the Bohemian Diet, the Czechs obstructed
in the Reichsrat. Government was carried on unconstitutionally
by the increasingly frequent application of Paragraph 14 which
legitimized authoritarian legislation. But all the time men of
intelligence and goodwill were trying to arrive at a real solution.
The Social Democrats made some of the more constructive proposals, beginning with their Brünn programme of 1899, which
advocated a democratic federal Austrian State and the abolition of
all the old provincial (*Kronland*) administrative divisions in favour
of national delimitation, as Löhner and Palacký had suggested in
1848. They denounced the idea that any nation should be more
privileged than the others, thus rejecting a state language, but
leaving the question of a *Vermittlungssprache* (i.e. an administrative
language of negotiation) open. These proposals did not bring

[1] Op. cit., p. 219.

matters farther; though the Czech Social Democrats condemned the *Staatsrecht* idea, it was certain that the Czechs as a whole would never abandon it unless the Magyars would give up the Slovaks to them so that they should have their whole ethnic area instead. But it was admirable that a German party should honestly give up the claim to national privilege, and take the line that if the Germans wished to retain the leadership it should be thanks to their natural qualities. Though it emphasized minority rights, the Brünn programme was not inconsistent with *Zweiteilung*, and the Socialists also agreed with a man like Jesser that it was not only generous but far-sighted to work for the raising of the standard of life of the Slav working class. If wages were protected all round the influx of cheap Czech labour into prevalently Sudeten German districts would automatically cease; if the Czech working-people were better off their birth-rate would fall and the population question would more easily settle itself. Men like Jesser felt profoundly that the Germans and the Czechs could not get away from one another because history, geography, and economics effectively forbade it. Since 1896 Masaryk, in his newspaper *Čas* and elsewhere, had advocated that the local government boundaries should as far as possible be drawn according to language, anticipating the German Socialists' proposals at Brünn.

More and more people spoke of a Swiss system for Austria. In September 1900 a leading article in Wolf's *Ostdeutsche Rundschau* rejected a Catholic suggestion of this kind. 'Every German must admit that a reconciliation with the Slavs is out of the question.... Nor do we need to negotiate, nor eagerly to clutch at the idea of a United States of the East based on a forged Swiss pattern.' Eisenmann's remarkable book, *Le Compromis austro-hongrois*, appeared in 1904, and ended with an appeal in favour of Swiss federalism. In 1906 came Renner's brilliant piece of work, *Grundlagen und Entwicklungsziele der österreichisch-ungarischen Monarchie*, urging a combination of Swiss methods with the Moravian personal system which had just been worked out. It is interesting, too, though he was only 24 and of no account at the time, that in 1908 Edvard Beneš wrote a thesis, *Le Problème autrichien et la question tchèque*, in favour of federalization. But there was something in what the *Ostdeutsche Rundschau* had written. Austria had problems which Switzerland did not know, and above all the tremendous problem created by a state of affairs in which the national so often coincided with the social question.

CHAPTER VIII

WAR

IN Central Europe the outbreak of the World War meant that the smouldering conflict between the Germans and the Magyars on the one side, and the Slavs on the other, flamed up into a mighty conflagration. For no territory in Europe did the War spell more terrible tragedy than for the Sudeten lands, Bohemia, Moravia, and Silesia. The Czechs found themselves called upon to fight and to die for German Imperialism, for that Germanic expansionism which they associated with oppression and with militarism in its most exact sense. To the Czechs the adulation of an officer caste, the attempt to live up to the Prussian example, were the outward expression of that brutal illiberalism which, in the German people, they felt it to be their mission to withstand The German tone of the army, its attitude of no weak pandering to the Slavs or to other insubordinate democrats, had repelled the Czechs from a military career. The democratic and rationalist tradition, which they were striving to build up, caused them to honour the professor rather than the general, and after the undreamt-of triumph of their liberation had taken place, the Czechoslovak Republic of post-War Europe was represented and led by Masaryk, Beneš, Krofta, and Hodža, all men of intellectual distinction.

Since the fall of Beck and the annexation of Bosnia and Hercegovina in 1908 the hopes of conciliatory men had been sidetracked by Aehrenthal and Berchtold at the Foreign Office, and by military influences. In 1878 it had been the Slavs of the monarchy who applauded the General Staff in the matter of occupying Bosnia, and the Germans as well as the Magyars who had objected to the further Slavification of Austria-Hungary. Plener always represented this view, and it has been seen how the German nationalist parties had wished to cut off, rather than annex, Slavonic territory. But although the last remnants of Schönerer's own following clung to their old opinion right up to the outbreak of war,[1] the situation as a whole had been reversed. Since her defeat at the hands of Japan Russia's interest was reconcentrated in the Near and Middle East, and particularly, after the 1907 Agreement with England with regard to Persia, in the Near East. She now collided with the outposts of Reich German and Austrian commerce and brought their interests into line. The new Karageorgević Serbia was hostile to Vienna, and Russia inevitably acquired the role of her protector.

---

[1] In the *Alldeutsches Tagblatt* the Schönerianer condemned the Government at the outbreak of war in 1914. See Molisch, op. cit., p. 238.

When in October 1908 Austria-Hungary at last annexed the mainly
South-Slav Bosnia and Hercegovina, her action came as an unfriendly move against an invigorated Serbia and her Great Power
patron.

Though Serbs and Croats were on none too good terms with
one another, both looked to Prague as well as to St. Petersburg for
encouragement. In 1908 the Czechs had lost direct influence at
Vienna, but Prague became a real headquarters for Southern
Slavs as well as for Slovaks. The summer of 1908 had actually
seen another Pan-Slav Congress summoned to Prague by Kramář,
a friend of Serb expansionism;[1] a new effort was made to remove
Polish dissidence, the fly in the Pan- or Neo-Slav ointment. In
1909 Masaryk further distinguished himself, in vindicating truth
against falsification, by his defence of the Serbo-Croats accused in
the Zagreb Treason Trial, and by his exposure of the forgeries—
for which the Ballhausplatz was at least indirectly responsible—
used by Professor Friedjung to incriminate the Southern Slavs.
Not only common Slav interests brought the Czechs nearer to the
Russians at this time, for the 1905 Revolution had aroused enormous enthusiasm among the Austrian Slavs and had reconciled
the really western-minded Czechs to the friendship of St. Petersburg; although the autocracy reasserted itself, it was felt that the
Russians would now be able to dispose of it in due course. And
after all the Czechs considered their own plight to be much the
same. Their ministers had left the Viennese Government, which
was headed by dictatorial premiers and which governed largely
with the help of Paragraph 14; their own rôle in Parliament could
now only be negative. As for the position between the Czechs and
the Germans in Bohemia, it had never been worse. There were
frequent anti-German demonstrations in Prague. The Germans
were able to obstruct all business in the Bohemian Diet, and in
particular to bar the democratization of the electoral system for
diet and municipal elections. For it must never be forgotten that
the franchise reforms of 1896 and 1907 had only affected elections
to the Central Parliament. The Germans had kept their full
advantages in the fairly wide range of affairs which were dealt with
by the diets, the districts, and the towns which, none of them,
boasted even a universal suffrage *curia*. Some believed that the
Germans had only been induced to accept Beck's reform on these
conditions; others held that the Government had taken good care
to preserve the old local hierarchies to balance them off against the
new forces, and to preserve the old Crownland administrative
frontiers which cut across the ill-defined but red-hot racial ones.
It was, at any rate, a provocative situation, reminiscent in some

[1] Fischel, *Der Panslawismus bis zum Weltkrieg*, p. 527 et seq.

ways of the early reign of Louis XVI when the *parlements* were
restored, as if intended locally to veto the reforming legislation of
Turgot at the centre. The impotence, thanks to German obstruction, of the Bohemian Diet brought about financial chaos,[1] and
finally, in 1913, the last remnant of Bohemian autonomy was
destroyed when an imperial commission was substituted for the
Executive Committee of the Diet. Czech-German negotiations for
a practical compromise, as we have seen, were never interrupted
for long, but the final pre-War efforts collapsed early in 1914
and added to the feeling of exasperation on both sides, although it
was not generally known that the Archduke Francis Ferdinand
was responsible for the abruptness of the break-down.[2]

The Balkan Wars had stimulated the feeling of Slav solidarity
against Turkey which represented the influence of Germany in the
Balkan peninsula. At last, when the Great War came, it came as a
war directly against the Serbian Southern Slavs, and it rapidly
developed into a war organized by Germany, and, in the eyes of
all Central Europeans, primarily a war against Russia who had
come to the rescue of the Serbs. In so far as the subjects of Austria-
Hungary were aware of the War in the west, the feelings of a
Czech at the Bohemian cross-roads were bound to be at least as
strongly aroused in sympathy with the small nation Belgium and
with the rationalist and intellectual French. Beneš wrote, 'Our
nation in the Bohemian provinces (not in Slovakia), both before
and during the War, through its historical development, its whole
psychology, its philosophical conceptions, its intellectual and social
structure, was bound to be in the West European camp.'[3]

Now the Sudeten Germans, one need scarcely point out, supplied the crack regiments in the Austrian Army; I have heard the
mildest and most Czech-friendly of them puzzling over the Czechs
because these peculiar people seemed to have no *Sinn für Militär*
(military bent). When it came to the outbreak of war, the
German Nationalist parties, but above all the *Deutsch-Radikalen*
of Bohemia, were filled with wild enthusiasm for the cause of the
Central Powers, and looked forward to a glorified fulfilment of
the Linz Programme, a great consolidation of Central Europe in the
German sense, as the final result of the struggle. The Czechs were
from every nationalist German's point of view the 'worst', the most
'treacherous' of the Slavs of the monarchy; even the Croats,
despite their closeness to the Serbs, had the *Kaisertreu* military
tradition of a peasant people. It had chanced that the actual
occasion of the outbreak of war had been created by the Serbs, but

---

[1] There were also industrial difficulties, with a good deal of unemployment
to add to the trouble.   [2] Sieghart, op. cit., p. 239.
[3] E. Beneš, *Světová válka a naše revoluce.*

in the eyes, especially of the Sudetendeutschen, the Czechs had been scheming to bring the catastrophe about. In the eighties Plener had said[1] the Czechs could never be for Russia in a war since it was clear that if they were they would 'simply be crushed— the Germans would never allow the Russians to take up a permanent position in the heart of Austria far into Western Europe'.[2] But since that time the Sudeten Germans had witnessed the diplomatic activity of the Bohemian Czech, Kramář, from the days of the Thun Government onwards. It was felt as singularly treacherous that the Slavs who lived in so crucial a position should break up the strength of the home front by allowing their sympathies to stray; it seemed particularly annoying that very cultivated Czechs like Kramář should question the values of German civilization from which they had admittedly profited so much. The proposals made at the Slav Congress in 1908 in favour of organizing Slav competition against German economic power were felt by the Sudeten Germans to be positively provocative. But above all, the Czechs were regarded as collaborators in the creation of the Triple Entente and the *Einkreisung*. In the spring of 1918 Dr. Wichtl, German Radical deputy for a Böhmerwald constituency and a man of academic standing, published an attack[3] upon Kramář, as not only the incendiary of 1914 but as the sinister architect of the alliance between London, Paris, and St. Petersburg. In 1919 Fischel,[4] in describing Neo-slavism, wrote:

In which direction his (Kramář's) goal and that of the other pillars of Neo-slavism lay, was already clear . . . to offer a helping hand to the Western Powers and to Russia in the destruction of the German Empire and its allies, the East Germans[5] and Magyars. Austria-Hungary must needs be disintegrated . . . in order that the Czecho-Slovak and Yugoslav States should be born.

These views were characteristic of the time, and have by no means disappeared since the end of the War.

It will, perhaps, have become clear that the situation in the Sudeten lands meant that, to the horrors of war in general, were added those of civil war, for in spirit, and increasingly in fact, the Czechs in Bohemia, Moravia, and Silesia were fighting with Russia and the Democratic Powers of the west against the Central Powers. In the very early days every one on both sides was optimistic and the Czechs expected the Russian steam-roller to be with them any

[1] Plener, *Reden.*

[2] To the Germans the frontier of Western Europe is, roughly, that between Germans and Slavs where in the eyes of the French the frontier comes roughly where the Roman Empire ended.

[3] *Dr. Karl Kramarsch der Anstifter des Weltkrieges* (Wien, 1918). Dr. Wichtl was director of the Austrian Civil Law School in Vienna and prominent in the *Bund der Deutschen.* [4] Fischel, *Der Panslawismus bis zum Weltkrieg*, p. 542.

[5] Academic and racial reference to the Austrians.

day. But then came two years of German and Austrian successes until about the time of the old Emperor's death in November 1916. What occurred in this period was as inevitable as it was ineradicable from the minds of the men of those days. Sudeten racial hatreds hardened. Czech soldiers, even regiments,[1] deserted to the enemy. Czechs in Russia and France and America worked with every enthusiasm for the cause of the Allies. Before the end of 1914 Masaryk had left Austria for ever to organize, together with his ex-pupil, Beneš, the new Czech Revolution thus launched abroad. The Czechs at home, like any other people in similar circumstances, kept up a show of loyalty, to the extent to which, as individuals, they happened to be cowardly or brave, cautious or rash. Their life became increasingly like that in a monster concentration camp. Many people were actually interned. War-time brought more than its usual restrictions, censorship, food regulations, ubiquitous military interference, &c. The Czechs were compelled to subscribe to war loans in the cause of the increasingly oppressive régime, they must work in the fields to eke out the diminishing food supplies of the monarchy at war. More and more, military influences, and more and more, out-and-out German influences, asserted themselves; more and more, the two tended to combine. Even before the end of 1914 Czechs were executed by the military authorities for speaking in some way or other of Czech independence, and as time went on the number of victims increased. 'Every capital sentence of the Austrian courts martial helped to cut the links which chained the Czech people to Austria.'[2] Among many similar actions the dissolution of the *Sokol* on November 23rd, 1915, may be mentioned. Kramář, and soon after him an outstanding young leader called Alois Rašin, were among those arrested in the summer of 1915. On June 3rd, 1916, Kramář, Rašin, and two other Czech leaders were condemned to death, against the wishes of the civil authorities. Though Kramář already stood too far on the Right for most of his countrymen— the working people increasingly combined socialistic opinions with their anti-Austrian attitude—he was immensely respected by the whole Czech nation, and that death sentence has never been forgotten.

What were the aims of Kramář and the other Czech leaders? To what extent were they inimical to Austria-Hungary? Before the War Kramář himself, as we have had occasion to see, had wished to make the foreign policy of Austria-Hungary consistent with the preponderance of Slavs among its inhabitants, and had consistently desired a Paris-Vienna-Petersburg alignment, a con-

---

[1] The 28th Prague Regiment was the most notorious; it went over to the Russians on Apr. 23rd, 1915.　　　　　[2] Strauss, op. cit., p. 99.

ception not necessarily repugnant to the Habsburgs themselves. Even on July 4th, 1914, he had declared in a lecture that the Czechs could not adopt a policy opposed to the monarchy.[1] But 'the day on which war was declared on Russia was the day of final farewell to Austria' for him.[2] 'Work for a great Slav empire,' he said to Dürich,[3] when Dürich was going abroad, and he henceforth hoped that Bohemia would become a principality ruled by a Russian grand duke. With Masaryk, who had long ago become Kramář's political opponent, the same thing had happened—July 1914 was the turning-point at which he abandoned for ever the hope of Czech co-operation within a federalized Austria. But of course the future Czechoslovak State he envisaged was to look to the west. As for the rest of the Czech politicians, how could they tell? They were all determined to get what they could for their countrymen when it came to a settlement, but some of them thought it best to strengthen their hand by correct behaviour, while others hastened to organize the Maffia, the exciting secret organization which smuggled in messages from abroad in the heels of shoes or spied upon the Viennese Chanceries themselves.

Though they certainly underrated the importance of Masaryk's activities abroad, it is far more surprising in the circumstances that the Austrian authorities ever allowed him to leave than that they resented his work which was, from their point of view, the frankest high treason. And the reprieve of Kramář[4] and Rašin through the young Kaiser Karl—their sentences were commuted to fifteen and ten years respectively—is astounding. The Germans would never have done such a thing; they shot Edith Cavell, and the British hanged Roger Casement. As Krebs says, 'Neither in the German nor in the Slav nor in the Magyar camp was any one in doubt that this war must be decisive one way or the other within the state too.'[5] Before finally leaving Vienna Masaryk had visited Körber, and Körber himself had said that an Austrian victory would mean the strengthening of the old system in its worst features since after victory the soldiers would decide, and they would be certain to centralize and to Germanize.[6] Already in January 1916 in Bohemia German was declared to be the only official language even on the railways, and thereafter the police often upbraided and even used their truncheons upon people they heard speaking Czech in Prague. The old German *Staatssprache* idea was to triumph again. One of the most admired

[1] Strauss, op. cit., quoting Dr. Jaroslav Werstadt.
[2] Kramář, *Pět přednášek o zahraniční politice* (Prague, 1922), p. 57.
[3] J. Dürich, *V českých službách* . . . (Prague, 1921), p. 13.
[4] He was known to be working, mostly via Sofia, with the enemy.
[5] Hans Krebs, *Kampf in Böhmen* (Berlin, 1936), p. 47.
[6] Masaryk, *Světová revoluce.*

characteristics of Prussian history, among the nationalist German Austrians, was the manner in which political had followed upon the economic Prussianization of Germany, the celebrated *Zollunion* policy. In 1915 Naumann's famous book, *Mitteleuropa*, was published; talk therefore increased of a German Central Europe binding together Hohenzollern and Habsburg territory by invincible economic links, and this talk culminated in the German 'Easter demands' in 1916.[1] According to this programme not only was German to be the one State language, but public minority schools were no longer to be allowed. *Mittel-Europa* was to extend specifically to the frontiers of Bulgaria, and, especially in the non-German southern and Adriatic provinces of the new empire, German colonization, and the setting up of new German industries and banks were to be promoted by the State. The notorious *Osterbegehrschaft* was signed by all German political parties, national councils, &c., with the exception of the Social Democrats. There were one or two individual exceptions, too, for intense German patriots like Jesser and Lodgman,[2] who were in real touch with Slav feeling, were horrified by the consequences they foresaw. It is of melancholy interest, too, that a Bohemian Compromise, if not one the Czechs would willingly have accepted for very long, was well on the way to signature when the Easter bombshell exploded about the ears of those who had not forgotten about conciliation and compromise even in war-time.

With the accession of the young Emperor Charles and with the year 1917, momentous developments occurred. The new ruler was anything but Pan-German in outlook and, aware of the stimulus provided by growing economic strain to the national hatreds among his subjects, he set to work upon a policy of appeasement at home and abroad. He appointed Seidler, a conciliatory if too insignificant figure, as Premier, called the Reichsrat together for the first time for over three years, proposed a federal Austria composed of the Crownlands become autonomous,[3] and released Kramář, who was escorted home by the citizens of Prague in what the police report referred to as a triumphal procession. The Emperor also began to put out peace feelers in the direction of France. But he was defeated all along the line by the enemies he was bound to encounter. William II later forced Charles to a fresh solidarity declaration. The Hungarians refused to have their frontiers touched by the young Emperor's reforms and thereby vetoed

[1] Naumann himself was far more liberal than the nationalists who framed the 'Easter demands'—see below, Chapter XVII. He did, however, visualize Prague as one of the organizing centres of *Mittel-Europa*, an unwelcome implication to the Czechs.   [2] See Chapter IX.
[3] Retention of the Crownland frontiers was in itself unlikely to satisfy any one at this stage.

South Slav and Roumanian demands and the Czech claim to Slovakia which was becoming daily more audible.[1] And finally Karl Hermann Wolf, in a famous speech in the Reichsrat, trod the ghost of Czech-German conciliation underfoot. In answer to a Czech speech in favour of Bohemian integrity, Wolf declared this to be the evil at the root of all Austria's troubles. Where the Government should have taken a strong line against *dieses Staatsrecht*, Wolf complained 'the Prime Minister behaved with a goodness, a gentleness, a delicacy, a sweetness in which one can perhaps indulge in highly civilized circles, but which one cannot show towards tigers. In a menagerie one does not work with promises and caresses, but with the whip.'[2] At this point there was some twenty minutes' interruption, after which Wolf, undaunted, continued in the same vein. I have heard people who knew him describe how he was constantly carried away by his own eloquence. The results, at any rate, were infinitely deplorable. The Czechs were hyper-sensitive enough—over their 'servants' language' and their uncouthness, which amused the Viennese so much—without being likened to wild beasts.

Already Czech literary and working-class indignation was rising against the caution of the political leaders at home. Strikes had been increasing; at Prostejov (Prossnitz), for instance, starving workmen who struck were shot down, so that 23 were killed and 40 wounded[3]—and this was by no means an isolated case. The Russian Revolution in its Kerensky phase was, of course, a source of great encouragement to the Czechs, and especially to those on the left.

Meanwhile Masaryk and Beneš were having a hard struggle abroad, and at first seemed unable to shake French diplomacy from Palacký's, and indeed to some extent their own earlier, views that Austria must not be destroyed. When Masaryk's friend Wilson brought America into the War in April 1917 the Czech leader's hand was very much strengthened. He was now eager to make more of the Czech legionaries who were actually fighting for the Allies in France, in Italy, and on a big scale in Russia, for Masaryk, like Cavour, believed that one must prove one's value to those from whom one asked help.[4] He therefore went to Russia in May 1917 to organize the legionaries there, and in July came their first success in the battle at Zborov. This battle, the baptism of

[1] Cf. the Manifesto issued by the Czech Parliamentary Club on May 20th, 1917, quoted in *A History of the Peace Conference of Paris*, edited by H. W. V. Temperley (subsequently referred to as *H.P.C.*), vol. iv, chap. iv.
[2] Austrian Parliamentary Debate, Sept. 27th, 1917.
[3] Strauss, op. cit.
[4] Masaryk once said, 'It was necessary to show that our freedom was dearer to us than life.' See Peroutka, *Budování státu*.

fire of the Czechoslovak Army, was a little too enthusiastically commemorated in 1937 as the 'death-blow' to Austria-Hungary. Nothing better illustrates than the matter of the legionaries the divergence of views between the uncompromising German Austrian and the uncompromising Czech. To the latter the legionaries were generous idealists who left everything and faced death to remind the world of the Czechs and strike a blow for their freedom. To the uncompromising German Austrian—who was, after all, more often than not a *Sudetendeutscher*—the legionaries were traitors, deserters, gangsters, and thieves, a rabble with nothing to lose, who betrayed the State to whom they owed allegiance. It is always the same. To the Austrians the Garibaldians were a set of roughs, and to the opponents of German National Socialism at home or in Czechoslovakia or in England or France Hitler's Storm Troops wore the same uncouth face. The Czech 'gangsters' had one remarkable characteristic, they respected and obeyed a professor of philosophy, who won the reputation of being the most upright man of his time.

In the autumn of 1917 came the Bolshevization of Russia, and consequently strained relations and finally conflict between the new Russian authorities and the legionaries, who prepared to retire to the Western Front via Siberia. Lenin's success cut the ground from under Kramář and Pan- and Neo-Slavism, and finally justified Masaryk's Westernism. On January 10th, 1917, the Allied note to Wilson had included a demand for 'the liberation of the Italians as also of the Slavs, Rumanes, and Czecho-Slovaks from foreign domination', an odd phrase which at any rate damned dualism. At last, in 1918, the efforts of the legionaries and the ceaseless industry of Beneš in Paris brought about the Pichon note of June 29th, by which France recognized the Czechoslovak National Committee in Paris as the first basis of a future government; British recognition followed very shortly afterwards. Meanwhile the Central Powers were collapsing and on October 16th the Emperor Charles's last offer of complete federal freedom to all the nationalities of Austria was spoken by nothing but a voice from the grave.

CHAPTER IX

BETWEEN WAR AND PEACE

THE question now arose what was this new Czecho-Slovak State of which the Allies had officially taken notice. What were its frontiers to be and who its citizens? Masaryk, who had spent all his political life fighting for truth in contempt for popularity, had become the man of the hour, and his conception would carry most weight with the Powers who now had to redraw the map. We have seen that Masaryk had originally taken the ethnical point of view; he had been in favour of an administrative frontier between Germans and Czechs—yes, *Zweiteilung* in so far as it could be practically carried out within Austria—and in this he had been at one with the Czech Socialists (and Beneš) in condemning dogmatic insistence upon *Böhmisches Staatsrecht*. But when the fronts hardened in the War he had come to believe that the Germans had so rigidly identified themselves with the Pan-German *Mittel-Europa* point of view of the *Osterbegehrschaft* that either that must triumph or Austria must go. The 'chief question' for him then became which is the lesser evil—that 10 million Czechs and Slovaks, a whole nation, should live in a German state or that 3 million Germans should live in a non-German state.[1] Since the fiasco of the Central Powers the question had decided itself, and the Pichon note had actually promised that France would do her utmost to bring about Czechoslovak independence within the 'historic frontiers' of the nation which implied the acceptance of *Staatsrecht*. The Peace Conference had yet to make the final decision.

The Germans of the Historic Provinces were mostly taken unawares by the downfall of Habsburg and Hohenzollern. They had felt the increasing hardship—which was extremely severe in the Bohemian industrial districts—but most of them had only read censored news and the official statements about imminent victory. Following upon Wolf's notorious declaration in September 1917, Pacher, another German Radical leader who was deputy for Komotau, had declared that the Germans would never go back to the old Prague Diet; he demanded the immediate materialization of *Zweiteilung* in the demarcation of a separate *Deutsch-Böhmen* which, in his view, already existed according to the frontiers of the parliamentary constituencies of 1907. In May 1918, at the time when Berlin was forcing him to a fresh declaration of Austro-German solidarity, the Emperor Charles acceded to the *Deutsch-*

[1] Masaryk, *Světová revoluce.*

Böhmen demand, and the Sudeten Germans gladly supposed that a strongly organized German *Mittel-Europa* with provincial autonomy for them was well on the way to realization just when the great German offensive in the west had failed. The Socialists of Vienna knew fairly well what the situation really was, and the men in the trenches were picking up enemy propaganda, but those who stayed at home at the 'heart of Europe' blamed the Czech peasants for the food-shortage and continued to trust in the powers that once were. I have often been told by friends who witnessed it how incredibly blind the Sudeten Germans were to the signs of the times. On October 28th, 1918, the Czech National Committee led by Rašin, Švehla, Soukup, and Stříbrný, took over the government in Prague in business-like rather than heroic fashion, and manœuvred the Austrian military authorities into a capitulation on October 30th, and the Germans at last began to realize that 'their' Bohemia, after a seventy years' struggle, might have fallen into the hands of an under-estimated enemy. In the previous April Kaiser Karl's Foreign Minister had publicly denounced Thomas Masaryk as a traitor to the State; before Christmas he was back in Prague hailed as the nation's saviour and its president to be.

The political chiefs of the Sudeten Germans were alive to the situation and wasted no time. Until the Peace Conference could get to work all national leaders were eagerly engineering *faits accomplis* so that their claims should be well grounded, and Pacher and his colleagues hastily gathered together on October 29th to declare themselves the Government of *Deutsch-Böhmen*, thus apparently established at last in the peremptory fashion threatened by the Reichenbergers before the War. It was obvious that the Czechs would not now accept the delimitation of 1907 which had clearly favoured the Germans and would mean the sacrifice of the vulnerable mining minorities of which we have heard so much. Pacher, nevertheless, declared the establishment of this German autonomous territory to be in accordance with Wilson's principles, and he was supported by all the political parties, including the Socialists led by Josef Seliger. A few days later he was summoned to be Austrian Minister of Education in Vienna, and Lodgman took his place as head of the provisional government of German Bohemia.

Lodgman was immensely sincere and idealistic; he had perhaps all along been too much isolated to make a successful political leader. He had been born at Hradec Králové (Königgrätz) in the Czech language area, where his father was an official, and he had been to a Czech elementary school; thus, unlike most of the Bohemian Germans, he could speak fluent Czech and was always to some extent in touch with Czechs. In a sense he was a follower of

BETWEEN WAR AND PEACE

Löhner,[1] though until about 1911 he believed in the possibility of a Bohemian solution, and for Bohemia alone he desired a plan comparable with that which had materialized in Moravia, i.e. a solution along personal rather than territorial lines. Later he convinced himself that the Bohemian question could only be solved as part of the whole problem of the Habsburg Monarchy, and, like the Social Democrats, he believed this to require a mainly territorial plan combined with observance of the so-called personal principle.[2] Thus he wished each individual freely to choose his nationality and was in favour of local autonomy within a federal system. In the summer of 1917 he appealed to the Emperor in this sense;[3] it was a time when a rigid German centralism was increasingly the vogue among all but the Social Democratic German deputies and it was rumoured that he was to be expelled from the nationalist deputies' union. Believing passionately in self-determination, he was profoundly susceptible to Wilsonism and new era hopes; he under-estimated other considerations, and above all the economic unity of Bohemia and the extreme dependence of its German industrial edges upon food supplies and railway lines from the Czech interior. On October 29th Lodgman negotiated with the Czech leaders, but they refused to accept his authority while he would not hear of co-operating with them, so that the meeting bore no fruit.[4]

It was relatively simple to establish an autonomous *Deutsch-Böhmen* on paper because *Deutsch-Böhmen* had for so long been under discussion. In the south of Bohemia, too, the German area was fairly homogeneous and lay along the frontier of Upper Austria; local leaders at Krumau took over control and hoped shortly to join up with the administration of Linz. The question of Moravia and Silesia was more complicated. Southern Moravia was rounded off by indisputably German territory and a German South Moravian authority was set up at Znaim (Znojmo), but its representatives wished to throw up a corridor to Brünn (Brno) which they said could not be left to the mercies of the Czechs. In the north at Troppau (Opava), the old capital of Austrian Silesia, the deputy Dr. Freissler set up a provisional government on October 29th, and was able, like the *Deutsch-Böhmen* authorities, to report to the Viennese Parliament on October 30th; his régime claimed to be responsible for the Germans of Austrian Silesia, of North Moravia, and the adjacent portion of Eastern Bohemia, and gave this combined territory the name of *Sudetenland*, after reject-

[1] See above, Chapter III.
[2] Information supplied directly by Dr. von Lodgman himself.
[3] His legislative proposals in 1917 were recently republished in *Die Junge Front*, June 1937.
[4] Peroutka, op. cit.

ing the proposed name of *Altvaterland*.[1] Most difficult of all was the problem of the Germans in the mid-Moravian towns, such as Olmütz, Zwittau, Iglau, &c., a category to which Brünn itself might be considered to belong, and at the same time as the above four provisional governments were established, a German national council for Brünn and Central Moravia was set up.

The Germans of Bohemia, Moravia, and Silesia preserved their autonomy and their association with Austria for something like six weeks. Before the end of November the Czechs began to occupy the German towns, and by Christmas 1918 they had all been handed over. According to the terms of the Armistice the Czechs were entitled to occupy necessary strategic points; they interpreted this permission as covering the whole German territory in the Historic Provinces.[2] No resistance was offered to the Czech troops and no bloodshed took place with the exception of one or two skirmishes, notably that at Kaplitz (Kaplice) in Southern Bohemia. From this it might be presumed—and indeed often has been— that the German population not unwillingly accepted the authority of the new Czechoslovak State; in the Czech *Mémoires* presented to the Peace Conference this was confidently asserted. It may be suitable at this point to attempt some further analysis of the state of mind of the Sudetendeutschen at the end of the War, both in general and in particular.

The Germans, especially those of the Historic Provinces, had been counting upon the achievement of a more centralized and economically more closely knit German structure stretching far into frankly conquered Slavonic territory and attached to the Berlin Empire. Suddenly they were forced to discover that far from the materializing of *Mittel-Europa*, the War was lost, and lost to the Slavs. The prospect of being included in an independent Czech State, after all that now lay been Czech and German, seemed at first too bad to be true. The War had brought the Sudetendeutschen closer to the Austrian State, and from October 30th, when the Parliament in Vienna claimed to keep their allegiance, they were eagerly Austrian in order not to be Czech. With all their tenets crashing about their ears, the non-Socialist Germans—Lodgman quite apart—reacted to Wilson and self-determination with almost childish eagerness, though they had long decried the 'Marxists' for speaking of such things; there was consequently a political land-slide to the left, stimulated also by defeat, by suffering, and by events in Russia. After his last-moment capitulation, the Sudeten Germans were happy to see the Emperor Charles abdicate on

[1] Freissler, *Vom Zerfall Österreichs bis zum tschechoslowakischen Staate*, p. 111.
[2] The Czech occupation came also in answer to Lodgman's appeal for help —see below.

November 11th, and delighted when, on November 12th, a provisional Parliament in Vienna declared German-Austria to be a democratic republic and a part of the German Republic; the Chancellor, Dr. Renner, declared to the deputies that, though it might be easier and more convenient to treat separately, 'in this hour our German people in every district shall know that we are one race and share one destiny,' and the House broke into the wildest cheers. 'Any one who experienced that moment can never forget it', wrote Freissler, the governor of the provisional Sudetenland. To the Sudeten Germans, more than all the others, a new day seemed to be dawning, for most of them lived nearer to Prussian Silesia, Saxony, and Bavaria than to the Alpine provinces of Austria and had, as we have had occasion to see, been torn between Hohenzollern and Habsburg.

Thus at the time when the provisional governments were set up at Reichenberg, Troppau, Krumau, and Znaim, these seemed the most sensible transitional arrangements until the *Anschluss* with Austria and Germany could be completed, and the political bitterness existing between the Social Democrats and the other parties who had decried them as traitors and pacifists up to the eve of the Armistice suddenly disappeared. The provisional governments in Reichenberg and Troppau proceeded to work very hard to adapt the administrative apparatus to the supposedly racial frontiers, which had hitherto only existed—in more or less the same shape —for electoral and educational purposes. It was a time of the greatest possible distress; the industrial towns were starving, the soldiers were coming home, bringing revolutionary ideas with them. Troppau had a difficult time disentangling the administration of its German from its Czech and Polish districts and taking on Germans from Moravia and Bohemia; it was cut off from its natural coal supplies around Ostrava (Ostrau) and its natural railway connexions, and all these things called for constant negotiation with the local Czech committees and later with the Czech military authorities. Communism spread, especially in the big lignite area in *Deutsch-Böhmen* with its partly Czech population, and the German middle classes were frightened of what might come, all the more when disorders broke out in Aussig early in November. Efforts were made to recruit National Guards, but old soldiers had little inclination to put on their uniforms again, and the Lodgman authorities asked for help from the Saxons and from the Czechs; the Saxons had enough troubles of their own, but the Czechs sent help and finally found it best to carry through their own occupation which then spread outwards from Aussig. Reichenberg was occupied by the Czechs on December 11th and Troppau on December 18th. The Lodgman Government had withdrawn beforehand into

Saxony, and turned up in Vienna on December 17th, never to return to *Deutsch-Böhmen*. The Freissler régime did not go into exile; its members held a meeting at Jägerndorf as late as February 1919 and made some sensible efforts to procure autonomy within the Czech State. The Böhmerwald and South Moravian German authorities melted gradually away, the deputy Teufel holding out longest in Znaim. As for the state of mind of the German population, it is true that the responsible people had considered resistance to the Czechs to be out of the question because the general atmosphere was one of profound war-weariness, and because they believed that violence would prejudice the Allies against their cause. It is true, too, to say that the old line between Socialist and non-Socialist parties was temporarily blurred,[1] because no party wished for incorporation with the Czechs. Resistance was contemplated by old soldiers here and there, apart from Kaplitz and a skirmish at Brüx. I have listened to would-be leaders in Southern Bohemia who collected comrades at an inn, who believed that arms were at hand at Aigen and Wels in Upper Austria, and who had had promises of help from Bavaria. But some one gave them away, a train full of Czechs mysteriously arrived, and the conspirators dispersed. The people, as a whole, had not been concerned. They were perhaps almost indifferent at first to the Czech occupation because they believed that a plebiscite would certainly be held and its verdict obeyed.

Indifference now rapidly changed into indignation which culminated in the tragic *journée* of March 4th, 1919. Shortly before this, elections were held to the Austrian Republican Parliament, elections in which the Sudetendeutschen expected to participate. This was made impossible by the Czech authorities, and the Sudetic German leaders in consequence summoned protest meetings in all noteworthy towns on the day upon which the new Parliament assembled in Vienna. The demonstrators do not appear to have been armed, but the Czechs were nervous and fired on the crowds in several places; at the end of the day 52 Germans had been killed and 84 wounded, the saddest case being the small town of Kaader (Kadaň), where 20 people lost their lives.

The causes and the effects of March 4th were entangled with one another. Actually, however deplorable, it would not be unintelligible that the Czechs, after those four years of war and bombas directed against them, should react resentfully to the German demonstrations. In addition there is no doubt that a lot of activity of a semi-military kind was going on beyond the frontiers in Upper Austria and Bavaria, accompanied by a good deal of talk of invading the Sudeten German territory. In Bavaria only private individual

---

[1] Until the communal elections in June 1919—see below.

were concerned, since the governments at the time were too much to the left to be in favour of anything of the kind. But in Austria, Renner's War Minister was the Egerland Pan-German, Josef Mayer. Mayer was an old enemy of the Czechs, who were convinced, not without reason, that he was working against them, for Mayer believed that, with war material which had been brought home to Bavaria, an invasion of Bohemia would be worth while. Julius Deutsch, his Socialist Under-Secretary, shared this opinion, and volunteers were being recruited. Lodgman and his very nationalist collaborator, Langenhan, were established in Vienna, and were, of course, in touch with the towns of *Deutsch-Böhmen*, while Seliger, who was Lodgman's deputy, had addressed the mass meeting at Teplitz on March 4th. Thus it was undeniable that activities officially encouraged in Austria, and unofficially in Bavaria, Saxony, and Prussian Silesia, were conducing to a state of unrest in the Sudeten German territory. On the other hand, a complaint which Beneš addressed to Clemenceau on March 8th against the neighbours of Czechoslovakia was supported by flimsy evidence, and Lloyd George and Lansing both condemned the Czech demand for retaliatory measures against Austria. The Teschen Commission was sent to investigate and reported on April 12th; it came to the conclusion that, in the words of Howe, the American representative, 'Though there is, no doubt, a strong feeling of discontent among the Germans of Bohemia fostered to some extent by Vienna and Berlin . . . the movement therefrom cannot be dignified by the name of a conspiracy.'[1]

Although the Sudeten Germans were embittered by March 4th, which to them had appeared as groundless massacre, and although in the local elections in June about 90 per cent. of the votes in *Deutsch-Böhmen* were given to German parties,[2] it would not be accurate to suggest that the Sudeten German population was by now entirely opposed to being incorporated in Czechoslovakia. All along industrial interests,[3] which depended upon the economic structure of a united Bohemia, had been opposed to a division between its German and Czech territory; the textile people of Asch, the little Bohemian peninsula which pokes up into Germany above Eger, were very much afraid of Reich German competition and therefore of the talk of handing them over. As the summer advanced it became increasingly clear that there would not be a plebiscite and that the

[1] D. Hunter Miller, *My Diary at the Conference of Paris* (published privately, 1924–6), vol. xvii, pp. 504–6.
[2] These elections were fought primarily on the socialist issue between the Germans themselves and are therefore not directly relevant to the national question.
[3] See Peroutka, op. cit., and Molisch, *Die Sudetendeutsche Freiheitsbewegung in den Jahren, 1918–1919* (Vienna, 1932).

Anschluss of Austria to Germany would not be sanctioned. This would leave Northern Bohemia and Freissler's Sudetenland as economically helpless Austrian enclaves unless they became part of Czechoslovakia. Even in the adjacent Böhmerwald territory, Krumau was on bad terms with Linz, which felt it had enough problems in Upper Austria, especially since the Central Government of Austria was so much weakened by the new federal constitution. A good deal of cautious middle-class opinion half preferred the bourgeois Government of Prague to the 'red' régimes of either Berlin or Vienna, which, they complained, had deserted them in poltroonish fashion; others again shook their heads over working-class movements in Czechoslovakia and remembered that Slavs were 'false' and Leftist at heart. It was not only the industrialists of Northern Bohemia, but also those of Northern Moravia who were now at any rate for the Czechoslovak State, while Silesian industry was strongly in favour of the whole of the old Austrian province going to the Czechs and not to the Poles. In Southern Bohemia and the *Böhmerwald*, where Social Democracy was particularly weak, both the industrialists and the peasants were against annexation to Socialist Austria, and the peasantry elsewhere seemed in favour of maintaining the ancient frontiers; small tradespeople, too, were for Czechoslovakia. The professional classes had long been the most nationalist and remained the most bitterly anti-Czech, and, strangely enough, it was now the Social Democrat working-people who shared their attitude towards the new state. There was always, of course, a stratum of silent opinion which was in favour of making the best of things and which was enlarged by the hope of getting good terms from the Czechs. It would be impossible to estimate proportions, and since there could be no satisfactory solution of the problem of the Historic Provinces, opinion divided all the more in its choice of lesser evils. One gains the general impression that extreme Pan-Germans, Big Business and Vicars of Bray apart, a good many people did cling to a moderately nationalist position, i.e. to being Austrians, and therefore to the hope of the enclaves originally indicated by Lodgman and Freissler. It is surprising how often one finds the same nationalist German declaring that to cut off East Prussia from the Reich was impossible, but that it was absurd to question the practicability of *Deutsch-Böhmen*. German emotional protest against the Polish corridor was, perhaps, commensurate with the emotional attachment of the Czechs to their ancient historic frontiers.

CHAPTER X

THE PEACE CONFERENCE

IT is difficult for most people, English, French, or whatever they
may be, to think back to the psychological atmosphere of the
Peace Conference, but it is quite impossible to understand its
behaviour unless one is willing to consider the terror and the havoc
which had gone before it. To-day public opinion has been so much
busied with exposing the injustices arising out of the Treaties that
it has forgotten the fear and the cruelty every one else then associated with Germany. Germany had for years seemed invincible
through that very remorselessness whose horrid features had been
distorted by hostile propaganda into an even more appalling
grimace. It is, moreover, almost impossible for members of old,
anchored States to imagine the intoxicated state of the 'liberated'
nations, especially that of the Poles and the Czechs who were now
to be put back on to the map of Europe after generations of feverish
yearning. To their irrational elation their leaders added a rational
determination to ask for too much rather than receive too little;
if they hesitated in this course, chauvinist pressure from at home
urged them on.

Among all the Small Power 'victors' who had to be satisfied,
Poles, Czechs, Greeks, Roumanians, Southern Slavs, the Czechs,
in the person of Dr. Beneš, stood out as the most sensible and the
most politically minded;[1] Dr. Kramář was also a Czech Peace
delegate, but by all accounts the part he played was insignificant.
Like every one else, the Czechs expressed their views and their
wishes to the Conference at Paris; these were contained in a series
of memoranda which, as it happened, were published in Germany
last year.[2] But the third of these *Mémoires*, the one which concerned itself with the Sudeten German problem, appeared in
Bohemia[3] as long ago as 1920, and has ever since been damned as
a piece of unscrupulous deception which misled the ignorant
innocents of Britain and America in the interests of Franco-Czech
chauvinism. Both indictments require consideration, since the first
has fostered a feeling of profound distrust on the part of the
Sudeten Germans towards Dr. Beneš, and the second a feeling of
unmitigated hostility towards the Peace Settlement.

It is true that the *Mémoires* were hurriedly and badly written

[1] Cf. Harold Nicolson, *Peacemaking 1919* (London, 1933).
[2] H. Raschhofer, *Die tschechoslowakischen Denkschriften für die Friedenskonferenz von Paris 1919–1920* (Berlin, 1937).
[3] Appeared Oct. 10th to 19th, 1920. *Bohemia* is a German newspaper
published in Prague.

and that they were thoroughly tendentious. The assertion, for instance, that the 1910 census figure for the German population of Bohemia (2,467,724) was an over-estimate (on account of the *Umgangssprache* method)[1] of 800,000 to 1 million was quickly disproved by the municipal elections of June 1919, and later, to a considerable extent, by the census of 1921. Actually, whereas Beneš suggested that Bohemia alone contained only about 1½ million Germans, the truth lay somewhere a little above 2 millions.[2] For the three Historic Provinces the 1910 census gave 3,512,682 Germans, and this was certainly an exaggerated figure; the Austrian Government, however, claimed at St. Germain to be pleading on behalf of some 4 million Sudeten Germans,[3] and thus added on about 1 million where Beneš deducted very much the same figure. As for an intention to deceive, the *Mémoires* were deliberate propaganda and as guilty or innocent as the propagandistic statements made by many governments then or now. Beneš was preparing them during 1918,[4] but he was much taken up by other claims on his time, he had been away from his country since 1915 and it was not always easy to get the material he needed; indeed it has been frankly admitted from Prague[5] that he used some statements in the Czech press which turned out afterwards to be without justification. The *Mémoires* naturally came out with all the old arguments about *Staatsrecht*, and emphasized the rôle of the Czechs as a barrier to the German *Drang nach Osten* in much the same way as Kramář had written in 1906. If Beneš's thesis in 1908 had adopted Masaryk's pre-War standpoint, Masaryk's view had changed by now, and in any case Czech sentiment about the historic frontiers was far too strong to escape emphatic formulation in Paris. Map 7, attached to *Mémoire* III, showing the advance of the German position in the *Randgebieten* since the time of the Hussite Wars, was an eloquent document, and expressed that feeling of encroaching encirclement within their own territory which may have been even more nerve-racking to the Czechs than Pan-Slav manifestations in Tsarist days ever were to the Germans. For Map 7 showed the steady German advance from the fifteenth to the nineteenth century, including that in the Mies-Pilsen area since 1700; this advance, if inaccurately indicated, had certainly taken place.

[1] The method of registering people according to the language in daily use—see above, p. 54.
[2] On Feb. 5th, 1919, Dr. Beneš made a similar statement to the representatives of the Great Powers at the Quai d'Orsay; in answer to a question from Mr. Lloyd George he admitted that the Sudeten Germans would vote against inclusion in the Czechoslovak State. See Hunter Miller, op. cit., vol. xiv, pp. 210–17.
[3] See Freissler, op. cit., and Molisch, *Sudetendeutsche Freiheitsbewegung.*
[4] Beneš, op. cit.
[5] *Prager Presse*, Oct. 12th, 1937.

It is the general opinion among Austrians, Reich and Sudeten Germans, and Hungarians that the Anglo-Saxon representatives at the Peace Conference were helplessly ignorant about Central Europe and blindly accepted propaganda such as that of the *Mémoires*. This theory may be immediately dismissed as untrue.[1] The British and American experts politely but hastily looked through the demands of the new nations, but they took no more notice of them.[2] They worked out their position on the basis of pre-War Austrian statistics, and it is interesting that, independently, they arrived at almost identical conclusions.[3] This was certainly so in the case of the Czech territorial claims. It is true that the atmosphere in general was anti-German, and that the additional expert advice which was available was mostly that of well-known critics of the Habsburg Monarchy; there was, moreover, lack of immediate contact because there was lack of time. Actually the Czech *Mémoires* suggested a great many small territorial readjustments in spite of the sanctity of the historic frontiers, and brought up the question of the Lusatian Slavs and the possibility of a connecting corridor across Burgenland to Yugoslavia (*Mémoires* II and VII). In the welter of problems which required solution the representatives of the Great Powers were anxious to avoid unnecessary change or complication, and they therefore completely ignored the Corridor and the Lusatian suggestions and only considered the possibility of simplifying the strangely jagged frontiers of the Historic Provinces in one or two places. The cession of Egerland to Germany and of Glatz by Germany were most discussed; Beneš would willingly have been rid of the Asch salient and was willing to exchange some territory around Friedland for Glatz (*Mémoires* IX and X).

Opposition came not from the Czechs, but from the representatives of France, who were still in a panic state of mind about the latent strength of Germany, and who had the exaggerated belief of many of their countrymen in the assimilative magic of centralization. According to Mr. Hunter Miller's *Diary*[4] there were disagreeable differences of opinion between Mr. Lansing and the French when the Czechoslovak Commission reported on the Czech-German frontier on April 1st, 1919. The Americans (not the British) thought Rumburg, also, should go to Germany, and Mr. Lansing suggested a plebiscite there. M. Laroche (France) replied that the Commission had decided that it would

---

[1] Cf. Great Britain: Foreign Office, *Bohemia and Moravia* (= Handbooks prepared under the direction of the Historical Section of the Foreign Office, no. 4, Jan. 1919). This is full of detailed information with one or two curious errors.   [2] See Beneš, op. cit.

[3] I am here largely guided by what Mr. Harold Nicolson has told me; he was a member of the Czechoslovak Commission.   [4] Vol. xvi, pp. 11–16.

be impossible to hold a plebiscite unless it were extended to all the German districts and this would reduce the Czechoslovak State to very slender proportions. 'The inhabitants of these regions', M. Laroche appears to have said, 'were accustomed to live in close connexion with the rest of Bohemia, and did not desire separation. . . . The result of the policy suggested by Mr. Lansing might be that the whole of Bohemia would elect to join Germany in order not to be separated from the German Bohemians.' In the matter of Asch and Eger, M. Jules Cambon, who was President of the Czechoslovak Commission, pointed out that the railway lines at Eger were all directed towards Bohemia. M. Pichon cut short the discussion by announcing that 'he could not allow Germany to be fortified by populations taken from what had been Austrian Dominions, taken, moreover from Bohemia, which, he trusted, would remain an ally of France, and handed over to Germany which, as far as he was concerned, still remained a country to be feared.' In the end the frontiers of Bohemia, Moravia, and Silesia remained unchanged, with four small exceptions, viz. part of the Teschen end of Silesia went to Poland, the small territory of Hlučin (Hultschin) near Troppau with its mainly Czech-speaking population was ceded by Germany, and two minor rectifications on the Czech-Austrian frontier were made, one at Gmund giving the station (a junction for Southern Bohemia) but not the town to the Czechs, the other at Feldsberg near Nikolsburg giving them, not the railway line, but a convenient piece of river.

The claim to the historic frontiers had never seriously been questioned, for it was true that to cut away the *Randgebieten* 'would have left Czechoslovakia so entirely defenceless as to be incapable of independent life'.[1] Mr. Lansing objected to strategic considerations, but it was not only the French but every one on the European continent who found American idealism exasperatingly inapplicable to the world in which they had to live. Economic considerations[1] all spoke for the preservation of Bohemian and Moravian unity as the food shortage in the Sudeten German districts, and the difficulties of Lodgman and Freissler in procuring supplies, had shown. In this connexion an interesting portion of the third Czech *Mémoire* deserves to be quoted because it gives an illuminating and by no means inaccurate description of Czech-German economic relationships:

Les populations allemandes de Bohême, en effet, ne se suffiraient pas économiquement [this paragraph begins]. Elles seraient donc obligées de nouer des relations économiques avec la population tchèque voisine, ce qui donnerait à l'Allemagne le prétexte, conformément aux conceptions connues des économistes et des politiciens allemands, d'étendre sa

[1] *H.P.C.*, vol. iv, p. 268.

sphère d'influence et d'expansion économique pour pénétrer dans la
Bohême même. Vu la grande masse de la population allemande et son
énorme force économique, et vu le caractère expansif de l'Allemagne,
en général, celle-ci éprouverait fatalement un sentiment de convoitise
à l'égard des régions tchèques voisines, sans lesquelles les régions allemandes ne pourraient pas vivre.

La conséquence fatale de cette séparation des régions allemandes de
la Bohême serait donc que la Bohême tout entière serait convoitée par
l'Allemagne, qui la prendrait sans violence par l'expansion et la péné-
tration économiques ou s'en emparerait par les armes.

With regard to the various salients which jutted out into Reich
German territory, it would, I believe, have been wise to cede them
to Germany, especially Egerland with its particular status and
traditions and its violent nationalism; indeed, the mountain frontier breaks before the Asch-Eger corner in a fairly convenient
fashion, and Rumburg and Friedland are beyond the essential
strategic line. It would also, I think, have been better to cede some
territory in the south to Austria, a suggestion accepted by Masaryk
in discussing the future with Dr. Seton-Watson in Holland in the
autumn of 1914.[1] One serious objection, however, had, already in
the summer of 1919, appeared to cessions of such a kind—this was
the resistance of the German inhabitants themselves. As soon as
they realized that the historic frontiers were sure to be preserved
en principe, the feeling arose that if any Sudetendeutschen were to
be the subjects of Czechoslovakia, then let it be all of them, so that
they should the better be able to make their weight felt;[2] this
feeling has increased fairly steadily since 1919.

In view of the legend of British and American ineptitude with
regard to the Central European settlement, it must be emphasized
that the Anglo-Saxon experts were experts and did not deceive
themselves about the difficulties involved in the preservation of the
historic frontiers. On June 16th at the 22nd Meeting of the Committee on New States, a report on Czechoslovakia was adopted
which included the following:

. . . [The Germans in Bohemia] have till within recent years been the
dominating influence in the State; they form a highly developed very
capable element, and, in the past, have been a very aggressive population.
It is clear that the prosperity and perhaps also the existence of the new
State will depend upon the success with which it incorporates the
Germans as willing citizens. The very magnitude of this task makes it
one quite different in character from the mere protection of the other
minorities with which the Committee have had to deal; it is one that

[1] See 'President Masaryk in Exile', in *The Slavonic Review*, no. 9, March
1925. The Coolidge Commission, also, advocated both these cessions to Austria,
and the cession of the salients to Germany.
[2] Freissler, op. cit.

goes so deeply into the heart of all the institutions that the solution of it is probably best left to the Czechs themselves.[1]

There is also a note in the Hunter Miller *Diary*[2] in which the writer says that it seems, and perhaps would be, absurd to leave the Bohemian frontier with all its mountains in German hands, but that as it is there will be a German population there

compactly situated, bitterly hostile to their Slav neighbours, and in sympathy with the Saxons, Bavarians (? and Austrians)[3] dwelling beyond their border and with the German capitalists and Germanized nobles within them.

Now while the peace-makers had no illusions about the intricacies, past, present, and to come, of the Czech-German problem, and while they had been quite unaffected by projects like that for a Burgenland Corridor, they had consoled themselves with the generosity of Dr. Beneš's suggestions with regard to the treatment Czechoslovakia's Germans were to receive. Here again the charge of deliberate deception has been levelled at the Czech representatives in Paris in 1919. On September 10th, the same day as that upon which the Treaty of St. Germain was signed with Austria, Czechoslovakia acceded to a generalized type of Minority Treaty, but she took on additional obligations such as the provision, not only of State elementary schools, but also of higher education,[4] for all her minorities. No special duties with regard to her Germans, as distinguished from her other minorities, were imposed upon her, though there was certainly understanding for the Sudetendeutsch tenet that the German Bohemians were not a minority, but joint dwellers in the land. The absence of special obligations was due to the general proposals which Dr. Beneš had made towards the solution of the problem—if he could offer these things he was to be left to carry them out. They were comprised in the Note of May 20th, 1919, and were, in fact, as follows:

Note on the régime of Nationalities in the Czecho-Slovak Republic.

1. It is the intention of the Czecho-Slovak Government to create the organization of the State by accepting as a basis of national rights the principles applied in the constitution of the Swiss Republic, that is, to make of the Czecho-Slovak Republic a sort of Switzerland, taking into consideration, of course, the special conditions in Bohemia.

2. There will be universal suffrage under the proportional system which will assure to the various nationalities of the Republic proportional representation in all elective bodies.

[1] Hunter Miller, op. cit., vol. xiii, p. 161. Much the same view is expressed in the *H.P.C.*, vol. v, pp. 145–6.
[2] Hunter Miller, op. cit., vol. xx, p. 342.   [3] *Sic.*
[4] *H.P.C.*, vol. v, p. 146 *n.*

3. The schools will be maintained by the State, throughout its territory, from the public funds, and *schools will be established for the various nationalities* in all the communes where the number of children, legally ascertained, proves the necessity of establishing such schools.

4. All public offices, in which in principle the two languages will have equal value, will be open to the various nationalities inhabiting the Republic.

5. The courts will be mixed, and Germans will have the right to plead before the highest courts in their own language.

6. The local administration (of communes and 'circles') will be carried on in the language of the majority of the population.

7. There is no religious question in the Czecho-Slovak Republic, hence there will be no difficulties on this subject.

8. The official language shall be Czech, and the State will be known abroad as the Czecho-Slovak State; but in practice the German language will be the second language of the country, and shall be employed currently in administration before the courts and in the central Parliament on an equal footing with Czech. It is the intention of the Czecho-Slovak Government to satisfy the population in practice and in daily use, but reserving a certain special position for the Czecho-Slovak language and element.

9. To express this in a different way we may say: the present State, in which the Germans had an overwhelming preponderance will remain; only, the privileges that the Germans enjoyed will be reduced to their just proportion (for example, the German schools will be reduced in number because they will be superfluous).[1] It will be an extremely liberal régime, which will very much resemble that of Switzerland.[2]

Paris, May 20th, 1919.

The reproaches of his enemies are levelled primarily against the phrase in the first paragraph in which, as in *Mémoire* III, Beneš spoke of making Czechoslovakia into a sort of Switzerland, an ill-defined dream which had, as we know, floated before the eyes of reformers in Habsburg Austria. It was unfortunate that the Swiss analogy should have been revived; it could have little application to the problem of the Czech miners in Northern Bohemia or the German minorities in the Moravian towns, but it is persistently cherished by people who have no conception of the cantonal complications of the Swiss Federal State. Moreover, the equilibrium of Switzerland depends, among other things, upon the fact that each of its three nationalities has a Great Power at its back; in Czechoslovakia, on the other hand, the smaller groups—especially the German one—have foreign Powers behind them, while the Czechoslovak majority has nothing, except in the view of those

[1] Alternative text = 'where they are superfluous'. See *Prager Presse*, Oct. 10th, 1937.

[2] The text given above is the translation published in Hunter Miller, op. cit., vol. xiii, p. 69.

who nurse the illusion that post-Lenin Russia is still Pan-Slav in outlook.

In the same breath in which Switzerland was mentioned in the Note of May 20th, 1919, the suggestion was qualified by reference to the special circumstances of Bohemia. It was also made absolutely clear in Clause 8 that the State was to be a Czechoslovak national State[1] with Czech as its official language, which reduced its 'Swissness' to nothing but a completely democratic electoral system and a degree of protection for those whose language differed from that of the State. There were certainly too many Swiss flourishes about this document, but there were no positive promises which were afterwards repudiated,[2] and it was clearly intimated that the number of German schools would be reduced. It is interesting, too, that when Dr. Beneš's note was brought before the Committee on New States it was observed that it went beyond the obligations imposed upon Czechoslovakia by the Minorities Treaty.[3] The examination of how the offer of May 20th, 1919, worked out in practice will constitute the main theme of the rest of this study.

The Czechs had retained the historical frontiers—without Glatz, Prussian Silesia, and the eastern portion of the Teschen territory[4] —not because they were historical but because no other solution was practically possible, particularly in the psychological circumstances of the time, which forbade the *Anschluss* or any other cession of territory to the German Reich. But the Sudeten Germans were irritated by the apparent discrimination which denied Hungary's historic claims to Slovakia while accepting the Czech historical claim to the Wenceslas lands. The leaders of the Czech nation were aware of their claim to the best of both worlds, but they believed that events since 1914 had justified it, though the Socialist M. Bechyně pointed out the danger in taking over so large a non-Czech population. They recognized that Sudeten German self-determination had been sacrificed to the event, and admitted, as the Czech publicist, M. Peroutka,[5] has said, a moral obligation to satisfy their Germans with as many national rights as could be reconciled with the unity of the State; it was presumed, for instance, when Dr. Beneš met the Prague political leaders in Geneva at the end of October 1918 that there would be a German minister in the Government. This was not only the attitude of the more liberal leaders, Masaryk, who was to become the first Presi-

---

[1] On Oct. 29th, 1918, Masaryk had wired home about negotiating with the Germans, adding that the new State would certainly be nationalistic, though it would be an advanced democracy. See Peroutka, op. cit.

[2] Except Clause 4, which was in fact contradicted by Clause 8.

[3] Hunter Miller, op. cit., vol. xiii, p. 68.

[4] The Teschen settlement was not completed until later. 　　[5] Peroutka, op. cit.

dent of the Czechoslovak Republic, and Beneš, its first Foreign
Minister, but also of its first Prime Minister, Kramář, who announced in Parliament that the Sudeten Germans 'had not the
smallest reason to fear anything for their national development'.

I believe [he continued] it is our duty to say to ourselves that every
emphatic insistence upon our victory is a sin against the future of our
state. We must at last learn consideration for the psychology of the
German people. . . . I am profoundly ashamed when I discover that
German inscriptions are torn down in a German town.[1]

For beneath this surface, none the less admirable because it
lacked the basis of provincial support, quite other forces had
immediately become active. No one could expect that vindictive
retaliations would not occur in the early days of victory and liberation; no one could expect the Czechs in the big lignite area to
forget the years of contempt they had known in what they had
always regarded as their own country. But chauvinistic action was
more systematic than this might suggest; for the Czech national
unions immediately set about exploiting the new situation to pursue
the old fight for land, for jobs, and for schools. Military influences
fanned the Národní Jednota flames, and there were political
leaders, too, who immediately resisted the programme of the
Note of May 20th. The most forceful among these was Rašin,
a very remarkable man, who immediately became the Minister of
Finance. He did not believe in the romance of magnanimity—he
would not, like Kramář, forget the death sentences of 1916. When
Seliger had come to Prague in November 1918 to negotiate with
the Czech leaders, it was Rašin who 'expressed the view that if
the Germans insisted upon having their own independent government, then the Czechs must direct their policy in accordance with
the old principle: no negotiations with rebels'.[2]

The trouble was that Rašin and the intransigent Czechs, like all
intransigent nationalists, were in one way—on a short view—right,
and the whole business, as it always is, a vicious circle. The
Sudetic Germans *were* rebels—as the Czechs had been until the
State was theirs. Even after Lodgman had left and Freissler
retired, it was not true that they only concerned themselves with
the peace negotiations and with looking after incriminated Sudetic
German officials. Mayer was trying to arrange for military help
from Germany in May 1919, but was told in the Reich that the
Sudetendeutschen must satisfy themselves with autonomy. Yet
although the German Foreign Office was anxious to avoid all
unnecessary complications, the Socialist Defence Minister, Noske,

[1] Peroutka, op. cit. But when Kramář received German complaints about
torn-down inscriptions he is said to have replied that the Germans should be
thankful nothing worse had occurred.   [2] Peroutka, op. cit.

was eager to come to the aid of the Germans across the Bohemian
and Silesian frontiers. Indeed, until after Germany's acceptance
of the Treaty of Versailles, there were bases all round Czechoslovakia in Bavaria, Saxony, and Silesia,[1] where Sudeten German
volunteers were collected and armed and trained. Though there
were not really very many of them, and they need not necessarily
have alarmed the Czechs, they themselves were certain of victory,
and survivors still tell one with some imprecision to-day that 'if only
the Germans had been united they could have won'. There was a
lot of scheming, and many old soldiers, in defiance of the German
Republican authorities, were busy on both sides—German and
Czech—of the frontier of Silesia, until after the Treaty of Versailles; there were hopes for some time of exploiting the tension
between the Czechs and the Poles around Teschen. Finally, when
their anti-Czech hopes were abandoned, these volunteers went off
to fight against the Soviet in the Baltic States, to join in the Kapp
Putsch, and directly or indirectly to prepare the National Socialist
—which was so largely an *Auslandsdeutsch*—Revolution in Germany in 1933. These were the people who finally did away with
the conciliatory policy of the Weimar Republic; their opposite
numbers—who were most aware of their activities and ambitions—
among the Czechs proceeded to distort as far as they could the
conciliatory efforts of Masaryk and Beneš. The deeply nationalistic
feelings of both Germans and Czechs make their most statesman-
like leaders, whether Stresemann or Beneš, very susceptible to
chauvinist criticism. Stresemann and Masaryk died undefeated.
It will be much more remarkable if the same should ever be said
of Beneš, who has to steer between the re-aroused chauvinists of
both nations, with armaments and anxieties heaping up around
him.

[1] The Austrian volunteers seemed to have dispersed after the Teschen
Commission's inquiry in the spring.

CHAPTER XI

THE GERMANS IN CZECHOSLOVAKIA[1]
(i) NORTHERN BOHEMIA

THE three million Germans who now found themselves to be citizens of the new Czechoslovak Republic had surprisingly little in common until they became members of the same so-called minority group. It has become customary, since the War, to refer to them by the general term of Sudeten Germans, a designation which was only exceptionally used until then, though since about 1910 various Bohemian and Moravian Germans had tried to fortify their unity by the adoption of a common name. The mountains which form the eastern frontier of Bohemia, the Riesengebirge, Adlergebirge, &c., are collectively known as *Sudeten*, and for this reason Dr. Freissler and his colleagues adopted the name *Sudetenland* for the territory whose autonomy they hoped to create.

(a) *North-Eastern Bohemia*

Even within the area which regarded itself as *Deutsch-Böhmen*, anything but uniformity reigned. To most people the gateway to Bohemia is certainly the Tetschen-Bodenbach (Děčin-Podmokly) Castle, which rises to one's left if one travels south from Dresden along the Elbe by train. This had belonged to *der lange Franz Thun*,[2] the evil genius of Francis Joseph as many Germans said, and the man who offended the German Emperor with that speech in the autumn of 1898.[3] The castle, now used as barracks by the Czechs—and 'serve the Thuns right', of course—is simple but beautiful *dixhuitième*, and it is exquisitely Austrian, or Bohemian if you will. Saxony, at any rate, is quite left behind. What this frontier means is elusive and difficult to describe, though it is physically actual enough with nothing but the Elbe cutting through the mountains. The people do not look nor speak very differently from their neighbours in the German Reich, and yet Austria has left her mark, her attitude to life. And what is that? Something Catholic, something faintly cosmopolitan, more than racial anyway. Something to do with really good coffee with whipped cream served with hand-kisses (spoken, not performed, but spoken with the sing-song drawl of the Bohemians) the moment one sits

---

[1] This chapter is intended to supplement the pre-War historical cross-section taken in Chapter VII by the taking of a post-War geographical cross-section. This may involve a certain amount of repetition, which can only be excused by the possible advantages of taking things in a different context.

[2] Cf. Sieghart, op. cit., p. 35, for an interesting indication of Franz Thun's contempt for anti-Semitism.   [3] See above, Chapter VI.

down in Bodenbach. Tetschen is the old town here and Bodenbach the new; together they are fairly characteristic—industrial
though small, with a socialist tradition and a sprinkling of Czechs
among the metal-workers. And in a moment one is out and away
into a fairy-story landscape with steep hills and pine forests and
old, delighting villages, and then down to that lovely Elbe valley
again. For Bohemia deserves the legendary reputation which its
name suggests to us in the west; it is still a land of castles and
forests, interspersed though they be with factories and mines. It
is easy to understand why young Sudeten Germans who are all for
Hitler and hate the Czechs will still sometimes tell you they could
have kissed the Czech officials at the frontier all the same, when
they came home last time.

From Bodenbach, if one goes up the Elbe, one comes to Aussig
(Ústí), a town which the Hussites de-Germanized for two or three
centuries. This has been the home of huge chemical concerns
since the Schaffners arrived in the fifties and the Schichts moved
from Reichenberg (Liberec) in 1882. In pre-War days Aussig was
Austria-Hungary's busiest port,[1] for it outdid Trieste with all the
goods to send off by the Elbe across Germany to Hamburg. To
the east, then, of Aussig is Reichenberg and a whole textile world
from Warnsdorf (Varnsdorf) to Trautenau (Trutnov), village after
village built round some factory. Reichenberg itself is a little
disappointing; having found one's way up its steeply inclined
streets—for it is almost among the frontier mountains themselves
—one discovers a citadel crowned by a late nineteenth-century
Gothic town hall, eager to remind one of its prototype in Vienna.
This was the self-appointed capital of *Deutsch-Böhmen* whose
claims to primacy were by no means accepted by a number of
rivals. Reichenberg town has a strongly national tradition. It was
characteristic that in the sixties when the Bohemian Diet for a
short time attempted to compel the learning of Czech as well as of
German in schools, the town of Reichenberg sent in a petition
which included the words, 'We cannot believe that the Government approves that Germans should be forced to send their
children to take lessons across the frontier',[2] i.e. into Czech-speaking territory. It was characteristic, too, that the Reichenberg
leaders disclaimed interest in people who spoke German but were
Jews, and that they had planned a little *coup d'état* of their own
before the War.[3] Reichenberg itself is typically North Bohemian
in that the town is relatively small with some 40,000 inhabitants,
but that another 60,000 people live in the surroundings; it is

[1] The Elbe is actually navigable from Mělník (Melnik), but all-important
loading is done at Aussig.
[2] Quoted in Eisenmann, *Le Compromis austro-hongrois*, p. 348 *n*.
[3] See above, Chapter VII, p. 68.

typical in that the actual town provides the nationalist element, while the weavers and so on, who live outside, have a strong Social-Democratic tradition. In the first decade following the War this tradition was maintained; the German-Nationals (in alliance with the Small-Traders' Party) ruled the town against strong Socialist opposition. The Reichenberg people are justifiably proud of the great reputation already won by Reichenberg cloth throughout Europe in the sixteenth century.

Next door to Reichenberg is the town of Gablonz (Jablonec), very little smaller than its neighbour, and surrounded by villages which depend upon its exporters of buttons and beads mostly made of some kind of glass. Gablonz is interesting because it is the only industrial centre whose surroundings are almost more nationalist than the town itself and in 1911 elected to the Reichsrat Fahrner, one of the first three German Working-men's Party deputies. This can be explained partly by an unusual Lutheran element round here, but still more by the mixing up with Czechs which is apparent in the neighbourhood and which introduces the competition of Czech glass-workers. Back and across the great frontier mountains are the two big salients which might have been ceded to Germany by the Peace. Friedland (Frýdlant), due north of Reichenberg, is the main town in the eastern one, with a famous statue in the market-place of Wallenstein, its duke, brooding over the future of the Holy Roman Empire; the western one, Rumburg (Rumburk) is the centre of the only Clerical constituency in pre-War Bohemia, though the Clericals were by far the strongest party in Austria proper without Vienna.

(b) The Lignite Area

Due south from Aussig is the long bitterly contested language-frontier district around Leitmeritz (Litoměřice), Lobositz (Lovo-sice), and Trebnitz (Třebenice), where Dr. Titta founded the Bohemian German Council in 1903;[1] fruit-farming flourishes here. At Aussig, too, the great lignite area begins and stretches to the west away to Kaaden (Kadaň). Close to Aussig itself is Teplitz-Schönau (Teplice-Šanov), a great German centre, where many historic demonstrations have occurred from the German protest against *Böhmisches Staatsrecht* in 1871, and the German celebra-tion of Rieger's surrender in 1890, to Seliger's speech to the pro-testing masses on March 4th, 1919, and the skirmish between police and Henleiners on October 17th, 1937. Teplitz Castle is the seat of the Clary-Aldringen family, and it and the buildings around it are old and beautiful. The modern town makes a very Reich-German impression; the sign-post at the centre of the town

[1] See Chapter VII, p. 64.

points to Prague and Aussig in small Czech and German Latin print, but to Dresden in large Gothic letters and in German only. Teplitz sets out, of course, to please visitors from the Reich, since it is, for many of them, the nearest of the Bohemian spas, and counts, though less than upon its industries, upon the drinking of its waters.[1] Apart from the lignite shafts in the neighbourhood Teplitz is also an important centre of the glass industry. From Aussig, west and south-west until beyond Brüx (Most), the population is considerably mixed, and the mining towns of Brüx and Dux (Duchcov) are about half and half German and Czech.[2] The poverty is great and the smell of lignite hangs about the air, but the miners' dwellings in the towns make a less sordid impression than bad working-class quarters in England, partly because the windows of the houses are larger. As for the textile villages in the Reichenberg area, even after the terrible impoverishment brought by the great slump of the early 1930's, they are far less depressing than much British poverty because the people at least have fields and fresh air around them. The soil in all the mountainous frontier region is poor, but many working-people are not quite divorced from it, and this helps them to be able to keep a cow or a goat, and to be able to grow potatoes.

Almost due south of Brüx is the beautiful old town of Saaz (Žatec), the centre of the hop-growing district. Like Leitmeritz, Komotau (Chomutov), České Budějovice (Budweis), and Prachatitz (Prachatice), Saaz, from being mainly German, became mainly Czech with the Hussite wars, and its Czech mayor, Hoštálek z Javořic,[3] was among the twenty-seven Protestant victims executed in Prague by the triumphant Habsburg authorities in 1621. In the course of the seventeenth century the city of Saaz was more or less re-Germanized. To-day it is one of the finest of the Bohemian towns, of which it is indeed a very lovely example. The character of the market-place and its surroundings is restrained early baroque, and the town seems to gravitate around those beautifully sculptured saints whom the Jesuits gave to Bohemia, and whom one finds, singly or in groups, in each town from one end of Bohemia to the other; even in a gloomy mining-centre like Dux they are there. It is they who make the country so different from Saxony and somehow more Austrian than Silesian or Bavarian.

(c) Karlsbad

Beyond Saaz the mixed region comes to an end, and one comes into a solid German triangle whose apex is in the corner of Asch

---

[1] The word Teplitz derives from *teplo*, the Czech word for hot.
[2] Brüx was actually about 35 per cent. Czech in 1930 and has become more so since then.   [3] *Českomoravská Kronika*, vol. v.

(Aš). The triangle is sometimes referred to as Egerland, but this is historically quite inaccurate, and only receives some justification in the fact that the Eger (Cheb) dialect makes its influence felt at least as far away as Karlsbad (Karlovy Vary). This world-famous town owes its origin to the great Bohemian Emperor, Charles IV, who, appreciating the value of its waters, is thought to have founded a small German city here so early as 1349. Thereafter Kaiser Karlsbad was the favoured protégé of the Kings of Bohemia, who granted it privileges and warned off the local nobles, the Schlicks of Elbogen (Loket), from interfering with its freedom. So famous and so Protestant had it already become in the seventeenth century that Ferdinand II preferred not to insist upon the full punishment and expulsion of Protestants in Karlsbad as he did elsewhere. Among the hosts of distinguished visitors to the city in later years were Peter the Great and Goethe; during the eighteenth century the city was the scene of much rococo pageantry, on account of its proximity to the brilliant Dresden of Augustus the Strong, Elector of Saxony and King of Poland.

Although Saxony was so near it was not until the last years of the eighteenth century that the Bohemian china industry was founded. There is plenty of china clay available in the neighbourhood, and Karlsbad became the centre of a network of small towns or villages where china was made. As the population increased the working-people settled largely in Fischern (Rybáře) next door to Karlsbad, and here in the late nineteenth century a strong Socialist movement grew up. North of Karlsbad the frontier mountains are known as the Erzgebirge, though they have produced no sign of iron since the sixteenth century. At Joachimsthal (Jáchymov) silver and copper used to be found and coins were consequently called thalers, and much later on and very far away they are still called dollars. Nowadays, since radium was discovered there, that has become the *raison d'être* of Joachimsthal.[1] So near the international luxury of Karlsbad, the Erzgebirge villages always lived in miserable poverty, for the soil is wretchedly poor and communication extremely difficult. A few rather specialized handicrafts, like the making of lace, of toys and musical instruments, have brought in money when times were good and the world had money for extras.

(d) Egerland

Close to the western frontier of Bohemia are two more watering-places, Marienbad (Marianské Lazně) and Franzensbad (Frantisikovy Lazně), which, with Karlsbad and Teplitz, make up a celebrated quartet. But Marienbad is almost, and Franzensbad

[1] See below, Chapter XIII, section (iii).

quite, in the old historic Egerland, indeed Franzensbad was originally known as Egerbrunnen (= Eger fountain). The people of Northern Bohemia, though often reminding one of Saxons, bring Thuringia to mind; many of them are dark, fine-featured, and not very tall, few of them recall Prussia in any way, and there is always a little of the Austrian veneer. As for the country-side it is difficult to find the adjective; it remains Bohemian until somewhere near Eger—still Central European. But by the time one has reached old Egerland, which actually included only the country around Eger and Wildstein (Vildštejn), one has left the Bohemian mountains behind and crossed some quite definite frontier into Western Germany. The people seem to be great strapping Franconians, or at any rate Bavarians. The land is fertile, the peasants rich and independent, for Egerland entirely lacks the feudal flavour of the rest of Bohemia, with its powerful landed nobility which, even since Land Reform, has not disappeared.

The town of Eger (Cheb) is one of the loveliest old German towns in existence. Romanesque, Gothic, Renaissance, and Baroque crowd upon one another, from the Romanesque hall at the castle which Barbarossa is said to have built, to the Renaissance house or Guildhall where Wallenstein was murdered in 1634 and the early eighteenth-century house where Schiller lived to contemplate the tragedy of Wallenstein. There seems to be a virgin or saint at every corner from market-place to castle, for the Hussites never took Eger, and, in the Thirty Years War, the Swedes did some damage but not a great deal. Until the fourteenth century Egerland, originally part of Franconia, constantly changed hands between Babenbergs, Swabians, and Přemyslids. In 1322, however, it accepted the suzerainty of King John of Bohemia in return for particular privileges; in 1350 Charles IV made fresh terms with the Egerländer, but they regarded the arrangement with Bohemia as conditional, kept their administration in their own hands, and never sent representatives to the Bohemian Diet until after the middle of the nineteenth century, though they could not entirely escape the centralizing attention of Maria Theresa and Joseph II.

The Egerländer are tremendously proud of themselves, of their songs, and their dialect, which they say has not changed these thousand years, and has spread outwards in influence to Karlsbad and Mies (Stříbro). They regard themselves as the most German of Germans. They attended the Reichsrat, sometimes under protest,[1] after 1860, but they supplied a high proportion of its most vigorous members in the heyday of Liberalism and of Plener.

[1] For instance, from the deputies Karl Iro and Josef Mayer.

1866 was a terrible blow most of all to the Egerländer, and within a decade or so they had eagerly accepted the doctrines of Georg von Schönerer; it is astonishing to find how many Schönerianer, but particularly how many German-Radical deputies—beginning with Karl Hermann Wolf himself—were born in Eger. It is almost impossible to discover to what extent the original Czech population survived here,[1] but old Czech inscriptions can be found, and the Czechs claim that the castle before Barbarossa's building was Czech. Nineteenth-century developments, at any rate, brought some Czechs in, for they were able to found a society in the town in 1883. But the Germans of Eger put an end to this in 1897, nor would they hear of even a private Czech school in the whole neighbourhood; even in Falkenau (Falknov), a small industrial town not strictly included in the Egerland, there were fierce struggles and on at least one occasion Czech parents, who had entered their children for a school which the Thun Government had promised to procure, were evicted from their houses. 'If a Czech wished to live in the Egerland, he was expected as a matter of course to accept German nationality.' This was said to me only the other day in Eger, in tones which implied that it was ludicrous to wish to remain a Czech and here one had never stood such nonsense. The attitude to Jews was equally disdainful. The self-respecting citizens of Eger were not expected to buy from Jews nor to have anything to do with them socially. This state of mind was all the more striking since there were few Czechs and fewer Jews in the Egerland—it was nowhere near the language frontier nor the big towns where Jews were powerful. Yet 'literature' used to be circulated, in the nineties, for instance, of exactly the same kind as the notorious *Stürmer* newspaper which is edited to-day by Herr Streicher, the most anti-Semitic of all Nazi leaders in Germany. Despite the town's devout surface the attitude of the Eger people to the Catholic Church was also one of hostility. Young Clericals were regularly thrashed by their Pan-German contemporaries at the *Los von Rom* time,[2] though there were actually less conversions to Protestantism here than in places like Reichenberg and Gablonz, and nowadays, though they applaud the persecution of the Catholic Church in Germany, the people of Eger cling to Catholic observances.

It is not surprising, then, that the most sensational German protest against the Badeni Decrees should have taken place in Eger.[3] On the day of this demonstration the following verse was

[1] i.e. the Czech population, which appears to have made some impression here, too, after the German Marcomanni and Quadi withdrew from Bohemia into Bavaria. See Chapter I.
[2] See Chapter VI.
[3] See Chapter V.

composed, and afterwards set up on a wall in the courtyard of the
Guildhall where Wallenstein died:

> Das höchste Gut des Mannes ist sein Volk.
> Das höchste Gut des Volkes ist sein Recht.
> Des Volkes Seele lebt in seiner Sprache.
> Dem Volk, dem Recht und seiner Sprache treu
> Fand uns der Tag, wird jeder Tag uns finden.
>   11. Juli. 1897.[1]

It was an unbearable thought in Eger that Czech should be heard
in its offices and streets with any official justification.

The collapse of the Central Powers in 1918 was such an overwhelming catastrophe to the people of Eger that even their
pugnacity was for a short time overtaken by defeatism, and when
the Czech troops were advancing towards the town in December
the Pan-German mayor himself went out to surrender to them.
But this state of mind did not last long. Already at Christmas,
when Lodgman declared his *Volkswehr* formations dissolved, the
people of Eger were indignant with his—as they saw it—passivity,
and constructed an organization of their own by which news and
orders could be passed round with lightning rapidity. The fierce
and famous Egerland soldiers had come home in the meantime,
but many of them had become revolutionary and they set up
soldiers' councils (soviets), which so much alarmed the middle
classes that these were not sorry for the Czech occupation, though
keen Pan-Germans were trying to arrange to become part of
Bavaria.[2] March 4th, 1919, brought only one death in Eger, but
Egerland feeling was rising. As in many other Sudeten German
towns, the Czechs immediately opened the elementary school they
had wanted for so long in Eger (though it was not until 1925 that
their own building was ready for it); in 1920 all its windows were
broken one night and Czech soldiers were brought into the town
the next day. In 1922 the Czechs wished to celebrate the six
hundred years' association of Egerland with Bohemia, but the
windows of the *Schützenhaus*, where this was to occur, were removed in the previous night; as it was winter, the celebration was
successfully vetoed. Not long after, Czech State police began to
replace some of the German municipal constabulary.

As a good many Czechs had foreseen, Eger was nothing but a
danger. Most Egerländer soon made no pretence whatever that
their sympathies were anywhere but with Germany; after all, they

---

[1] The most precious possession of Man is his people;
    The most precious possession of a people is its right;
    The soul of a people lives in its language;
    The day found us true to the people, its right and its language, and every
      day will find us so.
[2] First-hand information.

had never had any real feeling for Austria as such. In the Czechoslovak Parliament once, when some speaker questioned the Egerland
people's desire to belong to the Reich, Josef Mayer interpolated
that they would go to Germany 'in the night and bare-footed'.
From that day to this the Czech authorities have never insisted
upon street and inn names being put up in the State language as
well as in German—the Egerländer say they (the Czechs) know
it is not worth their while. North-west of Eger is Asch (Aš), a
small industrial town, which looks as Reich German as the position
would indicate. For Asch is modern and predominantly Protestant
and is thus more thoroughly alien in Bohemia than Eger. The
station of Eger and the four lines into Germany, including that via
Franzensbad and Asch, had belonged to the German State since
the sixties, when Germany, with Austria's permission, had constructed them. This arrangement was maintained by the Peace
Settlement, and it has certainly seemed very fitting to see the
employees of the German State railways at the stations at Eger
and Asch; it has also involved a considerable Reich German
population in Eger. In 1937 an agreement was made between
Berlin and Prague by which the Czechs were to take over control
of the passenger traffic at Eger station though the goods traffic is
still left to the Reich Germans; adjustments have also occurred on
the Zittau-Reichenberg line, which belonged to Germany, as
against a small portion of Czechoslovak line which ran into Bavaria
at Furth-im-Walde.

As late as 1929 the men of Eger put up frankly Pan-German
candidates in their municipal elections. But the feeling (and with
it the number of German National Socialist votes)[1] was growing
among them that the fiery Germanism of Eger could and should
help to ignite that of the other Germans in Czechoslovakia, and
leave political Pan-Germanism to be realized later. There is no
doubt that the Czechs would have been rid of their most dangerous
irredenta if Eger and Asch had been given to Germany in 1919.

(ii) THE BÖHMERWALD AND SOUTH BOHEMIA: 'LANGUAGE-ISLANDS'

Immediately south of Marienbad (Marianské Lázně) in the
neighbourhood of Tachau (Tachov), the Böhmerwald begins and
stretches away down the Bohemian-Bavarian frontier. There is a
strip of very old German population all along the forested mountains here, that is to say, German peasants have almost certainly
lived on the Bohemian side of the frontier since at least the time of
Ottakar II, and here, if anywhere, the Bretholz continuity theory
might have been justified.[2] The Czech cuts into the German

[1] See below, Chapter XIV, for the Nazi successes in Eger in 1933.
[2] See Chapter I.

population practically up to the Bavarian frontier around Domažlice (Taus), thus separating the big Egerland triangle from the Böhmerwald. In the neighbourhood of Wallern (Volary), near the point where German meets Austrian territory, the Böhmerwald becomes South Bohemia, and the German area thickens across to Gratzen (Nové Hrady). Whereas the Germans in the Egerland triangle or in North-East Bohemia number something not far short of a million, in the Böhmerwald and South Bohemia together there are only about 250,000 of them. This is an exceptionally poor population living on very poor soil. The whole area presents the sharpest contrast to the Egerland, for astonishingly feudal conditions prevailed until after the end of the War. The greatest seigneurs of the region were the Schwarzenberg family, who incidentally had estates in Northern Bohemia too, and altogether owned about 140,000 hectares; in South Bohemia around Kaplitz (Kaplice) and Gratzen, the Buquoys, also, were great landed proprietors.

Perhaps the most gigantic of the Schwarzenberg castles is that which dominates the town of Krumau (Krumlov), the chief German town in Southern Bohemia. Indeed, even to-day, to enter the gateway of Krumau is to enter something like the domain of a medieval princeling, but for the anachronism of Prince Schwarzenberg's guards whom, since the Battle of Leipzig in 1813, he has been privileged to dress in a particular uniform of the Napoleonic period. All Krumau revolves around the castle from whose towers each hour is trumpeted during the day. The people of Krumau, and of Southern Bohemia in general, are to the inexpert eye indistinguishable from those across the frontier in Austria—they seem small and pinched by comparison with the Egerländer—and they speak in the Austrian way. Until after the War most of the peasants, having gained next to nothing in 1848, were poor foresters who paid the Schwarzenbergs or Buquoys a low rent for the huts they lived in. They might not marry without the landowners' approval, for they would be subject to eviction; the customary greeting of these pseudo-serf foresters to their lord was to address him as *Brotvater*.[1] The roads were bad, or did not exist, and the villages were cut off from one another. The more spirited Southern Bohemians, however, went to Vienna to make their fortune, and it was only as a Viennese repercussion that Social Democracy even managed to appear. The Böhmerwald people wandered off into Bavaria to earn a bit more in the good season every year.

Krumau is almost unbelievably unspoilt; it is another Rothenburg which has hitherto been successfully concealed from the foreign tourist. This exquisite little town, with the Moldau

[1] = literally 'bread-father'.

(Vltava) winding about it before that river becomes more ambitious and embraces the stones of Prague itself, is another scene of controversy. For the Czechs believe that the Witigonen who built the original castle—now no longer to be seen—were purely Czech, and that their successors the Rosenbergs (or Lords of the Rose, who began to build the castle of to-day) spoke Czech as they spoke German. Actually, even the expert finds it difficult to judge, since medieval criteria were entirely different. It is certain that the activities of both Witigonen and Rosenbergs took them much into Upper Austria as well as Bohemia; as for language distinctions, before these were social as well, nobles of the kind no doubt spoke whatever it suited them to speak. Another lovely old town not really very far from Krumau, although it still takes many hours to travel around the mountains and hills which divide them, is Prachatitz (Prachatice). This was conquered by the Hussites, but became predominantly German again in the seventeenth century, and in the nineteenth century, when the Czechs turned the tables on the Germans and began to push them back a little, Prachatitz, like Leitmeritz (Litoměřice) and Lobositz (Lovosice), soon found itself right upon the language frontier, the battle-front indeed; in the 1910 census already a quarter of its population was admitted to be Czech, and with the emergence of the Czechoslovak Republic the fight was bound to become intense since the local Czech nationalist societies could push with little restraint while the Germans were left without many of their previous resources. It was not, however, until the municipal elections of 1935 that the Czechs were able to scrape together the barest majority.[1]

Southern Bohemia is the stationery department, and to some extent the brewery, of the land, for its biggest town, Budějovice (Budweis), is not only famous for beer, but it is the head-quarters of Hardmuth and other pencil manufacturers, while Spiro, the biggest paper factory of old Austria-Hungary, is situated just outside Krumau (Krumlov). Budějovice, like so many Bohemian towns, had a German period before the Hussites, and became mainly German in the sixteenth and seventeenth centuries, though it is admitted by anti-Czech Germans that a considerable proportion of the population continued to be Czech, and it is interesting that the first mayor elected after 1848 (i.e. before the main period of the expansion of the Czech population) was a Czech. In the sixties, in spite of Schmerling, the town council was about one-third Czech, and it was not until 1876 that it became wholly

---

[1] The Germans claim that workmen only temporarily in the neighbourhood were allowed to vote, and that there were even irregularities in the counting of the votes; this is the only case I know of a definite charge of irregularity in any kind of Czechoslovak election.

German;[1] thus, as in the Leitmeritz area, there was a German offensive in the late nineteenth century. A tremendous tussle now began, the Czechs pushing to conquer the propertied *curiae*[2] and therefore to buy up property—it was not until the nineties that they were able to get hold of one of the valuable old houses on the market-place. After the electoral reform of 1896 the Czechs were able to send their candidate, Prince Schwarzenberg, to the Reichsrat, but it was not until 1907 that they were able to win the third *curia* in the town council elections. In 1911 a tentative agreement was arrived at between the German mayor, Dr. Taschek, and the leader of the Czechs, Dr. Zátka, by which Germans and Czechs were to be divided into national *curiae*—as in Moravia—with fixed representation very favourable to the Germans. With the coming of the Czechoslovak State the artificial strength of the Germans was quickly eliminated, and with the census of 1921 the Germans were counted as only 17·5 per cent. and were therefore deprived of a legal claim to minority rights.

The famous town of Plzeň (Pilsen) is another of the so-called German 'language-islands'[3] of Bohemia. Germans consider that in about 1850 Pilsen had about 14,000 inhabitants, of whom some 4,000 were Czech. After this the Škoda concern drew in an ever-increasing Czech population from the Czech country-side. By 1883 the Chamber of Commerce was half German and half Czech, but it is typical of things as they then were that old Škoda, who brought up the foundry in the sixties, was a Czech who Germanized himself and arranged for his children to be educated in Vienna. The famous breweries were entirely in German hands until the Czechs founded a co-operative brewery in 1894. In 1912 the *Živnostenská Banka* financed the foundation of another brewing concern, and after this about 40 per cent. of the capital invested in Plzeň brewing was Czech. This unusual Czech achievement in the acquisition of property had led to the town council becoming entirely Czech some time before the War, so that in this case the Germans had nothing to lose and something to gain from the introduction of proportional representation when the Czechoslovak Republic was established. It should perhaps be mentioned that when in 1890, for instance, 41,593 Czechs and only 8,071 Germans were counted in Plzeň, the Germans complained, as they did in Prague, that the Czech authorities had misused the language-in-daily-use method of deciding nationality. In 1921 a Czech bank

---

[1] The population figures according to the Austrian census were:

		Germans	Czechs
1880	. . 11,829	Germans,	11,812 Czechs
1890	. . 11,642	,,	16,585 ,,
1900	. . 15,436	,,	23,421 ,,

[2] In 1883 the Czechs won control of the Budweis Chamber of Commerce. See Chapter V, p. 40.   [3] *Sprachinseln.*

was able to buy up most of the shares in the oldest Pilsen brewery, the *Bürgerliches Brauhaus*, which had belonged to the German banker Bleichröder before the War. Thus to-day some 75 per cent. of the Plzeň brewery capital is Czech, while there are seven Czech to five German directors.

Some little way west of Plzeň, across the language frontier, was the best-known Czech 'language-island' in the villages around the small silver mining town of Mies (Stříbo). Mies can only be considered to have been German since the eighteenth century, though German settlers had been arriving in the century before. Already by 1880 the villages to the west of Mies counted as German, and by 1890 the Germans had gained a majority in those to the east. It would be entirely misleading to generalize from those areas where there was a German 'advance' in Bohemia in the last quarter of the nineteenth century, but it would be equally inaccurate to suggest that the Czechs were gaining all along the line.

Bohemia's capital, Prague, was another German 'language-island', and much energy was expended in the fight over this. The Germans tried to insist, e.g. in the Whitsun Programme of 1899, that as the capital city and the seat of a German University Prague must provide perfect language parity for German and Czech. But, as we have had occasion to see,[1] the Germans in the town were almost melting away, and after a period of street names in both languages, German disappeared from the streets of Prague as it had from the streets of Plzeň.[2]

With regard to Bohemia as a whole, it is important to point out that while the whole province was densely populated, the predominantly German regions were even more crowded than the Czech ones. This is misleading to those who look at a racial map of Bohemia, since the map shows the Germans to occupy a smaller area than they would if the population were evenly distributed.

(iii) MORAVIA

There is a certain pugnacity and a certain suspiciousness about both the Germans and the Czechs of Bohemia, where for so long war has been waged with the instruments of peace. It is of the Bohemian Czechs that the other Slav peoples are thinking when they speak of the Czechs as the too Germanized, or even too Prussianized, Slavs. It is typical that Hussitism in Moravia was mostly the later contemplative religion of the Brotherhood, and it is typical, too, that Kramář was Bohemian and Masaryk Moravian. For Moravia and the Moravians are altogether gentler and more friendly. Just as the hills south of Brno (Brünn) are soft and

[1] See above, Chapter VII, p. 58.
[2] More fully treated below, see Chapter XV, section (vi).

charming, so the people have something of the Viennese about them. Bohemia is a half-way house between the Danubian world and the north and west, but in Moravia one knows that the Danube, together with the colour it lends to life, is very near. To the north and the south there are patches of what the Germans called 'closed' or 'locked'[1] German territory, but the problem of Moravia is much more the problem of the 'language-island', like Budějovice or Plzeň, i.e. the problem of important German minorities in towns with a Czech population around them, towns like Olomouc (Olmütz), Moravian Ostrava (Mährisch Ostrau), Jihlava (Iglau), and above all the Moravian capital, Brno (Brünn).

It has been seen how, in June 1848, the influence of the German aristocracy upon the Moravian peasants, combined, no doubt, with a certain quite natural 'Moravian' feeling, had caused the Moravians, Czechs though most of them were, to oppose the orders which came to them from Prague;[2] that Palacký himself was a Moravian made no difference at the time. By the Schmerling constitution the Moravian Diet had 100 members; at first 56 Czechs and 44 Germans were elected, but this soon changed and a German majority was created, and remained until 1905, though Moravia was all along something like 70 per cent. Czech.[3] These and other circumstances, such as the economic developments indicated earlier, aroused the indignation of the Czechs of Moravia, and by 1871 their attitude was changed. On October 13th, 1871, at the time when the Czechs were hoping to obtain much the same recognition as the Hungarians had received in 1867, the Moravian Diet definitely accepted Bohemian *Staatsrecht* and the so-called Fundamental Articles,[4] in spite of German opposition. The introduction of the personal principle in Moravia by the Compromise of November 1905 has, on account of its general importance, been dealt with above;[5] a territorial division in Moravia was always out of the question, and this simplified all Czech-German negotiations in the province. The result was that the extreme German National parties were never strong in Moravia though Clerical influence only remained strong among the Czechs. At the same time the language quarrel was far gentler, and in Brno, both before and since the War, people have been much readier to speak the other language than in Prague, though of course it is the Czechs who know German rather than the Germans Czech. It is characteristic that Körber's compromise proposals in 1900 included the full equality of the Czech language in Moravia, where the Germans

---

[1] = *geschlossen*.
[2] See Chapter III, p. 22.
[3] 70·34 per cent. according to the first serious census in 1880.
[4] See Chapter IV, p. 35.
[5] Chapter VII, pp. 51–2.

were not violently hostile to the idea[1]—nearly all the Badeni excitement had been in Bohemia.

In the circumstances of Brno (Brünn) the problem of Moravia was neatly summed up, for if its greater homogeneity, as compared with Bohemia, was a simplification, this brought with it a more clear identification of capital with the Germans and labour with the Czechs, and a consequent emphasis of the Social Question. It is perhaps for their architectural achievements that posterity has most reason to thank the Jesuits, and old Brno is essentially a beautiful late seventeenth-century Jesuit town; for most of a century now, it has been increasingly surrounded by textile and machine factories. The employers, and the secretarial and administrative staff in each factory, until after the War, were almost exclusively[2] German and the working-people Czech. The employing class mostly supported the Progressive Party, which ruled the town and supplied its representatives in the Reichsrat in Vienna.[3] These people were not intransigent followers of Wolf, on the contrary they were susceptible to many genuinely liberal ideas, but the Moravian Compromise had not affected municipal elections and the German Progressives eagerly preserved a German and a social ascendancy in Brno itself by clinging to the *curia* system. Though the Czech minority in the town was rising above 40 per cent. in the last year or so of peace, there was not one Czech on the town council, and no street name in Czech might be seen. The injustice was increased by the fact that the Czechs had an overwhelming and growing majority in the big suburban area around the city; after all, the suburban population depended on conditions in Brno although it was not included in the municipal area for municipal elections, &c.

One of the biggest Czech grievances was that the Brno town authority would never in pre-War days permit a single Czech *Bürgerschule*, i.e. upper elementary school, within the town. This meant that Czech parents had an interest in evading the *Lex Perek*[4] by calling themselves German in order to send their children to a German *Volksschule* or lower elementary school, so that these children should be able to continue their education from the age of 10 to that of 14. Otherwise a Czech working-class child in Brno could only get schooling from 6 to 10. In view of the Czechs' remarkable thirst for education, this circumstance involved a real grievance; even in the suburbs there were very few

[1] Hugelmann, op. cit., p. 216. The Moravian Compromise was partly descended from Körber's efforts to find a solution.

[2] More so than in Budějovice or Plzeň.

[3] The admirable Professor Redlich was a Progressive deputy, from 1907 onwards, for a South Moravian constituency near to Brno.

[4] See Chapter VII, p. 58

Czech *Bürgerschulen*. German resistance to the foundation of a Czech University in Brno has been considered elsewhere.[1] It is interesting that in the matter of secondary schools, the Czechs had nothing to complain of in Brno, with four boys' schools to five German ones; there was a girls' secondary school apiece and— which is characteristic—the Czechs ran another private girls' secondary school. The ample generosity accorded to the Czechs in the matter of secondary schools is explained by the fact that the State was chiefly responsible in the matter, while the communes were mainly responsible for both kinds of elementary school. In Moravia as a whole, as also in Silesia, the lack of Czech upper elementary schools was general.

Thus although the Compromise of 1905 worked fairly well, it is comprehensible that Czech indignation was rising in the years before 1914. To the Germans the compromise arrangements represented a stabilization, a truce in the struggle to keep the Czech masses 'in hand'; that there should be 73 Czechs to 40 Germans in the Diet seemed to them all that the Czechs could possibly desire, but the Czechs regarded this as a merely temporary gain, and eagerly awaited the day when numerical justice should be done, and a flexible system introduced by which the increase in the Czech population would always be able to make itself felt. This would immediately mean something nearer to 27 Germans to 73 Czechs in the Diet and the complete disappearance of the class *curiae*. The moment the Austrian authority vanished from Brno, the Compromise of 1905 was obviously doomed to disappear.

There are two stories told of the *Umsturz*, i.e. the collapse of the old régime, in Brno, illustrating that *Gemütlichkeit* which was as characteristic of Brno as of Vienna itself, and which distinguished Moravia so strikingly from Bohemia and Silesia, and all the more from Northern Germany. When the Czech National Committee in Brno requested the Austrian Governor (*Statthalter*), Baron Heinold, to resign, he asked who was to succeed him. They told him his assistant, Dr. Černy, whereupon Heinold telephoned to Vienna and begged that Černy should be promoted, since his official rank hitherto was insufficient for the governor of a province.[2] At the same time friends warned the German mayor of Brno that it would be wise to negotiate immediately with the Czechs, because the latter intended to incorporate the suburbs with the town in order to create a large Czech majority. 'But', the mayor answered, 'they could not do that without passing a law.' . . . In the seventeenth century the imperial forces did not overrun Moravia until

[1] See Chapter VII, p. 63.
[2] Peroutka, *Budování státu*.

some years after Bohemia was crushed. In 1918 the Czechs took over Brno as soon as they heard that the National Committee was in power in Prague, and the Republic empowered them to extend the frontiers of the city, so that the Germans suddenly became a a small minority. Much the same fate overtook the Germans in Olomouc (Olmütz) and Moravian Ostrava (Mährish Ostrau), and may be regarded as typical of the immediately post-War Moravian situation. For the time being the Germans in these towns were able to claim the rights appertaining to minorities of at least 20 per cent., for unlike Budějovice, they survived the census of 1921 with the German minority admittedly above that figure.

In Moravia and Silesia, but especially in Moravia, the post-War census figures of 1921 showed a steeper falling away from the supposedly German to the supposedly Czechoslovak population than in Bohemia. Apart from the possibility of undue pressure from officials,[1] the difference is to be explained by the relatively larger number of people who spoke both languages and the less harsh demarcation between the two nationalities. This meant that there were more unpolitically minded people who accepted the pro-German influences before the War and the pro-Czech ones after it. Thus in the Czechoslovak Republic the German minority in Moravia was counted in 1921 as 547,605 and only 20·93 per cent. of the population of the province, though in 1910 the Germans had been reckoned as 27·53 per cent. The Germans of the Jihlava (Iglau) 'language-island' (almost on the Bohemian-Moravian frontier) and their bigger textile region around Zwittau (Svitavy) in Northern Moravia also lost in numbers. In Znaim (Znojmo) on the Austrian frontier, perhaps the strangest changes of all occurred. Before the War only some 18 per cent. of the population had called itself Czech, yet in the communal elections of 1919, the Czechs were able to gain a bare majority. This was due partly to a great many apparently Germanized Czechs thinking better of their Germanization, but also to the presence of a garrison of some three thousand Czech soldiers who were at that time entitled to vote if they had been stationed in the town at least nine days. These 'election-battalions' naturally aroused much German resentment and the members of local garrisons[2] were later disfranchised. Where, as in Znaim, control of the town council was immediately lost to the Czechs, official appointments and school policy henceforth meant a steady undermining of the German position; even in Moravia the local Czech nationalist societies were zealous to recapture the Slav past of Znaim.

[1] See below, Chapter XII, section (i).
[2] The large garrisons at Olomouc and Troppau also weakened the position of the Germans there in the earlier municipal elections under the Republic.

(iv) SOUTHERN SILESIA

In discussing the problems of Bohemia and Moravia it is not always possible to cover the circumstances of Southern Silesia nor to break off in order to attend to them, and yet they must not be neglected. Its historical vicissitudes make Silesia difficult to treat. The whole of the province, with its then Slav population, was united to Poland in about A.D. 1000. In 1138, however, there was a quasi-separation and Silesia came under strong German influence, and in the course of the next hundred years was considerably Germanized. The Tatar invasion which culminated in the Battle of Liegnitz in 1241[1] involved a tremendous amount of destruction, and this in its turn was followed by further German colonization. Thus when in 1335 Silesia was finally joined to Bohemia, it brought a marked reinforcement of the German element in the kingdom, and at the time of the Hussite wars Silesia fought for the Emperor against the Hussites. With the German Reformation it became predominantly Protestant, only to be re-Catholicized in the period of the Counter-Reformation. In the eighteenth century important economic developments began to take place, but most of the province was annexed to Prussia by Frederick the Great. Though this involved a diminution of the German element, there were still enough Germans in that part of Silesia which remained to Austria to be of importance in the German-Slav struggle in the Historic Provinces, and the rulers of Austria continued to bring in German weavers from Saxony.[2]

The Austrian remnant consisted of the Freiwaldau (Frývaldov)–Jägerndorf (Krnov) territory and the districts of Troppau (Opava) and Teschen (Těšin), and was oddly invaded by a north-eastern tip of Moravia which came almost up to the new Prusso-Austrian frontier, a corner where the modern town of Moravian Ostrava has subsequently sprung up. In 1782 Joseph II, more resigned than his mother could ever bring herself to be to the conquests of Frederick the Great, united the Austrian fragments of Silesia with Moravia for the purposes of imperial administration. This arrangement was reversed by his successors except for a second brief period from 1860 to 1861. Moravian Ostrava and the Austrian-Silesian territory around it became of growing importance in the nineteenth century because of the coal-mines which are concentrated here and which are easily connected with the north by the River Oder. Around the mines several great iron furnaces have been constructed beginning with Vitkovice (Witkowitz) in 1828;[3]

[1] See above, Chapter I, p. 5.
[2] For tariff quarrels with Prussia, &c., see above, Chapter II, p. 13.
[3] Started as a small puddling-plant by the Habsburg Archbishop of Olmütz. See Chapter III, p. 19.

they mainly use Swedish ore sent up the Oder, or ore from the great iron supplies of Styria. Nineteenth-century industrial development brought in one sense a fresh Germanization since a good deal of capital and management and technical advice were supplied by Germans, not so much from German-Austria, but actually from the Hohenzollern Reich. But industrialization also created a labour demand mainly supplied by Slavs, by Czechs, Slovaks, by a good many Poles and a great many so-called *Wasser-Polaken* and *Slonzaken* who were thoroughly mixed and scarcely knew nor cared what their nationality might be. The Moravian class-race situation was repeated, but the proportion of Germans was probably higher, because there was a bigger German element among the miners and metal-workers themselves.

Politically Austrian Silesia retained a German complexion until the days of the Czechoslovak Republic. Its deputies to the Reichsrat until universal suffrage in 1907 were nearly all German; after 1907 it sent 10 Germans, 2 Czechs, and 3 Poles. The Silesian Diet was entirely dominated by the Germans, though the actual 1880 population figures were 49 per cent. German, 23 per cent. Czech, and 28 per cent. Polish, the Slav element gradually increasing from 51 per cent. in 1880 to 56 per cent. in 1910, and the Poles more quickly than the Czechs. Whereas the Moravian Diet accepted the Bohemian lead in 1871, the Silesian Diet was strongly opposed to incorporation in a Parliament representing the lands of the Bohemian Crown, and protested sharply against the Fundamental Articles. The Stremayr language ordinances of 1880 and the abortive Badeni decrees of 1897 were never applied in Silesia.

The problem presented by Silesia in 1919 was possibly more intricate than the questions arising with regard to Bohemia and Moravia. The eastern section was claimed by the new Polish State, and the Teschen frontier was not finally settled until July 1920; it left a small Polish minority in the north-east corner of Czechoslovakia which has caused a good deal of friction ever since. As for the Silesian Germans, though exceedingly nationalist, they were restrained by their industrialists who had every interest to avoid the competition of Reich German heavy industry. The mines and the furnaces, as a matter of fact, belonged, to a considerable extent, to people like the Rothschilds, who were without local interests. The capitalists, while disliking the partition of Austrian Silesia, much preferred a Czech, i.e. more western, to a Polish prospect, and exerted their influence towards pushing the Czech-Polish frontier as far to the east as possible. When the census was taken in 1921 in what now remained of Austrian Silesia, the Germans formed only 40·5 per cent. of the population, the Czechoslovaks 47·5 per cent., and the Poles 11·2 per cent. The position of the Germans in the province had deteriorated, but they formed a bigger proportion of the population than their brothers in Bohemia or Moravia, though it totalled only 252,635.

The German population of ex-Austrian Silesia makes a Prussian impression upon the traveller, for its links with Prussian Silesia are close. Here, as in Egerland, there has been irredentism ever since the Czechoslovak Republic, and before; Jews were regularly excluded from the Silesian national societies of Austria in the eighties of the last century. Troppau, the old provincial capital, linked in one's mind with Metternich and congresses and Laibach, has none of the beauty of the Slovene capital, for fires have destroyed its most ancient buildings. Once it was a great commercial centre, for the trade-routes from Danzig to the Adriatic and from the west into Hungary crossed one another here. When Joseph II's combinations were reversed in the nineteenth century, as capital of Austrian Silesia, Troppau became head-quarters for the provincial bureaucracy, but it did not become an industrial centre. The surroundings remained agricultural. Indeed, the villages around this old German town contributed to ethnical confusion by being inhabited by Czechs.[1]

Beyond heavy industry, textile activities have been continuously important in Southern Silesia. Jägerndorf, a violently irredentist town, is a great centre for woollens; linen is manufactured especially at Freiwaldau (Frývaldov) and Freudenthal (Bruntál). Freiwaldau is also a stone-cutting centre, and Friedeberg (Frydberk) specializes in granite. Timber is another important product of this region.

Just north and north-east from Troppau is the small territory of Hlučin (Hultschin)—with about 50,000 inhabitants—which was taken from Germany and given to Czechoslovakia in 1919. About 80 per cent. of the Hlučin people speak a Moravian-Czech dialect and they used to give the Prussian authorities a good deal of trouble. The Hlučin country is mainly agricultural and of no particular value; the population are for the most part poor agricultural workers, and described as unreliable and querulous by people who should know them pretty well. It appears that the transfer of Hlučin was based upon the straightforward application of linguistic Wilsonianism to a territory where this principle need not conflict with other considerations. It is also said that the Czechs were only too eager to win more covering territory in order a little to protect the vulnerable industrial district around Moravian Ostrava (Ostrau) so near to the point where Czechoslovakia, Germany, and Poland were to meet; in their Second Mémoire to the Peace Con-

[1] The small Czech town of Katharein (Kateřinky) claims to be older than its neighbour Troppau.

ference they suggested that their country should stretch as far as to Ratibor, but only this small portion of Frederick the Great's booty was handed over to the heirs of St. Wenceslas.

An outline of German-Czech history followed by this pere-grination around the German and the mixed districts of Bohemia, Moravia, and that part of Silesia which fell to the Czechoslovak Republic in 1919 should have made clear that the German-Czech situation, with all its local variety, and with changing impulses here and there, was a situation which in its essence was infinitely old. With all the gains that their development had brought to the Czechs the situation was artificially regulated to their disadvantage under Austria; a change of régime in their favour automatically swept the old artifice away, but with it went the old arbiter. The Habsburg State had given full play to the wealth of the Germans, attaching great social prestige to it. Meanwhile the German and Czech Defence Societies had scored a point whenever they could, but the imperial, unlike various local, authorities were beyond the range of their influence. The absolutely democratic character of the Czechoslovak Republic increased the power of popular agita-tion, while its insistence upon the Czech language and tradition meant that, in spite of fairly liberal laws, the new State was fre-quently tempted to accept an alliance with the Czech societies against the Sudeten German organizations.

CHAPTER XII
CZECHOSLOVAKIA, 1919–1933

(i) NEGATIVISM

AS Dr. Gustav Peters has written, the Sudeten German regards the Czech as

a half educated . . . creature, to some extent saved by German influence, who is politically intolerable and unreliable, socially never satisfied and always pushing for his nation, while the Czech sees in the Sudeten German the invader, the remorseless conqueror, the apostle of German world hegemony, the economic tyrant who only lives in the land in order to subject the Czech people socially, politically and in every other way.[1]

In 1919 the Great Powers had nevertheless accepted the inevitability of the political union of the Czechs and the Sudeten Germans, and had left them to fight out their old day-to-day quarrels with the cardinal difference that the State was now to be controlled by the Czechs, and not by a super-national régime with a German complexion.

The strongest emotions of the Czechs toward the Germans were the indignation of the poor man towards the snob, and again that of the small nation towards bombastic imperialism. In a thousand little ways the Czechs, in the early days of their Republic, set out to humiliate the Germans. At Břeclav (Lundenburg), the chief Czech-Austrian frontier station, French words replaced German ones, as if to say—or so it seemed to the Austrians and Sudeten-Germans—'The language of our allies, the French, who have beaten you, is a good enough "world-language" for you.'[2] On the new Czechoslovak paper-money the four languages of the Republic correctly appeared, but German came third on the list, following the Cyrillic script of some hundred thousand Ruthenes. And yet when Czechs say, 'If the Germans had won the War it would have been worse', are they wrong? Of course the officers of the old Austrian Army were insulted, but that sort of thing happened in other countries and had nothing necessarily to do with national enmities. Street-names in German were torn down to the chagrin even of Kramář,[3] and an apparently ridiculous chauvinism was enforced in Prague.[4]

The bad manners displayed by the Czechs in the days of their triumph were unfortunate but not very different from those

---

[1] G. Peters, *Der neue Herr von Böhmen* (Berlin, 1927).
[2] The Germans had always justified the pre-eminence of German in Austria, because German was a 'world-language'. See above.
[3] See above, Chapter X, p. 95.
[4] See Chapter XV, section (vi).

of other liberated nations in comparable circumstances. What mattered very much more was the series of laws in 1919 and 1920 by which the political and social future of Czechoslovakia was to be shaped. Of these the most important were the Constitution and the Language Law, which were passed on February 29th, 1920, and, on the social and economic side, the Land Reform Acts which began with the law of April 16th, 1919, the final establishment of an independent currency by the law of April 10th, 1919, the law of April 8th, 1920, legitimizing a capital levy and the laws of 1920 for the liquidation of War Debts; preparations had also to be made for a census to be taken, since its results would be of first-rate political importance in the new mixed State, supplying, as they should, a correction of false emphasis and inaccurate conjecture since the last imperial count in 1910. All this basic legislation was necessarily the work of a Constituent Assembly, which consisted of the Czech deputies surviving from the elections of 1911 with the addition of a certain number of Czech and Slovak nominees. The Germans and Magyars stood angrily aside, while the Ruthenes were far too disorganized to know whom they should send to Prague.

The Constitution of February 1920 registered a revolution indeed. Privilege and titles—unless the titles indicated office or occupation—were swept away. There was to be absolute liberty, equality, security, privacy, and right of agitation throughout the Republic. The bicameral principle was accepted, but the Senate, like the Chamber of Deputies, was to be elected 'by universal, equal, direct, and secret suffrage on the principle of Proportional Representation'. Thus, while it was intended to supply the indispensable brake, it was not differentiated, like the French Senate, by representing the localities, but only by consisting of 150 members where the Chamber of Deputies consisted of 300, by being elected by citizens over 26 from those over 45, instead of by those over 21 from those over 30, and by being elected for a possible eight, instead of a possible six, years. The Government was to be responsible to the Chamber of Deputies, and while the Senate, like the Government, was given the full right of initiating legislation, the Chamber of Deputies could veto the Senate's suggestions; on the other hand, a three-quarters majority in the Senate could veto the wishes of the Chamber of Deputies only if they turned out to be the wishes of not less than three-fifths of its members. A President was to be elected every seven years, and to exercise functions similar to those of the French President or the British King, the chief one being the choice of the Ministers forming the Government.

Chapter VI of the Constitution was entitled 'Protection of

National, Religious and Racial Minorities', and, together with a special Language Law passed on the same day, virtually incorporated the relevant portion[1] of the Minorities Treaty signed at St. Germain on September 10th, 1919. There were certain differences between the corresponding sections of the two charters, but these differences do not appear to justify the charge of trickery which is frequently levelled against the Czech Constituent Assembly. In the Minorities Treaty it was laid down that

> Notwithstanding any establishment by the Czecho-Slovak Government of an official language, adequate facilities shall be given to Czecho-Slovak nationals of non-Czech speech for the use of their language, either orally or in writing, before the courts.

In their Language Law the Czechs began with a clause declaring Czechoslovak to be the official language, and proceeded to restrict the use of their language in the courts to local minorities not smaller than 20 per cent. Technically the restriction might be considered to be inconsistent with the Minorities Treaty, but it is scarcely conceivable that the Great Powers ever thought of insisting on the possible use, in every court of law, of every recognized language spoken in the Republic, regardless of the composition of the local population.[2] The strongest adverse criticism which is—though not legally—valid is that which points out that the Czechs had always been bitterly opposed to a State language in pre-War Austria but immediately discovered the need for one in their own State.

The Language Law adopted the old Austrian 20 per cent. rule also as the meaning of the words 'a considerable proportion of Czechoslovak citizens' used in the Minorities Treaty when the circumstances requiring minority schools were defined. Indeed, the last article of the Constitution declared, 'Every kind whatsoever of forcible denationalization shall be forbidden. Violation of this principle may be declared by law to be a criminal offence'; these were far stronger words than any in the Minority Treaty. On the other hand, cutting across the unmitigated democracy of the Constitution ran the words of Article 113:

> Restrictions may be imposed by law, particularly as regards meetings in public places, the formation of associations for purposes of profit, and the participation of foreigners in political associations. The law may likewise determine what restrictions may be placed on the application of the principles of the preceding Sections in case of war or of the outbreak of internal troubles seriously threatening the Republican form of the state, the Constitution, or public peace and order.

[1] See above, Chapter X, p. 92.
[2] According to the later Language Law of 1926 an arrangement was made for non-Czech-speaking citizens to receive justice in their own language even if their own home lacked the 20 per cent. minority. See below, p. 126.

In the Minorities section, too, with regard to freedom of access to public employment and the free and general use of 'any language whatsoever', it was also stated that 'the foregoing provisions shall be without prejudice to the rights of State authorities in such matters in virtue of laws at present in force or hereafter promulgated for the purpose of ensuring public order, the safety of the State, or effective supervision by the State'. It is not to be supposed that the Peace Conference would have opposed these constitutional safeguards which appear in some form in every written constitution, but in critical times the minorities were most likely to be the suspects to whose disadvantage the laws would be—legally—waived. The minorities afterwards complained very much of the rules of parliamentary procedure, and the insistence upon Czech or Slovak as the language of the Chamber and the Senate,[1] so that the authentic text of a debate could not be procured in anything else. They also asserted that the 'Initiative Committee' always killed their Bills before they ever came to be debated,[2] though that must have happened to Czech oppositionals too. Later, in the spring of 1923, after the murder of the minister Rašin,[3] a law for the defence of the Republic was passed, which provided for the severe punishment of treason, conspiracy, and violent attacks against the Republic or against responsible persons. Although the Defence Law also decreed penalties against those who stirred up racial or religious hatreds,[4] it was felt by the Germans to menace their rights, and was bitterly opposed by many of them, as it naturally was by the Communist Party.

The Constituent Assembly was additionally engaged up to the last moments of its existence with economic legislation of the utmost importance, legislation which will be discussed in the economic section below. In the middle of April 1920 it dispersed, and elections to be held under the new Constitution were announced for April 18th (election of deputies) and April 25th (election of senators). The minorities decided to participate, and among the Germans, as among the Czechs, the spirit of the times was reflected in the large Social-Democratic vote; the Socialist, M. Tusar, who had succeeded Dr. Kramář as Premier after the the 'Red' communal elections of June 1919, continued in office for

[1] All deputies had the right to use their own language in speaking in Parliament.

[2] *Denkschrift der Deutschen Sozialdemokratischen Arbeiterpartei in der Tschechoslowakischen Republik an den Internationalen Sozialistenkongress in Hamburg* (Mai 1923).

[3] See Chapter XIII, section (i), p. 143. In Dr. Klepetař's book *Seit 1918*, p. 189, the Defence Law is likened to the measures taken in Germany after the murder of Rathenau in 1922.

[4] E. Sobota, *Das tschechoslowakische Nationalitätenrecht* (Prague, 1931) p. 342.

some months. On May 27th, 1920, the two houses met in joint session to form the National Assembly and proceeded to elect Professor Masaryk as the first President of the Republic.

Leaving aside the Slovak, Hungarian, and the Ruthenian questions, both Czechs and Germans now looked more foolish than they liked to contemplate. The elections, whose strict correctness has never to my knowledge been questioned, had revealed 1,586,060 German voters (72 representatives in the Chamber of Deputies), i.e. about 25 per cent. German citizens by their own declaration, in the State. In other directions, but particularly in this one, the Czechs were weaker than they had pretended, or than they had actually believed themselves to be. This was extremely embarrassing for the majority party, the Social Democrats, who had never much favoured the historic frontiers with the numbers of Germans it involved. Inevitably the local National Unions were strengthened in twisting the laws chauvinistically. The unitary Constitution had probably been intended from the beginning, but anxiety now continued to strengthen centralistic tendencies— decentralizing theories had no chance. 'It may well be', Mr. Macartney writes, 'that the experiment [of a federal state] was too hazardous; that equality would not have satisfied the Magyars and Germans, accustomed so long to domination. But rightly or wrongly it was not tried.'[1]

The Sudeten Germans were the unhappy victims of circumstances, but they had manœuvred themselves into an untenable position. From the very beginning they had rejected even the more generous Czech suggestions of co-operation, because it was a matter of principle with them to insist upon their right of self-determination; it was for this reason, and not merely on account of Rašin, that Seliger's conversations in Prague, in November 1918, had proved abortive. Since they kept up this attitude, upon which Dr. Lodgman and the Bohemians rather than Dr. Freissler insisted, the Czechs could hardly be expected to sit idle without Constitution or laws meantime; nor was it very new for the Germans to boycott parliamentary business in Prague. At last in April 1920 the Germans decided to put in an appearance, only to protest bitterly[2] against the Constitution which had been 'forced' upon them by the Constituent Assembly with which they would have nothing to do. When it came to the election of the President they refused to take part,[3] as a protest against Masaryk's first message to the nation after his return, in which he had said, 'We have

[1] Macartney, *Hungary and Her Successors.*
[2] Dr. Lodgman in the Chamber, June 1st, 1920.
[3] They also protested against the magnitude of the constitutional powers of the President as undemocratic; in view of the political past of many of the Sudeten German deputies, this was a curious objection to raise.

created our State, and that will determine the political status of our Germans, who originally came into the country as emigrants and colonists.' The Sudeten Germans felt immensely injured by these words, but it was unwise of them to take up a hostile attitude towards the man who would certainly try hardest to be just to them. And again his declaration was not wholly wrong. It was maddening for people with profoundly Bohemian feelings, living in districts which had been German six or seven hundred years, but Germans from the Reich had arrived in every century, including many an entrepreneur since 1850, and in the Czech view the fact that these foreigners had rarely accepted the 'Bohemian' language justified Masaryk's words. In the new Czechoslovak Parliament, moreover, the Germans had a way of behaving as if it were still the old Diet at Prague where even numerically they had represented a third of the people; they now represented rather less than a quarter of the population of the Republic.

Apart from endless strife over land, financial, and commercial questions, the next main issue between the Germans and the Czechs was the census arranged for in 1920 and carried through in 1921. The Government decided that nationality was to be judged primarily according to the 'mother-language' or language first spoken by the citizen, but choice, descent, and language in daily use might also be considered. Although the official instructions dictated the most careful veracity, the Germans and Magyars afterwards complained of every kind of irregularity on the part of the census-taking officials. On behalf of the Czechoslovak Government it must be pointed out that the decision to allow Jews to report themselves as a separate nationality was one which most German nationalists should have welcomed, though, as between German and Czech, it meant that the consequent numerical losses were almost entirely losses to the Germans. This and the mother-language test, heavier war casualties among the Germans, and the withdrawal of old officials to Austria and young recruits to Germany, all accounted for a reduction of the German population, as compared with that living in the same area in 1910. Before the War indifferent or ambitious people of ambiguous nationality would mostly have been entered as German,[1] though, in some Czech regions, circumstances might have pushed them in the other direction.

There can be no doubt that in 1921 there was a good deal of pressure in favour of registration as of Czechoslovak nationality. Czech officials were sent round to take the census and many of them were much more influenced by the reconquering National Unions than by the Law. It was a time of economic anxiety, and

[1] It has been seen that this happened a great deal in Moravia.

non-Czech or non-Slovak officials, who feared dismissal, had the greatest interest in a public acceptance of Czechoslovak nationality such as the taking of the census made possible. The census results also offered a strikingly high proportion of stateless or foreign inhabitants. This was partly due to the inevitable confusion with regard to citizenship which followed the disintegration of the Habsburg Monarchy, and partly to the fact that many business men distrusted Czechoslovakia's economic future and continued to call themselves Austrians.[1] There can be no doubt, however, that chauvinist officials often exploited the general confusion in order to reduce the numbers of the minorities.[2] For the census was a political battle of the first importance. Each national group hoped to be able to justify its exaggerated pretensions. And minority rights stood or fell by whether the local minority[3] could reach 20 per cent.—a few false entries and hundreds of people might be left without local schools and without the right to be governed or judged in their own language. It should be remembered that a minority which is too small to have rights is likely gradually to melt away, since the children will probably go to the State schools and find it convenient to accept the racial nationality as well as the citizenship of the State they inhabit.

The final result of the census of 1921 was 13,613,172 inhabitants of Czechoslovakia, of whom 238,943 were not citizens of the Republic; the number of German citizens counted was 3,123,624, making 23·36 per cent. of the whole, the number of Jews 180,535, making 1·35 per cent. It is reasonable to compare these figures, obtained by open declarations to officials, with the secret voting in the General Election in 1920. The 2·22 per cent. more Germans according to the election figures certainly indicates that the benefit of the doubt went against the Germans in a number of cases in 1921. But I do not believe it to be accurate to leave the matter there without enumerating several other considerations. (1) Voters exclude the population under 21; of this a lower proportion was then German. (2) The 1·35 per cent. Jews were mostly German-speaking and German-voting; in spite of the anti-Semitism of so many Germans it is remarkable to what extent Central European Jews clung to a 'German orientation' until after 1933; even to-day they discard it with difficulty. (3) The election of 1921 was fought upon social as well as upon national issues. (4) The election figures of 1911 also gave a higher German percentage than the census figures of 1910. This is difficult to explain. Some Czechs genuinely wished to be Germanized. Industrial workers in the

[1] Subsequently at the time of the inflation in Austria many of those who were able to do so proceeded to claim Czechoslovak nationality.
[2] This actually occurred more in Hungarian than in German districts.
[3] The unit taken was the *Gerichtsbezirk* or judicial district.

villages of Northern Bohemia were intimidated by German employers, peasants were intimidated by a few anti-Czech landowners, since continental villagers are seldom convinced of the secrecy of the ballot. But in the atmosphere of 1920 even the mildest intimidation by German property-owners must have been almost out of the question.

It is probably true to conclude that, in spite of the array of shocking incidents brought up in the Chamber by the German deputies,[1] the error in the German census figure was about 1 per cent. This is not excusable, but in view of the violent feelings of the time, when anti-German and anti-Czech demonstrations occurred any day, it is almost surprising that the passionately nationalist new officials of a new State behaved as correctly as they did.

From 1921 to 1925 the peoples of Czechoslovakia rubbed along somehow. There was an enormous amount of adjustment, mainly of an economic nature, to be done. The Sudeten Germans looked on disdainfully while the Czechs quarrelled with the Vatican over homage to Hus,[2] but joined with the Church in protesting against the confiscation of big landed estates. There were constant Sudeten German demonstrations against the closing of German schools. The Germans complained that Czech officials with large families were sent to the most German districts whereupon the Ministry of Education found it necessary for a Czech school to be built for the children of the officials. The Germans had forgotten that their fathers had often complained in just the same way, and that they themselves still on the whole preferred to look for more variety and profit than is offered by the life of the small bureaucrat. On the other hand, the fact that the State itself now put up Czech minority schools in German and language-frontier districts was a very big change; even when Czech peasant-settlers[3] had also arrived the Czech school was often fairly empty, and the local Czech union did what it could to tempt German children to help fill the emptiness. 'Forcible denationalization and a crime by your own laws', said the Germans; 'Unthinkable that any one should coerce you', said the Czechs. The truth, of course, was half-way. The Czech chauvinists made tempting promises, but if German parents stood up to them, mostly nothing more happened, for the promises were not authentic, not made by any authority; meanwhile the Germans generalized from a few bad cases.[4] The Czechs were undoubtedly too eager to be rid of German officials, but these

---

[1] They cited cases of schoolchildren, of soldiers, and of prisoners being brought into towns or villages *ad hoc*. See Hassinger, *Die Tschechoslowakei*.
[2] The Czechs insisted upon dedicating July 6th to Hus; the Vatican disliked the honouring of a heretic. See below, Chapter XV, section (x).
[3] See Chapter XIII, section (ii) below.
[4] See Chapter XV below for a fuller examination of the schools question.

German officials, just as undoubtedly, seldom knew the State language to any degree. Their demeanour, moreover, was sometimes that of the deputies—i.e. some of them were frankly negative towards Czechoslovakia, and made it clear that they believed the Republic to be merely a temporary misfortune. It was in December 1924 that a drastic economy law with regard to officials was passed which led to a great many German dismissals, but the final regulations about the official use of the State and minority languages only appeared in the Language Decree of February 3rd, 1926.[1] This piece of legislation was drafted by conscientious lawyers enough; so conscientious were they that the complicated character of their work lent itself the more readily to red-tape tiresomeness on the part of little officials. There were several rather fussy clauses about the State language always preceding the others, and, if the Czechoslovak and the minority version of an official text differed, the Czechoslovak sense was to be adopted;[2] there were detailed arrangements for the language tests to be applied to the minority citizens who wished to be officials; a Czechoslovak who was to act as a judge, or other official,[3] in non-Czech or non-Slovak districts, was to be competent in the relevant minority language, but need not be subjected to an official test. The Czech renaissance in the nineteenth century fully explains their hypersensitiveness with regard to their language—perhaps they could never have re-emerged from the German ocean without a little fanaticism, since the German language, understood by so many millions, had so great a practical pull. As for the feelings exchanged between three Czechs[4] and a German official being put through his paces in a test in the 'servants' language', they are easily imagined. Taking it all in all, the 1926 Language Decree was severe, but neither oppressive, nor dishonest with regard to Czechoslovakia's international obligations to the minorities. According to Article 3 officials were to help applicants who were ignorant of the language in local use as much as they could, and by Article 18 it was made possible for non-residents to apply to the courts or local administration, so that a German resident in Prague could go to Karlsbad in order to conduct a law-suit in his own language. The Nationalist Germans, nevertheless, demonstrated vigorously against the February Decree, as their fathers had demonstrated against the Badeni Decrees in 1897. Since 1880 Czechs could claim to be dealt with in Czech throughout Bohemia and Moravia, though the 1897 attempt to allow Czech to be used between officials had failed. With 1926, and in Silesia as well, only a 20 per cent. Czech minority entitled a Czech to deal in Czech with

[1] Sobota, op. cit., p. 361.
[2] Ibid., p. 392, Article 53.
[3] Ibid., Article 68.
[4] Ibid., Article 63.

;German town council, but where the German town council would often have ignored Czech rights after 1880, after 1926 they could be strictly enforced.

(ii) FOREIGN POLICY OF DR. BENEŠ: RELATIONS WITH GERMANY

The foreign policy of the Czechoslovak Republic in the first decade and a half of its existence was energetic and competent. It was based, as it was bound to be, upon a strong emphasis of the new *status quo* and upon high hopes of Geneva. The realism of Dr. Beneš, who was Czechoslovak Foreign Minister until he succeeded President Masaryk in 1935, prevented him from ever losing sight of the conditions by which the diplomacy of a small State must be restricted, and he held it to be of the first importance to Czechoslovakia to be well provided with actively co-operating friends. In the course of 1920 and 1921, together with the representatives of Yugoslavia and Roumania, he launched the Little Entente upon its anti-revisionist career, thus binding together the three small States whose existence depended upon the maintenance of the Treaty of Trianon.

The Sudeten Germans regarded the Little Entente with infinite distaste—it was a form of 'subjection to France', Roumania and Yugoslavia were 'wretched little States', the Serbs were the 'ruffians' who had started the War. In the early days they felt that they could only be reconciled with the Republic if it co-operated closely with Austria and Germany—a demand which implied that the Czechs were to obliterate memories of the past as completely, of course, as the extremer Czechs expected the Germans themselves to indulge in oblivion.

As a matter of fact the relations of Czechoslovakia with the Austrian Republic in its democratic days, if a little cool, were not bad, while Czechoslovak relations with Weimar Germany were officially good. The liberal German Republic all along took the typical Reich German, as opposed to the nationalist German-Austrian, point of view; that is to say, it regarded Czechoslovakia with far less fear and contempt than Poland. In the summer of 1919 Count Brockdorff-Rantzau had not only sent word from Paris that he wanted no complications from anti-Czech volunteering, but it seems that the German Government had even got into direct touch with the Czechs with regard to the possible cession of Egerland.[1] The Treaty of Versailles internationalized the Elbe from its junction with the Vltava (Moldau) at Mělnik, and the Oder from its junction with the Oppa just south-west from Moravian Ostrava (Ostrau), and the Czechs were given the right to a free zone in the harbour at Hamburg and also at Stettin. They

[1] Molisch, *Sudetendeutsche Freiheitsbewegung 1918–1919*.

never actually made use of their rights at Stettin, but the Hamburg arrangement worked satisfactorily and gave Czechoslovakia a fragment of that sea-coast which she so notoriously lacked. In the course of the original Elbe negotiations,[1] the Czechs took the opportunity to protest against the recruiting against them which had continued to occur on German territory, and again the responsible German authorities did what they could to hasten the winding-up of the Sudeten German 'Freedom Movement' (*Freiheitsbewegung*). Thus if the danger from Hungary, which had been vividly illustrated by Charles of Habsburg's two attempts to reestablish himself there in 1921, made the Little Entente too rigidly hostile to Budapest, official relations between Prague and Berlin were satisfactory. There was, however, a strong tendency, not only among the Sudeten Germans, but also in the Reich, to regard Dr. Beneš as a particularly venomous enemy of Germany, and the French occupation of the Ruhr exacerbated German-Czech differences over France. It was inevitable that the Francophile tradition of the Czechs and Dr. Beneš's Parisian career should combine with the French desire to block German expansionism and create a strong Franco-Czech diplomatic friendship; a treaty of friendship and alliance was signed on January 25th, 1924, and duly registered at Geneva. Dr. Beneš is anything other than fanatical and never held the Germanophobe opinions of some of the more intransigent of his countrymen. In March 1924, however, the *Berliner Tageblatt* published a document which professed to be a secret military pact between France and Czechoslovakia for an attack upon Germany. Though the document proved to be a forgery, probably deriving from German National and Tsarist Russian circles, it poisoned the political atmosphere. The election of Field-Marshal von Hindenburg as President of the German Republic in the spring of 1925 was, in its turn, thoroughly distasteful to France and the Little Entente.

The years 1925 and 1926 brought, however, a very real appeasement, with the Treaties of Locarno, the appearance of Germany at Geneva, and that semblance of economic prosperity which now began to make itself evident. Dr. Beneš, who had already become a prominent figure at Geneva,[2] participated in the discussions at Locarno, and in addition to the Rhineland Pact, Germany signed arbitration treaties with Czechoslovakia and Poland at the end of the year, though the German-Czech and German-Polish frontiers were not, like the German-Belgian and German-French frontiers, precisely guaranteed. Earlier in the year the friction between Czechoslovakia and Poland, due to disputes over

---

[1] Molisch, *Sudetendeutsche Frieheitsbewegung 1918–1919.*
[2] He was rightly regarded as one of the architects of the Geneva Protocol.

the Teschen frontier and to Polish irritation that the Czechs had not definitely taken their side against Soviet Russia in 1920 and ever since, had been relaxed by a valuable treaty[1] which regulated Czech-Polish relations—roughly speaking—until January 1934.

Dr. Beneš actually presided on the day upon which Germany was admitted to the League of Nations in September 1926 with a permanent seat on the Council. This was an event of potentially great importance for the Sudeten Germans, since their complaints with regard to infractions of the Minority Treaty were now a great deal more likely to be sponsored by a Great Power. As a matter of fact the situation at Geneva remained from this point of view virtually unchanged, for Dr. Stresemann immediately made it clear that he was not inclined to look for trouble with Prague since he regarded the issues between Berlin and Warsaw as the serious ones. He considered there were enough Sudeten Germans to look after themselves and he indirectly advised them to co-operate actively with the Czechoslovak Government. In an election speech in the spring of 1925, just after Locarno, Dr. Beneš claimed that the Sudeten Germans could now no longer complain that Czechoslovakia had not taken every possible step to be on good terms with the Reich. But complain they certainly could; there has never been much interruption in the stream of Sudeten German condemnation of Czechoslovak foreign policy because, in general, it showed greater sympathy for France than for Germany. It was probably unfortunate that Dr. Beneš's position at Geneva was so strong that he could easily forestall Sudeten German petitions, which never, in fact, came before the Council of the League. The League of Nations should have succeeded the Habsburg dynasty as Central European arbiter, but, as it was, the Sudeten Germans believed that Geneva was nothing but a Franco-Czech trap.

Although the representatives of the Weimar Governments kept the Sudeten Germans at a distance, their régime was extraordinarily liberal, particularly in its attitude towards reactionary and chauvinistic or racial organizations. The old Pan-German Union, while continuing itself to exist, had been prolific in its offspring. Its most prominent heirs were (1) the *Verein für das Deutschtum im Auslande* (V.D.A.); (2) the *Bund Deutscher Osten*, mainly occupied with anti-Polish activities until 1934; and (3) the *Auslands-Institut* at Stuttgart, which made a study of German questions abroad. All these bodies were founded round about the time of the end of the War, and all of them collected money to distribute to the German citizens of foreign countries, especially for so-called cultural purposes. There was also something called

[1] A common anxiety over Germany's imminent *rapprochement* with the west drew Czechoslovakia and Poland together at this time.

the *Deutscher Schutzbund* organized by a certain Herr von Loesch at an office in the Motzstrasse in Berlin, while the *National-Sozialistische Deutsche Arbeiterpartei*, founded at Munich in 1920, with its emphasis (point 1 of its programme) upon the need for the union of all Germans in one Greater Germany,[1] soon began to play its part as a link between Germans within the Reich frontiers and beyond them. Immediately after the War young Sudeten Germans, besides those who had joined the battalions recruited to fight against the post-War frontiers,[2] frequently took refuge in Germany in order to avoid Czechoslovak military service. Deserters as they were, they were precluded from going home to Bohemia, Moravia, and Silesia, and they formed a company of highly disgruntled exiles. Mostly from their ranks an organization called the *Sudetendeutscher Heimatbund* sprang up in Dresden, then in Berlin and other cities, soon after the War. This society welcomed any German refugees from Czechoslovakia so vigorously that Prague sometimes protested; in those days the Berlin Government would then shake a mild finger at the exiles.

Until 1931 the activities of that transcendental Germanism which hovered above the earthy limits of frontiers were taken up chiefly with the relation of Austria to Germany. Here the Socialists were enthusiastic, too, and the Reich-German Socialist leader, Herr Löbe, was president of a society for promoting the *Anschluss*. When two German-Austrian Nationalists visited Berlin in January 1925 there was some agitation in the Little Entente. On the other hand, when the projected Austro-German Customs Union was prevented in 1931, Germans of all kinds blamed Dr. Beneš exaggeratedly. The Czechoslovaks, though far from being alone in their opposition to the plan, believed that Germany meant to compel them to join the Berlin-Vienna customs alliance in order that the old *Mittel-Europa* economic programme should be realized.

Meanwhile the V.D.A. and kindred organizations 'made contacts' with and financed the other Germans outside Germany, and it is obvious that their relations with the Sudeten Germans were the most easy to establish, whatever the Wilhelmstrasse or even the Prime Minister of Saxony or Bavaria might have to say. Among Germans who were interested in their own race rather than in more widely human ideas, the defeat of Germanism in the World War had stimulated an enthusiastic determination to establish their values by a German unity in the future closer than the past had allowed. Thus the success of the Entente from 1914 to 1918 appeared, ironically enough, to have killed Pan-Slavism while

[1] Point 1 of the German Nazi Party's programme ran as follows: 'Wir fordern den Zusammenschluss aller Deutschen auf Grund des Selbstbestimmungsrechtes der Völker zu einem Gross-Deutschland.'

[2] See above, Chapter X, p. 96.

revivifying Pan-Germanism. The Pan-German racial conception was not inconsistent with the romantic ideals of nineteenth-century heroes like Garibaldi and Mazzini, but, like the Germans and Czechs of 1848, it ignored the bases of the western political phrases which it freely adopted. After all, the French no longer cast longing eyes at French Switzerland nor at Western Belgium because they spoke French, nor do the English insist on the restitution of North America to make national unity good. When French and Dutch immigrants settled in Prussia in the eighteenth century they certainly felt as far from civilization as the Germans who were sent to the Banat by the Habsburgs at about the same time, yet they had not insisted upon the retention of a separate national existence. Even if the extraordinary national tenacity of Germans the world over were recognized, post-War Europe could scarcely be expected to ignore the distinction once made by a Czechoslovak diplomat between *civis Germanicus* and *homo Germanicus*.

(iii) ACTIVISM

Czech-German feeling had run very high in 1923, with the French in the Ruhr, but after that, gradually, a local Locarno-spirit set in, and, encouraged by Dr. Stresemann, that section of Sudeten German opinion which condemned the entirely negative attitude of the Sudeten German political leaders to the State grew. The most striking thing about the Sudeten Germans, politically, was the number of parties into which they had redivided, and the squabbles between these groups. Before the elections in the autumn of 1925 Dr. Lodgman made an appeal for German unity, but the National Socialists[1] made difficulties, and he was unsuccessful at the polls and finally withdrew into private life. The Germans returned to the Chamber of Deputies 24 Agrarians (*Bund der Landwirte*), 18 Social Democrats, 12 Clericals, 10 German Nationals, and 6 National Socialists. The striking thing about the elections was the great increase of Communist votes at the expense of both German and Czech Social Democrats. This fact helped M. Švehla, Czech Agrarian Prime Minister since 1922, in negotiating for German participation in the Government to fortify the State against revolutionaries. The outstanding German friend of a change from 'negativism' to 'activism' was the German Agrarian leader, Dr. Spina, a professor of Czech literature[2] and a convinced believer in the possibility of sensible co-operation between Germans and Czechs. Within a year of the elections, to the particular satisfaction of President Masaryk and with the approval of Berlin,

[1] See below. Not to be confused with the Czech National Socialist Party to which Dr. Beneš belonged.
[2] See above, Chapter VII, p. 59.

activism was realized in the inclusion of two German Ministers in the Cabinet. Dr. Spina became Minister of Public Works, and the rumour was soon circulated that the Czech officials at his Ministry were being gently reproved when they used bad (Czech) grammar by the German scholar now in their midst. Dr. Mayr-Harting, an amiable Viennese professor, was made Minister of Justice as representative of the German Clericals.

The next few years were prosperous and relatively easy. Many Germans were hopeful of activism and willing to give it a chance. After the 1929 elections, when—in general—Clericals[1] and Communists lost and Socialists gained, Dr. Mayr-Harting followed M. Švehla out of office. Dr. Spina remained in the Cabinet, and, which was at the time important, Dr. Czech, the leader of the biggest German party, the Social Democrats, became Minister of Social Welfare. This meant that a more definite majority of the Sudeten Germans was represented in the Government than in 1926, and the German Clericals, though out of office, were not merely negativist. In 1926 34 German deputies (apart from the Communists) were in sharp opposition to the Cabinet; with 1929 it seemed that only 15 remained bitterly intransigent.

Meanwhile in 1927 an administrative reform of some importance had been passed. At least two of its provisions considerably affected the German population. In the first place the rump of Silesia lost its independence as a province, and was, as it had been by Joseph II,[2] attached to Moravia. A glance at the map will justify the change, for the settlement of 1920 had reduced non-Prussian Silesia to even smaller dimensions than the wars of the eighteenth century, and it would obviously be more economical in every way to administer it from Brno (Brünn). But of course the new law struck a blow at the German town of Troppau, whose provincial officials had to be pensioned off; here was one of the many natural occasions for Germans to lose positions, occasions which the Germans regarded as created purely by malevolence. Some Czechs positively rejoiced, others were not sorry to see the German officials go; but in no State east of Switzerland would it have seemed possible to dismiss the minority nation officials only in proportion to those of the majority, least of all in a province like Silesia, where the Germans had had so marked and so artificial a predominance. The union with Moravia was welcomed by the Moravian Germans because they would be strengthened, but it robbed the Silesian Germans of the advantages they had derived from being a 40 per cent. minority.[3]

[1] The German Clericals excepted.
[2] See above, Chapter XI, section (iv), p. 114. Before 1614, also, Moravia had claimed the right to annex Troppau, but in that year the claim was dropped.
[3] See census 1921.

In the second place the law of 1927 revised the new administrative divisions of the Republic and centralized its local government. Each of the four provinces Bohemia, Moravia-Silesia, Slovakia, Ruthenia[1] was divided into districts (*Bezirke*) and subdivided into circles and communes. The Germans had hoped against hope that the frontiers of the district would be the so-called national frontiers which they had always claimed, but this would have been an approximation towards federalism; the Czechs were determined to risk nothing of the kind[2] and arranged what was often the geographically obvious thing, e.g. that the Germans south of České Budějovice (Budweis) should be in a mainly Czech district administered from Budějovice. It was now further legislated that a third of the members of the provincial diets and of the district councils should be nominated from Prague, and only two-thirds be elected; the commune or town councils were still to be entirely elective, as both Houses of Parliament were. I have heard a very nationally minded Sudeten German support this change with fitting arguments in favour of the nominated expert rather than the chance local favourite on a district council. In general, however, the Germans regarded the introduction of these nominations as yet another blow aimed at them,[3] and it proved true that the nominations tended to overweight the Czech element. If not that, the Czechs usually chose a German who was not 'emphatically national' —inevitably, since the others were probably disloyal to the Republic; then seeking for anti-Czech arguments, the emphatically national German found this one, that the Czechs put a premium upon being lukewarm and internationally minded. Quite recently I discussed the 1927 law with a Sudeten German lawyer, who, with—as I believe—absolute sincerity, assured me that it had made local government in Czechoslovakia far less democratic than in pre-War Austria where the whole of each diet or council was elected. It had entirely escaped his attention that those elections in pre-War Austria had been weighted by privilege and wealth[4]—such, apparently, is the effect of national conflict upon a reasonably honest and educated man.

The Local Government Reform of 1927 was followed by another Language Decree in 1928, which slightly extended the right of a mainly German district council to conduct its business solely in German;[5] the influence of the German Ministers was thus perhaps felt.

[1] Bohemia and Moravia had previously had a slightly different local organization from one another.

[2] Involving, as it must, the surrender of Czech minorities to local German rule.

[3] At one time the Germans had feared the introduction of larger districts (*Gaue*) containing the *Bezirke* and so constructed as to minimize German proportions; a plan of the kind was, however, not carried through.

[4] Our time was up, so that I could not begin an argument on the point.

[5] Sobota, op. cit.

It will here be convenient to refer to the results of the census held in 1930. The Germans in the Republic were found to have increased from 3,123,624 in 1921 to 3,231,688, but the Czechs, Slovaks, and Ruthenes had increased each more quickly than the last, so that the Sudeten German minority was reduced from 23·36 per cent. to 22·32 per cent. of the whole population of Czechoslovakia. The Germans had increased in Bohemia, Slovakia, and Ruthenia, but, as its special circumstances might lead one to expect, in the new province of Moravia-Silesia their numbers had actually decreased by 184. The judicial districts of Olomouc (Olmütz) and Moravian Ostrava (Mährisch Ostrau) had lost their 20 per cent., while Brno (Brünn) and Hranice (Mährisch Weisskirchen) were very near that significant margin and Znojmo (Znaim) had lost its German 50 per cent.[1] One hears less doubts cast upon the accuracy of these 1930 figures as compared with those of 1921, but the open rejoicings of the local Czech unions of Olomouc and Moravian Ostrava at the now justified banishment of the German language from among them made these German losses more painful than necessary.

(iv) NATIONALISTS, NAZIS, AND YOUTH

After 1929 only the emphatically national parties remained in complete intransigence. The German-Nationals, corresponding to the party of the same name in Germany, were descended from the pre-War People's and Progressive and German Radical parties which had mostly worked together in the German National Club of the old Austrian Parliament. In the Czechoslovak Republic they had followed the leadership of Dr. von Lodgman until his retirement in 1925. Theirs was a party of propertied people.

Perhaps more native to Bohemian soil was the—at first—small party of German National Socialists. They were descended directly from Karl Hermann Wolf's proletarian allies of the German Working-men's Party, and were alternatively frowned upon as revolutionary, or helped as anti-Marxist, by the German-National employers. Ever since the appearance of the Czechoslovak Republic these people have publicly claimed that they stood for nothing but national demarcation and the complete autonomy of every racial group within its own frontiers. It should, however, be observed that at a meeting of their Bohemian section on November 25th, 1917, they protested against the 'war-prolonging peace whimperings of the Bourse papers and of the Socialists', and declared that 'a greater German Empire, and an Austria-Hungary which economically dominates the Balkans and the south-eastern States, are war demands which are justified by our superior mili-

[1] These are all the judicial districts (*Gerichtsbezirke*) concerned.

tary position'. In Vienna in the following May the German Working-men's Party, which was already explaining that it represented a complete *Weltanschauung*, expanded its name into *Deutsche National-Sozialistische Arbeiterpartei* (or German National Socialist Working-men's Party), usually abbreviated to D.N.S.A.P. With the disintegration of Austria-Hungary the Sudeten Nazis were forced to separate from the Austrian Nazi party under Dr. Riehl's leadership, the party which was to be suppressed later on by Dr. Dollfuss. The leaders of the Sudeten Nazis were still Herren Knirsch and Krebs and Jung. Early in 1920 Adolf Hitler, a man born not many miles away from Bohemia, who had also grown up in pre-War Austria and reacted strongly to the ideas of Schönerer and of Wolf, founded his *National-Sozialistische Deutsche Arbeiterpartei* or N.S.D.A.P. in Munich. The Sudeten Nazis were delighted to hear of this,[1] and Reich German, Sudeten, and Austrian Nazis all assembled in a Pan-German conference at Salzburg in August 1920; Herren Hitler and Drexler represented the Germans from the Reich. Herr Krebs has written an enthusiastic description of frequent visits to Munich at this time, of the depression caused in the Sudeten German Nazi movement by the Hitler fiasco of November 1923, and the invigorating effect of Hitler's release at the end of 1924.[2] Like the twin Hitler movement, the Czechoslovak D.N.S.A.P. was keenly anti-Semitic and anti-democratic; it was racialist and Pan-German, desiring the union of all German-speaking people in one Reich; it even adopted the very same banners and uniforms as the Nazis in Germany.[3] It was thus clearly inimical to the Czechoslovak Republic from every point of view. For the time being the Sudeten Nazis busied themselves with emphasizing Pan-German cultural unity and with endless protests against activism; although they claim always to have worked for Sudeten German union, other German parties blamed them as the group which put most obstacles in its way. In 1927 they produced a national autonomy programme based on a nationalities map,[4] which blotted out a surprisingly large number of Czechs. But the Sudeten Nazis were not to be ignored. Their numbers in Parliament rose from 5 in 1920 to 6 in 1925 and 8 in 1929 (when the German National deputies fell from 10 to 7), for they attracted young people. From 1929 youths over 21 were organized by the Sudeten Nazis in the so-called *Volkssport*, which behaved exactly like Hitler's Storm Troops in the Reich, wearing a similar uniform.[5]

There were many young Sudeten Germans at this time who,

[1] Krebs, *Kampf in Böhmen.*   [2] Ibid.
[3] See photographs in the same.   [4] Ibid., p. 177.
[5] Krebs, op. cit., photograph, p. 158.

determined though they were to remain only negative towards the Republic, found the German-Nationals too reactionary and the Nazis too drastic—at any rate to start with. They consoled themselves in supporting the old cultural and gymnastic societies. The old *Turnverband* and the *Schutzvereine*, with a changed name here and there,[1] had taken up their historic activities; among the choral societies the *Finkensteinerbund* was most prominent. After the War many young Germans in Germany, Austria, and Czechoslovakia were diligent members of Youth Movements, *Wandervögel*,[2] &c., and, since they wished to have nothing to do with Czechoslovak politics, the young Sudeten Germans clung to the romantic mysticism which this kind of thing provided very much longer than young Germans elsewhere. Those of them who later joined the *Volkssport* organization took a good many of their *Wandervögel* dreams into it with them, with serious political consequences to follow. The mystically inclined joined together in the now famous *Kameradschaftsbund* (usually abbreviated to K.B.), which was founded in about 1926 and came into the open in 1930 with its monthly review, *Die Junge Front*.[3] Among its founders were Heinrich Rutha, Walter Heinrich, and Walter Brand,[4] all young men who devoutly believed in something mysterious and untranslatable called *das Bündische*—an organic binding-together, perhaps. The *Wandervögel* themselves were reorganized in 1930 by Josef Suchy into a more severely disciplined *Bund*. While the Sudeten Nazis and the *Volkssport* youths were more and more for the expansion of the Berlin Reich, the K.B. people still clung to an Austrian allegiance. Heinrich, Brand, and many another studied at Vienna University, and there responded with enthusiasm to the teaching of Professor Othmar Spann. In academic circles Professor Spann was regarded rather as a delightful romantic than a first-rate scholar. He believed in organic—*bündisch* or *ständisch*—social grouping, a vaguely back-to-the-guild medievalism, which shut the door with a slam upon western democracy. What was perhaps more to the point was that he believed in a resurrection of the Holy Roman Empire of the German nation, a tidying-up of the whole of Central and Eastern Europe by the Germans. For the Germans, he held, were the cream of humanity and the only possible saviours of civilization; as Fichte had exclaimed in 1809, if the Germans went under, it would be the end of mankind.[5] The

---

[1] The old *Schulverein* had been refounded as the *Kulturverband* in 1920.

[2] Founded in Austria in 1911.

[3] See Pfitzner, *Sudetendeutsche Einheitsbewegung*. A new 'anti-liberal, desirous-of-authority' generation was to be brought up. Since then *Die Junge Front* has changed its political tone, for in 1935 it became purely Nazi.

[4] Brand, who was only born in 1907, started these activities while still at school.

[5] Othmar Spann, *Vom Wesen des Volkstums*. See also the *magnum opus, Der wahre Staat* (Leipzig, 1923).

young men from Bohemia dreamed happily of Bohemia's medieval traditions and the German mission to save it again. They came home to preach this gospel, and gained many followers; indeed, they soon won a dominant influence in the various Sudeten German nationalist societies. This was in strict accordance with a Platonic element in Professor Spann's teaching, which emphasized the importance of an intellectually trained *élite* to take over political leadership, since the proletariat, in his view, is composed of a racially inferior stratum of the population. It is interesting, too, that the K.B. people were in touch with Hans Zehrer's famous *Tatkreis* in Germany which advocated a conservative socialism, and whose influence only disappeared with the abrupt elimination of its patron, General Schleicher, on June 30th, 1934. Edgar Jung, who also met his death on that day, represented a kindred ideology, and had, while he lived, been regarded as the political mind, as it were, of Herr von Papen.

The K.B. was a North Bohemian group,[1] while the Nazis and *Volkssportler* were strong in Eger (Cheb), Gablonz (Jablonec), Leitmeritz (Litoměřice), and in Southern Bohemia. *Bündisch* ideas were also increasingly popular with the Germans in Czechoslovak Silesia. Indeed, the Spann *genre* of ideology was widespread among the professional classes and simple-life youth of Troppau (Opava) and Teschen (Těšín). Not necessarily under Spann's direct influence, these people longed for a *bündisch* new order under German leadership in Central Europe. Some of them believed that the Historic Provinces should form the heart of the new German Empire to come; a certain Dr. Patscheider, Tyrolese by birth, but now a schoolmaster at Troppau, urged the reunion of Prussian, Polish, and Czechoslovak Silesia,[2] so that united Silesia should be Germany's 'gate to Moravia and her bridge to the valley of the Danube'. At Olomouc (Olmütz) in 1930[3] an organization called the *Bereitschaft* was founded by people of this way of thinking. It was to be the centre of a network of five guilds, of an *Ordensring*, an *Arbeitsring*, &c. The *Bereitschaft* leaders were in touch with the *Volkssport* people, and at first with the K.B., with whom they had more, perhaps, in common. But the K.B. quarrelled with them on at least one point. Rutha, Heinrich, and Brand were eager to strengthen Sudeten German unity so as to be able to speak with more emphasis within the Czechoslovak Republic.[4] Patscheider

[1] Böhmisch Leipa was headquarters, since it was the home of Dr. Heinrich and of Herr Rutha. Dr. Heinrich subsequently became Professor Spann's assistant in Vienna. At Reichenberg a certain Professor Lehmann provided a centre of nationalist influence, but he belonged rather to the *Bereitschaft* set—see below.   [2] See articles in the *Schlesische Jahrbücher*.
[3] Pfitzner, *Sudetendeutsche Einheitsbewegung*, says 1929. The moving spirit here was Herr Staffen.
[4] The *Volkssport* leader, Haider, also took this view.

and his friends, on the other hand, were romantic believers in the sanctity of kin and tribal ties, and consequently dreamed of the direct reunion of the Czechoslovak Silesians with the Prussian and Polish ones, of the descendants of the Saxon settlers in Northern Bohemia with the Reich Saxons, and so on.

The *Bereitschaft* people, therefore, had many connexions with Germany. Patscheider himself was closely associated with the *Arbeitskreis für gesamtschlesische Stammeskultur* in Breslau, with the *Verein für das Deutschtum im Auslande* (V.D.A.), and with something called the *Bündische Front Nord-Ost*. Speakers and mass visits were naturally enough exchanged across the German-Czech frontier, and a good deal of money came to the Sudeten German associations from Germany. Whenever the Czechs looked doubtful, the *Bereitschaft*, the *Volkssport*, &c., insisted that they were only working to strengthen the cultural link between the Sudeten Germans and the Reich, and the old pre-War Pan-Slav, Neo-Slav, and Pan-German arguments were revived. That many Sudeten Germans had Pan-German thoughts no law could forbid, and from 1930 Czech mistakes, economic decline, and the rising tide of Hitlerist propaganda increased Pan-German thinking. But if National Socialism was, as it claimed to be, a complete attitude to life, the boundary between cultural and political activity would be effaced. And the projects of the Nazis (whether in Germany or in the Czechoslovak Republic), of the *Bereitschaft*, and of the other societies more or less in sympathy, all involved the political annihilation of Czechoslovakia, both as to its frontiers and its political, i.e. democratic, character.

The *Volkssport* young men were the ones who sailed closest to the wind. They belonged to the D.N.S.A.P. which, at Salzburg in 1920, had regarded itself as the very same thing as Hitler's party,[1] and which enthusiastically received Dr. Goebbels as a visiting speaker in 1927 and Dr. Frick in 1928.[2] They dressed as the German S.A. did, and indulged in as much military training as they could provide for themselves. Already in 1929, to take one example, they had sent a big group to the N.S.D.A.P. annual rally at Nürnberg and had marched beneath the motto *Treu zu Hitler*.

In 1931 Nazi and *Volkssport* uniforms were forbidden in Czechoslovakia,[3] and at last in the summer of 1932 the Czechoslovak

---

[1] The delegates from Austria, Czechoslovakia, and Germany, at Salzburg described themselves as the National Socialist Party of the German people; at Linz in 1921 they referred to themselves as the representatives of National Socialist *Grossdeutschland*. See Krebs, op. cit., p. 222.

[2] Krebs, op. cit., p. 182.

[3] It may be remembered that Nazi uniforms were forbidden for a short time in Germany itself in the spring of 1932.

Government decided to indulge in the dangerous luxury of a great treason indictment, and launched the famous *Volkssport* Trial.[1] Seven young members of the *Volkssport*, most of them students or not much more, were accused of having prepared armed rebellion in connexion with a foreign Power, and with having planned the destruction of Czechoslovakia in order to bring about a Pan-German union. The trial was held in Brno (Brünn) because there was the requisite apparatus there for trials to be conducted in German. The charge was foolishly big and relied to a disagreeable extent upon the secret evidence of Czechoslovak staff officers as to the military character of the *Volkssport* organization. No arms of a serious kind had been discovered by the police, and when the case came up on appeal in September 1933, the armed rebellion charge was dropped. But the defendants had frankly acknowledged their acceptance of the Pan-German first of Hitler's Twenty-Five Points,[2] and though not condemned for conspiring with a foreign State, they were sentenced for conspiring against the Republic and its democratic constitution. Haider, Illing, and Metzner, the three who were considered most dangerous, were originally condemned to three years' imprisonment, now reduced to two and a half, of which they had already served one. There was a great German outcry against the sentences. If the Czechs had handled the business clumsily, it would yet be unjust to ignore the incomparably heavier sentences which dictatorial States have provided for comparable crimes. At the time of the Brno sentences the alien imbecile, Van der Lubbe, was already on trial in Berlin for a piece of incendiarism which many experts believe was evidently performed by others and which was nevertheless to cause his execution.

With the *Volkssport* Trial, the great world depression was making itself more and more acutely felt in Czechoslovakia, and an examination of the whole economic aspect of the German-Czech question can no longer be delayed.

[1] Some of the defendants believed that the German Activists had incited the Czechoslovak Government to prosecute them, because the Activists feared the growing strength of their opponents.
[2] See above, section (ii), p. 130 n.

CHAPTER XIII

THE ECONOMIC ASPECT

THE relations of the Germans with the Czechs in Czecho-slovakia have all along been embittered by economic developments. We have seen that the social changes which followed in the wake of the Industrial Revolution had, long before the War, brought about readjustments which worsened the position of the Sudeten Germans as a whole. Such a process was accelerated by the War itself, and was, within certain limits, inevitable. Roughly speaking, wealth, though decreasingly, had been in German hands in the Historic Provinces before 1914; after the War the owners of wealth everywhere in Europe were subjected to various forms of impoverishment. The perfectly normal unwillingness of those who have property to part with it, however much the rest of the community lacks, blended with the racial animosities of Czecho-slovakia to an extent which cannot be exactly measured. It is true that the new Czech authorities were bound to feel less mercy towards German property than the old Austrian authorities might have shown. But it is equally true that many Sudeten German complaints were extraordinarily similar to those of the wealthy or ex-wealthy in any other country in Central Europe at the time. The property-owners of post-War Austria talked in almost exactly the same way, only the citizen of Vienna who had been rich blamed his Government because it was Socialist, and the German citizen of Brünn or Aussig blamed his because it was Czech. It was also characteristic of the situation in Czechoslovakia that the natural clash between industrial and agricultural interests easily appeared as a German-Czech conflict. While the racial quarrel certainly intensified and embittered normal economic friction, it would be quite inaccurate to ignore the fact that there were rich industrialists who were Czechs and poor working-people who were German, though their interests were at first very rarely in conflict in the same industrial concern; in the Škoda works at Plzeň a small proportion of Germans were employed by a Czech firm.[1]

(i) FINANCIAL POLICY

Among the new Czechoslovak State's most immediate needs at the beginning of 1919 were financial measures. Perhaps the most forceful of all the Czech leaders was the first Finance Minister, Alois Rašin. Condemned as a youth in a great political trial in the

[1] Škoda's counted as a German concern under Austria; after the War its German shares were partly bought up by the French firm of Schneider-Creusot.

nineties to two years' imprisonment, he had become, after Dr.
Kramář, the most prominent of the Young Czechs; we have seen
how he was sentenced to death in 1916. He believed whole-
heartedly in the sanctity of the Czech historic frontiers; to him,
therefore, 1918 was an act of historic retribution and the German
immigrants were now to fulfil a long-overdue act of allegiance to
the State—that they questioned its frontiers was therefore rebellion
in his eyes.[1] Dr. Rašin was an untiring patriot. He was immensely
industrious and unhesitating in action when his goal was perceived.
The Germans regarded him as their uncompromising enemy, but
one whom most of them must needs respect. He has been described
as a Puritan on the Anglo-Saxon model, indeed he demanded from
his countrymen a republican discipline and self-denial after the
Roman or even the Spartan manner. His personality was a powerful
factor in a world which was still gasping for peace and for paradise.

At the beginning of 1919 the old Austro-Hungarian currency
was still circulating in Czechoslovak territory, but it had been
steadily losing in value as the amount of paper money in circulation
had been increased with nothing but debts to cover it; the volume
of money circulating had risen from about 2·4 milliard crowns on
June 28th, 1914, to at least 33·5 milliards in October 26th, 1918,[2]
and Austria continued to inflate. At that time the Austro-Hungarian crown was quoted in Zürich at about a quarter of its pre-War
value, but already there was a tendency to quote the Prague crown
separately at a slightly better rate. About 8 to 10 milliards of the
money circulating was in Czechoslovak territory and people were
hoarding money in spite of the great need to replenish stocks.
Dr. Rašin, as one would expect, was a great enemy to inflation, and
he was determined to launch a 'sound' Czechoslovakia into the
new world. He now carried through with efficiency and speed the
first part of an integral financial project which he and the Maffia
had planned. On the night of February 25th, 1919, the frontiers
of Czechoslovakia were closed for a week, all the paper money in
circulation in the Republic was called in, and stamps transforming
it into Czechoslovak currency were stuck on to the notes. But the
opportunity was also to be seized to make an inventory of the
nation's wealth and temporarily to confiscate about half of the
notes, &c., in circulation in order to levy a tax on capital out of the
confiscated sum; actually owing to cases of immediate need, only
about one-fifth of the circulating money was retained in the end.[3]

[1] See above, Chapter X, p. 95.
[2] Dr. Engliš puts it at 35 milliards in *Ten Years of the Czechoslovak National Bank*.
[3] According to Dr. Engliš, op. cit., the confiscated money was transformed
into a nominal loan to the State at about 1 per cent.—i.e. a sort of forced loan.
As the sum each person owed, according to the scale for the capital levy, was
worked out, any surplus they had paid was returned to them.

By this means Dr. Rašin intended at one and the same time (i) to remove enough money from circulation as to prevent or curtail inflation; (ii) to correct social injustice by taking from the rich (especially from war-profiteers) to give to the whole nation; and (iii) to supply the State with some capital with which to begin its career. While becoming the mistress of ex-Austrian and Hungarian State and dynastic properties within her territory, the Czechoslovak Republic was compelled to take over several liabilities; she took over 42 per cent. of the ex-Austrian and 16 per cent. of the ex-Hungarian State debts and was also obliged to pay a Liberation Debt to the Allies.[1] In addition, then, to a steeply graded capital levy, a levy was planned on the increase in the value of private wealth from 1913 to 1918; this was aimed, not only at the ordinary war-profiteer, but at the landowners, because of the steep rise in the value of land during the War—since owners of land were far less impoverished than owners of other kinds of property, it was considered just that they should contribute something more.

Dr. Rašin's conception was undoubtedly bold and brilliant, but things did not work out exactly as he had hoped. For some three months after the re-stamping of the currency, the new Czech crown—the Kč—strengthened steeply, but then, despite the Canute-like frowns of the Minister, the tide of inflation set in, and by February 1920 the Kč had depreciated from its peak figure of over 34, to 5, Swiss centimes. There were a number of reasons for this. Although Rašin had hoped to isolate Czechoslovakia from her steadily inflating neighbours, it was difficult to resist the contagion. He himself found it necessary during 1920 and 1921 to put a little more money in circulation after all.[2] In the summer of 1919, moreover, M. Tusar's Socialist Cabinet had come in and naturally insisted upon importing food and raw materials at a heavy price from abroad into the more or less denuded ex-Austrian territories of the Republic, although these imports could not be paid for by normal exchange but involved a tremendous drain upon the funds which Rašin had attempted to amass. All this led to another quick change and Bohemian industry suddenly boomed.

[1] There were also debts to France on behalf of the legionaries. The Liberation Payment was finally fixed at The Hague Conference in January 1930. (In view of these facts Dr. G. Peters's statement in *Der neue Herr von Böhmen*, p. 78, is a little obscure; he says, on the one hand, that Czechoslovakia had no State debt to take over, but, on the other, that she had to take over pre-War debts in a certain proportion.) These liabilities were, of course, recurrent. Payment of the Liberation Debt has been suspended since July 1931. Czechoslovakia was not entitled to reparations payments, with the exception of an infinitesimal sum from Bulgaria. For further details see H. G. Moulton and L. Pasvolsky, *World War Debt Settlements* (New York, 1926), p. 74, and J. W. Wheeler-Bennett and H. Latimer, *Information on the Reparation Settlement* (London, 1930), p. 154.
[2] J. Čakrt, *Rašin als Währungsreformer* (1926).

The ex-combatant world was eager to replenish its stocks, and Karlsbad china and Reichenberg textiles could be sold to the tune of what people had broken or worn threadbare for years; while the Czech currency fell they could be quoted more and more cheaply abroad. The State, however, was very hard hit by this inflationary period which Rašin had so much wished to avoid, for the rise of prices meant that official salaries must be raised while payments abroad cost more and more, and it was almost impossible to borrow.

From early in 1920 until the middle of 1922, owing to the boom, the currency improved in value, varying round about 10 Swiss centimes to the crown, in spite of the scare in 1921 on account of the ex-Emperor Karl's abortive Hungarian coup which dragged the Kč momentarily down again to 5. By the end of the year (1921) Czechoslovakia's foreign trade had a surplus of 4,878 million crowns. It was in 1922, however, that Rašin's almost abandoned dreams of improving the value of the crown actually became possible of realization on account of the complete collapse of the German, Austrian, and Hungarian currencies. Capital took refuge in Czechoslovakia as fast as it could—indeed, the Czechoslovak Republic became the 'savings-bank of Central Europe'.[1] The Ministry of Finance emphasized the consequently stronger tendency of the Kč by seizing the opportunity to borrow in London and New York, though on disadvantageous terms; £3,300,000 sterling and 14 million dollars were borrowed at 8 per cent., for Rašin was now apparently putting the prestige of the Kč before everything else.[2] The result of all this was that by September 1922 the Kč stood at nearly 20 Swiss centimes, and bankruptcies, unemployment, and the reduction of officials' salaries followed. Indeed, so embittered was the social atmosphere that in January 1923 Rašin was shot by a Czech revolutionary youth named Šoupal.[3] His successors appear, unfortunately, to have 'been troubled by his spirit, for from 1923 they stabilized the Kč at about 15 Swiss centimes. In 1926 the control of the currency was no longer left to a department of the Treasury, but became the task of the newly founded National Bank of Czechoslovakia. In the early days Rašin had worked perforce without a gold cover, but now the currency was linked to a gold and foreign exchange reserve. But it was stabilized at the 15 centimes level, or 50 per cent. higher than the estimate made of its 'natural' value by most financial experts.[4] It is even said that Rašin himself, had he lived longer, would have opposed so high a figure.

[1] Charles Rist, *La Déflation en pratique* (Paris, 1927).
[2] The rise in the Kč was, of course, a help from the point of view of paying foreign debts.   [3] Cf. Klepetař, *Seit 1918*.
[4] e.g. Dr. Engliš on the Czech side; Dr. Rosche, Dr. Gustav Peters on the German side.

Another financial operation of some importance in the early post-War years was the liquidation of the Austrian and Hungarian War Loans held by Czechoslovak citizens. At first the Czechs had taken the view that money contributed to finance a war to which they themselves had been wholly opposed, a war which had indeed been waged against their national interest and desire, could not be honoured by them.[1] This view was, however, modified in view of the pressure which had been exerted upon people to subscribe, and in view of the now impoverished people who had done so. By the law of June 24th, 1920, a War Debt *arrosement*[2] was legislated as follows:

Holders of War Debt, if they wished in future to receive any interest were asked to pay up in cash 75 per cent. of the War Loan capital they held. They were then divided into two categories:

   (a) Privileged. This included banks, churches, communes, orphans. They were to receive 6 per cent. on the cash they now contributed, and 5 per cent. on their original amount of loan (but this was reckoned at something a little under its nominal value).

   (b) Unprivileged, i.e. every one else. Here $5\frac{1}{2}$ per cent. and $3\frac{1}{2}$ per cent. respectively were offered.

About 8 milliards of War Loan had been held in Czechoslovak territory and of this over 6 milliards was converted, nearly 5 milliards belonging to the privileged category. Those who would not, or could not, convert on these terms had their share of loan repudiated, with the exception of people who owned less than 25,000 Kč capital; the latter, by a regulation made in 1924, received 3 per cent. interest upon 75 per cent. of their capital. Nearly a milliard of War Loan capital was dealt with in this way. There was one further complication—how should War Loan be counted when it came to working out the levy due on this capital? The original law of April 8th, 1920, had decreed that War Loan holdings, which then still seemed likely to be repudiated, should not be affected by the capital levy. However, by the law of September 30th, 1924, it was laid down that all those who held converted War Loan must pay a levy reckoned on 30 per cent. of its nominal value.[3]

The capital levy was a measure which seemed socially admirable to the majority of Czechs in the elation of the first years of their national liberation, and in the socialistic enthusiasm of the early post-War period. Some Czech patriots were with Rašin in pursuing financial prestige; others, again the majority, regarded the conversion of War Loan as a quixotic concession to pro-Habsburg

---

[1] They were not compelled by the Peace Treaties to honour these debts.
[2] Often referred to as the 'Fourth Loan'.
[3] By the law of June 24th, 1920, the levy was to be reckoned on 40 per cent. of the nominal value, but this clause never came into operation.

capitalists. To the Sudeten Germans, however, the whole financial reorganization of these post-War years seemed to be malevolently directed against them. On the whole the Germans were still the rich men, industrialist or land-owning, of the country, who were consequently assessed at the steepest rate in the capital levy and the levy on the increase of wealth from 1913 to 1918. As for the War Loans, they were held in the Sudeten provinces almost exclusively by Germans,[1] for the *Živnostenská Banka* and other Czech bodies which had originally been compelled to buy them had resold at the earliest opportunity while the War was still being fought. Here it was not merely a matter of the wealthy Germans only, but of people whose last savings, perhaps, were invested in War Loan. Though the Czechs point out that War Loan holders in post-War Austria and Hungary were harder hit on account of the Austrian and Hungarian currency collapse, this brought little consolation to maiden ladies who were vaguely aware that the crown only went about one-fifth as far as it did in 1913 even when the oscillations of the period from 1919 to 1924 were over. Indeed, Germans nearly always speak of the War Loans as having been wholly repudiated.

The deflation which set in in 1922 suited people with State loans, but it ruined many manufacturers and threw thousands of work-people out of work. In the boom of 1921 a number of quite unsound concerns were undoubtedly launched and enjoyed a spurious success while the Kč was low. But this only very partially accounts for the industrial collapses of 1922 and 1923, when many of the soundest concerns only kept alive by living on their already diminished capital reserves. The suffering industrialists were exporters and the exporters were to a very great proportion Sudeten German, whose export was, again to a very great extent, to German and ex-Austro-Hungarian territory. Thus they were caught between millstones by the German and Austrian currency collapse, which sent up the Kč while at the same time annihilating the purchasing power of the chief customers of the Sudeten Germans. In 1923 there were about 450,000 unemployed in Czechoslovakia, of which, clearly, the majority were Sudeten Germans normally employed by Sudeten German firms.

It would be ridiculous for an impartial judge to attribute the economic suffering in Czechoslovakia in 1922 and 1923 to deliberate maltreatment of the Germans by the Czechs. The disaster was partly inevitable and partly the result of a mistaken, but not a malevolent policy. In the background, however, racial animosity can be descried, rather psychological than actual in its results.

[1] According to a German estimate about 6 out of the 8 milliards were in German hands.

The Czechs were inclined not to be very sorry for the German working-people when their wages fell or vanished, because the German standard of living was higher, and the Czechs thought it was time that Czechs lived as well as Germans in their own country. And then, as the Czechs were not slow to point out, the Sudeten Germans had been so keen about economic union with Germany, but now it was Germany that was letting them down; indeed, the Czechs exaggerated the harm done to Czechoslovakia by Reich German speculation.[1] The Sudeten Germans, on the other hand, cursed the megalomania of the Germanophobe Rašin who seemed to take the prestige of his wretched little country so seriously while he destroyed its real wealth. So great an authority as Dr. Engliš, the present Governor of the Czechoslovak National Bank, condemns—in measured but quite clear terms—the deflationary policy on the same grounds, and points out that it led to a too great dependence of industry on the banks.[2] There was even, perhaps, something of the contempt that Germans feel for French financial caution in the attitude of the Sudeten Germans towards the currency policy of Czechoslovakia; they were scornful, too, because Czechoslovakia was unable to balance her budget until 1926.

On the other hand, the non-Socialist Germans complained that post-War social expenditure kept taxation so high,[3] though it is difficult to see what else would have been possible at a time when socialism was the favourite political creed. With regard to the capital levy the Sudeten Germans resented not only the initial 'theft', but also that the assessment, according to the law of April 8th, 1920, was very much heavier by the time they came to pay up in appreciated crowns. Indeed, the Czech financial experts admitted that owing to bureaucratic delay, the levy was heavier than had been originally intended. The Germans also pointed out that Bohemia paid about two-thirds of the total capital levy,[4] although its inhabitants only constituted 48·6 per cent. of the population of the Republic; thus Slovaks and Ruthenes, in this view, were favoured at the expense of Germans and Czechs. That the much greater poverty of the Slovaks and Ruthenes should be regarded as enviable is, however, an argument which is not very difficult to meet.

Apart from their annoyance at being 'robbed' by capital levies and the so-called repudiation of the War Loans, the Sudeten Germans complained of the infinite delay, complication, and uncertainty which all these measures involved. It was well into the thirties before every one's share of the capital levy was assessed

[1] See Čakrt, op. cit.
[3] Peters, Der neue Herr von Böhmen.
[2] Engliš, op. cit.
[4] Ibid.

and squared up, but that, no doubt, was just as annoying for a once wealthy Czech like Dr. Kramář, who by now was completely impoverished. In addition to all the purely financial adjustment, the tremendous enterprise involved in the Agrarian Reform Law complicated matters more, since, in the case of most landowners, compensation for confiscated land had to be balanced off against capital levy payments. It will, therefore, be convenient to turn now to the whole matter of Agrarian Reform.

(ii) LAND REFORM

Nothing illustrates more exactly the conflict between Germans and Czechs, nothing so accurately sums up its history, as the Land Reform question; over nothing has there been more misunderstanding, more incapacity to see the other point of view; nothing has been more fruitful of propaganda based upon half-truths.

It is incontestably true that the Historic or Sudeten Provinces, while Austria-Hungary lived, had remained fantastically feudal in territorial organization.[1]

More than one-quarter of all Bohemia was owned by less than 2 per cent. of the landowners. Nearly one-third of the soil of Moravia belonged to less than 1 per cent. of the landowners, while one-half of the total number of holdings were less than one half-hectare in size. Much the same state of affairs existed in Silesia.[2]

Count Clam-Gallas, the Liechtenstein, and, as we have seen, the Schwarzenberg families owned vast stretches of land. The peasants, especially in the Czech interior of Bohemia and Moravia, had tiny holdings or no land at all; this had led, in pre-War days, to large-scale emigration to America, as well as to the flow of Czech population to the Bohemian and Moravian *Randgebieten* and on a great scale to Vienna. After the War, America was to close her doors, while Vienna, once the capital of a fifty-million empire, was faced with her own catastrophe.

Long before the War the need for land reform was spoken of; indeed, the Habsburg Government had benevolent intentions which were only weaker than the feudal foundations upon which it rested. In the national and social elation of their 'liberation', and amidst the varied dreams of a millennium which floated in the air in 1919,[3] it was inevitable that the big landed estates should

[1] The Foreign Office Handbook of Jan. 1919 on *Bohemia and Moravia* points out that from 1869, when it became possible to transfer land freely, large estates had tended to increase and small-holdings to be more than ever subdivided.

[2] L. E. Textor, *Land Reform in Czechoslovakia* (London, 1923). These figures are based upon the Austrian statistics of 1896. (N.B. 1 hectare = about 2½ acres.)

[3] The agrarian aspect of the revolution in Russia aroused particularly strong hopes and desires among the peasantry of the other Slav countries.

be claimed 'for the nation'. Every kind of emotion from Utopian idealism and practical benevolence to the meanest greed and the narrowest chauvinism furthered this demand. Not only did the Czechs and the Slovaks (who had emigrated even more) wish Czechoslovakia to provide a new home for their nationals who had previously prepared to leave Austria-Hungary, but there was a host, now, of legionaries and war-invalids for whom particular provision must be made. In the revolutionary spirit of those times, the big parties on the left favoured the nationalization[1] of the land without compensation. Compensation seemed quite superfluous, too, to many of the very nationally minded Czechs who intended to put right the historic wrongs of the seventeenth century.[2] Among the members of the Czech national defence societies, the big land-owners were decried, rather as the descendants of the men to whom the Habsburgs had forcefully transferred Czech properties, than because they were rich and privileged. Like their German counter-parts of the *Bund der Deutschen* or the *Böhmerwald Bund*, the Czech chauvinists wish to conquer, or still more often—since it sounds more justifiable—to reconquer, territory; nor was it only the violent chauvinists who felt apprehension at the German character of the mountainous frontier districts at a time (1919) when the Sudeten Germans were still frankly hostile to the new State—we have seen that the Czechs had discovered themselves to be weaker in the country than they had originally expected.

It was essential to act quickly, for the land-hunger of the peas-ants was rising, and home-comers from all over the world were adding to the general social explosiveness. On April 16th, 1919, a week after Rašin's second law for the inauguration of the cur-rency, the Law providing for Expropriation was passed. According to this all the larger estates were put at the disposal of the State—they might not be sold, leased, mortgaged, or divided without official consent. It was decreed, as a general rule, that a landowner might retain 150 hectares of arable land or 250 hectares altogether, in no case more than 500 hectares. The question of compensation for the property of which he was deprived was left over, but it was there and then enacted that no compensation would be paid to any of the Habsburgs (except as stated in the Treaty of St. Germain, Article 203), to citizens of an enemy State, or to 'people who had committed grave offences against the Czechoslovak nation during the World War'.

This enabling legislation was then further developed by a num-

---

[1] This word, if literally translated into German, has a much more nationalistic flavour than the English word, which should be translated *Verstaatlichung*.

[2] Professor Pekař pointed out in a famous publication soon after the War that Ferdinand II had confiscated land from Germans as well as from Czechs and drew attention to other fallacies in the extreme Czech point of view.

ber of later enactments. The law of June 11th, 1919, provided for a special Land Office to be created; this was to be the body to administer the new Land Laws, and was in its turn to be supervised by a committee of twelve chosen from the National Assembly and termed the Board of Control. Great struggles followed over the constitution of the Land Office, but when, in October, the Agrarian Party (who already controlled the Ministry of Agriculture) were able to supply its President, the future of Czechoslovak land reform was settled in the sense of private property rather than socialization. Tenants enjoying long leases were given the right to buy their holdings provided they would not then become the owners of more than a fairly small farm.[1] The Law of Allotment of January 30th, 1920, arranged for the distribution of land, in which legionaries, war invalids, and returning emigrants (if they were farmers) were to be specially favoured. While forests, pastures, and fish-ponds were in general to go to communities, recipients of agricultural holdings might get credits from the Land Office up to a maximum of 90 per cent. of the price of the land and 50 per cent. of the cost of the buildings it had or required.

The Compensation Law was passed on April 8th, 1920; it represented a compromise, for compensation was in general to be paid, though it was to be calculated at a fairly low rate. Deprived estate-owners were to receive the price of the land taken from them at its 1913–15 value calculated in pre-War Austrian gold crowns but paid in Kč.[2] The recognized price was to be lowered $\frac{1}{10}$ per cent. for every hundred hectares above 1,000, but in no circumstances by more than 30 per cent.; from the year 1923, there was to be a very slight reduction for every year until the estate was actually taken over; all equipment was to be paid for in cash and at the full current price. Former employees on estates now required for distribution or nationalization, in so far as they could not still be employed, were to be indemnified with land, a suitable job, a pension, or with money compensation.

At first nothing very drastic was done with regard to the large tracts of forest land owned by the big landowners, beyond measures to prevent the trees from being cut down. While the big proprietors owned some 50 per cent. of the forests in the Republic, only 15 per cent. belonged to the State, the rest being owned mostly by various local government authorities. But by far the major part of the forest land was situated in frontier regions, and there was strong nationalist pressure upon the Government to take most of it over; in July 1922 it was announced that 300,000 hectares were, in fact, to be nationalized.

[1] Originally limited to 8 hectares by the law of May 27th, 1919.
[2] See section (i) of this chapter.

The position about agricultural industries such as distilleries, breweries, and sugar factories—all very important in Czechoslovakia—was rather obscure. According to the law of April 16th, 1919, industries which were economically independent of confiscated land were exempt from expropriation, but it was extraordinarily difficult to determine the exact meaning of economic independence in the context. A number of breweries were, accordingly, taken over, but the sugar factories were not at first touched; by 1933, out of 72, 15 had come into the hands of new owners, while out of 698 private distilleries 215 came under the management of co-operative societies.[1]

The transformation involved in all these laws was bound to be a gradual process. Indeed, even to-day, there is still land under sequester, land which has not been distributed, but over which the last owner is not allowed to exercise full rights because it may yet be required. Up to January 1st, 1937, apart from the area retained by the State, 1,272,934 hectares had been redistributed to individuals, or to communities of one kind or another.[2] I think it is true to say that a great and necessary piece of work has been done. If it has been faultily done, that is true of every piece of work of the kind; it would not be just to decry either the work of Stein in Prussia or the great Russian emancipation of 1861[3] because they did not achieve all that their initiators intended, nor even because they sometimes defeated their own ends. The sharp pre-War inequalities in land-tenure could not have continued, and the Czechoslovak reform has been less drastic than that carried through in various other countries in post-War Europe. In view of the revolutionary feeling, idealistic or destructive as the case might be, just after the War, it is surprising that the Czechoslovak measures were as moderate as they were; one is constantly astonished by the amount of sequestrated land which has been returned to its former owners. Although on the whole the Agrarian Party succeeded in putting through the principle of individual small-holdings, a good deal came into the hands of the communes or of co-operative societies, according to the programme of the Socialists. Whether the small-holdings principle or that of large-scale farming, such as both the big proprietor and the advocate of the collective farm favour, is more applicable to the soil of Czechoslovakia is a debatable point, and depends upon varying local conditions.

Agrarian reform easily lends itself to jobbery. If it was right to take the land it was wrong to allow its distribution to depend upon

[1] M. A. Pavel (of the Land Office and Ministry of Agriculture in Prague), in a lecture held on Feb. 23rd, 1933, at the Czechoslovak Agricultural Academy.
[2] Information supplied by M. A. Pavel.
[3] There is not, perhaps, a direct parallel between these emancipation laws and Czechoslovak Land Reform, but many of the problems involved were the same.

the bargaining of political parties. The Land Office, and the board which controlled it, were frankly chosen with a view to giving the parties, *qua* parties, a say; on the other hand, because a certain number of unsuitable people received 'estate-remnants'[1] through the influence of a political friend, it would be ridiculous to suggest, as hostile critics do, that most of the land did not go to peasants who needed it. A certain number of unsuitable people were settled and have subsequently resold the land, but it would be difficult to say whether the number of bad choices was above the average, if an average could be taken of comparable miscalculations whenever land has been redistributed upon a considerable scale.

The question now arises of how the Sudeten Germans have been affected by land reform in Czechoslovakia. If the country were treated as a territorial unit and the reform put through according to principles of social justice it was absolutely inevitable, since the big landed proprietors were predominantly German and Hungarian, that a very high proportion of German and Hungarian land should be taken for redistribution. And again, since it was the Czech and Slovak population which was predominantly agricultural and often landless and whose birth-rate (especially the Slovak birth-rate) was high, and since a much higher proportion of the German population was mainly industrial, it was inevitable that the peasants to whom the land was allotted should be predominantly Czech or Slovak; the legionaries, moreover, were to be preferred, and they were all Czechs or Slovaks. The Czechoslovak Ministry of Agriculture points out that in the Czech-speaking interior of the Historic Provinces, 198,909 more hectares were expropriated than in the mixed or German districts,[2] and that apart from the definite category of the settlers, the claims of applicants for land were only considered if the land applied for was not more than 5 kilometres from their homes so that, on these grounds alone, Germans were often less eligible. At first no statistics could be obtained which considered the nationality of the persons who were allotted land by the Land Office, but they have subsequently been compiled, although the Ministry of Agriculture does not regard them as exhaustive, and points out that, in earlier years, since they were not recorded as such, a larger number of allotments to minority nationalities may have occurred. Up to January 1st, 1937,[3]

[1] i.e. the farm buildings, &c., which had formed the centre of each farm, and which were kept together to form larger allotments; the original owner could often exchange less indispensable areas for them, according to local conditions.
[2] Information supplied by M. Pavel.
[3] The distribution of land still continues, though to a diminishing extent. In the *Prager Presse* of Feb. 10th, 1938, plans for distribution in 1938 were published, e.g. 1,440 hectares at Mnichovo Hradiště (Munchengrätz) and so on.

the following land is known to have gone to Sudeten Germans:

In small allotments .	.	.	.	. 42,925 hectares to 48,685 families
In larger „	.	.	.	. 14,345 „ „ 135 „
Total	.	.	.	. 57,270 „ „ 48,820 „

This is, in fact, 4·5 per cent. of the 1,272,934 hectares allotted in all up to that time. 'As the land allocated to the German applicants', a Ministry of Agriculture statement continues, 'is to the extent of four-fifths agricultural land, of which a total area of 862,410 [hectares] was distributed, it may be said that this minority participated in the allocation of agricultural land to the proportion of 5·2 per cent.'[1]

I have never heard the more serious Sudeten Germans, however anti-Czech they may be, deny that the German tenants working on expropriated land were quite justly treated in being allowed to become its owners:[2] 'The German farmer received land even from a Czech landowner', Miss Textor writes. In Southern Bohemia and the Böhmerwald it is always admitted, however grudgingly, that the German foresters, who have now become masters of their own huts and of the plots of land around them, have been changed from serfs into men only by the land reform carried through by the Republic—neither Joseph II nor Kudlich had been able to help them. Finally, in view of the particular circumstances, if it be remembered how high a proportion of the expropriated land in the German districts was forest land and unsuitable for individual allotment, it is not certain that, if the Germans received 5 per cent. of the distributed land, they were unjustly treated from this point of view.

There are three main categories of German complaints in the matter of land reform: (a) the complaints of former employees on big estates; (b) those based upon the big landowners' point of view; (c) those based upon the tradition of the Czech-German racial struggle in the Historic Provinces.

(a) All the evidence suggests that the former German employees were harshly treated and suffered very much. The hostility of both Czech and German employees to the new legislation became vigorous from the time that they realized that they would be victimized; their opposition became conspicuous at the beginning of 1922, and it was soon after enacted that big estate ex-employees were to be added to those who were to be preferred in the allotting

---

[1] M. Pavel, as above. The figure of 1,272,934 hectares excludes about 500,000 hectares taken over by the State.

[2] In the *Land- und Forstarbeiter*, Feb. 20th, 1926, it is rather scornfully admitted that 31·8 per cent. of the land so distributed went to Germans, because it depended upon decisions in the courts and not upon the Land Office, the paper asserts.

of land. The owners were also obliged to use the compensation they received, before they spent it in any other way, in providing pensions for their employees.[1] Though the latter were entitled to compensation from the State the lower officials of the Land Office often interpreted their ill-defined claims as unkindly as possible; a Bohemian German might be offered as his compensation under the law a piece of land in Eastern Slovakia. To the German that would spell sentence of exile, and he perhaps refused, whereupon the Czech official was entitled to say, 'He would not have the compensation offered him by the law—very well, he has chosen to do without.' I have heard a Czech say, of a case of the kind, 'After all, we could not be sentimental over things like that.' Where money compensation was given, it was very little, and a Sudeten German who had lived well on some flourishing estate in 'Friedenszeiten'[2] was bad at adapting himself to a lower standard of life in a cold, hard world with no *grand seigneur* protection.

(b) These *grands seigneurs* of the old Austria, though more western than their Hungarian counterparts,[3] preserved the mentality of a pre-industrial age; like their superb Baroque palaces[4] in Vienna and Prague, their standards retained a magnificence and a Catholicism which were in direct contrast with the puritanical simplicity of the best Czech tradition, of the Brethren, of Komenský, of Masaryk. Many of the aristocrats maintained a fine patriarchal sense of responsibility towards all their retainers and dependants, but in others it had degenerated into the assumption that they were born into the world in order that others should work for them, and indeed—I have heard this sort of thing pronounced without reticence—that they required the poor men at their gate in order that they might practise charity without effort. And whether genuinely benevolent or not, a big landowning class—one is reminded of the notorious East Elbian Junkerdom with its opposition to Dr. Brüning's '*Agrar-Bolschevismus*' in 1932—seems invariably unable to comprehend or even to contemplate other than aristocratic forms of society; certainly in Central or Eastern Europe, one seems to discover something like a physical incapacity, among members of this social stratum, to think in other terms.

To these people the new Czechoslovak land laws were simply immoral. They could never understand that there was often the same profound moral conviction behind the idea that property is

[1] Textor, op. cit., p. 97.
[2] = peace times, the usual way of referring to pre-War days.
[3] A good many big landowners had held land on both sides of the Leitha, but, according to my own experience, the difference of mentality on the near and the far side of that frontier must have been really considerable.
[4] One has only to remember the Kinsky, the Clam-Gallas, Harrach, Czernin, and Lobkowicz palaces.

theft, or that it is easier for a camel to go through the eye of a needle than for a rich man to enter into the Kingdom of God, as behind the aristocratic conception of life. They still explain to one that land reform outraged the moral instincts of their good German employees too, though it needs to be repeated that the big estate employees only appear to have become indignant when they began to realize that they would lose their own jobs.

The more precise and tangible arguments of the German big landowners were fully expressed in the numerous memoranda they drew up, and are ably set out in their complaint to the League of Nations in September 1922.[1] They objected, of course, to the fact that the sequestration of the land was voted by the Constituent Assembly in the absence of German representatives of any kind— this argument naturally turns up again and again. Further, they complained that the Land Office was staffed entirely by Czechs and controlled by the board of twelve Czech deputies—they even indicated that a good many of the Land Office officials were undesirable Czechs. Here it should perhaps be mentioned that the landowners were sometimes represented in various *enquêtes* though they took the view that no attention had been paid to them. They also pointed out, with a great deal of justification, that production would be reduced by breaking up the big units. Indeed, in December 1919 they wished to make any surrender of land dependent upon the proper qualification of the people who were to receive it.[2] With regard to this group of objections in general, and in view of the particularly inelastic mentality of the landowning class, there is something to be said for the Czech official who remarked that 'when you want to drain the swamp you do not consult the frogs'.[3] Another source of irritation to the big land-owners was the decree of June 18th, 1919, according to which a mismanaged estate could be placed under the compulsory super-vision of the Ministry of Agriculture, and later under that of the Land Office. Food was short at the time, and it was clear that the big proprietors, after April 1919, would be tempted to realize what they could by selling things off while prices were good and before their property had been somehow transferred. The State was bound to try to prevent this, but it is obvious that many small Czech officials were thus given the occasion to supervise properties in a fairly offensive way; they would have been more than human if they had not represented the aristocrats as something like ogres in order to assert their new power with righteous emphasis. And the aristocrats themselves would have been more than human if

[1] *Beschwerde der deutschen Grossgrundbesitzer der Tschechoslowakischen Republik . . . gerichtet an den Völkerbund . . . überreicht . . . im September 1922.*
[2] *Denkschrift des Verbandes der deutschen Grossgrundbesitzer Böhmens*, Dec. 1st, 1919.   [3] Textor, op. cit., p. 119.

they had not resented these representatives of the new democracy, who were perhaps less confident and therefore less courteous than revolutionary officials in the first French Revolution.

The rate of compensation naturally aroused the indignation of the *grands seigneurs*; indeed to refer to it as compensation at all seemed to many of them to be mere hypocrisy. Their annoyance was increased by their contempt for the Republic and its currency, which would, according to their expectation, sink to still lower levels. At the time (April 1920) of the Compensation Law the Czech crown was standing at scarcely one-eighth of the old Austrian crown to which it was for this purpose to be considered equivalent; in 1922 it rose steeply and in 1924 settled down to a rate somewhere between one-fifth and one-sixth of the pre-War value, while the value of land tended to fall. It would, I think, have been literally impossible to pay compensation at a higher rate in view of the spirit of the time,[1] and in view of the important fact that it is worse than useless to redistribute the land unless the peasants can acquire it sufficiently cheaply, and unless there are funds to supply them with essential equipment. But the temperamental inability of the big landowners to see the non-conservative point of view was embittered by the irritating fact that their land was valued at a definitely higher rate when it came to their paying capital levy. Many of them were habitually in debt, and in addition to the above discrepancy in valuation, they now found themselves paying interest on ordinary debts and upon the capital levy payment they owed at 7 or 8 per cent., while the State paid them 3 to 4 per cent. on the compensation which was recognized to be due to them. Bitter indignation was also felt that people who had displayed hostility towards the Czechs during the War were not to be compensated; as the German landowners pointed out,[2] this was a penalization of patriotism. Here the more nationalist Germans and Czechs were mutually blind; it was—and still is—impossible to get them to admit that a keen Sudeten German was morally bound to exert himself against the Slavs in the War to exactly the same extent as an enthusiastic Czech was bound to work against the Central Powers. That their land should go to the legionaries whom, as we have seen, they regarded as traitors and thugs, further exasperated the German or Hungarian landowners. In practice each landowner could negotiate with the Land Office with regard

---

[1] It was a concession to the landowners to take into consideration the value of their land up to the end of 1915, since this had steadily risen after the outbreak of War.

[2] See the 1922 complaint to the League of Nations mentioned above. Dr. Sobota (in *Das tschechoslowakische Nationalitätenrecht*, p. 190) says that this exception with regard to compensation was never put into practice, and was overridden by the law of April 8th, 1920.

to the compensation to which he was entitled, and more often than not, if he was not openly inimical to the Republic, the Land Office was glad enough to let him keep more than the law implied in return for paying him less.

The 1922 complaint (referred to above) to the League of Nations was particularly vehement against the nationalization of forest land which had been announced that July. This hit the German nobility very hard, and was not needed for redistribution to peasant farmers. On the other hand, it is scarcely possible to conceive of a Central European State which would be willing to risk—even when Germany was weak—that frontier districts of first-rate strategical importance should be in the private possession of a group of people who were, socially and nationally, at least unfriendly to the State, and of whom several were the nationals of the neighbouring states.[1]

(c) The recurrent refrain in all the German complaints was that the whole land reform project was aimed at denationalizing the minorities, and above all, as they felt, the Sudeten Germans.[2] This was true and not true. The reform was essential, if faultily carried out, and it was bound to bring more to the Czechs and Slovaks than the Germans. In view, however, of the traditional tussle over every house in a market-place, over every building site and especially over hotel property because of the economic attraction involved,[3] it was inevitable that the Czech National Unions should wish to exploit the new land laws to the utmost. The chauvinists on both sides had been busy, at least since the eighties, in 'conquering' territory from one another.[4] The nationalist Czech press can be indefinitely cited by the Sudeten Germans to show that the Czech nationalist societies were pushing for the installation of Czechs in the place of 'foreigners', by which minority citizens were nearly always meant. Legionary and other Czech colonists were gradually settled on the available arable land all around the lignite areas where the population was most mixed, and to a lesser extent in Northern Moravia, where the local Czechs demanded to have the minority strengthened.[5] In the old battle-ground territory between Brüx and Leitmeritz, Teplitz and Třebenice, the effects of land reform are interesting to observe. Much of the land around here belonged to the Schwarzenbergs. One passes expropriated

[1] Many aristocratic families held estates in, e.g. Germany, Poland, and Czechoslovakia or in Austria, Czechoslovakia, and Hungary. In 1937 I was interested to meet a big landowner who was the national of an unfriendly State but had been allowed even then to keep forest land right on the frontier.
[2] See, e.g., *Land- und Forstarbeiter* quoted above.
[3] Cf. Hassinger, *Die Tschechoslowakei*.
[4] See Chapter VII above.
[5] Quoted in *Mitteilungen des Verbandes der deutschen Grossgrundbesitzer Böhmens* no. 11/12.

farm buildings bought up by Czechs since the republican land laws; sometimes they have changed hands once or twice because the original buyers did not take kindly to a farming life. In many of the villages the German peasants tell one how Czech farmers began to arrive in about 1925 though there were never any Czechs there before;[1] there will be caustic references to the new schools[2] for the Czech children, or to the Czech girl in charge of the post office who has just begun to learn the German numerals since she has become interested in a German young man. (The sterner members of either nationality do not think that this kind of interest should be allowed to stray from one race to the other.) In one village here there are about twenty Czech families brought in from Russia because their ancestors are said to have been exiled as Hussites— dirty Russians, the Germans call them. At Lobositz (Lovosice), which has always been considered of particular importance in the national struggle,[3] the Germans complain that with land re- form, officials and Czech schools, nearly 40 per cent. of the population is now (1937) Czech, though, as they tell one, there were no Czechs to notice in Austrian days. And yet so long ago as 1900 there were 15 per cent. Czechs and in 1902 bitter com- plaints about Czech officials and the Czech private school which had just been started.[4] Although my German informants in Lobo- sitz were thus revealed to be careless about accuracy, I am inclined to believe some of what they told me about the objections made by the local branch of the *Národní Jednota Severočeska*[5] when a German tries to buy land from a Czech, and even when a Czech politician accepts hospitality from a German in Lobositz.

The German big landowners had tried to defend their property by protesting against the disturbing of old traditional German ownership. Of the forest question they spoke with particular vehemence because they declared that it involved the confiscation of the most ancient Sudeten German national territory. The frontier of national ownership, it has been seen, had wobbled backwards and forwards, and everything depended upon the arbitrary choice of a date which should count as the beginning of lawful possession; if the years 1100 or 1450 were taken the Ger- mans would have much to lose, but if either 1400 or 1800 were chosen they might have something to gain. In any case the forests, if one thought in racial terms, must be counted as German. Further, cases like that of Graslitz (Kraslice), where the local authorities applied to buy the woods from the local big landowner,

---

[1] This frequently occurring assertion has to be received with caution. See below.　　　　　　　　　　　　　　　　　　　[2] See Chapter XV below.

[3] See above, Chapter VII, p. 62 n.

[4] Zemmrich, *Sprachgrenze und Deutschtum in Böhmen*.

[5] = North Bohemian National Union.

but were not allowed to do so, aroused bitter resentment. The town of Graslitz announced in July 1922 that

> The attack on German home land will meet the united resistance of the whole German population, since our German people is bound indivisibly to its soil and its woods, and will never divorce itself from this inheritance.[1]

The case for the State in nationalizing the forests has been put, and it is not destroyed by its decision to stick to the woods near Graslitz (which is exceedingly near the German frontier) rather than handing them over to a Sudeten German commune. Where the Czech authorities went wrong was in frequently replacing the German foresters by Czechs, either immediately or as occasion arose. This meant that Sudeten Germans who might have been willing to accept Czechoslovakia fairly happily were rendered inimical. There were plenty of Czechs who regretted the tendency to dismiss Germans, but since the Land Office depended upon political parties it could not afford to resist pressure from the Czech nationalist societies, or if one party's representatives would have ignored the pressure those of another could scarcely help seizing the advantage this gave. Among the emphatically national people on both sides there was also a great deal of friction over the *décor*, as it were, of the frontier districts which had always attracted many tourists from abroad. The Czechs said this was their country and the traveller should be made aware of the difference between it and Germany. They tried to insist that hotels and inns should be designated in Czech as well as in German, and when an opportunity offered they bought up the hotels.

In conclusion, a redistribution of land was desirable and inevitable. Like any revolution of the kind, it involved personal hardships, and disorganization, and a certain amount of bargaining of a not exactly high-minded nature. Well-run estates were sometimes broken up and made far less productive than they had been before. The Bohemian fish-ponds, involving the important industry of fish-breeding, have been cited as a case of a change for the worse[2] when the fish-ponds were handed over to the local authorities. The argument, which one constantly hears in big landowning circles, that much employment was destroyed is not valuable since a good deal was certainly created; there is no reason to suppose that the distilleries run by the co-operatives, for example, employed less people than before. On the whole one is struck by the mildness of a reform which was bound to take place, and the frequency with which the 500 hectares limit has been disregarded;

[1] *Kundgebung der Stadtgemeinde Graslitz vom 18. Juli, 1922.*
[2] Textor, op. cit., p. 85.

of the land originally put under sequester, over 40 per cent. has been returned to the original owners.[1] It is no secret that the Schwarzenberg family has retained nearly 50,000 hectares, and several other big proprietors on reasonably good terms with the State, though they are considered to be Sudeten German, and though their estates are in the frontier districts, have kept a great deal. Indeed, although the constitution abolished hereditary titles, and although the State dislikes social display, they appear to keep up old forms without let or hindrance. The Roman Catholic Church shares with the Schwarzenbergs the honour of having been left in possession of very wide territories.[2]

As for the Czech-German national situation, it is a question of a point of view. If Czechoslovakia be accepted at all as a unit, and if social justice and the will, and the greatest happiness, of the greatest number be admitted as standards, Czechoslovak land reform was justified in removing land from big German land-owners and distributing it among poor Czech and Slovak peasants. Despite a certain number of irregularities, the principles of western democratic thinking were, on the whole, observed.[3] If, on the other hand, one thinks in terms of racial organisms and is guided by the principles of Schönerer, K. H. Wolf, and Adolf Hitler, and if the racial organisms can be exactly related to certain territorial areas, the giving of Sudeten-German-owned land to Czech or Slovak peasants or to the Czechoslovak Republic itself can be condemned. Here again, however, there is a difficulty because the relation of a racial group to the soil is considered to be determined by the dynamic of events; it is difficult to be certain whether this can be taken to cover the appearance of a new State which passes new laws, but probably it can.

The whole question of land reform certainly emphasized the rough tendency for the Czechs to take up a western, democratic, egalitarian standpoint and the Sudeten Germans a more mystical organic position. Whether the Czechs would have been so constant to the western or Masaryk position if it had not suited their interests is another question—Masaryk was never so prominent as Kramář before the War, but Palacký and Rieger had in their way been more western than eastern. At the time of Austria-Hungary's collapse a friend of mine travelled in a train with a poor Czech bricklayer who kept on exclaiming happily, 'Now we shall be the masters! Now we shall be the masters!' but whether he meant 'we, the Czechs' or 'we, the working-people' probably he himself

---

[1] *Statistisches Jahrbuch der Čechoslowakischen Republik, 1937*, p. 64.
[2] See Chapter XV, section (x).
[3] The main legislation was all unanimously voted so that even if German representatives had been present, the laws would not have been rejected in the Assembly—still less so by the first elected Assembly of 1920.

did not know. The accident of coinciding interests has often had long-term political consequences.

About the further agrarian history of Czechoslovakia there is not a great deal that it is relevant to the subject to add.[1] In spite of the predominantly industrial character of the Sudeten German population, the German Agrarian Party has played a certain role in the Czechoslovak Parliament, and was, indeed, the largest German party between the elections of 1925 and those of 1929. The Czech Agrarian Party, representing the peasant proprietor, has from the first been the predominant party among the Czechs, and there has consequently been a tendency all along for other interests to be sacrificed to those of agriculture. Thus it has been easier for the *Bund der Landwirte* (= Farmers' Union) or German Agrarians to adopt an activist policy, and to co-operate with the Czechoslovak State; they did this without a break from 1926 to 1938, though the Egerland Farmers, led by Herr Josef Mayer, were strongly opposed to activism from the beginning.

(iii) INDUSTRY

The Sudeten German districts had, during the second half of the nineteenth century, become the workshop of the Dual Monarchy, an empire whose population had grown beyond 50 millions by 1910. It has been seen how Bruck's abolition of tariff barriers in 1851 had formed the whole of Austria and of Hungary into an economic unit. This unity was, however, challenged from Budapest in the last few years before 1900, since the Hungarians wished to emphasize their national integrity by building up their own industries instead of depending upon those west of the Leitha. There was a very anxious period for Austrian industrialists until, after endless negotiating, a fresh 'Compromise' with Hungary was arrived at in 1907, and the Dual Customs Union preserved. The Magyars continued, nevertheless, to invest a great deal of money in Hungarian industry, and thereby threatened the immense prosperity of the Sudeten German industrial concerns for the future. It has been pointed out above that the Czech Agrarians had, during the same period, shown similar intimations of post-War autarchy by desiring protection from Hungarian wheat. Up to the outbreak of war, however, Sudeten German industry, while heavily protected against Reich German and other foreign competition, retained a home market which was able to absorb some 80 to 90 per cent. of

[1] A number of minor Sudeten German grievances could be cited, e.g. in the Böhmerwald, South Bohemia, and elsewhere one hears that the Czechoslovak Ministry of Agriculture does not do enough for stock-breeding because it involves the German population rather than the Czechs and Slovaks of the lowlands.

its production.[1] The unfortunate peacemakers, scapegoats for all Central European original sin, have had the whole blame thrown upon them for the economic disruption of Austria-Hungary, though they wished, as Article 222 of the Treaty of St. Germain[2] shows, to preserve such cohesion as they could in the ruins of the Habsburg edifice. It was absolutely inevitable, however, that Silesian industry, for example, should now be deprived of the Galician market upon which it had relied. How thankful indeed Bohemian industry may well have been that no frontier was drawn between Reichenberg (Liberec) and Prague such as that which arose between Troppau (Opava) and Lwow (Lemberg).

An astonishing proportion of the old Cisleithan sources of production were incorporated in the new Republic of Czechoslovakia. These included the whole china industry, of which 55 concerns were Sudeten German and 4 Czech. The Republic also took over:

21 out of	24	ex-Austrian	window and bottle glass factories of which 16		were Sudeten German	
1,218	„	1,524	„ cotton factories	„ 819	„	„
281	„	333	„ wool factories	„ 201	„	„
239	„	267	„ linen factories	„ 167	„	„
47	„	55	„ hemp and jute factories	27	„	„
55	„	65	„ silk factories	„ 44	„	„

This works out at about 80 per cent. of the cotton industry, 85 per cent. of the woollen industry, 90 per cent. of the linen industry, 85 per cent. of the hemp and jute industry, 85 per cent. of the silk industry,[3] and since the Hungarians had been making efforts to develop industry in Slovakia the percentages, if reckoned on the whole of the ex-Habsburg territory, are even higher than this.[4]

[1] The Historic Provinces were nevertheless susceptible, even in pre-War days, to the state of the international market; the Foreign Office handbook on *Bohemia and Moravia* (Jan. 1919), already quoted, refers (p. 89) to the depression in the cotton industry in 1912 'owing to the Balkan War and the extended credit demanded by Serbia, Bulgaria and Roumania . . .'. A little farther on (p. 94), in describing the general pre-War situation, it states that 'The Bohemian glass industry often suffers from depression, owing to severe competition with Germany and Belgium, in which countries manufacturers have the advantages of cheaper inland freights and raw materials, while taxes and other expenses are lower. Japan also is trying to oust the Gablonz manufacturers of glass jewellery from the Indian market.'

[2] Article 222 runs as follows:

Notwithstanding the provisions of Articles 217 to 220 (by which Austria promised Most Favoured Nation treatment to the Allies) the Allied and Associated Powers agree that they will not invoke these provisions to secure the advantage of any arrangements which may be made by the Austrian Government with the Governments of Hungary or of the Czecho-Slovak State for the accord of a special customs régime to certain natural or manufactured products which both originate in and come from those countries, and which shall be specified in the arrangements, provided that the duration of these arrangements does not exceed a period of five years from the coming into force of the present Treaty.

[3] Peters, op. cit., p. 77. The percentages are reckoned on the whole number of factories taken over by Czechoslovakia.

[4] See Dr. Miloš Horna on 'Industry' in *Ten Years of the Czechoslovak National Bank*, who gives, for instance, 97 per cent. as the figure for the linen spindles taken over, 90 per cent. for silk, but otherwise just about the same as Dr. Peters.

With all this, the Sudeten German industrialists were left with an internal market of just over $13\frac{1}{2}$ million consumers instead of just over 51 millions. Quite apart from impoverishment due to the War, for which all critics of the Czechoslovak Government perpetually blamed it, this internal market was not a potentially wealthy one, since it consisted mainly of small peasants and shopkeepers and many working-men; in the east it included, in Ruthenia, perhaps the most backward area of the old Hungary. Further, the Sudeten German entrepreneur now found himself more dependent upon raw materials from abroad, and with higher freight charges to face upon goods going south, since so many frontiers had arisen between Bohemia and the Mediterranean. Unless Sudeten German industry could keep the custom of the pre-War Austrians and Hungarians in post-War Austria, Hungary, Poland, Yugoslavia, and Roumania, as well as that of Germany, her most valuable pre-War customer abroad, she was threatened, in the long run, just as British coal-mining was, with irreparable disaster. As in the case of other highly industrialized areas, which had been built up upon Manchesterian assumptions of the progressive development of international trade, it was not for ten years that this grim fact emerged clearly from a background of hope and illusion. It has been seen[1] that in 1920 and 1921 Sudeten German industry indulged in a post-War replenishment boom before the post-War tariff barriers had arisen. Not only did textiles and china sell well, but the lignite miners were kept very busy. The glass exporters, above all, flourished, since they were able to profit from the fact that French and Belgian glass were not yet back on the world market. Those were wild days of wealth, and many are the stories of the working-people who suddenly burst into dress shirts and dinner jackets. In 1922 came inflation abroad and deflation at home and widespread ruin.[2] It is almost a truism by now that industry in Central Europe is much more closely related to the banks than is industry in Great Britain. This tendency was quite unduly emphasized by the economic disasters of 1922 and 1923 which were accompanied by the new egalitarian capital levy payments, heavy losses for larger incomes on War Loan investments, and severe taxation. Many industrial concerns, which were guilty of no undue rashness, were forced to live on their capital and to borrow heavily from the banks at a high rate of interest. The banks with which the Sudeten Germans were accus-

---

[1] See section (i) above.
[2] The flax industry in Trautenau (Trutnov) never really recovered from its losses in 1922, nor did the glass industry nor the china industry grouped around Karlsbad. This slump actually took place in a series of jerks beginning in September 1920. See Great Britain: Department of Overseas Trade, *Report on Economic Conditions in Czecho-Slovakia* (to June 1921).

tomed to deal were themselves in a state of considerable confusion, since many of them had had their headquarters at Vienna, and while the Czechs pressed for their 'nostrification', i.e. separate organization at Prague, they themselves were not quite dissociated from the financial break-down of Austria in 1922 and 1923; the *Böhmische Escompte Bank (Česká escomptní banka)*, for example, was the direct heir of the *Osterreichische Kreditanstalt*.

In 1924 Czechoslovakia passed a financial reorganization law by which certain funds were placed at the disposal of the banks now in trouble, but the Sudeten German banks made little use of the assistance thus rendered available. The old defence society tradition that no German should depend financially upon a Czech (or vice versa, of course) made them unwilling to do so; they preferred to borrow abroad, especially, once the mark was stabilized, from Germany. A certain amount of Sudeten German capital now found its way into Reich German investments, for the Sudeten Germans continued to regard the Czechoslovak Republic with distrust and disdain. With the stabilization of the mark, the period of American investment in Europe, Locarno, and so on, the nominal prosperity of the later twenties set in. Sudeten German industry picked up again, and, like industry the world over, became too confident, though its prospects—in the eyes of the far-sighted—must remain gloomy. Not only was it heavily indebted and dependent upon foreign markets which would certainly be reduced, but many of its branches were particularly sensitive to the Japanese competition which made itself seriously felt at least as early as 1925. Much Sudeten German activity had always been fairly precarious because it produced luxuries or their equivalent, such things, for instance, as the toys or musical instruments made by the home-workers of the Erzgebirge, or the beads and buttons of Gablonz (Jablonec). In the post-War world, which was fundamentally impoverished and democratized, even a boom was not so immensely profitable for makers of these things, while they themselves mistook the boom demand for post-War normality. The German districts of Bohemia were particularly attractive to tourists, especially short-term tourists from Germany, and tourist traffic swelled to unknown dimensions in the later twenties. The Sudeten Germans exerted themselves to provide for this, but they forgot that this sort of travelling is a luxury, too, and is immediately curtailed in bad times. Karlsbad (Karlovy Vary) and Marienbad (Mariánské Lázně) were more admittedly luxury affairs, which could never again hope to see visitors in the grand manner of pre-War days when they had been the favourite resorts of the Russian aristocracy; they, too, were unwilling to admit that the World War had inevitably effected a great levelling down, an economic revolution.

The erection of tariff barriers between all the Succession States was bad enough for Sudeten German industry, but its ulterior object, the economic self-sufficiency of the States concerned, was a more serious menace still. Even Czechoslovakia's intimate friends, her partners in the anti-Magyar Little Entente, were building up their own industries for all they were worth. Already in 1928 Czechoslovakia's export to both of them was falling. In 1927 she exported to Roumania goods to the value of 907,500,000 Kč, in 1928 to the value of 870,000,000 Kč, in 1929 to the value of 769,500,000 Kč.[1] The corresponding figures for Yugoslavia showed a similar development, where Reich German exports to Yugoslavia steadily rose. The expansion of the Polish textile industry, too, was ominous for the future.

The Sudeten German industrialists blamed the Czechoslovak Government for everything that went wrong. They complained that Czechoslovakia was a small country which could not negotiate on equal terms with Great Powers; they complained that it pursued a chauvinist tariff policy although the German textile people at Warnsdorf (Varnsdorf), for example, had themselves demanded higher tariffs against Germany and Austria soon after the War. The Sudeten Germans also complained that the Government favoured backward Czech firms, and, in doing so, injured quality standards. Of course people who know each other are more likely to help each other, and the people they do not know will therefore call them corrupt, with what justification it is difficult to determine. In the old days the German-Austrian firms had had the advantage in the matter of State contracts; after all one of their directors may have been related to the Minister's secretary. Now the Czechs had those opportunities, though a law was passed giving a local firm preference with regard to State contracts, even if its estimate were up to 5 per cent. higher. In the old days the Austro-Hungarian diplomats and consuls were nearly always German-Austrian or Hungarian, and recommended the representatives of a German-Austrian, rather than those of a Czech, firm abroad; now the case was undoubtedly reversed, in spite of the great number of high quality Sudeten German producers. Unnecessary insistence upon the use of Czech was also sometimes a hindrance to trade, especially to tourist traffic. It has been seen that the Kč had been stabilized at a level which experts mostly considered far too high. The Czechoslovak Government certainly made little use of Article 222 of the Treaty of St. Germain, largely because the Agrarians wished to keep foreign corn out. Indeed, in 1930 they broke off

[1] See a publication of the Deutscher Hauptverband der Industrie in Czechoslovakia entitled *Warum verträgt die Industrie der Tschechoslowakei keine Erhöhung der Erzeugungskosten?* (1930).

commercial relations with the Magyars for this reason, and dealt a bad blow at the already diminishing market of the Sudeten German manufacturers in Hungary. But Czechoslovakia could not have altered the general economic trend, nor could it alone re-create that great free-trade area in the Danube Valley which each of the Successor States wanted, provided the others were willing to make sacrifices. Nor could the Czechoslovak Government prevent Czech industrialists from absorbing the internal Czech- and Slovak-speaking market, any more than it could prevent Sudeten German manufacturers from themselves setting up factories in Roumania and Yugoslavia, and consequently employing less German labour at home. Examples of Sudeten German firms which emigrated were Peschel (hats), or Klinger (textiles), while the Aussig Chemical Company[1] (Aussiger Chemischer Verein) established plants abroad.

The figures for Czechoslovak foreign trade from 1926 to 1933 were as follows:

(In thousand Kč)

	Imports	Exports	Balance
1926	15,276,601	17,755,025	+2,478,424
1927	17,960,410	20,133,448	+2,173,038
1928	19,190,718	21,205,057	+2,014,339
1929	19,962,258	20,496,921	+534,663
1930	15,712,400	17,471,881	+1,759,481
1931	11,764,187	13,118,574	+1,354,387
1932	7,486,710	7,342,659	−144,051
1933	5,831,091	5,854,696	+23,605[2]

The fall in value from 1929 was, of course, much greater than the fall in volume. Since Czechoslovakia was dependent upon importing many of her raw materials, and since she had no foreign investments to speak of,[3] she was unable to afford an unfavourable balance—only in 1932 was she actually faced with one.

Thus the devastating slump, which, beginning with the Wall Street collapse of 1929, spread across Europe, had cast a faint shadow before it upon Czechoslovak foreign trade, while rationalization within various industries was paving the way towards large-scale unemployment. The Czechoslovak economic machine did not, on the other hand, break down so suddenly as did that of her neighbours; while Germany's production figures touched their lowest point in 1932, 1933 was the year of blackest depression in Czechoslovakia. The greater stability shown by the Republic

[1] See below.
[2] These are the official Czechoslovak figures. The Sudeten German Hauptverband der Industrie figures and those sent home by the British Legation in Prague vary a little, but the variations are insignificant.
[3] There were, of course, a number of Sudeten German investments in Germany and Austria.

in the slump years is partly accounted for by the steadiness of her banks and by the fact that she was not, like Germany, living on imported capital. Czechoslovak industry was, nevertheless, particularly dependent upon the availability of raw materials from abroad, i.e. she could not live comfortably without importing a good many. Further, the Central European area with which she was bound to be most intimately associated was precisely the one where, in 1931, the whole financial apparatus suddenly collapsed. It was in May of that year that the *Österreichische Kreditanstalt* broke down in Vienna (with repercussions in Hungary), and two months later the Danat Bank in the Reich, and the whole capitalistic system seemed to be crumbling away. Germany, Austria, and Hungary were all suffering so acutely from the flight of capital, that they introduced severe restrictions on the movement of money. Poland and Roumania were the only neighbouring countries which, like Czechoslovakia, struggled on for some time without introducing restrictions; indeed, Czechoslovakia was the first of these three to adopt certain minor limitations.

If the effects of the world slump were more gradual they were none the less serious for the Republic in the long run. It was now perforce that the economic disruption of old Austria-Hungary was completed, the efforts of the economic Little Entente[1] notwithstanding. Czechoslovak, and especially Sudeten German, industry understood how to cater for ex-Habsburg and Reich-German consumption, but showed a lack of adaptability to demands from further west. In any case when Great Britain had left the gold standard in 1931 the sterling-block markets became more difficult. Until 1931 there had been in effect a circulation of goods between Czechoslovakia, Great Britain, and the British Empire so that Czechoslovakia had sold cheap goods to Great Britain and imported raw materials from the Empire, but this was now well hit on the head, all the more with the British tariff of 1932.

Sudeten German industry was from every point of view the most vulnerable section of Czechoslovak industry, and nothing has so greatly envenomed the relations between Czechs and Sudeten Germans as this incorrigible fact. In the first place the German financial disasters of 1931, since the Sudeten Germans had chosen to place capital in the Reich, struck a direct blow at them; both the *Böhmische Escompte Bank*[2] and the *Böhmische Union Bank* found themselves with considerable sums frozen in Germany at a time when deposits were being hastily withdrawn, and some of them transferred to the *Živnostenská* and the *Zemská* Banks.

---

[1] See below, section (iv), p. 186.
[2] This bank, particularly, is considered to have taken too speculative risks with its Reichsmark holdings.

Secondly, quite apart from Germany itself, the Sudeten German banks, including the savings banks, were deeply involved in industry and had taken very grave risks.[1] The *Zentralbank der deutschen Sparkassen* was a striking case of a bank which had combined too great ambition with too little ability, and the dismay of many savings-bank investors was acute when it was forced to stop payment in 1932. The Sudeten Germans were now compelled to turn to Czech bankers who sometimes made hard offers about credits. They were scarcely in a position to do anything else at the time, but of course closer personal relations between Czech and German business men might have facilitated special consideration here and there. In 1932, moreover, the Czechoslovak Government felt called upon to pass a new reorganization law by which the banks were to be more severely controlled. In return the *Böhmische Escompte* and the *Böhmische Union* banks were to be helped out by the Czechoslovak National Bank, the *Zemská Banka* and the *Živnostenská Banka*; indeed, the National Bank provided the two Sudeten German banks with 300 million Kč without conditions. The National Bank also provided a loan of 111 million Kč to the Sudeten German savings banks in April 1933 at relatively low interest, and this figure rose later to a maximum of 327 million Kč.

The textile industry, in nearly all its branches, had become dependent upon the banks since 1922. With the great slump its financial foundations appeared to crack up beneath it, while its foreign markets, especially in the neighbouring countries, disappeared. To some extent the Sudeten German textile people had dug their own grave. Rationalization was an inevitable process; as soon as employers began to lose confidence they were bound even more to try to economize, and to worsen the general situation, at any rate for a time, by reducing the number of people they employed. But in textiles, as in glass and beads, the pressure from Japan early compelled Sudeten German entrepreneurs to reorganize. The tendency to emigrate into Hungary, Roumania, and Yugoslavia, though possibly an intelligent response to the autarchistic economic policy pursued long before 1929 by all the small countries, had deplorable results in the labour market at home, and accorded ill with the sentiments of responsibility towards their own people which were customarily uttered at large gatherings of employers. In addition to reliance upon Sudeten German and Reich German banks, whose weakness was now revealed, a number of German industrialists had themselves taken

[1] The following among other Sudeten German banks, at any rate in Czechoslovak opinion, are held to have behaved too rashly: *Karlsbader Volksbank, Reichenberger Volksbank, Deutsche Landbank* in Leitmeritz, *Deutsche Landbank* in Moravian Ostrava. The management of the *Kreditanstalt der Deutschen* is, on the other hand, generally praised.

unwarrantable financial risks; the direction of Liebig's great textile firm is criticized for devoting enthusiastic attention to technical achievement at the expense of blithely disregarding finance.

The slump descended upon Northern Bohemia like the plague. The figures, take them where you will, for the years from 1930 to 1933 tell a story of unmitigated catastrophe.

On 31st December, 1932, there were in Czechoslovakia 3,620,000 fine spindles for the spinning of Indian, American, Egyptian or similar cotton yarns. . . . Of this total number some 650,000 spindles are out of commission, and the remainder are in use at an average of 70 per cent. of capacity

wrote the Commercial Secretary to the British Legation in Prague, early in 1933;[1] the spindles referred to were very largely Sudeten German. The export of Czechoslovak carpets, for which Rumburg (Rumburk) is one great centre, fell from 60 million Kč in 1931 to 18 million Kč in 1932.[1] Of flax and linen the same authority reports that 'Of the 25 (flax) mills inherited from the Dual Monarchy only ten are working at present and these at only 40 per cent. of capacity'; Trautenau (Trutnov), Freiwaldau (Frývaldov), and Freudenthal (Brunthál) were the great linen centres.

According to the census of 1930, about 350,000 people, including clerks, technicians, and casual workers, were employed by the textile industry in Czechoslovakia. The majority of these were Sudeten German and all bound to lose in pay or in work or in both by the slump situation. The Union of German Textile Workers held an inquiry in 1937, when a certain degree of recovery had unquestionably taken place, into the number of concerns which had been ruined since 1929 in the Sudeten German *Randgebieten* area, from Asch (Aš) to Römerstadt (Rýmařov), in which it functions. It established that in:

West Bohemia (Asch)	11	concerns employing	945	people had	closed down
North-West Bohemia (= Bensen, Teplitz-Schönau, Weipert)	8	,,	1,870	,,	,,
Rumburg	5	,,	558	,,	,,
Warnsdorf	18	,,	1,420	,,	,,
Reichenberg, including Friedland, Kratzau, Gablonz, &c.	40	,,	6,005	,,	,,
Trautenau, including Braunau and Hohenelbe	44	,,	8,877	,,	,,
Moravian Schönberg	5	,,	1,810	,,	,,
Zwittau, including Moravian Trubau	3	,,	970	,,	,,
Jägerndorf	6	,,	696	,,	,,
Freudenthal	5	,,	807	,,	,,
Römerstadt	21	,,	2,221	,,	,,
making altogether	166	,,	26,179	,,	,,

[1] Great Britain: Department of Overseas Trade, *Report on Economic Conditions in Czechoslovakia* (March 1933).

Of these it was believed that for only thirty-four concerns even a slender hope of their reopening could be entertained.

If one goes into the villages around Reichenberg one discovers what the textile break-down meant for the people. In the village of Weisskirchen (Bílý Kostel) there were three textile factories which normally employed some 800 people. In 1931 they closed down because they had lost their markets. The machines have already been sold to competing countries abroad, and in 1937 the factory buildings were being pulled down. Perhaps no one but the working people whose lives depended upon those factories can altogether realize the psychological effect of the demolition of the factory buildings; the village has become a cemetery; the people prefer to stay indoors so that they shall not see that their source of life has dried up. In Weisskirchen it is not quite so bad as elsewhere because some one has opened a chocolate factory which provides unskilled work for a few hundreds for miserable wages. Conditions in a chocolate factory are not inspected as they would be in an important industry, and there is a conspiracy of silence among employers and employed, because the people are terrified that even the chocolate factory might go if there were complaints about the conditions.

In Görsdorf-Grottau the textile firm of Kosmanos used to employ 800 people until 1932, since when they have been dismissed and the village ruined. At Kratzau (Chrastava) the firm of Klinger & Co. is employing some 50 people instead of the 600 or 800 who worked for them previously; the same owners employed over 800 people in two other concerns. Their management wasted its resources on impressive offices in Vienna until the confidence of their bankers was forfeited. At the village of Haindorf (Hejnice) the textile firm of Simon, formerly employing 300 people, has broken down. Near Friedland (Frýdlant), at Heinersdorf, the Heintschel textile factory has been closed since about 1930 and destitution has overtaken the villagers, though the Heintschel manor-house looks prosperous enough. In a typical family which had hitherto lived comfortably there, while the husband gets 3 or 4 weeks' (paid) annual relief work on the roads, his wife and, say, mother or sister can get work to do at home—interlacing shawl fringes, to be quite exact—by which each woman, working as long as she is able, earns about 5 or 6 Kč a day. This was occurring in 1937, when there was a little more work about but prices had risen; the work is provided by a middleman who is able to keep up a few of the Heintschel connexions; though the sterling exchange was about 140 Kč, prices are a good deal lower than in England and 5 Kč can be said to go about as far as 1s. At Dittersbach (Dětřichov), also near Friedland, two Reich German brothers owned several mills, but when the depression had reached its nadir in 1933 they shut down and disappeared into Germany, where one became an S.A. camp commandant at Görlitz and the other was given a post in Berlin. Meanwhile a foreman managed to keep some of the people at work for some time.

It is not surprising if such scenes give rise to inaccurate narration, and it will perhaps be simpler to add one or two comments at once, before fully embarking upon the Czech-German controversies born of the slump. Though these districts are overwhelmingly German, a third of the unemployed in Weisskirchen in 1937 were, to my knowledge, Czechs, a surprisingly high proportion. It is customary, in German circles, to suggest that the Government sees to it that the Czechs are always in work. It is customary, too, to declare *tout net* that Czechs deliberately removed the textile machines from German factories at Kratzau and Heinersdorf, and set them up at Hradec Králové (Königgrätz), and Dvůr Králové (Königinhof). The actual fact is that in both these towns there was an old-established Czech textile industry which catered mainly for the Czech interior. When the slump descended and the German concerns near by were ruined, the German entrepreneurs were glad to realize something on their machines by selling to any one who was willing to buy them, and the buyers happened to be these Czech firms.

The woollen industry of Czechoslovakia declined less suddenly than the cotton and linen branches of the textile industry as a whole, but it has also encountered almost greater difficulties in recovering a little, and finds it easier to pick up on exporting yarns which can only build up competition abroad. In addition to home markets, the woollen industry of old Austria-Hungary had supplied large amounts to Turkey, Roumania, and Germany,[1] while Austria exported 109 million pre-War crowns' worth of woollen goods to Hungary in 1913 in spite of Hungary's efforts to produce textiles in Slovakia. The most famous centre for woollens was and remains Brno (Brünn), which, for obvious geographical reasons, depended particularly upon the Hungarian demand. In July 1914 the Brno woollen industry was employing 17,419 factory-workers and in 1928 it attained its post-War maximum of 16,814. In 1933 it was down to 8,405, continued to decline very slightly until 1935, but at last began to show signs of improvement after that. The Brno industry is relevant from two points of view—(a) the direction and clerical staff have always been German and continued to be so after the War; and (b) the employees, as long as any one can remember, have been preponderantly Czech. Thus it is clearly shown that the Czechoslovak Government could do no more to

[1] e.g. in 1912 11 million pre-War crowns' worth to Turkey.

	10·8	,,	,,	,,	Roumania.
	8·6	,,	,,	,,	Germany.

protect the Czech weavers of Brno from the slump than the German weavers around Reichenberg; indeed, the economic breach with Hungary in 1930 probably injured Brno more. Actually the Brno workers suffered less, but solely on account of the structure of the Brno industry where the factories are nearly all in the town. This avoids the risk of whole village populations depending upon one factory. The Brno wool-workers often live a long way out, for their dearest wish is to own a cottage and garden, however small they may be; once equipped with these they are less sensitive to economic depression, for the soil of Southern Moravia is fertile and it is easy to keep poultry and grow vegetables. Sweating conditions do not exist because the work is all done in factories, and the Brno woollen industry is the heir to an enlightened social tradition.

According to the calculations of the Deutscher Hauptverband der Industrie in 1930,[1] while 54·2 per cent. of the cotton goods, 61·7 per cent. of the woollens and 67·6 per cent. of the silk goods produced were normally being exported from Czechoslovakia, the figures for plate glass were 79·2 per cent., for bottle glass 77·3 per cent., for Gablonz glass ornaments, &c., 95 per cent. Of the glass industry, which is mainly centred in Teplitz-Schönau (Teplice-Šanov), headquarters of the big Mühlig glass concern,[2] and, of course, in Gablonz (Jablonec), it is also worth noting that the number of glass-workers employed sank in 1933 to about 30,000,[3] where in the early post-War years more than 60,000 were kept busy. It is, however, difficult to get unquestioned figures here, since so many glass-workers in the Isergebirge villages to the north of Gablonz work in their homes with their families and are not organized; a great many others work in small workshops. South of Gablonz a considerable number of Czechs are involved in glass-making. The dependence of this town upon world prosperity is also conveyed by the fact that, small though it is, it contains between 500 and 600 exporters, mostly concerned with buttons, beads, and buckles made of some kind of glass. In foreign markets it is protected against the Japs only by greater proximity to the dictators of European (not American) fashions.[4] The potters and porcelain-makers are just as vulnerable, and indeed the china industry, which had been exporting to the extent of nearly 90 per cent., seems the most hopeless of all. The chief firm, Epiag, of

[1] Op. cit. The textile percentages are reckoned on quantities produced, the rest on value.
[2] Produces mostly glass for windows, but also bottle glass.
[3] *Deutsches Wirtschaftsjahrbuch für die Tschechoslowakei, 1937*; that the main collapse for Gablonz was 1922–3 is clearly shown in Fig. 52 in E. Winkler, *Die Tschechoslowakei im Spiegel der Statistik* (Karlsbad, 1937). The Diagram is based on Czechoslovak official statistics.
[4] As a matter of fact, Japanese pressure has recently lessened on account of the Sino-Japanese War which broke out in 1937.

Karlsbad (Karlovy Vary), was formed at the end of the War by the grouping together of a number of small local industries in the neighbourhood. It had startling successes in the first post-War boom, only to collapse in 1922. Until then it had been financed by the Vienna *Handelsbank*, but was subsequently bought up by the 'Anglo-Bank',[1] by whom it has ever since been entirely controlled. With the slump of the thirties Epiag lost about two-thirds of its foreign trade, and whereas in nearly all other industries some recovery has taken place, in this one, where the break-down was so immensely severe, very little improvement has occurred or seems likely to do so. While the home market has expanded a little, international insecurity, sanctions (in 1936), and self-sufficiency have effectually cancelled out that gain. Epiag employs about a third of the china-workers in Czechoslovakia; for the remaining two-thirds the story is very much the same. Being almost entirely in the Karlsbad district, they are almost all Germans; even among those who have work, there is, of course, a great deal of short time.

The North Bohemian lignite mines had difficulties of their own with which to contend in the post-War years. For one thing, any inclination of the Ministry of Railways to use hard coal rather than lignite was justified by the greater efficiency of the former, and a perpetual tussle went on between the direction of the mines around Brüx (Most) and of those worked by mainly Czech miners around Ostrava (Ostrau); it was genuinely difficult for the State railways to stick to the inferior product, though the Germans inevitably felt injured when they failed to do so. Again, house-heating technique was changing and called for smaller pieces of coal, which were in fact more expensive to produce. But of course lignite mining was particularly vulnerable in the great world depression since the fall in glass, china, and textile production automatically reduced the demand for the lignite from the mines which were so closely linked with the North Bohemian industries.

It will be seen that the improvement in 1934 was not maintained in 1935, and though there was some improvement in 1937 the outlook is a fairly gloomy one, largely owing to German autarchic determination.[2] The privately owned[3] Brüx shafts are cut out by those owned by the State[4] when it is a question of State tenders, and to this extent the Czech miner has a very slight advantage over the German, since the proportion of Czechs in the employ of the State is a little higher. Roughly the Brüx (Most) mining popula-

[1] Anglo-Czechoslovak and Prague Credit Bank.
[2] The Saxon mines have offered serious competition ever since the War, but the effect has been intensified by the policy of Nazi Germany.
[3] Mostly owned by branches of the Petschek family or by Herr Weinmann.
[4] The State owns about 15 per cent. of the Brüx shafts.

tion is half and half; it is some four times as large as the almost entirely German mining population of Falkenau. The figures show that the drop in the export of lignite affected the Falkenau people relatively less than those around Brüx.

The position created by the slump was as follows:[1]

Production

	In the whole of Czechoslovak territory	In the Brüx shafts	In the Falkenau shafts
	tons	tons	tons
1913	22,600,000	18,087,000	4,095,000
1929	22,655,000	17,393,000	4,262,000
1932	15,910,000	12,063,000	2,990,000
1933	15,125,000	11,503,000	2,795,000
1934	15,258,000	11,377,000	2,919,000
1935	15,226,000	11,464,000	2,787,000

Export figures

	From the whole of Czechoslovak territory	From the Brüx shafts	From the Falkenau shafts
	tons	tons	tons
1913	8,425,000	6,757,000	1,659,000
1929	3,123,000	2,064,000	1,050,000
1932	1,544,000	857,000	684,000
1933	1,655,000	915,000	740,000
1934	1,837,000	993,000	844,000
1935	1,717,000	953,000	764,000

On the whole figures and observation concur to show that the chemical and heavy industry suffered a great deal less sharply than textiles or china.

The chemical industry is represented by the huge Schicht concern at Aussig (Ústí) which employs perhaps 2 to 3 per cent. of Czechs, and the Aussig Chemical Company, whose chief factories are at Aussig, Falkenau, Lobositz (Lobosice), and in Slovakia; thus the industry as a whole employs a majority of Germans. Heavy industry concerns the German population relatively little, though there are metal-works scattered about the mainly German territory, at Komotau (Chomutov), where the Reich German firm of Mannesmann works, at Teplitz-Schönau (Teplice-Šanov), Bodenbach (Podmokly), Böhmisch Leipa (České Lipa), and at Eger

[1] These figures are taken from the *Deutsches Wirtschaftsjahrbuch für die Tschechoslowakei*. They do not exactly coincide with those published by the Czechoslovak Statistical Office, but show the same tendencies. These statistical discrepancies frequently occur, not, I think, for any reason other than different bases of calculation. I happened to use the German figures because they gave a longer sequence of figures of production, *not* because I have more or less faith in them. In any case there are Germans in the Government Statistical Office in Prague.

(Cheb), where the bicycle industry flourishes. If on the whole the employees in these industries have suffered the least, the most terrible distress of all—even worse than that in the villages dependent on the textile factories—overtook the people who depended upon the home industries of the Erzgebirge, and the one large-scale disaster in the metal industry served to blacken the gloom in a region whose outlook was already sufficiently dark.

The small towns of the Erzgebirge, such as Graslitz (Kraslice), Joachimsthal (Jachymov), Neudek (Nejdek), and Rothau (Rotava), had always lived dangerously. They suffered, like the towns and villages on the Saxon side of the frontier, from very poor soil, few communications, and the extreme disinclination of their inhabitants to leave their homes in the mountains. In pre-War depressions their poor standard of living had degenerated into distress, but pre-War depressions were short; even in those days it had been thought necessary to plant a State tobacco factory at Joachimsthal to provide relief. After the War fashion proceeded to destroy the markets for the lace-makers scattered about the Erzgebirge; the *Zeitgeist*, after all, had turned against frills and lace curtains. Graslitz, which has been made into a by-word for Sudeten German distress to-day, has since the sixteenth century been a centre for the making of musical instruments,[1] and for musical and other toys which require minor varieties of similar skill. Firms like Kohlert's[2] made the musical instruments for the old Imperial army, but the Czech army patronizes an old Hradec Králové (Königgrätz) firm. Here, as in textiles, Japanese competition[3] was injurious, yet from about 1925 until 1930 the Graslitz industry did well, and the propagandist picture of quite unlimited distress tends to be misleading. The development of the wireless industry has not, in actual practice, proved injurious for the best Graslitz firms; on the contrary they believe it has stimulated demand. Although on the eve of the slump the musical instrument industry was 90 per cent. dependent upon export,[4] Kohlert's themselves never did better than in 1937,[5] partly, no doubt, because their best customer is the United States.

While Kohlert's employs about 300 people in the factory and 200 people working at home, the position in Graslitz as a whole is best summed up by the fact that whereas the five biggest firms in the

[1] When the supplies of iron were exhausted (see note 3, p. 175 below), the inhabitants took to making musical instruments because of the lavishly available wood provided by the forests.

[2] Kohlert's itself was founded in 1840, but the music instrument industry upon a larger scale dates from some thirty years later.

[3] In Germany later rival industries have also grown up.

[4] See Deutscher Hauptverband der Industrie in der ČSR, op. cit.

[5] Even before 1914 this firm lived mainly upon export. Since 1936 they have been sending a good deal to Great Britain.

town paid out 19 million Kč in wages in 1929, in 1936 they paid about 6 million Kč to about half the same number of workers.[1] The practical result of these figures is an appalling amount of sweated labour at home. Two representative examples are as follows:

(a) A family of four, each of them working 10 or 11 hours, are able to turn out about 20 dozen toy trumpets in the day; for this they receive 20 Kč altogether, but are forced to spend about 2 of the 20 Kč upon necessary raw material. Thus there remain about 18 Kč, say the equivalent of 3s. 6d. for the four of them per day.

(b) In another family of four, one woman was embroidering at the rate of 5 Kč (equivalent to the value of 1s.) for two days', and another at the rate of 25 Kč for a fortnight's work.

Payment at these rates destroys any claim to relief and is yet too low to entitle its recipients to any kind of insurance.[2]

Terrible though these conditions are, no government of a fairly small State in very hard times could have brought any great alleviation. It has been seen that the victims themselves condone the sweating which might otherwise be legally prevented. One firm which employed over 1,000 people upon the manufacture of musical toys has closed down in Graslitz because the combination of its natural indebtedness and the fortuitous accumulation of death duties frightened the *Bank für Handel und Industrie* into refusing further credit. Perhaps a more magnanimous government might have proved helpful. But there are other cases in Graslitz of a reasonable generosity from the Czechoslovak National Bank.

The most tragic village in the Erzgebirge is that of Rothau (Rotava), near Neudek (Nejdek). The local *grand seigneur*, Count Nostitz, owned an iron and steel works there before the War,[3] and employed altogether some 1,100 people in the neighbourhood. The position, however, was unfavourable, partly because the railway connexion was bad, the works being a long way from a very small station on a branch line; even in pre-War days a removal had been spoken of. After the bad period 1922–3 the foundry was nevertheless tremendously improved, and produced first-class steel of world-wide reputation; indeed by 1926 it was scarcely able to

[1] While the men are mostly musical instrument makers in Graslitz, the women find employment in textiles when times are not too bad.

[2] There are homes in Graslitz which are a lamentable sight, but some of the photographs of them which have been shown in foreign countries were taken in the sheds to which nine families were temporarily transferred after a tenement house had been burnt down.

[3] Iron had been mined in the Erzgebirge until the sixteenth century, and though the local supplies then came to an end, a smithy tradition survived and had been continuously developed, adapting itself to the new processes of the nineteenth century.

carry out its orders. Whereas in 1922 it was employing 2,350 people to produce 14,270 tons of sheet-metal, in 1929 it employed 1,780 to produce 31,400 tons.[1] These figures indicate the degree of rationalization, a distressing problem in itself. Branches of the concern were employing hundreds of men at Neudek and Schindelwald as well. From 1926 working conditions were improved, so that the men only did six-hour shifts, wages were kept up, and production continued to increase until 1929. In 1922 a certain Herr Doderer had come from the Poldi Hütte to be managing director of the Rothau-Neudek Foundry. His attitude was that of the typical German national employer and he was dissatisfied with the inconveniences of the Rothau site. In order to make bigger profits still he looked round for a better position, though the finances of the company were in excellent condition; whereas in 1922 it had had debts to the value of 53 million Kč, already in 1927 its assets were up to 27 millions.

In 1929, then, unprecedented catastrophe overtook Rothau, for Herr Doderer, in that most critical year, brought about a fusion of his concern with the big *Berg- und Hütten-Werk* at Frýdek (Friedek), near the Silesian hard coal-mines. News of the transaction was first made public in November 1928, to the consternation of the metal-workers' trades union. Inquiries were held in 1930; at first it was airily suggested that 800 workmen could be transferred, but it then became clear, on the one hand that orders were falling off, and on the other that neither the authorities of Moravia-Silesia nor the population around Frýdek would allow a serious infraction of the population proportions (83 per cent. Czech, 17 per cent. German) in any factory round there. In the end about 200 men were transferred to the east, for 68 work was found at Škoda's, and a handful were kept on at Rothau and Neudek themselves. Indirectly it was a blow, too, to Falkenau mining and to dependent concerns such as a perambulator factory at Graslitz.

After very careful inquiry I am satisfied that the transfer from Rothau to Frýdek was not in any way due to official or unofficial Czech pressure, though hints to this effect are generously distributed. The decision to move was due to the simple desire to gain greater profit in apparent indifference to the social results. Rothau to-day is a cemetery indeed. The enormous foundry buildings stand empty, deserted, and largely dismantled. The population fell from 3,782 in 1930 to 3,188 in 1937. There seems to be no one with a properly paid job. People work at home on toys or needlework; the Social Democrats have started a co-operative organization which is able to organize work for about 180 people. The sweet-faced woman at the central village inn tells one that

[1] Figures supplied by the International Metal-Workers' Union.

before the foundry was closed she sold as much beer in a month as now in a year. Real efforts have been made to relieve the distress. From 1930 to 1937 the Metal-workers' Trades Union paid out 42 million Kč in relief under the Ghent system,[1] the State contributing about two-thirds of this total; further, the Ministry of Social Welfare has provided large amounts of bread, milk, potatoes, &c. Still more important, every avenue has been explored in the hope of establishing new and permanent employment of some kind. Here every imaginable difficulty has been encountered, obstruction from rival industrialists, unsound propositions from persons who only wished to get hold of a subsidy from the State; the Metal-workers' Union hoped at one point to put up a scythe factory of their own, but were foiled by the obstinate fidelity of the peasants around to the scythes they have always imported from Styria. At the moment of writing (January 1938) a satisfactory plan has at last been reached by which an entrepreneur from Neuern in the Böhmerwald is to expand his optical instruments concern by taking over the foundry buildings at Rothau. He should be able to take on 400 workers there without reducing the numbers he employs at Neuern. Dr. Czech,[2] Monsieur Nečas,[3] and the Director of the *Berg- und Hütten-Werk*, Monsieur Kruliš Randa,[4] are warmly supporting the project, and the Ministry of Defence has given the consent which is necessary in a district so near to the Saxon frontier. Whether the Czechs are to deserve any blame in this question will now be decided by the willingness or unwillingness of the Ministry of Finance to provide the financial guarantee required by the entrepreneur from Neuern.[5]

The rise of Sudeten German nationalist feeling since 1933 has been so much associated with Sudeten German economic distress that the political complexion of a place like Rothau deserves consideration. In the elections of May 1935, after some five years of destitution, the Rothau people still gave 1,038 votes to the Social Democrat Party and at the same time 698 to the S.d.P.[6] and 294 to the Communists, the other parties being negligible here. These figures showed a gain of 70 votes for the S.d.P. as compared with the local elections of 1934. They do, however, correct the too easy assumption that the S.d.P. is a refuge for all Sudeten Germans in economic distress, and suggest the extraordinary tenacity of the old pre-War Socialist tradition of the Erzgebirge.

[1] See below, section (v).
[2] Minister of Health and leader of the Sudeten German Social Democrats until April 1938.   [3] Minister of Social Welfare until March 1938.
[4] M. Kruliš Randa has offered to help finance the new venture.
[5] The situation has been transformed by this gentleman's arrest in Austria after the annexation of Austria by Germany.
[6] See chapter XIV.

A little way west from Rothau and Neudek, high up in the Erzgebirge, is the small town of Joachimsthal (Jachymov), from whose mines, since the days of the Curies, early in the century, radium has been extracted. From these mines, like those at Schneeberg[1] across the Saxon frontier, mysterious emanations induce a form of what is now diagnosed as cancer; this has hitherto cut short the lives of at least half the miners. Nationalistic Sudeten German propagandists do not hesitate to announce that the Czechoslovak authorities make no attempt whatever to safeguard the miners because they are German,[2] and in fact that the Czechs are content that the miners should die. Such propagandists do their utmost to embitter the men themselves, and it is necessary, therefore, to examine the case with particular care.

The Joachimsthal mine belonged to the old Austrian State, and in 1919 was taken over by the Czechoslovak Republic. Until 1929 it was managed very much as it had been before—certainly no worse, for conditions under Austria were admittedly bad. In 1929 Dr. Löwy of Prague established for the first time with certainty a clear case of cancer in a miner who sickened in the usual Joachimsthal way, and President Masaryk immediately gave 300,000 Kč for further research. In the next year or so the mine's direction, at the dictation of the doctors, inaugurated a system of ventilation to dispel emanations, and a system of watering to lay the dust of the splintered rock surface in the mine; arrangements for the medical examination of the miners were also made,[3] baths put in, &c. The medical advisers say that all their recommendations have been carried out. They themselves are in touch with Reich German medical authorities; neither the Czechoslovak nor the Reich German doctors know what else to recommend, and the results of the measures hitherto taken can only be gauged by about 1940.

In addition to the ventilation and watering, the doctors recommend that the standard of living of the miners shall be as high and as easy as possible. The ordinary miner in Czechoslovakia is entitled to ten days' holiday in the year, but the Joachimsthal miners have nearly twice as much. Their wages are about 10 per cent. higher than elsewhere in the Republic, but this is neutralized by the fact that, partly in the interests of their health, they were reduced in 1935 to a forty-hour week. About the same time a law was passed by which a man who becomes ill through his work is entitled to a pension, which goes to his family if he dies; in the case

[1] Cobalt, nickel, &c., but not radium itself, are mined at Schneeberg.
[2] At the moment under 300 miners are employed and of these about 5 per cent.—a mere handful—are Czechs. The propagandists also tell one that in the Reich the cancer problem has been solved and no miner falls ill.
[3] One Czech and one German doctor is always available, and the miners are examined four times a year.

of Joachimsthal the miners, once ill, die very soon, so that this is a help to their families, not to themselves.

Joachimsthal is a particularly difficult problem for the Czecho-slovak State. The value of radium to humanity is so great that every one agrees that it far outweighs the penalty paid by some of the miners. In recent years, however, Canada and Belgium have been producing radium far more cheaply than Czechoslovakia. Thus Joachimsthal is run at a loss, yet requires more and more outlay on behalf of the miners. The men, egged on by those who have a political interest in exploiting the situation, tell one that the ventilation and watering are all no good, and that nothing can help them but to work only for twelve years. Tragic though the circumstances of their life clearly are—on an average they have hitherto lived to 42 or 43—it is an unprecedented demand that a miner at Joachimsthal should work, say, from 18 to 30 and be pensioned by the State for the rest of his life,[1] the more since the doctors expect that the improvements in the mine will prove to have lengthened the miners' lives a good deal. As for the behaviour of the Czechoslovak authorities it seems true to say that it has been characteristic. They have done what could be done conscientiously but ungracefully. By placing Czechs in the responsible positions in the management of the mine and the associated laboratories they have allowed it to appear as if Czech officials were profiting from a deplorable situation; it would have been wiser not to have introduced a new identification of the national with the social question in Joachimsthal.

Apart from the radium mine, Joachimsthal depends upon the tobacco factory mentioned above, upon glove-making, and upon tourists or invalids; all mountain sport is available for the former, and radium treatment on the spot is available for the latter.

The North and North-West Bohemian tourist and spa 'industry' must now be considered, since a large population had been accustomed to get through the winter on their earnings as waiters or chambermaids in the hotels during the season, and the Erzgebirge people had relied upon selling their toys to the foreign visitors in Karlsbad (Karlovy Vary).

At (1) *Karlsbad* the record pre-War year was 1911, with 70,935 *Kurgäste*, i.e. visitors drinking the waters, exclusive of merely healthy tourists.

The best post-War years were 1928 with 67,675 *Kurgäste*
1929 ,, 66,802 ,,
The worst post-War year was 1933 ,, 37,818 ,,

[1] The only possibility of an arrangement of this kind would arise if the miners were willing to be transferred to some other job for a time, but the Joachimsthal people are particularly conservative and unwilling to leave their homes and traditional jobs, come what may.

It should be borne in mind that although the 1928 figure was very near to that of 1911, the post-War visitors had less to spend.

(2) *Marienbad* (Mariánské Lázně):

Pre-War record	1911	.	. 34,508	visitors staying longer than 5 days.		
Best post-War years	1928	.	. 39,362	,,	,,	,,
	1929	.	. 41,226	,,	,,	,,
Worst post-War year	1933	.	. 21,503	,,	,,	,,

(3) *Franzensbad* (Františkovy Lázně):

Best post-War years	1928	.	. 18,402	*Kurgäste*
	1929	.	. 18,287	,,
Worst post-War years	1933	.	. 9,786	,,
	1935	.	. 9,512	,,
	1936	.	. 9,640	,,

(4) *Teplitz-Schönau* (Teplice-Šanov):

1929	.	. . 8,606	*Kurgäste*
1933	.	. . 4,820	,,
1936	.	. . 4,700	,,

Thus in the German spas the average drop from 1929 to 1933 was a reduction of guests by nearly a half; for 1937 there was in each of these four centres a very definite improvement. The total figure for *Kurgäste* from abroad[1] to all the spas of Czechoslovakia was in

1929	.	.	.	158,139
1933	.	.	.	60,144
1934	.	.	.	75,777
1935	.	.	.	76,578
1936	.	.	.	72,680

The Slovak must therefore have suffered more severely in 1933 than the German spas, with regard to foreign visitors upon whom, however, they depended less. It seems reasonable, therefore, to conclude that, although the Czechoslovak authorities certainly take more trouble about publicity for Piešťany[2] than publicity for Karlsbad, the Sudeten German spas in the Republic have not suffered more than the others.

Lastly, industry in Southern Bohemia deserves consideration. It is on a much smaller scale than in the north; the great depression, therefore, did not spell such tremendous ruin, but for the same reason the outlook for the future is gloomier, since the essential reorganization of small-scale activities is worth no one's while Timber[3] from the *Böhmerwald* districts, and graphite, are the chief natural products, so that Budějovice (Budweis) has become the head-quarters of Hardmuth and other pencil production, while it

[1] These are figures kindly supplied by the Central Association of Czecho slovak Spas and Health Springs.
[2] One has only to go into the *Čedok* office in Prague to see this, but the Czech say every one has heard of Karlsbad after all.
[3] Furniture and *Solo* matches are consequently made in South Bohemia.

has been seen that the big Spiro paper-mills have been working at Krumau (Česky Krumlov) since 1862. For a narrow strip of mostly poor and mountainous territory, where communication was always difficult and bad, the creation of the Czech-Austrian frontier was a disaster in itself. Spiro found itself mainly dependent upon river communication, for the Moldau (Vltava) fortunately connects Krumau with the Elbe, and therefore with Hamburg and the world. While this firm employed about 2,300 hands in 1930, it is now down to about 1,650,[1] a slight improvement on the worst slump years; rationalization has countered the effects of recovery on employment, and the prospects of capturing fresh markets are dim. There is another paper-mill (Porak) at Kienberg (Loučovice). The graphite situation is frankly a bad one because the graphite is running out. In September 1937 the closing down of graphite production at the village of Schwarzbach (Černa) was expected at any moment, and about 80 people would thus be deprived of their living. And there is the same story to tell as in Northern Bohemia, viz. Hardmuth's has found it more profitable to reduce production at home and open factories abroad; thus though this German firm still employs a mainly German clerical staff,[2] that staff has had to be reduced with consequent hardship for Germans. New Czech firms have appeared since the War, but they obviously take on Czech clerks in a town like Budějovice where the Germans now form only 14 per cent. of the population. The fact that the German population has been steadily losing ground for so long in Budějovice has economic results of this kind which inevitably radiate outwards to the disadvantage of the Germans in the country around. Czech competition in the Budějovice breweries began long before the War, and has naturally continued to grow. Apart from this, a concern such as Westen's enamel-ware production in the circumstances of to-day is fortunate to be employing about two-thirds of the numbers it employed in 1913. This, by the way, is a very nationalistic firm, founded by a Reich German in 1892, where only Germans are engaged, but there is little evidence to show that it is any the worse off in consequence; its management complains of neglect in the matter of State contracts, of course. And, as elsewhere in the Bohemian *Randgebieten*, post-War, and still more post-slump, circumstances have enormously reduced tourist activity in the Böhmerwald. Tourism here was never in the grand manner, but rather a matter of people with rucksacks crossing the frontier for the

[1] Spiro employ rather less Czechs than the Czech-German proportions of Krumau (about 24 : 76) would indicate. Even according to the Austrian census of 1910, the Czechs in Krumau were about 18 per cent., so that very little change has taken place.

[2] The hands have always been predominantly Czech, and the Koh-i-noor pencil is claimed as a Czech discovery.

week-end and bringing money to small inns; the innkeeper's income has been quite as much reduced as that of the *Kurhaus* proprietor of Karlsbad, but it is more difficult for him to ventilate his troubles or for any deliberate action to be taken to alleviate them.

(iv) DIFFICULTIES WITH GERMANY OVER COMMERCE AND CURRENCY QUESTIONS

With a country so dependent upon foreign trade as Czechoslovakia it is virtually impossible to disentangle the complex of industry from that of finance and commerce. The Czechoslovak Republic had commercially continued her historic association with the old Alpine provinces which constituted post-War Austria, and, although this fragment of an empire had only some 6 million inhabitants, it was not until the middle twenties that Czechoslovakia was able to sell a little more to the 65 millions of Germans in the Reich; even in 1930 her exports to Austria (2,443 million Kč) were only some 500 million Kč less in value than her exports to Germany (2,971 million Kč).[1] The financial break-down in both German-speaking countries in 1931, as I have already suggested, was thus a catastrophe on the very doorstep of Czechoslovakia. In the matter of that curious exporting medium, the foreign visitor from abroad, the repercussions were most immediate, since the Germans and Austrians were the greatest frequenters of Karlsbad (Karlovy Vary) and Marienbad (Mariánské Lázně), and now their National Banks became unwilling to allow them enough currency for them to continue to travel abroad. The visitors from Germany to the Czechoslovak spas fell from 83,156 in 1930 to 59,991 in 1931, and to 30,110 in 1933; the Austrians fell from 14,708 to a minimum of 8,823 in 1932.[2]

Although it has been seen that the Slovak spas were about as severely paralysed by the slump as those in the Historic Provinces, the Sudeten Germans assumed that the Czechoslovak Government was indifferent to their own deprivation and made no effort to counteract it; indeed, it is often suggested that Czechoslovakia was so inherently anti-German that she was perfectly willing to see her commercial relations with Germany injured.[3] It would seem more

[1] Germany's imports were kept down by the inflation crisis until 1924. It should be noted that Germany mostly imported from Czechoslovakia for direct consumption while Austria did a great deal of re-exporting.

[2] Figures kindly supplied by the Central Association of Czechoslovak Spas and Health Springs.

[3] Many Sudeten Germans speak as if Czechoslovakia had refused to be on normal terms of commercial relationship with Germany. Actually there was a hiatus owing to delayed negotiations in 1926, but nothing worse. It is true that Czechoslovakia did not become part of a tariff union with Germany as the Sudeten Germans in the old *Mittel-Europa* tradition desired, but her other treaties did not in any case permit her to do so; moreover, a tariff union of this kind would have been injurious to a great many Sudeten German industries.

accurate to say that, quite apart from sentiment and prejudice, the Czechs had too much common sense for this to be true. Czech-German negotiations over tourists were opened in September 1932, and the Czechs granted special terms for the visitors from Germany only; because of their importance to the Sudeten spa towns, Reich German guests were allowed to draw money on German blocked accounts in Czechoslovakia. These accounts, however, were soon used up, indeed overdrawn, since some German visitors managed to bring cheques which were not really covered; against these they ran up debts which the *Reichsbank* gradually paid off later. Czechoslovakia, caught up in the throes of foreign exchange regulations herself since 1931, was, after all, incapable of making unreciprocal concessions.

In 1934 new tendencies made themselves abruptly felt. On their side the Czechoslovaks in February of that year effected a long overdue change, i.e. they depreciated their currency by about 17 per cent. In the Reich, on the other hand, the character of the new National Socialist régime received economic expression.[1] Germany, having defaulted not only on her financial but also on her commercial debts, began[2] the policy of importing large quantities of goods from smaller countries, in return for which, since she had not enough foreign exchange to pay, she virtually compelled them to accept large amounts of the manufactured goods for which she required markets. Since 1928 Germany had exported more to Czechoslovakia than she received from her. Indeed, the Czechs had been finding their German bill altogether too large. In April 1933, therefore, they negotiated a special agreement with Germany according to which it was agreed that the ratio of German goods going into Czechoslovakia to Czech goods coming into Germany should be somewhere about 5 : 4. Soon after this Germany began to make high bids for Czechoslovak as for Yugoslav goods, and during 1934 the import of Czechoslovak goods into Germany steadily rose, until, in November of that year, Czechoslovakia found herself with nearly 30 million marks owing to her. Fresh negotiations had been opened with Germany late in September. They proved exceedingly difficult since both sides now wanted to buy raw materials and sell finished goods; a few raw materials from Germany, for instance small quantities of Brandenburg sand and Brunswick salt for glass, were almost indispensable to Czechoslovak, and especially to Sudeten German, industry, while Reich German manufactures were expensive and of deteriorating quality. It was also annoying to other countries at the time that Germany

[1] Cf. the rigid control of all imports introduced by Germany on Sept. 24th, 1934.

[2] German commercial policy in Weimar times had shown the actual beginnings of this development which was, in itself, a return to pre-War tendencies.

was reselling their produce in order to acquire more foreign exchange, though their own credits in Germany remained frozen. The Czechs now tried to safeguard themselves against these German practices; they also pushed very hard for lace, glass, buttons, and beads, i.e. for the Erzgebirge and Gablonz (Jablonec), rather than for the textile manufacturers, whom they regarded as better able to take care of themselves.[1] It came to bargaining that with so much timber, the Reich Germans should also help Gablonz or Graslitz (Kraslice) to such and such an extent, to do which, however, they showed no inclination at all. At last a compromise was reached on November 20th, 1934, and Czechoslovak exports were stabilized at a figure slightly short of 100 million marks' worth per annum, divided roughly as follows:

  (i) Lignite,[2] 20 per cent. of this total.
  (ii) Agricultural goods, 30 per cent.
  (iii) Raw materials, 10 per cent.
  (iv) Semi-finished goods, 12·5 per cent.
  (v) Finished goods, 25 per cent.

Lignite involved several German employers and a good many German miners; the finished goods would, to a considerable extent, be made by Sudeten Germans; these two together accounted for about 43 million marks' worth. The semi-finished goods included the yarns produced at Trautenau and Hohenelbe (Vrchlabí) in East Bohemian German territory. Even the agricultural goods and raw materials were not to bring any striking advantage to the Czechoslovak, as opposed to the Sudeten German, population. The first involved a great deal of timber produced chiefly in State or German-owned forests, but 4 million marks' worth of hops were included and these would be produced by the German concerns of Keller and Sonnenschein at Saaz (Žatec)—if, like the lignite-owners, these firms were German-Jewish, most of their employees were innocent of any racial flaw. Neither Czech-produced sugar nor geese were allowed for by the quotas now fixed. Raw materials included a good deal coming from the Czechoslovak interior, but also 3 millions' worth of china clay which was partly contributed by the Karlsbad district. It would be difficult to show that the Czech negotiators sacrificed Sudeten German interests by this agreement, indeed, they seem, as no doubt they should, to have considered them carefully in spite of the difficulties made by their Reich German opposite numbers. The 1934 Agreement has remained the basis of Czech-German commerce, and although the Czech

[1] The Sudeten German cotton manufacturers, by the way, were pressing for the facilitation of the sale of cotton products against marks while they wished to acquire raw cotton against gold payments.
[2] There had long been a special agreement for keeping the exchange of Czechoslovak lignite against German anthracite level; this continued to operate.

balance in Germany continued to rise until the middle of 1935, by the beginning of 1937 it was reduced to about 8 million marks, only, as it happened, to rise again later. The Czech-German Agreement of November 1934 incidentally created a precedent, in that Czechoslovakia agreed to limit her own exports; it supplied the model for similar treaties between Germany and other countries, though Czechoslovak opinion was very critical of the sacrifices which it was felt the country had made.

Since then Czech-German commercial negotiations have remained upon the basis of the 1934 Treaty. In November 1937, at Hamburg, adjustments for the year 1938 were agreed upon, and a slight increase of the total volume of trade was arranged. The Reich negotiators agreed to take rather more finished goods from Czechoslovakia, but only on the condition that Germany also received a corresponding increase of Czechoslovak raw materials and foodstuffs.

It will be convenient here to refer to the later tourist negotiations. In 1935 an agreement was made by which Reich German visitors were allowed to use, in Czechoslovakia, the proceeds of various Czech State purchases and of the Czechoslovak import of Reich German cars. In 1936 a definite percentage of the payment for goods from Germany was put aside for German visitors to the Czechoslovak spa towns. For some time the German Government had only allowed even long-term visitors doing a cure in Czechoslovakia an allowance of 500 marks a month, and this figure was reduced in 1937 to 350 marks. For that year Germany did at last accept an old Czechoslovak proposal to set aside a small proportion of the value of German exports to Czechoslovakia as a special spa-account, and for 1938 a larger figure has been made available. It should not be forgotten that short-term German tourists (without exceptional permission) had long before been reduced to an allowance of 10 marks, while people in frontier districts were limited to 3 marks. The utterly desolate impression made nowadays by some village on the Czechoslovak side of the frontier, say Herrnskretchen (Hřensko) in the Elbe valley, a village which lived for the reception of week-end visitors from Saxony, has to be experienced to be believed, for one sees—even on a Sunday—nothing but empty table after empty table in restaurant after restaurant.[1] The tourist negotiations were carried on in a not unfriendly manner without any smell of political malice. Nazi economic policy made it simply impossible[2] to allow more money to be spent abroad; though this meant bitter resentment among

[1] The writer happened to be there in June 1937.
[2] Vigorous anti-foreign-travel propaganda occurred in the Reich from the time of the Nazi revolution and doctors discouraged visits to health resorts abroad, but this was perfectly consistent with the aims of the régime.

the Sudeten Germans against the Czechoslovak, not the German, Government, the Czech representatives did not have the impression that the Reich German negotiators were aiming at this. It should be mentioned that Sudeten German representatives from the spa towns are always consulted when the agreements are being discussed, and they go to Berlin when the transactions occur there.

The devaluation of the Czechoslovak currency in February 1934 brought an immediate alleviation of the general foreign trade situation, at least in many branches of industry. In 1934, also, the Czechs made great efforts to strengthen economic co-operation within the Little Entente, which they hoped to develop into a small *Mittel-Europa* with Slavonic foundations. It was clear that Škoda and Živno capital might be put to profitable uses in developing Roumania and Yugoslavia, and might with advantage compete with Krupps, though the Sudeten Germans were infinitely scornful about the uselessness of plans of the kind. The most serious obstacle was Czech Agrarian opposition to the importation of agricultural produce from two countries both of which were 80 per cent. agricultural themselves. France and Czechoslovakia, also, were too similar in economic structure to be able to intensify their interchange of goods to any noticeable extent. At the end of 1935 came League sanctions against Italy which robbed Czechoslovakia of a market and impeded the recovery of the Sudeten German china industry; into the bargain Germany succeeded in snapping up a large amount of Yugoslavia's trade with Italy. Germany's buyings in Yugoslavia in 1935 were altogether in the grand manner, and though the Yugoslavs called a halt in 1936, this development also occurred at the expense of Epiag hopes, and German china ware appeared in Yugoslav kitchens.

In 1936 the commercial situation was substantially improved. Commercial relations with Hungary had been provisionally resumed[1] in June 1935, and from 1936 regular Czech-Hungarian treaties have been signed. Some fairly solid extension of economic co-operation between the Little Entente Powers was negotiated at Bucarest just after the Bratislava Conference in September 1936, and about the same time, following the French devaluation, Czechoslovakia reduced the value of the Kč a little further—from about 120 to about 140 to the £ sterling. This fresh depreciation reinforced efforts to achieve a change in the orientation of Czechoslovak trade, so that it should be less dependent upon Germany

---

[1] From 1924 to 1930 Hungary annually sent about 900 million Kč worth of goods to Czechoslovakia and Czechoslovakia over a milliard Kč worth of goods to Hungary. From 1931 to 1936 Hungary sent about 140 millions' worth to Czechoslovakia and Czechoslovakia's exports to Hungary decreased from 289 millions' worth in 1931 to 157 millions' worth in 1936, with a minimum of 139 millions' worth in 1935.

and the Succession States and their currency weaknesses. In 1936, for example, 31 per cent. of Czechoslovakia's exports went to the sterling bloc countries as compared with 24 per cent. in 1933; with regard to the gold bloc there was also an improvement in those years.[1]

The Sudeten German industrialists, entrenched behind cartel agreements within the Republic, continued to complain that the Government did nothing whatever to help them. They continued to grumble when the rate of interest came down, they resented financial help from any Czech bank, and, forgetting the price paid by German industry as a whole, they demanded praemia such as Reich German exporters enjoyed. Indeed, I have heard responsible business men complain in the course of the very same conversation that the Kč stood so low that it had no prestige and so high that they could not compete in foreign markets. What was a serious hardship for them was that they knew the German and Succession State markets, and it was really difficult for them to adapt their goods to British, French, and American taste.

(v) LABOUR

In the 'days of plenty' before 1914 there were nevertheless great extremes of poverty and wealth. Austrian social legislation, thanks to the work of men like Steinbach and Vogelsang[2] in the days of the Taaffe régime, was not far behind that of Germany or Great Britain. There was accident and sickness insurance and factory inspection, in the bigger industries trades-union organization had become fairly strong, and there was a certain amount of self-government in the factories. Conditions in home industry, as in the Erzgebirge, were terribly bad, housing, especially in Vienna, was often deplorable, and there was no old age or unemployment insurance. Above all, wages were uncontrolled by law; it was this which created national feeling among the working-people, since the Slav worker, owing to the lower standard of living the farther south and east one went, was willing to accept less pay than, say, the Sudeten German, and was therefore able to cut him out, especially in unskilled work.[3] It was for this reason, of course, that the Industrial Revolution had brought a turn of the tide in German-Czech population movements, and it was for this reason that well-known Sudeten German textile firms like Liebig and Brass set up

---

[1] See Dr. Ivan Jež on 'Foreign Trade' in *Ten Years of the Czechoslovak National Bank*.

[2] See E. K. Winter, *Arbeiterschaft und Staat*.

[3] This should not be taken to mean that the Slavs were necessarily less competent. Czech craftsmen were famous for their quality and Slovak agricultural workers were not merely cheap, but were considered specially good at, for example, sugar-beet cultivation.

factories in Czech-speaking country before the War, preferring to pay what Czech weavers would take. The Sudeten German earned less than the Reich German, and this similarly brought Reich German entrepreneurs, like Mannesmann, from Düsseldorf across the old Austro-German frontier to Komotau (Chomutov). On the other hand, the smaller significance of frontiers in those happy passportless days made it relatively easy for the Sudeten German workman to get work in the Reich, and facilitated a lot of seasonal earning by poor Böhmerwald peasants—to take only one example —who could go over the mountains to Bavaria. This pre-War mobility lessened the effect of pre-War trade depressions, which were not long drawn out and did not, therefore, drain people's resources to the last drop. It should, however, be emphasized that the mountainous edges of Bohemia and some North Moravian districts had for years lived with destitution at their doors; it has been seen that State tobacco factories were set up before the War to provide employment in areas with the complexion of distress at places like Joachimsthal (Jachymov), Sternberg (Šternberk), and Tachau (Tachov). The most striking evidence of the terrible conditions which prevailed in the nineties was supplied by several publications from the pen of the Social Democrat, Herr Max Winter (afterwards vice-mayor of Vienna). In *Zwischen Iser und Neisse* he described the miserable lives of the glass-workers who seldom lived beyond the age of 40. In a book about the china industry area he described the wives and children of the china-workers queueing up for the refuse from the kitchen of a big Karlsbad hotel. A few years later he published *Die Blutsauger des Böhmerwaldes*, in which he examined the wretched conditions in which the foresters lived.

During the War it is undoubtedly true that the working-people of the Sudeten German districts had an extraordinarily bad time. Some of them were already physically degenerate. Their own soil was quite incapable of nourishing them. The produce of the Czech interior was to a large extent commandeered, and the enemy blockade was intensified by the refusal of the Hungarians to spare food to Austria, and even a little by the Bavarian peasant's determination not to go short. The short-lived post-War boom was followed by very great deprivation in 1923 and 1924, intensified as it was by the miserable conditions in Austria, Hungary, and Germany at the time. From Southern Bohemia and Southern Moravia in the old days, the enterprising working-man had often found his way to profitable openings in Vienna. Even when the ex-enemy Powers were financially rehabilitated after 1924 there were frontiers and complications now between Gratzen (Nové Hrady) or Znaim (Znojmo) and Austria.

Under the Czechoslovak Republic the eight-hour day had been immediately established for all work in factories and mines. The Government supplemented the social legislation inherited from Austria by a comprehensive Insurance Act in 1924, supplying all workers[1] with sickness and old age insurance; employers and employees shared the contributions to which the State then added; the employers alone were made responsible for accident insurance. As regards unemployment the Ghent insurance system was introduced, according to which relief was paid to their members by the trades unions,[2] the Government supplying at least half the expense, while the employers were completely exonerated. As between Czechs and Sudeten Germans perhaps the worst difficulty in the twenties was that the Czechoslovak authorities admittedly had more money to spend upon social purposes in Czech or Slovak areas because they said they must raise their conditions of living up to the Sudeten German level. The Sudeten Germans regarded the expenditure as unjust, and tried to remind the Czechs of their sufferings during the War and the 1922–3 slump.

It was, of course, the 1930 economic break-down which thoroughly embittered the Sudeten German working-people against the Czechs. In the first place unemployment among the Sudeten Germans rapidly developed on a much greater scale than among the Czechs or the Slovaks. This was not only due to the more agricultural character of the Czech and Slovak population, but also to the fact that Czechoslovak (as distinguished from Sudeten German) industry inclined to be heavy industry with a margin of indispensable work to do, or, like Bat'a shoes, had a solid mass of consumers at home for whose tastes and needs it set out to provide. The Czechs in Northern Bohemia, miners, glassworkers, &c., were, if hardier, in just as terrible distress as the Germans. In this connexion the following incident should perhaps be recalled. In the winter 1936–7 a prominent Sudeten German deputy invited a Czech National Socialist deputy from Southern Bohemia to visit the North Bohemian distressed area with him. The Czech agreed and was led to a disused cemetery at Kosten (Košt'any) near Teplitz-Schönau (Teplice-Šanov), where a man was living in the vault where corpses had been kept. But when the visitors spoke to the man in German he answered, 'Já jsem Čech' (I am Czech).[3] Thus the contention was strangely well illustrated that the economic suffering of the thirties was by no

[1] All, that is to say, whose wages were above a certain low figure.
[2] The biggest Sudeten German trades unions were, of course, the free or Socialist ones, but there were also Catholic unions and the National Socialist ones which the Socialists denounced as 'yellow'.
[3] The Sudeten German deputy agreed to pay a return visit to inspect Czech distress, but within a year's time he had not found it possible to do so.

means the monopoly of the Germans but hit a great many Czechs; to take a further example, the building industry was particularly hard put to it, and this actually affected more Czechs than Sudeten Germans. But of course it was absolutely inevitable that the mainly German districts should suffer appallingly in a world crisis of the magnitude of the slump in question; the Sudeten German territory became—what some of its industries had foretasted since 1922—a gigantic distressed area without hope of recovery. Where no national problem existed, say in Great Britain itself, such a situation caused the bitterest reproaches of indifference and incompetence to be flung at the Government. How much the more exacerbated was the position between the Sudeten German unemployed and the Czechoslovak Government; the presence of activist German Ministers in the Cabinet served only to cause them to be regarded as national traitors by many of their own people who had never hitherto adopted a chauvinist posture.

It is peculiarly difficult to make at all an exact estimate of the relation of the Sudeten German to the Czech unemployment figures at any time during the crisis. For one thing the districts one refers to as Sudeten German—even the purest of them—are scattered with Czechs; suddenly a few Czech villages or a group of Czech glass-workers crop up in the most unexpected places, Czech officials quite apart. In the Czech and Slovak districts there are, of course, the German language-islands indicated above[1] and several smaller surprises here and there. The Czechoslovak Government, like all governments, used the figures which made the economic situation seem least gloomy, that is to say they published the figures of applicants for work at the labour exchanges. The Sudeten Germans pointed out quite justifiably that this concealed short-time workers and that there were many unemployed who did not go to the labour exchanges. The Government has also sometimes used the sickness insurance figures, where it often occurs that people are left on the lists after they have lost their job. The Germans, on the other hand, used standards which made their own plight seem even worse than it was, and often made the impression that all the unemployed—say in the textile or the glass industry—were Germans, whereas in fact in textiles German to Czech unemployed were about as 2 to 1 and in glass as $2\frac{1}{2}$ to 1;[2] these proportions weaken the force of the statement[3] that in 1935 and 1936 35 to 48 per cent. of the unemployed in the Republic lived in what the Sudeten Germans called German territory which

[1] Chapter XI.
[2] These figures are a compromise between those of the Czechoslovak Ministry of Social Welfare and those of the Deutscher Hauptverband der Industrie in der ČSR.
[3] Winkler, *Die Tschechoslowakei im Spiegel der Statistik*, Fig. 47.

always included the lignite mixed districts, &c. There appears to be nothing misleading about the list of places in the Republic in which the *Deutsches Wirtschaftsjahrbuch* for 1936 found the highest proportion of unemployment among able-bodied adults[1] between March and July 1935, viz.:

	Per cent.		Per cent.
Graslitz	37·9	Pressnitz	26·9
Sternberg	31·0	Römerstadt	26·0
Neudek	30·4	Elbogen	26·0
Vsetin	28·9	Rumburg	25·2
Friedland	27·4	Karlsbad	23·5
Freudenthal	27·1	Jägerndorf	22·7

Of these only Vsetin was predominantly Czech.

A variety of circumstances made the economic catastrophe particularly enraging for the Sudeten Germans. There was still no comprehensive minimum wage system. The trade unions over a certain area habitually agreed with the employers in their industry upon a certain schedule of wages, but though it was rare it was not impossible for employers to remain isolated and offer lower wages; if they did so, they were likely to take on Czechs rather than Germans because Czech unskilled workers could still adapt themselves more easily to a lower standard of life. In 1935, as a matter of fact, a law was enacted by which the textile industry, if 70 per cent. of the textile workers (or rather their representatives) in a certain district agreed upon a minimum wage, it became possible to prohibit the paying of wages beneath this figure. But this law was not extended to industry as a whole. In the case of people like unorganized glass-workers who worked at home it was particularly easy to reduce their pay, and the Ghent system left them with no claim to unemployment relief, since it did not cater for non-union labour. Secondly, when staff was reduced and people dismissed, the tendency was for Czechs to be kept and Germans not. Some big German employers were more likely to do the reverse, but in any concern which had reason to wish to please the Government, the Czech workmen had the advantage, and in the crisis it became of unprecedented importance to employers to get contracts from the State; in order to do so, it was made clear to them that they had better adapt the German-Czech proportions in their factories to those of the local population as a whole. The official proportions in the local districts were, in Sudeten German eyes, distorted by the number of Czech officials at the stations, the post offices, &c. And yet, in very desperation, keen Germans would now sometimes try to make themselves out

[1] Or rather what the Germans call *Berufstätige* (i.e. those pursuing an occupation).

to be Czech rather than be faced with destitution. Their inward resentment against a State where they had to seem renegades was at least as violent as that of Czech workmen who had been turned into the streets unless they called themselves German in the Austrian days.

The pressure in favour of the dismissal of Germans was strong in the main Škoda factory at Plzeň (Pilsen) and in other Czech towns where a good many Germans were still employed, for the Czechs said, 'Why should we starve while the "foreigners" can earn?' The State tobacco factories for historical and geographical reasons employed 35·8 per cent. Germans to 60·9 per cent. Czechs in 1931,[1] and there was Czech nationalistic feeling against this. But what Czech nationalism had all along particularly resented was the attitude of a firm like the Aussig (Ústí) Chemical Company, or again the character of the management of the great Vitkovice (Witkowitz) iron works.

The Aussig Chemical Company after the War removed its head-quarters from Vienna to Karlsbad until 1930, and then to Aussig. The management—certainly as seen by the Czechs—was aggressively German. Among the directors 10 per cent. were actually Germans from the Reich; there were no Czechs at all on the clerical staff, and business was perforce conducted solely in German. Meanwhile the company's financial resources in Vienna were drying up, and its shares were accumulating in the hands of the *Živnostenská Banka*. Through the influence of the *Živno*, a Czech managing director, Dr. Basch, was appointed in 1934, the head-quarters were removed to Prague,[2] and the proportions among the employees were gradually adapted to the population ratio in the various factories of the company at Aussig (Ústí), Falkenau (Falknov), Handlova, Lobositz (Lobosice), and Hřušov. This chiefly involved the dismissal of German technicians on the grounds that economy measures were indispensable and that their ignorance of Czech was a too great practical disadvantage in what was, after all, a Czechoslovak concern. When recovery began to set in, out of ten German engineers who had been dismissed by the Aussig Chemical Company at the blackest time only two were successfully reinstated. It is characteristic of the Czech-German situation that while the Czechs believe that only these two applied to return, the Germans are convinced that the other eight were kept out because they had not learnt Czech in the meantime, although it had not been made clear that they were to do so. It appears to be one of many cases of genuine misunderstanding.

[1] See *Freiheit* (published in Teplitz-Schönau), June 10th, 1937.
[2] Concerns whose head-quarters are not in Prague are subject to very slightly heavier taxation.

The Vitkovice (Witkowitz) iron works were originally owned by the Rothschilds and Gutmanns; since the War Dutch, and then British, capital has come into the concern and a certain amount of Czechoslovak (Živno) money, especially from the time of the financial crashes of 1931. Though the population around Vitkovice is only something like 20 per cent. German, to this day the proportion of Germans among the ordinary hands is well above that figure. On the clerical staff, engineers, &c., 85 per cent. (out of some 3,000) were German until 1929. When it came to dismissals during the slump it would have been really impossible, in the sight of the surrounding population, to dismiss Czechs, so the Germans had to go. Indeed, when a new managing director, Herr Federer, was appointed, he undertook in 1932 gradually to modify the Czech-German ratio to 50:50. This was not an excessive request from the Czech side, but of course it brought great hardship to some hundreds of Germans.

It seems to be impossible to reconcile the Czech and German point of view over cases like these. The Czechs feel that the Germans are living upon an historical privilege, the Germans, as often occurs in such circumstances, substitute for privilege the word merit, sometimes with justice and sometimes not. At any rate the world slump had given a new grievance to small middle-class Germans by cutting the ground from under their feet as *Beamten* in important industrial concerns, and this social stratum had always been particularly susceptible to violently nationalistic doctrines. At the same time, among its economy measures, the Czechoslovak Government now passed a law depriving ex-officials of their pensions if they had other means, and many an ex-official in Troppau (Opava) found himself robbed, as he saw it, of his pension because he had succeeded in providing himself with a tobacconist's monopoly from the State.

While Czech feeling was able to make itself felt through the influence of the exceedingly competent *Živnostenská* Bank and through the choice of firms to carry out State contracts, the Czechoslovak Government made a serious mistake in frequently allowing Czech unemployed workmen to be brought into predominantly German territory to mend roads or engage upon the other public works which were naturally launched in the slump in order to mitigate unemployment. It was a maddening experience for unemployed Germans to witness the importation of Czech labour into districts which they regarded as their national territory—it seemed to them like a deliberate caricaturing of their trouble. One explanation of these provocative occurrences—in so far as the work was not organized directly by the State—was that Czech firms always seemed able to offer to do a job more cheaply than their German competitors,[1] so much more cheaply, indeed, as to escape the safeguarding law,[2] and force the hand of an economizing régime. If a Prague firm consequently got the Government order to build a police station or whatever it was, it naturally imported the requisite labour. The invariably lower quotation from the Czech firms was a little mysterious. Sometimes they were paying slightly lower wages, and in general their carriage was a little more modest. It seems, too, that they sometimes under-estimated costs and sent in a supplementary bill later. Finally it was easier for them to get credits from the Czech banks than for the Sudeten German firms, whose own banks, it has been seen, had been virtually paralysed by the slump. Circumstances, indeed, had by now reduced the Sudeten Germans to financial dependence upon the Czechs, a condition which seemed to them to be a surrender of their national tradition, indeed of their national integrity; to the Czechs, thinking in terms of a Czechoslovak national State, the state of affairs merely seemed to have become normal.

In general the old curse remained—incredible ignorance of local conditions. Czechs living in Prague simply did not believe in the poverty of the Sudeten German workers. They said, 'Oh, our Germans have always been noisy fellows, always crying wolf —always extravagant, too, and expecting to live better than we do; it is our duty to be cautious and financially careful.' History had made the Czechs sceptical and evasive, and the influence of the peasantry, as in France, was an influence in favour of parsimony. Even before the Nazi Revolution in 1933 the German tendency was to do things on a grand scale. But the passions now aroused among the Sudeten Germans were stimulated by darker suspicions. It is probably true that, even if all the rules of the game are kept, the minorities in a multiple State are likely to dwindle in their proportion to the majority nation. Roumanian statistics go to show that the Hungarian minority, partly because it is often urban and needs to be replenished from the country-side, may in the long run die out, even if it is justly or even generously treated. The Czech *národní jednota* people had celebrated the disappearance of

[1] I happen to have an example of the Czech and German tenders made actually a little later (i.e. early in 1937, when efforts had been made to prevent the Czech firms from using any particular advantage) for a tax office in Hohenelbe (Vrchlabí).

Eight Czech offers were made by 2 Prague firms,
　　　　　　　　　　　　　　　　2 Pardubice (Pardubitz) firms,
　　　　　　　　　　　　　　　　2 Kostelec firms,
　　　　　　　　　　　　　　　　1 Hradec Králové (Königgrätz) firm,
　　　　　　　　　　　　　　　　1 Jilemnice (Starkenbach) firm,
and they varied from an estimate of 497,000 to one of 596,000 Kč. Four German offers were made by 3 Hohenelbe firms and 1 Freiheit (Svoboda) firm, and varied from an estimate of 657,000 to one of 699,000 Kč.

[2] See above, section (iii), p. 164.

the 20 per cent. German minorities in Olomouc (Olmütz) and Moravian Ostrava (Ostrau) in 1930. Now, in the misery of 1933 and the next year or so, the Sudeten Germans easily believed that the Czechoslovak Government would do nothing to help them because it positively wished them to die out.

Everywhere on the Continent there are certainly chauvinists and other fanatics who deliberately discriminate in the relief of social distress in favour of their own people—Central and East European anti-Semitism gives examples enough. Though I know of no positive proofs of it,[1] it seems probable that, here and there, a Czech local official showed malevolence in the matter of Sudeten German distress. It has been seen, however, that without anything of the kind, acute and widespread distress were bound to occur and that the Sudeten German birth-rate was on the decline. The Ghent system of unemployment relief was quite unsatisfactory for a period of prolonged distress. Not only did it fail to provide for the relatively high proportion of non-union labour in the Republic, but it was originally intended to supply unemployment relief only for thirteen weeks. This thirteen weeks' period, under the stress of slump circumstances, was soon extended to twenty-six; after this a third quarter of 'Crisis-relief' was provided, but then for the last thirteen weeks of the year the unemployed man was entitled to nothing from his trade union. At the beginning of the second year of unemployment the union offered him relief for another thirty-nine weeks, but at the end of two years out of work he technically ceased to belong to his industry. As far as they were able, the trade unions ignored these restrictions, but it was not always possible for them to continue to do so.

It is to the German Social Democrat, Dr. Czech, who was Czechoslovak Minister of Social Welfare from 1929 to 1934, that the introduction of unemployment relief for unorganized labour is due. Ever since June 1st, 1930, when the so-called 'Czech cards' were introduced, the single man who is not enrolled in a trade union, and who passes a means test, can claim 10 Kč', the married man 20 Kč' worth of food and other necessities from the local authorities. This is little enough but it is infinitely more than nothing; sometimes more than the minimum has been allowed. A great deal of relief in kind, other than that provided against the Czech cards, has also been distributed by the Ministry of Social Welfare in the most distressed regions.[2] I have spoken to Germans who have regularly helped to distribute coal, potatoes, and bread in the Reichenberg district, and they assured me that they had

[1] On occasions when Germans have wished to prove this kind of thing to me, the evidence has always broken down.

[2] Cf. article by Monsieur Nečas, Czechoslovak Minister for Social Welfare, in *The Slavonic Review*, April 1937.

never been witnesses of any kind of discrimination in favour of the Czech population. The people who are least provided for are the young unemployed, for technically the recipient of a 'Czech card' is supposed to have established that he was employed for at least three months in 1929 in a job with sickness insurance attached to it. In the distribution of food direct from the Ministry of Social Welfare, also, children under 15 are sometimes excepted. Of course there are shelters and hostels[1] for young people, but there is room here for a harsh attitude on the part of officials; members of the Czech Agrarian Party, who tend to take the view that unemployed people are nothing but lazy, are liable to behave in a rigorous and short-sighted way, thus driving Sudeten German youths to desperation and irredentism.

[1] Cf. figures given by M. Nečas in *The Slavonic Review*, April 1937. M. Nečas is generally regarded by the Sudeten Germans as the least chauvinist and most enlightened Czech Minister, in spite of the fact that he is a Socialist.

CHAPTER XIV

THE RISE OF THE SUDETEN GERMAN PARTY

IT has been seen that Bohemia was the cradle of German National Socialism, and that this way of thinking had been regaining ground in the Historic Provinces since before the elections of 1929. In 1931 and 1932 the slump swelled the columns of the Reich-German S.A., and the Sudeten Nazis and their *Volkssport* were able to expand their activities in sympathy, until the Czechoslovak authorities called an abrupt halt. On January 30th, 1933, the National Socialist régime of an Austrian was established in Berlin with devastating repercussions to disturb the equilibrium of Czechoslovakia. The militarist trappings, and the racial and anti-democratic phraseology of Hitlerism, encouraged the least Germanophobe Czechs to believe that the Germans were now re-revealed in their true light, and that the speeches of Karl Hermann Wolf had, after all, expressed Germanism more exactly than a Stresemann or even a Bismarck régime. As Professor Pfitzner is never tired of emphasizing, Sudeten German unity can trace back its origin to the eagerness of all the Sudeten German deputies to participate in the work of the Frankfurt Parliament in 1848, and National Socialism, too, goes back to the Pan-Germans of the *Paulskirche*.[1]

Thus the National Socialist Revolution in Germany was a revolution in all Central Europe. For the first time in modern history the Pan-German idea, in that alliance with Socialism which the pre-War Sudeten German Working-men's Party had initiated in 1904, had successfully ousted the *Kleindeutsch*[2] standpoint from a key position; henceforth the *Auslandsdeutschen*, scattered in minorities right away to the Black Sea, were bound together in a new species of imperial unity. This unity was psychological, and—in so far as post-1933 politics can be distinguished from psychology—not political yet. A strange state of war broke out between the new German spirit and those non-Germans who wished to protect their political independence; Germans who retained other than national values often found themselves forced to take their position on the non-German side, non-Germans sometimes found reasons to range themselves with German nationalism. It would be difficult to overestimate the importance of the revolution which had occurred, although it was often un-

---

[1] The Frankfurt deputies met in the *Paulskirche* in 1848.
[2] The *Kleindeutschen* in 1848 were chary of annexing Austria to the rest of Germany; subsequently the *Kleindeutsch* position implied the acceptance of 1866 and the frontiers of Bismarckian Germany.

noticed by the casual or inexpert visitor. It created a state of psychological war, fought with propaganda and the fear of actual war. Large sums of money were used, not only upon armaments for a future war, but upon pamphlets and broadcasting. Attacks were launched, not yet against physical fortifications, but upon people's nerves—every effort was made to induce mass hysteria. Political opinions became less related than they had perhaps ever been before to facts, but were based upon unreasoning conviction; even the opponents of the National Socialist *Weltanschauung*, with its frank insistence upon a subjective standpoint, found it more difficult to be faithful to their own search for objectivism. Outside Germany proper, the Saar and the Free City of Danzig, Austria and Czechoslovakia were the most acutely affected by the change which had taken place. A kind of new Taaffe coalition between most of the Czechs and the German Clericals in both countries put an end to any ill-feeling between the Vatican and Prague. The Social Democrats, too, were bound to be on the anti-racial side, though attempts at negotiation between the Austrian Clericals and Socialists proved abortive, and this led in February 1934 to the catastrophe of open war between them; although the Clericals triumphed they now depended upon making constant concessions to the Pan-Germans in their midst.

In Czechoslovakia the demarcation between German activism and negativism hardened. This was illustrated by reactions to the news from Germany. The activists learned uneasily of the persecution of Pacifists, Liberals, Socialists, Catholics, and Jews, and shook their heads over the economic risks which the Berlin Government was prepared to take. The negativists believed that Germany had become a heaven on earth filled with happy enthusiasm and jobs for everybody; this was the pleasanter view to take, and the activists continued to lose and the negativists to gain. It was particularly satisfactory to believe that unpleasant news from Germany derived solely from Jewish refugees who had arrived in Prague, and the racially minded Sudeten Germans protested against the toleration of émigrés.

The majority of the Czechs, though less startled than Western Europe by the fanfares from the Reich, believed that the only way with this sort of thing was to take a strong line. One must defend democracy against any form of fascism by stealing the enemy's weapons, rather than holding up one's hands with the helplessness of the would-be defenders of the liberal Weimar constitution. The *Volkssport* Trial had already been launched in 1932,[1] and on the strength of the Sudeten Nazis' association with their fellows in Germany, which had thus, in Czech opinion, been clearly revealed,

[1] See above, Chapter XII, section (iv).

the Czechoslovak Government prepared to follow the example of the Austrian Government[1] and to suppress the D.N.S.A.P. In October 1933 the Sudeten Nazis in fact forestalled the authorities by dissolving themselves, and, as the German Nazis had done in the case of the Socialists and Catholics in the Reich, the Czech authorities forbade the *völkisch* trade unions and confiscated their funds. Pressure was also brought to bear upon the German National Party in Czechoslovakia to dissolve itself. As a consequence the German National and Nazi mayors or members of municipal bodies were temporarily replaced by activist Government nominees in suitable proportions, a flagrant, but possibly necessary, interference with municipal democracy. Sudeten German indignation was particularly strong in nationalist strongholds like Gablonz (Jablonec) and Eger (Cheb). In Gablonz the municipal elections of 1931 had returned 9 German Nationals and 12 Nazis, together 50 per cent. of a council of 42.[2] In Eger local elections were held on March 19th, 1933, exactly a fortnight after the famous Reich elections which followed the Reichstag fire. The results gave 17 town council seats to the Nazis, 3 more to a separate Pan-German block, 8 to the Clericals, 7 to the Social Democrats, and 3 to the Czechs; after the dissolution of the Nazis their 17 seats were distributed as follows:

2 to the German Agrarians (*Bund der Landwirte*).

5 to the Clericals.

7 to the Socialists.

3 to two smaller tradespeople's groups.

There was no attempt to add to the Czechs, but a Clerical was nominated as the mayor of Eger.

While the strange new Central European tension which had been created by Hitler's rise to power synchronized exactly with Czechoslovakia's most acute economic distress, it created an intense and direct anxiety among the Czechs with regard to the new militarization of Germany. This process, which had obviously begun immediately in 1933 and was combined with Germany's brusque exit from Geneva in the autumn, received its first overt expression in the restoration of conscription in the Reich in March 1935. Czechoslovakia's adherence to the Masaryk, rather than the Hitler, point of view, her mainly Slavonic character, her proximity to Germany, her small area and population which lay behind enormously long frontiers, and above all the character of her frontier population, physically starving and emotionally intoxicated as it was at the time, created an intelligible nervousness and a deter-

---

[1] The Nazis were suppressed in Austria in June 1933.
[2] Reichenberg (Liberec) at the same time only elected about one-third of its municipal council from German Nationals and Nazis.

mination to take early precautions. From the time of the Enabling Law of June 1933 the local German police were frequently replaced by Czech State police officials.[1] This measure, together with its effects, was characteristic of the dilemma in which the Czechs found themselves. The municipal policeman in the Sudeten German towns usually belonged to that lower middle-class which had always inclined to the *völkisch* state of mind, and in that case he was certainly not to be trusted from the Czech point of view, for the only Germans against whom he was now likely strictly to enforce the Czechoslovak law were the Socialists and Communists, although the former remained a Government party. If, on the other hand, Sudeten German Socialists were appointed as policemen, the very national Germans were indignant at being supervised by Marxists. On the other hand the appointment of Czechs seemed to the citizens of Reichenberg (Liberec) and Karlsbad (Karlovy Vary) like the provocation of a foreign occupation, and involved the pensioning off of Germans, thus accentuating a situation where everything seemed to be depriving the minority of its daily bread in favour of the majority.

In circumstances such as these, elections fell due in Czechoslovakia in May 1935, and the Sudeten German population was called upon by its most enthusiastic nationalists to emulate the 90 per cent. pro-German vote in the Saar in the previous January by voting for a new Sudeten German Party.

In 1925 a Reichenberger called Konrad Henlein became instructor in the *Turnverband* at Asch (Aš). He was 27 at the time and had nothing very remarkable behind him. He had fought in the War, been taken prisoner by the Italians, then returned to his actual birth-place, Reichenau (Rychnov) near Reichenberg, to become a bank clerk at the local branch of the *Kreditanstalt der Deutschen*. By 1929 Herr Henlein, who was in close touch with Heinrich, Brand, and Rutha, the leaders of the as yet secret *Kameradschaftsbund* (K.B.), had become a *Verbandsturnwart* and one of the leading people of the whole German *Turnverband* of Czechoslovakia. Konrad Henlein was a tremendous admirer of the great protagonist of German gymnasts, Ludwig Jahn, and cherished the same notions as the Czech *Sokol* leaders of achieving a grand-scale non-party—because non-political—national unity[2] via the gymnasium or its equivalent. But all the talk, from this

---

[1] The appearance of the State police had begun earlier here and there, in Eger, for instance, see Chapter XI, section (i) (d). In Gablonz until 1928 there were 40 local German policemen, but within two or three years they had been replaced by a much larger force of State police, the big majority of which was Czech. The State police often took on a certain number of Germans; in a suburb of Aussig, for instance, out of half a dozen German policemen, two were enrolled in the State police and four got better-paid jobs as local officials.

[2] J. Pfitzner *Sudetendeutsche Einheitsbewegung* (Karlsbad, 1937).

time onwards, among Germans both within the Reich and outside it, of a *Volksgemeinschaft* was ambiguous; if, as opponents pointed out, the *Volk* was to mean all the Germans in the world—and it was never made plain that it did not—then to advocate the *Volksgemeinschaft* was to propound a new gospel of Pan-Germanism indeed.

While his K.B. friends emphasized *das bündische*, Herr Henlein strongly supported the leadership principle; they all condemned any kind of individualism and the accepted forms of western democracy. From about 1930 Konrad Henlein expressed these opinions in various articles published here and there. One appeared in 1931, under the title of *Völkische Bedeutung der Leibesübungen* (= the national or, literally, 'folkish' significance of physical drill), in which was said, among other things:

'We declare war to the death upon Liberalism even behind the disguise of the cult of personality. Disciplined mass unities rule the present —the Fascists, the *Heimwehr*, the Hitler movement. For men wish to be led in manly fashion. . . . We all know that an un-German parliamentarism, an un-German party system, which divides our people into inorganic parts, will and must break down some time.'

Herr Henlein also at this time condemned all forms of compromise.

Events in the German Reich in 1933 both disturbed and exaggerated the opinions of the existing Sudeten German parties and strengthened the cry for the attainment of some kind of Sudeten German political unity. For years the so-called bourgeois parties had had a common political organization, the offspring of the old conglomeration of German National parties which shared the German National Club of the old Austrian Reichsrat. The post-War organization was called the *Deutsch-politisches Arbeitsamt*, and after 1926 both activist and negativist parties belonged to it.[1] After a time Herr Kundt, a leading member of the *Kameradschaftsbund*, had become its secretary; in 1933 he pressed the candidature of Herr Henlein as leader whenever the question of a more real Sudeten German political union was debated. Meanwhile the *Deutsche Turnverband* of the Republic, now largely officered by members of the K.B., was becoming increasingly active; in July it held a big festival at Saaz (Žatec) at which Herr Henlein was the outstanding figure and was indeed for the first time hailed by members of his audiences as *Führer*. 'We have become the educational organization of the Sudeten Germans', he declared; 'these days [at Saaz] have shown it.'

During September, with the National Socialists already under

---

[1] After the withdrawal of Dr. von Lodgman from political life in 1925, German-National co-operation with the German Clericals and Agrarians was facilitated.

ban in Austria, and with the *Volkssport* trial going on, it was fairly clear that the days of at least the D.N.S.A.P. were numbered, and all kinds of negotiations took place as to future political groupings. On October 1st, a day or so before the *Volkssport* Trial verdict had been spoken, Herr Henlein suddenly appealed to the Sudeten German people to rally round a Sudeten German Home Front. 'I appeal above all parties and estates . . . to the Sudeten German people', he declared, 'and place myself at the head of this movement.' The movement, he announced, accepted the 'fundamental demands of democracy', yet it was to be built up on the basis of division into *Stände*, i.e. estates or corporations. A few days later the Nazi and Nationalist parties perforce disappeared, and there was no political organization left to which the 'emphatically national' Sudeten Germans could lawfully belong other than that of Konrad Henlein. From the Czech side suspicious views were expressed on the assumption that the new front would be nothing but disguise for a new Nationalist-Nazi combination on the Hitler-Hugenberg model, and it was observed that in fact a high proportion of the old members of the German National Party and of the D.N.S.A.P. was soon absorbed by the *Sudetendeutsche Heimatfront* (S.H.F.). Representatives of the latter, however, were quick to point out that its officials were new men without a political past, and indeed they nearly all came from the membership of the K.B. which had suddenly decided to wind itself up. This led to a temporary complication because in November three of the most prominent ex-K.B. people, Herr Kundt, Dr. Brand, and Herr Oskar Kuhn, were arrested on a charge of conspiracy,[1] the police having found ambiguous papers in their possession. Herr Henlein during this period, however, showed a remarkable talent for compromise. While recruiting successfully among disgruntled negativists, he made the public presumption that he was in fact to be regarded as an activist independent of any organization other than the S.H.F.; Herr Kundt, on behalf of Herr Henlein, had stated this to be the case to Dr. Jesser, for instance, and Herr Henlein himself subsequently concluded a Gentleman's Agreement with the Agrarian Activist Minister, Dr. Spina,[2] by which the S.H.F. and German Agrarians (*Bund der Landwirte*) were to co-operate and not to compete.[3] Dr. Spina's intervention, incidentally, brought about the release of the three ex-K.B. leaders in February 1934, and all

---

[1] Actually for *Geheimbündelei*, an offence against the 1923 Law for the Defence of the Republic.

[2] See Dr. Spina's evidence at the Dauba trial, Dec. 1937, reported in the *Deutsche Landpost*, Dec. 11th, 1937. This trial was initiated by Herr Henlein in repudiation of assertions that he had broken his word.

[3] The German Small Traders' Party (*Gewerbepartei*) allowed itself to be absorbed directly into the S.H.F.

positions of importance in the S.H.F. remained in the hands of ex-K.B. men, who were thus carrying out their programme of occupying key-positions through members of a team of trained leaders.

During 1934 it continued to appear as if Herr Henlein's movement might perform the valuable work of enrolling the negativist Germans behind an activist banner. Late in the year[1] his speech at Böhmisch Leipa (Česká Lipa) developed more fully the neo-activist standpoint he had outlined at a press reception on October 8th, 1933. The Böhmisch Leipa speech,[2] to which Dr. Walter Brand is thought to have contributed a good deal, was a constructive and impressive declaration. It first of all repudiated both Pan-Germanism and Pan-Slavism as inevitably leading to the catastrophe of war. It claimed that, at a time when the Sudeten Germans were disloyal and *désorientés*, the S.H.F. had sprung into the breach, and, by pressing for a co-operative in place of a coercive policy, had brought them back to allegiance to the State, while insisting, of course, that they could never cease to be Germans. Herr Henlein then proceeded to repudiate any identification with Italian Fascism or German National Socialism, and to make the following statement, noteworthy in view of his earlier and later condemnation of liberalism: 'We shall never abandon liberalism, i.e. the unconditional respect for individual rights as a fundamental principle in determining human relations in general and the relations between the citizen and official authority in particular.' The speaker next made a declaration against the restoration of the Habsburgs and the revision of the Peace Treaties, thus laying emphasis upon two favourite and, as they believed, indispensable tenets of the Czechs; Herr Henlein even went out of his way to refer to the improvement in the position of the Germans in Slovakia and Ruthenia since the fortunes of war had transferred those provinces from the Magyars to the Czechoslovaks. Later in the speech he pressed for decentralization, while expressly stating that the unity of the State must be ensured. 'It is therefore senseless to suppose that self-government could mean a Sudeten German Parliament or anything like it.'

This speech should have provided the signal for a more promising co-operation between Czechs and Sudeten Germans than ever before, and it may be that the Czechs should have quickly requested of Herr Henlein to be allowed to take him at his word. But from the very beginning of the S.H.F. an uncomfortable feeling existed that it represented a compromise which was so complicated and self-contradictory as to lack sufficient substance

[1] Oct. 21st, 1934.
[2] See *Konrad Henlein spricht*, a Collection of Speeches (Karlsbad, 1937).

to exist.[1] Herr Henlein's position as *Führer* seemed inconsistent with the fidelity which he professed towards democracy, and as the elections approached and it became clear that he would not stand for the Chamber[2] the inconsistency seemed more conspicuous. Further, in practice, in spite of his tribute to liberalism at Böhmisch Leipa, the behaviour of the S.H.F. leaders incorporated the totalitarian technique of the Nazi Party in Germany, for they condemned criticism from their supporters as indiscipline. Indeed the curious situation arose that the ex-K.B. people who had created the Henlein movement were condemned by old Sudeten German National Socialists on the one hand because they held the oligarchical views of a Spann or Hans Zehrer or of an Edgar Jung, and on the other had adopted the totalitarian conception of which Bohemian National Socialism had hitherto been innocent.[3]

The *Sudetendeutsche Heimatfront* (Sudeten German Home Front), from at least the beginning of 1935, began an election campaign of astounding vigour and thoroughness, astounding, that is to say, only for those who had not observed the pre-election activities of the Nazis in the Reich both in the spring and in the autumn of 1933. The energy and the methods employed in both countries were strikingly similar. At least as early as January 29th[4] elaborate instructions were prepared for meetings and the distribution of propaganda. Members of the S.H.F. were made responsible for canvassing each street, *Sprech-Chöre*, i.e. groups of people to shout slogans in unison (e.g. 'Who have betrayed us?—The Social Democrats'), were organized, and it was even announced to party organizers that on the Friday before the election the S.H.F. must have procured the largest meeting-hall in every locality in order to hold similar last-moment meetings far and wide. On May 14th the Eger S.H.F. reminded its members that it would show a lack of responsible feeling to have left a single pamphlet or slogan forgotten in a drawer and so undistributed.[5]

The S.H.F. propaganda had three main themes—down with the Jews, down with the Reds, and unite in the spirit of the front-line

[1] As it was known that the Government was considering the suppression of the S.H.F. at the time, the Böhmisch Leipa speech was regarded by Herr Henlein's opponents as a manœuvre to prolong the existence of his movement.

[2] Various reasons have been given at different times for this decision, e.g. that Herr Henlein did not speak Czech (he could, of course, have spoken German in Parliament) or that he had vowed to gain nothing (e.g. not even the parliamentary salary) from his leadership.

[3] Innocent, that is to say, apart from Krebs who supported the idea, and in 1933, until his departure, was negotiating with Henlein and the K.B. Of course the totalitarian attitude towards criticism is always more welcome to those in command of a movement than to those who feel critical towards it.

[4] I have seen very full election instructions of that date issued by the S.H.F. at Eger and signed by the person responsible *Mit deutschem Gruss*.

[5] These instructions were headed *Weisung no. 98* (*Letzte Weisung vor den Wahlen*), i.e. Instruction no. 98 (last instruction before the elections).

soldiers like the leader Konrad Henlein who fought in the Great War. Fat Jewish Socialists, corrupt party bosses, were displayed as responsible for the people's misery in numberless cartoons, and the drive was directed, not so much against the Activist Parties as a whole, nor against the Communists, nor—since it would not have been allowed—against the Czechs, but against the German Social Democrats in Czechoslovakia. At the last moment, incidentally, the S.H.F. was told by the Czechoslovak authorities that a Home Front did not comply with the normal conception of a political party, and if they wished to take part in the election as such they must alter the name. The Henleinists, therefore, changed their name to Sudeten German Party (*Sudetendeutsche Partei*) and their initials to S.d.P.; in this way they re-emphasized their claim to represent the whole Sudeten German 'Folk', and underlined their refusal to recognize that the other German parties in Czechoslovakia were capable of doing so.

The Henleinists made the most of the new Central European circumstances. They not only announced that everything across the frontier in Germany was excellent, plenty of work with plenty of pay. They not only made out that the Czechoslovak Government had put up the inland price of sugar out of sheer malevolence, although the Sugar Cartel and its monopoly prices were a direct inheritance from Habsburg Austria. They also succeeded in surrounding the doubting voter with a sense of shame and fear—shame that he could hesitate to back the rescuers of his people, and fear lest, according to the rumours freely circulated, Hitler should march in any day and activist heads should roll. The effect of whispers such as these was greater, perhaps, than anything actually circulated in print. Although I have never encountered a suggestion from any quarter whatever that parliamentary elections in Czechoslovakia are not correct and that the secrecy of the ballot is not strictly maintained,[1] simple people in small towns and especially in villages (and there are no really big Sudeten German towns) are never insensitive to the bully who goes round saying, 'I shall know how you vote.' Sudeten German employers mostly welcomed the anti-Marxist (i.e. anti-class war) *Sudetendeutsche Partei*, subscribed to its funds and made it clear to the people around that the *völkischer* workman would stand a better chance for a job than his Socialist, Communist, or even Christian (Catholic) Trades Unionist competitor. In a big firm like Schicht's it would not be accurate to suggest that the direction showed any signs of

---

[1] Though the parliamentary constituencies are weighted against the Hungarians and the population of Ruthenia, this is not the case in the Historic Provinces; only greater Prague has a very slight advantage over the rest of Bohemia and Moravia-Silesia.

discrimination, but, since the clerical staff was usually overwhelmingly Henleinist, pressure was nevertheless brought to bear.

While the Sudeten German Party had borrowed from the Reich a technique which introduced a new emotional element into an election campaign, it would be completely misleading to suggest that there was not a great deal of perfectly spontaneous enthusiasm for Konrad Henlein's 'List 12' in the elections of May 1935. The idea of dropping all the old party differences attracted very many people; many were delighted with a movement, which, as they believed, had adopted the best things in Hitlerism, without the most brutal methods employed in the Reich. Finally, there were many old nationalists who declared that Herr Henlein's conditional loyalty to the Republic had made it possible for them to become loyal citizens for the first time since 1918.

The elections took place on May 19th, 1935. They revealed no very great change among the Czechoslovak voters who still returned the Agrarians (1,176,593 votes) and Social Democrats (1,034,774 votes) as their largest parties. The Sudeten German results, on the other hand, were impressive, for 1,249,530 votes— or 62 to 63 per cent.[1] of the German electorate—went to Herr Henlein's party. And yet, in view of the appalling distress at that time in Czechoslovakia, where circumstances had brought the economic depression and therefore the subsequent recovery later than in Austria and Germany, it is almost more surprising that the activist parties did not lose even more. While the Social Democrats lost less than half of their 1929 votes,[2] their supporters decreasing from 506,761 in 1929 to 299,942, the German Catholic and Farmers' Parties were more susceptible to the attractions of Henleinism, and did in fact lose about 50 per cent. of their electorate each.[3]

[1] The S.d.P. always states their percentage as 67·4, thus ignoring the four German Communist deputies who represent about 120,000 votes; owing to the absence of national distinctions in the Czechoslovak Communist Party it is not possible to estimate the number of German votes cast in 1935 more exactly. In the two predominantly German constituencies of Böhmisch Leipa and Karlsbad the Communists polled 24,475 and 20,638 respectively, and there were a good many German and a good many Communist voters—of whom some were certainly the same—in the constituencies of Mladá Boleslav, Louny, Plzeň, and Olomouc.

[2] The 1929 figures were unusually favourable to both German and Czech Social Democrats.

[3] Each of these parties had fought the elections in a larger block in 1929, so that it is impossible to calculate their exact loss.

CHAPTER XV

CULTURAL QUESTIONS

(i) ELEMENTARY SCHOOLS

THE school question continued under Czechoslovak rule, as it had in Habsburg days, to provide the occasion for intense national conflict between the Czechs and the Germans in the Historic Provinces; and, as in other directions, the poverty of the bad post-War years envenomed the fight because the enemy appeared, in Sudeten German eyes, to exploit the people's need.

In the old days it has been seen[1] that the Sudeten Germans had had every advantage in enticing Czech children into German schools which seemed likely to equip them for a more successful future. The Germans, too, had had wealth on their side, and were able to provide the best school summer outings and Christmas parties. Where the Czechs had at last achieved minority schools they had had to content themselves with the educational disadvantage of far bigger classes.[2] Under the Czechoslovak Republic the tables were turned, though it would be inaccurate to suggest that the situation was exactly reversed. The Czechs had all along objected to the disproportionate number of German schools, and Dr. Beneš had made it clear at the Peace Conference[3] that German schools would be closed. The Republic certainly shut down a number of them, while providing Czech schools for various Czech minorities in the lignite area and elsewhere where German opposition had hitherto offered an effectual veto.[4] A very much higher proportion of German schools disappeared in Moravia and Silesia than in Bohemia, but this was the perfectly natural consequence of the differing local circumstances, of the more brittle German surface which towns like Brno have been seen to have preserved. Another natural cause for the reduction of Sudeten German schools was the more rapid decline in the Sudeten German birth-rate; the War years meant less children for the elementary schools from about 1920, and even after the end of the direct consequences of the War the Sudeten German birth-rate continued to fall. Many of the very nationalistically minded Germans were unable to consider these circumstances; they had never been able to understand why a Czech miner in Dux (Duchov) or a Czech weaver in Brno (Brünn) resisted Germanization, and they now

[1] See Chapters V and VII above.
[2] See Chapter VII, p. 57, above.
[3] See the Note of May 20th, 1919, referred to in Chapter X above.
[4] See above, Chapter VII.

complained that these people were being stolen by the Czechs. Every German school closed seemed to them a local defeat in the national battle.

What action, more precisely, did the Czechoslovak Government take with regard to elementary education? It closed 293 out of 3,376 German lower elementary schools[1] between 1918 and 1928, most of them actually before 1926; in the decade (1926–36) since then this same category of German schools has increased again by 14 per cent., or in other words the number of classes in these schools, which stood at 10,657 in 1918, was down to 7,966 in 1926, and up to 9,142 with 333,072 children in 3,331 schools ten years later. This gives the Sudeten Germans 21·4 per cent. of all the lower elementary schools in the Republic, i.e. just under their due proportion of 22·32 per cent. With upper elementary schools the figures were rather more favourable to the Germans in this 1926–36 decade; the number of these schools is now almost exactly 22·32 per cent. of all such schools in the State, and though the number of German classes is a little smaller, it increased by 29 per cent. from 1926 to 1936.[2] Czechoslovakia further took over from pre-War Austria the division of the Bohemian and Moravian provincial school councils into German and Czech sections. As against this the school councils were now under a Czech President whose powers were increased, while the centralizing authority of the Ministry of Education in Prague was emphatically asserted.

By the law of April 3rd, 1919,[3] the old Austrian figure of 40 children speaking a minority language in any commune was enacted as justifying the establishment of a lower elementary school for them, and if this school were visited by 400 children, then an upper elementary school could also be opened in conjunction with it. In view of pre-War local squabbles over schools, minority schools were now placed directly under the Ministry of Education. The law for providing minority schools was, nevertheless, mainly put into practice to provide Czech schools in predominantly German districts or in the vicinity of the 'language-frontier'; scarcely any German minority schools were opened. The Czechs had a genuine enthusiasm for education, and an array of fine new schools sprang up all over the country. It constantly occurred that the Germans perforce went on using their old school building dating from 1900 or 1890 or even earlier, while a much

---

[1] Figures supplied by the *Deutsche Kulturverband*. Lower elementary schools supply the first five years' schooling for children from 6 to 10 inclusive, and upper elementary schools supply a further three years up to the child's fourteenth birthday.

[2] All these are official Czechoslovak figures taken from Czechoslovak State statistical publications. Classes are very frequently taken as a unit, rather than schools or pupils.

[3] Sobota, *Das tschechoslowakische Nationalitätenrecht*, p. 183.

smaller number of Czech children was housed in the most up-to-date quarters; the new Czech 'palaces' became a sour joke among the Sudeten Germans, who, as they grumbled, paid their taxes to the Government only to be thus 'provoked'.

One of the 'language-frontier' regions in which new Czech minority schools are most conspicuous is the area south of Winterberg (Vimperk) down to the villages south of Krumau (Český Krumlov) in the Böhmerwald and Southern Bohemia. Up to 1929 Czech *Volksschulen* had been built in the following predominantly German villages mostly for a mere handful of Czech children:[1]

Scheiben	Eleanorahain	Rosenberg
Wessely	Böhmisch Röhren	Gross Gallein
Freiung	Oberschlag	Salnau
Kuschwarda	Sablat	Höritz
Ottau	Priethal	Kalsching
Hohenfurth	Kienberg	

Several more have been added in this district since 1929. A number of genuinely German children go to these schools. In the early years of the Republic, and especially in Moravia, a number of indifferent families willingly changed from German to Czech schools, but in Southern and South-Western Bohemia it is rather a question of poverty and pressure. The population which, it has been seen, has always had a hard struggle for existence is offered some local advantage or that the Christmas treat at the Czech school will clothe the children for the winter. Local members of the *Národní jednota pošumovská* (Böhmerwald National Union) make much of these advantages and, where it applies, remind parents that they live on State forest land and had best please the State. The Ministry of Education may not know how the Czech minority schools are filled; it naturally does nothing to empty them. When the slump made itself felt in the thirties, economic pressure was more resented because it counted more; into the bargain the Government was proclaiming the need for economy, yet new minority schools[2] continued to appear. The Germans also complain that Czech minority schools have occasionally been built in villages with a Czech majority, and since only one minority school is allowed in a commune, the Germans then lose their chance. Albrechtsried (Albrechtice) and Raudnig (Roudníky)[3] are examples

[1] The law gives the Ministry of Education discretion to establish minority schools for less than 40 children where desirable.

[2] Since 1935 officially known as State Schools. It should be added that in the case of at least one of these schools opened in the Böhmerwald in 1937 it had been asked for by activist Germans because their children were too much victimized by young Henleinists in the German school.

[3] In February 1935 the *Völkischer Beobachter*, for instance, put Raudnig in a list of places in Czechoslovakia, some of which had a German majority and were yet allowed only a German minority school.

given, but both these places are in mixed areas, and with the population position so fluid as it is, it is often uncertain who has the majority—such are the problems of the Sudeten provinces. It would perhaps be unjust not to mention that the first thing I saw in the German village of Hohenfurth (Vyšší Brod) in Southern Bohemia in 1937 was a new German *Volksschule* (with *Nutze den Tag* writ large across it) which cannot have been more than a year or so old. Nor should one forget that the *Deutsche Kulturverband* and the *Bund der Deutschen* compete, where they can, in offering Christmas and other attractions. The fact, however, remains that there are about 16,000 German children at Czech elementary schools and only about 5,000 Czech children at German ones. The figure of 16,000 is composed also of the children of Germans (often officials) living in Czech districts where the Germans are nowhere near 20 per cent. and no one would dream of putting up a German school. The *Deutsche Kulturverband* does what it can to emulate the pre-War activities of the *Ustřední Matice Školská* and had in 1937 137 kindergartens, 70 nursery schools, 34 lower elementary schools, 2 upper elementary schools of its own.[1] Some of its schools—the one, for instance, at its headquarters in Prague —have been taken over by the State, and the State contributes to the others.[2] Great importance is, of course, attached to nursery schools and kindergartens by the keenest nationalists among both Sudeten Germans and Czechs, for the child cannot be captured too early. Attendance at these institutions is perfectly optional, but it is, perhaps, of interest that an analysis of the educational position in a nationalist German fortnightly on September 1st, 1937, complains that of the 1,004 Czech kindergartens in Bohemia 538 are supported by the State, which, however, only maintains one out of the 482 German Bohemian kindergartens.

Away from the language-frontier districts there are few genuine complaints about elementary schools as a whole. The municipal authorities of Eger (Cheb), Karlsbad (Karlovy Vary), and Aussig (Ústí) are able to provide adequate schooling for the Sudeten German children. It has been seen that minority schools apart,[3] the German-speaking population is about as well off as the Czechs and the Slovaks. New legislation in the summer of 1937 has improved the position with regard to the size of classes, so that the continued fall in the number of schoolchildren is not accompanied by a proportional reduction in the number of classes, and some

[1] Information supplied by the *Deutsche Kulturverband*.
[2] For the last ten years the *Deutsche Kulturverband* has received about 700,000 Kč from the State.
[3] The minority, or more correctly State, schools are obviously not included among the ordinary Czechoslovak schools whose numbers are counted up among those of the various nationalities in the official statistics.

earlier anti-German discrimination with regard to the size of classes appears to be vanishing.[1]

Many Sudeten Germans do not, of course, accept the school statistics published by the Government. They believe, for instance, that German schools which have been closed have remained on the official lists, especially since the law of December 20th, 1935, for the reorganization of the upper elementary schools; they also believe that German children at Czech schools are sometimes registered as Czech. It should, moreover, be borne in mind that the remarkable lack of schools for Germans in the ex-Hungarian territories of Slovakia and Ruthenia have caused a high proportion of new German schools in Czechoslovakia to be established there; this helps to justify the Sudeten Germans when they find it difficult to observe that much educational expansion has accrued to their benefit in Bohemia and Moravia-Silesia. They, for their part, often claim that, in the mountainous country in which they are at home, a relatively higher number of schools is required—on account of the difficulties of communication—than in the Czech interior. It would be difficult to find a régime which could accept this claim from a minority. On the other hand, it can scarcely be doubted that the Czechoslovak Government, as in the case of unemployment figures, gives itself the benefit of any doubt when statistics are compiled—is there any Government that does not?

(ii) PUBLIC LIBRARIES AND ADULT EDUCATION

On July 22nd, 1919, the National Assembly passed a generous law for the provision of public libraries, with special provision for minorities in any commune where there was a minority school, or where the minority numbered at least 400 people; where the minority was less than this, but constituted 10 per cent. of the population, it was to share in a library belonging to several communes.[2] With regard to the administration of this law one hears of few grievances. In the matter of adult education the State offers small subsidies to the Germans, who again complain that they receive so little. For the German Adult school at Brno (Brünn), for instance, the State provided 100,000 Kč, while 1,800,000 Kč was raised by the Brno Germans themselves. Multi-national cultural claims do, of course, strain the resources of a small State very severely.

(iii) SECONDARY SCHOOLS

With regard to secondary schools there are, strangely enough, very few tangible German grievances; the most embittered Sudeten

---

[1] See an article by the deputy, Herr Jaksch, in *Der Sozialdemokrat*, 'Um Schule und Zukunft', Oct. 27th, 1937. [2] Sobota, op. cit., p. 190.

Germans will say that the Czech National Unions know they cannot denationalize the secondary school children so they do not waste their time trying. The one big complaint is in the matter of the *Gymnasium* at Reichenberg (Liberec) which in 1935 was taken on economy grounds—for Czech[1] pupils; the German secondary school children have all since then had to go to the German *Realschule*. A similar change was spoken of for Arnau (Hostinné) near Trautenau (Trutnov), but it did not take place.[2]

It is significant of the strained atmosphere in the Historic Provinces that conciliatory people who would like to send their children for a time to a school where the language of instruction is not what they speak at home are mostly prevented from doing so because they would be thought nationally disloyal or because the children would feel themselves outsiders. The question mostly arises, of course, for the parents of children attending secondary schools. It arises, however, relatively seldom because the Germans feel Czech to be not merely difficult but antipathetic, a subjectivism which the course of history has shaped. It should not be forgotten that most Czechs pronounce German with obvious difficulty.

(iv) TEACHERS AND INSPECTORS

With regard to teachers there are no important Sudeten German grievances; indeed, the Sudeten Germans never mention the teaching profession when complaining of the eviction of Germans from State, provincial, and communal jobs, because, as a whole, German teachers are equitably employed. The only sign of discrimination is that while Czech is taught by Czechs in German schools, German in Czech schools is often taught by Czechs. With regard to inspection it is not denied that German schools are only inspected by Germans, though the final authority is in Czechoslovak hands; actually one of the heads of all school inspection is President Beneš's elder brother, a man rightly honoured for his liberal attitude in the national question. Emphatically nationalist Germans object to the fact that the inspectors are expected to maintain a neutral attitude, i.e. it is *mal vu* for them to belong to the German *Kulturverband*; in the German camp, especially since 1933, it is said that the Czechoslovak authorities thereby compel the German inspectors to behave in an un-German manner.

(v) 'HIGH SCHOOLS'

By 'High Schools' Central Europe understands universities polytechnics, and all kinds of training colleges for particular jobs

[1] The Reichenberg population is now about 18 per cent. Czech.
[2] A girls' secondary school at Troppau (Opava) has been closed and the girls attend what was previously only a boys' school, but it is not clear that reduced numbers did not justify the change.

The struggle for these institutions was one of the pivots of the German-Czech situation before 1914. The very German view that *Kultur*, at any rate east of the Rhineland, was altogether a German affair was the greatest obstacle to the complete emergence of other nationalities; for *Kultur* covered, after all, intellectual and skilled technical achievement, and sought to perpetuate a German hegemony in the administration, in industry, and in that world which provided society with its main directions of thought and of feeling. It was here that language rivalry was more than mere bickering, for each language undoubtedly has a particular expressiveness of its own, and the one which is most generally accepted by any society inevitably moulds the form of its thinking.

In Austrian days, not only had the Czechs been unable to get their Moravian university,[1] but they had suffered from the slighter support they received from the State and the smaller resources of their students, who had mostly to struggle against very great poverty. It was inevitable and justifiable that after the War they immediately established a second Czech University at Brno (Brünn), just as they proceeded to found a first Slovak university at Bratislava. It was at first inevitable and justifiable that the Czechoslovak authorities supplied larger funds for social help to Czech and Slovak than to Sudeten German students; the Slovaks were particularly poor. As time went on, however, the old differentiations between Sudeten German, Czech, and Slovak means became, as the legislation of the Republic had intended, invalid; the Czechoslovak authorities easily forgot the extent to which their own levelling-up policy had succeeded by the time of the acutest depression in 1933 and 1934. When economies became essential they took it for granted that the Germans could best afford to make them. While this had not always ceased to be true, it was undoubtedly the case that since openings for young Germans in the army and in the administration had melted away to a minimum, they were therefore more eager than before to be armed with academic qualifications.

A new Brno (Brünn) crisis arose in 1934 when the Prime Minister, M. Malypetr, suddenly announced to the principal of the German *Technische Hochschule* or Polytechnic there that this institution must close down within two or three days, although, like the Czech Polytechnic in Brno, it had over 1,200 students. Owing to the intervention of the Foreign Minister, Dr. Beneš, this misfortune did not overtake the Moravian Germans. A year later,[2] however, the official German technical school for textile workers, which had enjoyed a flourishing career since October 1860, lost its independence, and was joined to the corresponding Czech

[1] See above, Chapter VII, pp. 63, 64.
[2] By an announcement dated July 18th, 1935.

institution in one bilingual State college. This was bitterly resented by the Germans of Brno as deliberately intended to obscure their technical prowess. The Czechs, on the other hand, felt that two technical schools at Brno were an unnecessary luxury and could not understand why the Germans so particularly treasured a separate existence.

It is, of course, in and around the university life of Prague that the intellectual battle most fiercely rages. Already at the beginning of 1920, before the German deputies had appeared in the Chamber, a law was passed according to which the Czech, not the German, university in Prague was declared to be the only true Charles University.[1] It is difficult to excuse the ever-recurring obstinacy with which Germans speak of Charles IV as having founded the first German University in 1348, now that the word *German* has acquired a racial sense entirely alien to medieval conceptions, but it is equally difficult to excuse the aggressive attitude of some Czech professors; after all, if any descent could be claimed, the vicissitudes of history had allowed greater continuity to the German University. It was actually not until after the Nazi revolution in the Reich that, following serious student disorders, the Ministry of Education in November 1934 compelled the German professors to surrender the Caroline insignia which were then handed over to the Czechs. There is a rumour that the famous insignia were discovered, after much commotion, not to be genuine—a pleasant little irony for all but the Czechs and the Germans concerned.

Under the Republic the German University in Prague has not been unfairly treated with regard to directly educational subsidies,[2] though it has been seen that the Germans were deliberately treated as youths who had less economic hardship to face than the Czech and Slovak students. A great deal of friction has occurred over university housing and laboratory conditions. These were all exceedingly bad in pre-War days, and too little has as yet been done to improve matters; on the other hand, I have sometimes been invited to deplore the historic character of academic quarters whose hygienic failings were certainly rivalled in Oxford or Cambridge until quite recently. The hospitals in Czechoslovakia are altogether very poorly equipped, and medical students, both Czech and Sudeten German, are often without the simplest surgical apparatus. Late in 1937 three new hospitals for the Germans in Prague were arranged for, and it is hoped that they will soon be available for patients and medical students alike. Another loudly voiced German complaint is that it has hitherto been impossible

[1] In the seventeenth century the Jesuit reorganization had led to the name of Charles Ferdinand University.

[2] According to information received from German, as well as Czech, University sources.

for a Sudeten German to study veterinary surgery in his own language in Czechoslovakia. In general, relatively more has been done for the 10,000 Czech students than for the 5,000 German students under the Republic, for the Czech University has acquired new buildings for its philosophical and its law faculties. The German law faculty is still lodged in the Carolinum (which belongs to the Czech University) because the arrangements for constructing a new building have encountered the most protracted delay; indeed, most Germans speak as if *they* never expect to see their new university building materialize. The obstruction is thought to have come from the city of Prague with regard to the site, but since 1936 when a conciliatory Lord Mayor succeeded the well-known Germanophobe, Dr. Baxa, it appears that the difficulties will now certainly be mastered. The German philosophical faculty will be provided for at the same time; it is at present housed in the Clementinum together with the University Library. There in the library, which the two universities share, and where Czech and German notices, with occasionally a few words of French in addition, share the honours, the peace which wisdom should provide seems to reign.

While the Czechoslovak Republic has hitherto provided all its universities with more academic freedom than, perhaps, any other country on the Continent,[1] the disappearance of Habsburg Austria undoubtedly inflicted a very great blow to the intellectual life of the Sudeten Germans. Like so many other post-War hardships, this was in the nature of things. The old Austrian academic ladder had been Czernowitz (Cernaŭti), Innsbruck, Prague, Graz, Vienna, and German-speaking professors and students had circulated, not only between these five 'inland' universities, but had also had the free run of those in the Reich and in German Switzerland. Before Europe was overtaken with the currency cramp of the thirties, the old area was not blacked out, but it was far less accessible for obvious economic reasons, and also because a Prague German student after the War was only allowed to count two half-years spent at a foreign university towards his final qualification. It has been seen that many Sudeten Germans studied entirely at Vienna, but in recent years foreign exchange difficulties have created further impediments. Thus the number of German students at Prague has considerably increased. It should, however, be observed that, whereas in the early days of the Republic many of the Sudeten Germans clamoured to have their university transferred to Reichenberg (Liberec) or at any rate to some Sudeten German

[1] Early in 1937 the Ministry of Education proposed to restrict this freedom, but all the universities, Czech, Slovak, and German alike, protested, and there has hitherto been no change, nor does it seem probable that any will now occur.

town, nothing is heard of this project to-day. On the contrary, the German students in Prague seem to be taking more trouble to learn Czech, and since many young Czechs are blind to the advantages enjoyed by their bilingual fathers, the tables are turned and it is the German young men who more often know Czech.

(vi) THE ROLE OF PRAGUE

The effect of post-War frontiers upon historical research at the German University at Prague has been interesting. In response to new boundaries people have chosen small local Bohemian themes for study. With the rise of German national feeling in the thirties, researchers, consciously or unconsciously, have been harping upon the German character which they claim for, at any rate, all the best things in Bohemia, and they lay emphasis, naturally, upon all that is German in the city of Prague. It will, perhaps, be most satisfactory to consider the complicated role of Bohemia's capital city here and now. To the Sudeten Germans the importance of Prague has become increasingly acute, since, in 1848, the temporary collapse of the *ancien régime* revealed how overwhelmingly Czech the town already was. This revelation showed Prague to be a Czech centre whose value as head-quarters of the Czech national movement was inestimable; to the extremer Czech nationalists, who hoped to 'win back' the 'Germanized' districts, the perfect position of Prague, as the centre towards which the German towns, too, were bound to gravitate, was a factor of first-rate importance. With industrialization the German towns grew, but they remained small and geographically divorced from one another, and indeed with the development of the railways they became more dependent upon Prague, where all the main lines were bound to intersect, than ever before.

Thus the struggle for control of the administration of Prague, together with the struggle for a Czech University and National Theatre, became of the greatest importance in the Czech-German situation. It will be realized that these things were closely interrelated since a Czech town council majority could do much to further Czech building projects and give the city so Czech a complexion as to make the German University appear as a foreign institution. So late as 1784 Czech had been the language in which Prague was mainly administered, but, from the time of the reforms of Joseph II, not only were university lectures given, but also the government of the city was conducted, in German. After a brief year or so (1848 and 1849) of equality for the rival languages in the city, German received back its monopoly until the reforms of 1861. In the municipal elections which then occurred the Czechs were immediately successful in all the *curiae,* and in the town council of

90 there were 75 Czechs—including both Palacký and Rieger—and only 15 Germans; this result was described by the newspaper *Bohemia* at the time as a 'Solferino for the hitherto powerful'. By 1882 the number of Germans had fallen to 4. On October 12th of that year the mayor, Tomáš Černy, proudly referred in a speech to 'golden and Slavonic Prague', whereupon the four German town councillors felt called upon to protest by withdrawing, and until the days of the Republic, German councillors never reappeared in the town hall; the last official report on the administration of Prague to appear in German was published in 1896.

The apparently childish exit of the Germans at the Czech claim to a Slavonic Prague expressed the intensity of the feelings entertained on this issue. To the Czechs, a small Slav island in a German sea, the assertion of the difference of national character was tremendously important. As communications developed, the assumption made by the Sudeten German, the man from the *Alpenländer* of Austria or the Reich German, that every waiter and porter in Prague must speak German, and that all public notices should appear in German as well as in Czech, made it increasingly difficult for the city to assert a non-German character of its own, a different identity from the purely German-Austrian towns. And if it failed to do so, geography and the presence of the German University and Theatres, with their close association with other German-speaking institutions, would make the Historic Provinces into a Germanic dependency permeated with Germanism to an extent which must sap the vitality of their non-German life. Such considerations account for the apparently trivial squabbles over the names of the Prague streets. Here Czech had been added to German some years before 1848. From 1861, however, the order was reversed, and *Václavské Náměstí* appeared above *Wenzelsplatz*. On December 21st, 1892, the Prague Town Council decided to eliminate the German names altogether. There were loud German protests at once, and the Governor (*Statthalter*) of Bohemia opposed the mayor. It is interesting that when the matter was taken to Vienna for a final decision the imperial authorities, as often before, were far less pro-German than the Bohemian Germans. Those were, of course, the Badeni times,[1] and from 1894 the German street-names were removed from Prague. The Germans, thereupon, put out their own street names on 201 houses, but again a decision from Vienna in 1896 denied their right to do so.[2] The Germans in Prague were diminishing rapidly at this time, and numbered only some 5 per cent. of the 190,000 inhabitants, a

---

[1] See Chapter V.
[2] See *Administrační Zpráva obce . . . Prahy za rok*, 1896, p. 311. The rest of these facts come also from the archives of the city of Prague.

much smaller minority than the Czechs in Vienna;[1] it has been seen that, in their Whitsun programme of 1899 they nevertheless demanded the restitution of complete language parity.[2]

With the emergence of the Czechoslovak Republic, in Prague, as in Brno and elsewhere, the suburbs were incorporated with the central quarters of the city, and the capital soon numbered some 900,000 and may to-day be counted as a town with a million inhabitants. The suburbs notwithstanding, the proportion of Germans has declined scarcely at all, partly because the centralization of administration, banking, and commerce in Prague, and the greater dependence of the Sudeten Germans upon their Prague University, has again raised the number of Germans living in the capital after a marked decline in their numbers between 1890 and 1914. Since 1918 they have been proportionally represented on the town council, and since the last elections in 1931 have four representatives on a council of 100.

There have, of course, been very bitter complaints of petty persecution of Germans and German in Prague since 1918. The lord mayor, Dr. Baxa, was undoubtedly an exaggerated enemy to Germanism in the capital, and even prevented shop signs from being exhibited in German, though no objection was made to other foreign languages. While that sort of thing seems petty and stupid it is not difficult to understand. More than ever the Czechs wished their Prague to be fundamentally Slavonic in character, though geography pressed so hardly against their desire. There was no possibility of Prague being absorbed into a French or an English world, and so the Prague people had nothing against a shop sign in French, and preferred to try to speak English with foreigners though they knew German much better and were perhaps making fools of themselves. In the experience of the present writer it requires nothing but two words in Czech[3] or an apology that one cannot speak their language to bring the Prague people who know German to speak it without restraint. The influence, moreover, of Dr. Zenkl, Dr. Baxa's successor since 1936, is making itself felt in the direction of a more liberal attitude, though the Prague Czechs resent a Sudeten German who has not to some degree mastered the 'first' language of the State.

With the growth of the feeling of Sudeten German unity the importance of Prague has increased for the Germans in the

---

[1] The Czechs in the early years of this century numbered about 12–15 per cent. of the Vienna population, but the proportion is always difficult to estimate because many of them had ceased to bother about their Czech nationality, more especially under the famous lord mayor, Dr. Lueger, whose remark 'Leave my Czechs in peace', became proverbial.

[2] See above, Chapters VII and XI, section (ii), p. 109.

[3] Cf. Naumann, *Mittel-Europa*, p. 253, where the same experience is indicated.

Republic, for no other town has proved really eligible as a Sudeten German centre; this is one reason why the talk of removing the German University has entirely ceased. Among the followers of Spann, of Patscheider, or among other varieties of Pan-German enthusiasts, while some emphasize the linking-up importance of Moravia, all of them believe that Prague has pre-eminent significance as a centre of the German *Mittel-Europa* of the future; for this reason, too, the German University has a great function to fulfil by remaining in Prague, and its historians, it has been seen, are, in one way and another, emphasizing the German aspect of the history and character of the capital of Czechoslovakia.

(vii) THEATRE AND OPERA

The theatre question had always played a big part in the intellectual battle between Germans and Czechs. For both peoples theatre and opera play a larger part in life than they do among the British. On the Continent, too, the State directly concerns itself with far more cultural activities than an Englishman naturally expects, and this is especially true of the theatre in all its branches. Thus political differences penetrate into the most unpolitical social crevices.

The Sudeten Germans had, and still have, an astonishing number of subsidized theatres.[1] This is due, again, to their many small towns, i.e. to geographical circumstances. So many theatres playing only for some months in the year constitute a very uneconomical system to which the Czechoslovak State, especially in lean years, naturally contributes with less satisfaction than did the old Habsburg authorities. The scattered character of the Sudeten German population further made Prague exaggeratedly important for them with regard to the theatre as with regard to university life. Thus at the time of the break-down of Austria, though Prague had done so much to assert its Slavonic character, there were two big publicly subsidized German theatres in the city and only one comparable Czech institution, the National Theatre, which had arisen at the beginning of the eighties.[2] The two German theatres were the 'New German Theatre', dating from the same decade as the Czech National Theatre, and the *Ständetheater* or theatre of the Estates. The latter was an aristocratic foundation dating from the eighteenth century, and in the days of Bohemianism had played in both languages; in the last days of the monarchy, however, it had long played in nothing but German. After 1918 it was scarcely to be expected that this two-to-one German-to-Czech situation could continue in a 95 per cent. Czech town and the capital at that.

---

[1] I believe I am right in saying that there are more German than Czechoslovak subsidized theatres in the Republic.   [2] See Chapter V, p. 40.

In 1920, indeed, Czech crowds demonstrated in front of the *Ständetheater* and occupied it. An arrangement was subsequently made[1] by which the Germans resigned their claims to it; in return they henceforth received a regular subsidy for the 'New German Theatre', and a substantial contribution towards a new German theatre called *Die kleine Bühne* which was started in 1923; the two German theatres are under joint management.

The change-over was perhaps more hardly felt in towns like Brno (Brünn) where, roughly speaking, the upper stratum of society had been German, thus supplying an unduly high proportion of the theatre-going public. In Brno there was only the one official theatre, and in the early days of the Czechoslovak Republic it was agreed that German plays should be given two nights in the week; the 1921 census showed Brno town and surroundings together to be nearly three-quarters Czech, so that the arrangement seemed not ungenerous. At the same time it is easy to feel with German Moravians if they found the banishment of Grillparzer and Lessing a saddening affair, the more since Brno's nearness to Vienna had pampered the city with frequent visits from the greatest actors and singers of the German-speaking world. The new arrangement, moreover, worked badly, there were mutual Czech-German recriminations, and after a time the theatre was only available for the Germans on Mondays. One night a week was found to be a very expensive plan, the more since the Germans of Brno decided to reserve it for opera and for important visitors, while running plays and operettas in two private halls of their own. The Germans, therefore, resolved to build a theatre for themselves; they have collected some $3\frac{1}{2}$ million Kč for the purpose and the Government is helping them out with a million or so more. The fact that Czech-German personal relations in Moravia are friendlier than elsewhere has helped matters forward, but there have been endless delays over this business, and the Germans accuse the Brno municipal authorities of obstruction. Official delay has the excuse in Czechoslovakia, as it has in Austria, Hungary, and the Balkan States that the old Habsburg tradition of *Schlamperei* still inevitably survives, but the new German theatre in Brno is now actually begun.

In the Sudeten German towns of Bohemia an arrangement is in operation by which the local theatre is placed at the disposal of the Czech minority one night a week or something of the kind. Even Eger (Cheb) is constrained to allow the Czech language to come across its theatre footlights once in a while. It should perhaps be mentioned in this context that the Czech municipal authorities of Budějovice (Budweis) are taking an interest in the traditional Ger-

[1] Largely through the influence of Dr. Beneš.

man passion play at Höritz (Hořice) in Southern Bohemia; they are helping financially, and the suggestion that they have attempted to 'de-Germanize' the performances appears to be malicious and meaningless.

(viii) EFFECT OF THE REICH GERMAN REVOLUTION OF 1933

The National Socialist transformation of German life from 1933, and the promotion of Herr Alfred Rosenberg to be the official exponent of a Nazification which involves not merely political change but a completely revolutionized point of view towards every aspect of life, has created a profound disturbance in the Sudeten German mind. If the Sudeten Germans were to remain in cultural unity with Germany they must now accept the permeation of literature, theatre, film with a racial, anti-democratic point of view according to which the Masarykian principles at the basis of the Czechoslovak State ceased to make sense. Even those Czechs who had all along had a fanatically nationalistic outlook[1] had been curbed by the fact that they had to do lip-service to Masaryk's views; their hypocrisy maddened the Sudeten Germans, but chauvinism is, I think, weakened by being compelled to wear a mask, and in Czechoslovakia, as many of the best judges believed, the time factor, if undisturbed by external events, was working against extreme Czech nationalism.

But now there came a clarion call from the Reich. All Germans must hold together and be truly German, i.e. subjective, for it was un-German to attempt objectivity. German *Kultur* must be based upon German *Volksgemeinschaft*, which, knowing no frontiers, must yet take its lead from the party which had been able to grasp power in the Reich. All political and aesthetic standards must be *völkisch* (= national or racial, literally folk-ish), not democratic, i.e. a man must follow his racial group rather than listen to reason or any aesthetic criticism which could be associated with two now condemned standards of value—the one individual and the other international. Herr Henlein[2] did not accept the pagan theses of

---

[1] The extreme *Národní jednota* people were, in the Nazi way, prepared to regard the needs of their nation as the highest moral law; as far as I am aware they did not, however, make *Herrenvolk* claims for the Czechs—they endowed Czech or Slav civilization with a certain sanctity, but did not claim that either the Czechs, or the Slavs as a whole, were born to supply the ruling caste among the nations, whereas the ruling caste theory has formed one of the bases of school teaching in Germany since the installation of the Nazi régime.

The Czech National Socialists, though sometimes very chauvinist, have always remained a party favouring democratic as opposed to dictatorial methods, and are therefore entirely distinct from German National Socialists. Though some of their members are keen National Union members, the National Unions are recruited rather from the National Democrats (followers of Kramář) and of course from the Agrarians.

[2] See his *Kultur* speech of Feb. 23rd, 1936, in *Konrad Henlein spricht*.

Herr Rosenberg though he wished Christianity to be kept out of politics. And it has been seen that Herr Henlein at first emphasized loyalty to the Czechoslovak State as against a frankly irredentist standpoint.[1] But in the Czech view his loyalty would involve a perversion of the State which Masaryk and Beneš had done so much to build up. In cultural, as in political matters—and the line between them had been blurred out of recognition by the Nazi, as by the Bolshevik, revolution—many Czechs now believed that he who does not coerce the would-be coercer is lost in a fight against a totalitarian creed.

Before 1933 there was of course some friction over the importation of school-books or newspapers from abroad. Sometimes, even then, Pan-German disloyalty to Czechoslovakia had given the Czechoslovak authorities grounds for interference. But again the action of officials was sometimes based upon their ignorance of German, or sometimes upon bureaucratic pettiness. The Sudeten Germans naturally resented the Czech official mis-spelling of the word Czechoslovakia in German State documents. The č, though so much simpler than the German equivalent, is not German, and it was foolish to try to compel the Sudeten Germans to write Čechoslovakei instead of Tschechoslowakei.[2] In school-books and elsewhere the fact that, in Czech, there is no distinction between the word for Bohemian and the word for Czech[3] led to ambiguity which was often irritating for the Germans of Bohemia.

The question of the text-books, atlases, &c., used in schools had caused a certain amount of trouble all along. In 1925 a decree[4] had been issued according to which educational accessories of foreign origin required the approval of the Ministry of Education in advance. It was intelligible that Czechoslovakia did not wish her future citizens to be educated with such old Habsburg and Hohenzollern text-books as Sudeten German schoolmasters would be happy to use; since the Sudeten frontiers had changed so little, she was not, as a matter of fact, so unwilling for pre-War atlases to be used by Sudeten German as by Magyar children. The Ministry of Education was free to make exceptions, but, *en principe,* books, &c., were only to be imported from countries which would also import educational material from Czechoslovakia, a fairly severe restriction. The 1925 decree was repeated in December 1932. Actually on the Continent, where private schools are exceptional, the State expects to exercise a strict control of the text-books in use, and exceptions in favour of old books were often made, especially when new ones would have involved too much expense

---

[1] Chapter XIV.
[2] In Czech *Československo,* so that Čechoslovakei means nothing.
[3] Cf. Chapter II, p. 15.
[4] Decree of the Ministry of Education no. 24, 943/24—I. Nov. 14th, 1925.

for the local authorities. But there were red-tape officials who not only removed all the traditional pictures of the Habsburg Emperors but were also capable of removing, say, a photograph of some figure painted on the roof of the Sistine Chapel because its country of origin was not Czechoslovakia. Moreover, for the Sudeten German secondary schools there was sometimes a genuine dearth of the less obvious school-books, because Sudeten German publishers found it too expensive to produce only for their own small market.

From 1933 onwards the foibles of some Czech officials received a justification which they could not have found before. If German school-books and encyclopaedias now became full of *völkisch*, un-democratic assumptions, and therefore implicitly anti-Czech, there was a much stronger case for banning their use. The school-book question had been more or less dealt with, but in the autumn of 1933 a stock-taking of the accessories at all elementary schools was ordered by the Ministry of Education in order to guard the Reich German frontier more carefully. The new Nazi encyclopaedias were troublesome, and for a time Brockhaus and Duden were for-bidden until more suitable versions could be prepared for Republi-can use. The extremer Nazi newspapers, too, were forbidden to come in from the Reich, and the censorship within the country became more severe. This censorship could be very annoying, sometimes, again, because the censors did not know German exactly enough, and always because, being a censorship that comes after a newspaper or book is ready for publication, these things now frequently appeared with large blank spaces. 'What sort of democracy is this?' the Germans would say, but the things with the blank spaces were circulated with an evident satisfaction never-theless; indeed they were often reprinted with the spaces headed *Beschlagnahmt*.[1] Every State claims, and probably must claim, the right to suppress directly subversive attacks made upon it, and most Czechs believed that the torrent of propaganda from the newly Pan-Germanized Reich, whose frontiers marched with three sides of the Bohemian quadrilateral, genuinely menaced the Re-public. The Reich papers now constantly published attacks upon Czechoslovakia from the Sudeten German *émigrés*, such as Dr. Viererbl, who had joined the staff of the *Völkischer Beobachter*, and Herren Krebs, Jung, and Schubert, who had made themselves scarce soon after the *Volkssport* Trial verdict, and who, at the first opportunity, were nominated and elected by the Nazi party to be members of the German Reichstag in apparent contravention of treaty agreements.[2] Within Czechoslovak frontiers, the interference

---

[1] *Beschlagnahmt* = confiscated.
[2] The Czechs protested against the election since the men in question had not cancelled their Czechoslovak citizenship and were therefore not eligible by

with the freedom of the Sudeten German press has all along, to the student of general conditions in Europe east of the Rhine, seemed astoundingly slight; when reading the Henleinist paper *Die Zeit*, one can often scarcely believe one's eyes that it should be allowed the liberties it takes. The German minority in Czechoslovakia is, in this respect, distinctly better off than the Magyar minority.[1]

If the Czechs disliked the election of Sudeten Germans to the Reichstag in 1936, the Sudeten Germans objected to the inevitable result of the totalitarian victory in the Reich, that German democrats and littérateurs took refuge in Prague. Indeed, the peculiar situation arose that Germany's greatest twentieth-century writer, Thomas Mann, asked for and received Czechoslovak citizenship. Thus the Czechs became the protectors of men whom the world had acclaimed as the best products of modern German *Kultur*, while Sudeten German children, following the example of their fellows of the Reich, despised Goethe as un-German because he had been a great European.[2] The Sudeten German activists, Catholic or Socialist, were bound to deplore the persecution of Socialists and Catholics in Germany, to help refugees and to try to keep their point of view alive. Thus the activists were attacked by the *Sudetendeutsche Partei*, not only as corrupt party chiefs who had allowed their people to be destroyed by economic distress, but as traitors to German civilization.

Meanwhile, though the Czechs and Slovaks were as a whole anti-Communist, old Pan-Slav traditions and a certain familiarity with the language gave them an interest in literary and film developments in the new Russia, more especially since the U.S.S.R. had apparently acquired stability and permanence. Communism among students, for instance, was, as it was in Yugoslavia, much rather a pro-Russian than a pro-Marx or -Lenin feeling. It would be difficult to be certain that there was at any time more Soviet, than French, or German, or Tsarist Russian, cultural influence in Czechoslovakia. The old legionary tradition inherited by the Czechoslovak army was, if mostly Kerenskist, strongly anti-Communist, while the influence of that eminent patron of *les beaux arts*, Dr. Kramář, until his death in 1937, was definitely Tsarist Russian.

The totalitarian cultural claims of Nazi Germany were disturbingly felt in every direction; there were occasions, now, when

treaty to become Reich German; the Czechs were told that they had nevertheless received German citizenship.
[1] Among other examples, a Magyar paper was, in March 1937, forbidden to publish a criticism of Dr. Hodža which habitually appeared in the Sudeten German press.
[2] I have encountered various examples of this.

activists who were keenly German really preferred to send their
children to a Czech school to avoid bullying by Henleinist children.[1] The German theatres in the Historic Provinces sometimes
stood empty because the Czechoslovak and activist German local
authorities allowed plays with an anti-Nazi flavour to be given.
Indeed, the Czechs of Brno (Brünn) now objected that if the
Germans did build their new theatre there, the Henleinists would
boycott it unless it gave seditious plays; meanwhile the acid dissensions which Hitlerism and Henleinism have brought about
among the Sudeten Germans themselves undoubtedly combined
with Czech hesitation to delay the building of the Brno German
theatre until late in 1937. At about the same time the Reichenberg
theatre had to be rescued from bankruptcy by a presidential subsidy, because the Henleinists had boycotted its productions on
account of collaborators whom they condemned as not racially
pure or as too much on the Left.

Many of the issues at stake were raised in one of Herr Henlein's
most important speeches delivered in Prague on February 23rd,
1936.[2] On that occasion he claimed that *völkisch* unity was the
only possible source of true art, and made it perfectly clear that
such unity required that the Sudeten Germans should accept the
leadership of the Reich.

As Germans in the Sudeten provinces [he said], in spite of our unusual
political position, we feel ourselves as members of the great cultural
community of the Germans in the whole world, and have here, as we
have always had, German cultural tasks to carry out characteristically.

The idea of an only partially German Bohemianism he rejected out
of hand.[3] 'It must be branded as a cultural scandal if it is attempted
to set up artificial frontiers in the realm of the spirit, frontiers
which make all creative exchange impossible.' The university, he
declared, could never give up the appointment of German professors from abroad, and he complained that the professors at the
German University, not being filled with the new (i.e. Nazi) spirit
of the times, were out of touch with the students. Actually the
autonomy of the German University in Prague had not been interfered with,[4] but it was scarcely possible to appoint frankly Nazi
professors from the Reich, while Liberal or Socialist or Jewish
exiles from Germany led to difficulties with the Sudeten German
students. There was, for instance, the notorious example of the
hostile demonstrations on the occasion, in October 1936, of the

[1] See above, section (i), p. 209, n. 2, of this chapter.
[2] See collection of speeches entitled *Konrad Henlein spricht*. Also published as
separate pamphlet in the *Bücherei der Sudetendeutschen, Die deutschen Kulturauf-
gaben in der Tschechoslowakei* (Karlsbad, 1936).
[3] This 'symbiosis' idea had always been favoured by Dr. Spina.
[4] See above, p. 215, n. 1.

inaugural lecture of Professor Kelsen, a man of great intellectual distinction and of wide popularity, even as it happened a native of Prague, but 'tainted' with genuine liberalism and Jewish descent. The Prague professors as a whole were, indeed, men who still valued a *démodé* liberalism, and believed that learning can only serve, or be served by, those who accept objectivity as at least a necessary aim. In making their appointments they were largely thrown back, now, upon Sudeten German resources by nothing but the force of events.

In his *Kultur-Rede* of February 1936 Herr Henlein *inter alia* complained that the German Music Academy received much less than the corresponding Czech institution, and that in the bilingual Arts and Crafts School in Prague the teachers are all of them Czech. He did not refer to the chief Art School, where, of twelve regular instructors, three remain German—it could only be objected that younger people should by now be appointed, for the three have been at work there since the birth of the Republic. In these various directions, the State has certainly done more for Czech than for German students until recently, but it has been influenced by the originally justifiable consideration, which has been seen to have carried great weight in the allocation of University subsidies, that the German students were backed by greater private resources. It will be seen[1] that in 1937 the Czechoslovak Government revised the subsidy policy it had hitherto pursued.

(ix) THE JEWISH QUESTION

In the Prague speech Herr Henlein had complained of 'un-German' professors and the greater liberty accorded to the 'un-German' newspapers appearing in German. It was un-German, of course, to refuse to accept the new Reich German point of view. Some of the professors to whom he referred, and most of the journalists, not merely favoured tolerance and criticism, but were of course 'un-German' in the sense that they were Jews. This was true also of a fairly high proportion of the theatrical and film producers to whose work he was taking objection.

The plight of the Jews in Central and Eastern Europe is one which most people in the west prefer to forget. The fact that Czechoslovakia is the one country where legal discrimination against them does not occur does not make their position in the Republic a completely happy one. Anti-Semitic Socialism was a product of old Austria; it sprang up, not only in the Historic Provinces, but also in Styria. In Germany the chief financiers were Jews, but, on the whole, the industrialists were not; in Austria and Hungary Jewish employers formed a conspicuous majority.

[1] See below, Chapter XVI, section (ii), p. 269.

Thus the anti-Semitism as well as the anti-Slavism of the socialism of contemporary Germany is essentially Austrian.

In the old days the Slavs, and among them the Czechs, were anti-Semitic because they regarded the Jews as Germanizers or Magyarizers as the case might be. They were right; the Jews were tremendously devoted to the cause of German *Kultur* in old Austria as they were to that of Magyar civilization in Hungary. Away in the east the University of Czernowitz (Cernaŭti) was a great centre for the dissemination of German *Kultur* to, but also by, the Jews. So long as the Court was there to condemn the Schönerer movement, the Jews under-estimated the anti-Semites, and they never took seriously enough the Reichenberg attitude of rejection towards themselves.[1] After the War it was surprising how many Jews still filled in the census as Germans, though they could now be entered as Jews, and though to enter as Czechoslovaks would be most advantageous. Even after 1933 it is often with infinite difficulty that the Jews of Eastern Europe withdraw their allegiance to the Germanism which spurns them.

Since 1933 the Sudeten Germans have, however, been able to attack Czechoslovakia as the State *par excellence* which is run by the Jews. This is not merely because a good deal of industry on Czechoslovak territory has remained in Jewish ownership, the privately owned lignite mines, Spiro's paper-mills, and, to some extent, Vitkovice (Witkowitz), for example. It is not only because Jews have taken refuge in the Republic. It is largely because Nazi Germany, with its remarkable conjuring qualities, equates Jewry, democracy, and Bolshevism, and the Sudeten Germans, in their enthusiasm not to be un-German, accept this *tour de force*. Finally, it is characteristic of the whole situation that the Germans, who are willing and able to learn Czech and willing to serve the Republic faithfully, are to a high degree Jews. Many a firm requiring a bilingual staff for practical reasons finds the Jews the best linguists, and therefore picks them out. For the service of the State, again, the non-Henleinist candidates with the best language qualifications tend to be Jews. During 1937, when the Czechoslovak Government genuinely wished to appoint more German officials,[2] this tendency became conspicuous. On these, as upon other, grounds the extremist Germans dismissed the move towards conciliation as eyewash. Perhaps the most delicate point of all for Czechoslovakia's Jews to-day is that the minority rights of towns like Brno will depend upon the nationality under which they register in the census due in 1940; indeed, it is generally admitted in Brno itself that enough Jews will withdraw their German registration to make

---

[1] See above, Chapter VII, p. 68.
[2] See below, Chapter XVI, section (ii).

certain that the German minority will sink below 20 per cent. The Jewish position is thus extraordinarily difficult. If the German-speaking Jews remain faithful to their German traditions it is only to be racially rejected by the majority of people who speak the same language; if, on the other hand, they register as Jewish or Czechoslovak, they help to reduce the rights of the language they prefer and are likely to be at least as bitterly reproached.

With every incitement to anti-Semitism supplied to them from within and without, the Sudeten Germans have been carrying out a minor anti-Semitic boycott on their own. The *Bund der Deutschen* is proud that it teaches the people to 'buy German', i.e. not from Czechs or from Jews. One sometimes hears quite small children in Sudeten German towns telling each other that of course they must not buy sweets at that Jewish shop. Just recently old Jewish shops in Eger and Rumburg, for example, have had to close down on account of the boycott against them; I am told by friends in Reichenberg that such a thing would to-day be very much less likely there. Jewish doctors, as I happen to know from the case of Aussig (Ústí), are finding their non-Jewish patients unfaithful, and not long ago, when a Jewish painter exhibited there, there were disorderly protests, and his pictures were injured and deco-rated with swastikas. At the same time the Jewish boycott against Reich German goods is proving advantageous to several branches of Sudeten German industry, notably the fabric glove factories at Asch (Aš).[1]

(x) THE CATHOLIC CHURCH IN THE HISTORIC PROVINCES

In pre-War days the Catholic Church, except around Rumburg (Rumburk), was unpopular among the Sudeten Germans; they disliked it as too international, and further they accused it of condoning Czechification. It has been seen that Czechs were far readier to go into the Church than Germans,[2] even in the heyday of the Young Czechs who were so strongly anti-clerical; the chief reason, perhaps, was that the Czechs were poor, while the Germans saw many more profitable openings around them. As for Czechifi-cation, it is interesting that in the case of the German region around Tachau (Tachov), for example, where, even before 1914, sixteen out of seventeen parish priests were Czech, in the eyes of German colleagues they did nothing which could fairly be con-demned as chauvinistic. Elsewhere, of course, one hears of intran-sigent Czech priests. Of Leitmeritz (Litoměřice), on the other hand, one reads in the pages of Dr. Zemmrich that, if a Czech

[1] See below, Chapter XVI, section (ii), p. 256, note 1.
[2] See above, Chapter V, p. 41.

priest dared to betray national feelings, the Germans soon put an end to that.[1]

After the rise of Czechoslovakia a very admirable Czech Primate, Dr. František Kordač, succeeded the German-Austrian Count Huyn at Prague; the new Archbishop openly expressed the view that a German Bishop should be appointed for the Sudeten Germans. Although this never occurred, relations between Czechs and Germans within the Church have not been bad and more Germans have become priests in the post-War years; in some old abbey like Hohenfurth (Vyšší Brod), where Czech and German brothers are living peacefully together, one seems to escape most completely from racial strife. It is regrettable that Cardinal Kašpar, the present head of the Catholic Church in Czechoslovakia, and some of the leaders of the Czech Clerical Party, have often made public declarations of a rather pronouncedly Czech nationalist nature. The nationalist Sudeten Germans complain bitterly of the policy of sending Czech priests into German districts and Germans into Czech districts, which Cardinal Kašpar appears to advocate.

It has been seen that in the early years of the Czechoslovak Republic the Neo-Hussitism of many patriots endangered the relations between Prague and the Vatican.[2] Difficulties also arose because of the discrepancy between political and ecclesiastical frontiers. In the ex-Hungarian provinces this was chiefly due to Peace Treaty changes of political frontier, but in the Historic Lands the discrepancy dated back to the eighteenth century. Curiously enough, the conquests of Frederick the Great had never been noticed by the Catholic Church, and the district of Glatz had remained within the diocese of Prague while much of Austrian Silesia had remained subject to the Archbishop of Breslau; a few parishes in Prussian Silesia, too, had remained in the diocese of Olomouc (Olmütz). In addition to the consequent confusion, the Church, though let off relatively lightly, found itself weakened and impoverished by Czechoslovakia's Land Reform measures. Disputes over Church land came to a head at about the same time as the differences over Hus, on the occasion (August 12th, 1925) of the announcement that the lands of Tepl Abbey at Marienbad (Márianské Lázně) would in future belong to the State. The Abbot of Tepl was a German, Dr. Helmer, and the district was, of course, overwhelmingly German; the cause of the Church appeared once again to be identified, as it had been in Hussite days, with that of the Germans.

After a difficult time the Republic and the Vatican, thanks partly to the negotiations of Dr. Krofta at Rome, came to terms in the

---

[1] Zemmrich, *Sprachgrenze und Deutschtum in Böhmen*.
[2] See above, Chapter XII, section (i), p. 125.

Modus Vivendi[1] which was ratified early in 1928. State and ecclesiastical frontiers were, according to this, to be brought into conformity; in the land question, such Church land as the Land Office had not decided to expropriate was to be freed from all restrictions, the Church regaining full control. The Church, especially the Archbishops of Prague and Olomouc, were altogether handled with leniency by the Land Office. As for the matter of the Glatz-Silesia rectification, subsequent amplifications of the *Modus Vivendi* concerned themselves with it, but no signs of a practical readjustment have yet become visible.

The post-War introduction of proportional representation gave the German Christian Social or Clerical Party in the Historic Provinces a political position entirely denied to it under the Habsburgs, amidst the racialist fervour of the Sudeten Germans. It has been seen that a German Clerical entered the Czechoslovak Cabinet as Minister of Justice in 1926, and, although he withdrew in 1929, his party joined the Government again with the appointment of Herr Zajiček to Cabinet rank in the summer of 1936. It was in the pre-1933 period that the German Clericals had political importance, since, as it has been seen, the differences between the Vatican and Prague had temporarily brought the Sudeten Germans and the Church on to the same side of the fence. The German Clericals in Czechoslovakia, by the way, remained rather Austrian than Reich German; they were more on the right, that is to say, than the Centre Party in Germany, because, though there were some keenly Catholic trade unionists in the Historic Provinces, on the whole the German Centre people, with their Rhenish and Silesian following, were much more associated with labour.

To no group or organization has German National Socialism spelt greater disaster than to the Catholic Church. At first the Vatican was loath to emphasize the ideological gulf which yawned between Catholicism and Hitlerism, or to face the new *Kulturkampf* which now succeeded the struggle with Bismarck by some sixty years. Finally, in the Encyclical of March 1937, the terrific conflict was admitted and faced. The Glatz-Silesia confusion might have entangled the Sudeten Germans[2] in the Reich German religious struggle more than it actually did. Although the Sudeten German population is nominally Catholic to such an overwhelming extent that it is unnecessary to devote any space to the handful of Protestants who live mostly around Asch (Aš), those who went Henleinist in 1935 were satisfied with Hitler's case against the Pope. A great many people, especially the youth, went over from the Clericals to the *Sudetendeutsche Partei*, and, among the Clericals

[1] See F. J. Vondracek, *Foreign Policy of Czechoslovakia, 1918–1935* (New York, 1937).   [2] Just under 250,000 souls.

themselves, groups like the *Staffelstein* youth were in fact won away to the nationalist fold. Even the devoutness of Rumburg (Rumburk) melted away to nothing.

Herr Henlein, it is true, had at the opening of his political career expressed himself respectfully towards the Churches, while insisting that they should have no political influence. That he had left the Catholic to join the Protestant Church on account of his wife was generally respected, though the significance of the action in the light of pre-War Bohemian history could not be entirely ignored. While the S.d.P. has never frankly adopted a Schönerer or Rosenberg attitude towards Christianity, one can scarcely fail to be impressed with its attitude of tempered approval towards Reich German treatment of the Churches. Occasionally one hears some speech of Dr. Goebbels deplored by supporters of the S.d.P., but on the whole they and their press speak as if it were time some one should rid Hitler of these turbulent priests—'Why don't they suppress these Confessional pastors?' is a question I have often heard among the Sudeten Germans.

At the same time there has been no break with the Church; members of the S.d.P., other than Herr Henlein, have not left it. In passionately nationalistic centres like Eger one gets the impression of a particularly devout population. While leading Catholics are well aware that the racial creed, justifying force, which comes from the Reich, and which it would be 'un-German' for the Sudeten Germans to reject, is diametrically opposed to Christian values, the Sudeten German rank and file is happy to be Catholic and Henleinist at one and the same time. The women specialize in what increasingly deserves to be regarded as inconsequence, as Henleinist and Hitlerist come more and more to mean the same thing. The out and out Nazi opposition to the S.d.P. would certainly be stronger if it were not for the old Habsburg Catholic tradition which cut short the *Los von Rom* movement[1] about forty years ago, and which moderates the reaction to Herr Rosenberg's philosophy in the Historic Provinces to-day.

(xi) THE HLUČIN (HULTSCHIN) TERRITORY

The thorny question of Hlučin is unique and difficult to place. These 50,000 people, of whom about 80 per cent. spoke a Moravian Czech dialect,[2] had been extremely discontented as the subjects of Germany before the War. The Prussian authorities in return had neglected their territory which was poor and undeveloped. Most of the population was agricultural, and many Hlučin people picked

[1] See above, Chapter VI. In this connexion it should perhaps be mentioned that Eger was in the German diocese of Ratisbon until the dissolution of the Holy Roman Empire.   [2] See Chapter XI, section (iv), p. 116.

up a seasonal livelihood in the neighbouring German country where there was more to be earned. When they became Czechoslovaks they continued to earn across the frontier in Germany until the slump and the Nazi Revolution barred the way. The hardship involved combined with other resentments to complete the irritation of this chronically intractable population against the Czechoslovak authorities.

The latter, from the moment when they took over the administration, had adopted the racialist attitude towards the population of Hlučin, i.e. that these people, who were clearly Slav by descent and by language, must be rescued from the semi-Germanization which had overtaken them until then. There were no technical grounds to compel the existence of more than a couple of German village schools, since the census taken according to the mother-language test elsewhere revealed something just under a 20 per cent. German-speaking minority. All other German schools were consequently closed, and the German-speaking children either went to school in Troppau (Opava) or learnt privately at home, and non-German Hlučin parents often showed great eagerness for their children to join the German classes which sprang up. Indeed, far from settling down to their newly regulated Slavonic allegiance, the Hlučin people now developed a perverse admiration for the Germany against whose authority they had previously protested. When this same Germany became Hitlerist, then proceeded to shut its doors and cut away their principal earnings, the Germanophile enthusiasm of Hlučin appeared only to increase. Economy measures meanwhile involved the reduction of German schooling facilities in Troppau,[1] and the German-speaking children from Hlučin were left in a difficulty.

Apart from the expense of private tuition, new legislation now complicated the Hlučin situation. In 1935 the *Lex Uhlíř*, named after a Czech deputy who particularly interests himself in educational questions, was passed, and it came into force on April 1st, 1936. Since 1869 it had been allowed that children could be privately taught, provided they kept up to State standards by passing the requisite State examinations. In post-War Czechoslovak days, good democrats disliked the possibility which was thus provided for the children of aristocratic families to be kept aloof in the care of private tutors, and many people considered the Uhlíř law long overdue, according to which all children were now compelled to attend school unless a specific exception had officially been made.

Nowhere did the new legislation create serious difficulties, save

---

[1] Several hundreds of Hlučin children had come into Troppau, which threw disproportionate expense upon that town.

for Hlučin. For both Czech and German-speaking children, who had belonged to private German classes there, were now compelled to attend the Czech schools in the Hlučin territory. In the elections of May 1935, this scarcely 20 per cent. German population provided something like an 80 per cent. vote for the *Sudetendeutsche Partei*; thus the atmosphere was already feverish when the Czech schools became compulsory. Private tuition after school was still legally in order, and the Hlučin people ostentatiously engaged German teachers. In so poor a district so much private teaching would have been out of the question had not Reich German funds been available. Pro-German partisans freely admit that the V.D.A.[1] has always provided lavish funds for German lessons in Hlučin since the early days of the Czechoslovak Republic. Indeed, the Hlučin situation is really grotesque. Genuine believers in *das Völkische*, such as the organizers of the V.D.A., should scarcely help to impede the, as it were, re-racialization of the Slav population of Hlučin, and the Hlučin Henleinists exchanging S.d.P. catch-words in their own Slav dialect, even when they find themselves in prison in Moravian Ostrava (Mährisch Ostrau), are a by-word in that part of the world. For, with the constant stiffening of the frontier tension between Prussian and Czechoslovak Silesia, the Hlučin people have become a serious political problem. It is scarcely denied on the German side that Hlučin disloyalty has been amply exploited, and V.D.A. money, as all public organizations have become the instruments of the party which rules the German State, has tended more and more to assume the guise of subsidization by an unfriendly Power. Mysterious free drinks flow in the Hlučin territory nowadays—nobody knows who has paid for them. As for German lessons there, since 1933 they have inevitably become lessons in Hitlerism and in the twentieth-century 'Mythus'[2] of Herr Rosenberg. The Czechoslovak police have consequently arrested many of the teachers for inciting people to action against the State[3] or occasionally for action contrary to the State Defence Law of 1936.[4] These arrests are consistent with the laws, and fully comprehensible from a Czech point of view. But to the Hlučin population and in the eyes of nationalist Germans, since private teaching outside school hours is allowed by the law, the action of the police has appeared grossly oppressive. The fact that the Hlučin teachers have been imprisoned not at Troppau, where

[1] = *Verein*—later *Volksbund—für das Deutschtum im Auslande*. See above Chapter XII, sections (ii) and (iv).

[2] Herr Rosenberg's best-known work is entitled *Der Mythus des Zwanzigsten Jahrhunderts*.

[3] Crime under the 1923 Defence of the Republic Act, see above, Chapter XII, section (i).

[4] See below, Chapter XVI, section (i). There was a particularly large number of arrests in Hlučin in April 1937.

the police and the Czech judges have a particularly correct reputation, but at Moravian Ostrava where the police record is probably the worst in Czechoslovakia,[1] has added to the embitterment. The Czechs find the Hlučin people particularly exasperating and for this reason, if no other, the Czech authorities have mismanaged the Hlučin situation. One often hears people in Troppau say, 'Bismarck could not make the "Hultschiner" into Germans, but where he failed the Czechs have succeeded.'

[1] See Chapter XVI, section (ii), p. 262 below.

SINCE THE ELECTIONS OF 1935

(i) *From the Elections in May 1935 to the Eger Speech in June 1936*

AS a preliminary to the consideration of the last phase, the period since the Czechoslovak elections of May 1935, it will be necessary to glance at international developments since 1933; the Czech-German situation within Czechoslovakia has reacted very sensitively to every important international event.

In the first place, the early frowns of Marshal Pilsudski notwithstanding, the accession of Herr Hitler to supreme power in the Reich brought about a German-Polish *rapprochement* in the Ten Years' Agreement of January 1934. This *volte-face* was received with chagrin in Prussian circles, but it was consistent with Herr Hitler's Austrian background; German Nationalism in Austria had always worked along the line of resisting Pan-Slavism by making advances to the anti-Russian Poles, advances which, both before the War and after it, in hard fact gave the Poles a free hand to oppress the Ukrainians or Ruthenes. The relations of Czechoslovakia with Poland had been none too easy in the early twenties, and the Poles never really resigned themselves to the Teschen frontier decision. A treaty, political and economic, had nevertheless been signed in 1925, and all but minor difficulties appeared to have come to an end.

From January 1934, however, Czech-Polish relations bristled with disputes again. The Poles perpetually found fault with the Czech treatment of the small 80,000 Polish minority in Moravia-Silesia; they refused, however, to submit the matter to arbitration as the second part of the 1925 Treaty[1] indicated, and in the following September, at Geneva, they renounced their own minority obligations, i.e. the treatment of minorities in Poland was declared to be a purely internal affair. This Polish action was taken partly as a precaution against the new possibility of Russian comments at Geneva upon Polish minority questions, since the Soviet Union was now admitted to membership of the League of Nations. In 1934 Dr. Beneš had taken various steps to refortify the Little Entente, and it was with the approval of Roumania and Yugoslavia that he had recognized Bolshevik Russia in June 1934. The Poles now borrowed the bilateral arguments of the Germans to destroy the Eastern Pact plans which had been launched by MM. Barthou and Litvinoff in the previous May. Dr. Beneš, feeling Czechoslovakia's need for diplomatic reinforcement to be

---

[1] See Chapter XII, section (ii), p. 129.

the greater, proceeded on May 16th, 1935, to the signature of that
treaty with the U.S.S.R. which has apparently caused such violent
commotion in the minds of all Russia's opponents. It is important
clearly to record that the Czechoslovak-Russian Treaty was an
appendage to the Franco-Soviet Treaty of May 2nd, 1935, and
Czechoslovakia, in her relations with Russia, was to form a diplomatic unit with France; she is only bound to assist Russia, when
attacked, if France has also decided to do so; she assumed no
extra-European obligations; Russia is bound immediately to assist
France and Czechoslovakia, if they are the victims of aggression,
without waiting for the Council of the League of Nations to state
that aggression has occurred. It was in this last point alone that
these treaties went beyond the Covenant of the League to which
the U.S.S.R. had now adhered.[1]

In view of the suspicious apprehension already expressed by the
Henleinists during the election campaign with regard to the relations of Prague with Paris and Moscow, and in view of the dislike
felt by the Czech Agrarians towards Soviet Russia, but above all
in view of the inevitable annoyance of the Germans and the Poles,
critics from all sides have questioned the wisdom of Dr. Beneš's
diplomacy in 1935. If it was an answer to the announcement, in
March 1935, that conscription was restored in Germany, they say,
it only helped to justify the German remilitarization of the Rhineland in March 1936. It would be difficult for any serious student
of National Socialist ideology to suppose that Herr Hitler's régime
would have suffered a limitation of Germany's sovereignty in the
Rhineland one minute after this limitation could be repudiated
with impunity. It is unquestionable, on the other hand, that
German troops in the Rhineland undermined the French-Czech
alliance, since it would be a great deal more difficult, in any
emergency, for France to come to the help of Czechoslovakia.

Germany's destruction of the Treaty of Locarno cancelled the
mutual guarantee of the German-Czechoslovak frontier, and the
German Chancellor's subsequent offers[2] ostentatiously omitted
any mention of Czechoslovakia. From this time onward, moreover, streams of abuse began to issue from the Reich German press
and wireless. Czechoslovakia, it was said, had become the tool of
the Bolsheviks, a Soviet spearhead in the centre of Europe directly
menacing Western civilization, pointing as it does at Bohemia's
neighbour, Bavaria, that ancient home of *Kultur*. The Czechs
shrugged their shoulders. 'Their Germans' had called Prague the

---

[1] The Franco-Russian Treaty was, incidentally, pronounced by the Law
Officers of the Crown in the United Kingdom to be consistent with the Covenant
of the League, and this pronouncement may be taken to have covered the
Czechoslovak-Russian Treaty by implication.

[2] e.g. those made on March 31st, 1936.

Western Moscow at frequent intervals since 1848, and a Czech gesture towards Russia had mostly been denounced as a stab in the German back. While some people thought it might have been wiser not to have presented Dr. Goebbels with the gift of the Czech-Russian Treaty of 1935, others considered that his brilliant ingenuity would in any case have discovered methods by which to produce the same effect. The Sudeten Germans readily believed that a terrible menace was let loose in their midst, and that they themselves had a mission to save Central Europe from the Reds. In the elections 10·3 per cent. of the whole electorate had voted Communist, so that the party had 30 seats[1] in the Chamber, 2 more indeed than the Czech National Socialists. Already in 1929, however, they had had almost exactly the same support in the country, and a Communist party which gains nothing from a catastrophic slump can scarcely be regarded as dangerous. The treaty with the Soviet, moreover, completely immobilized the Communists in the Chamber, for they now appear to have had orders from Moscow to make no difficulties for the Czechoslovak Government, predominantly Agrarian though it was.

The Czech Agrarian Party, which had already emerged into political prominence before 1914,[2] had been very greatly fortified by the post-War Agrarian Reform which had distributed land to its peasant supporters, and also by the tact and ability of its leader, M. Švehla.[3] Once land reform was a *fait accompli* the party was bound to become conservative, and, standing for small individual peasant holdings as it had,[4] it was certain to be intensely hostile to Communism. At the same time, its large following of small peasants ensured a democratic programme, and, since it had contributed so much to the sociological architecture of the Czechoslovak Republic, the Agrarian Party was genuinely republican. It had had many links with M. Witos and the Polish Agrarian Party; it was large and various in its composition, but its very influential Right Wing was above all susceptible to the fear of the Communist message. With the Soviet Treaty and the consequent paralysis of the Communists, the Agrarians, though numerically in much the same position as before the elections, had gained strategically all the way round. The Sudetendeutsch Party was a little larger than they had bargained for, but they had encouraged it behind the scenes and were not sorry to have a strong new block on the Right, a block of which they hoped to make use in all political manœuvres. That Czechoslovakia should be denounced for its Bolshevism at a time when the now conservative Agrarians were consolidating their

[1] Of the 30 Communist deputies it may be remembered that 4 were German.
[2] See above, Chapter VII, p. 65.
[3] See Chapter XII, section (iii), p. 131.
[4] See Chapter XIII, section (ii), p. 149.

position was one of the prettiest ironies of history. It caused a good deal of bitterness on the Czech Left and Left Centre that precisely that party whose economic egoism had penalized industry, and therefore the Sudeten Germans, and whose rank and file produced some of the most stupid Germanophobe bureaucrats, should coquet with the Henleinists and, in 1935 and 1936, advocate an agreement *à la polonaise* with Germany. It must not be forgotten that the Agrarians were not only responsible for the denunciation in 1930 of the commercial treaty with Hungary,[1] but also for the maintenance of high sugar prices and for the quota system which, in the interests of butter, restricted the production of margarine. All these things made life more expensive for the industrial working-classes and aggravated the sufferings of the bad slump years; even the Corn Monopoly of 1934, though agreeable to the German and Hungarian, as to the Czech and Slovak, peasantry, was of doubtful advantage to Czechoslovakia as a whole. And though the Agrarian leader, M. Švehla, who died in 1931, had pronounced the desire to see the Sudeten Germans take their place as 'equals among equals', Agrarian party propaganda before the elections in 1935 had positively preached the de-Germanizing of the Germanized districts.[2]

In December 1935 President Masaryk, at the age of 85, finally retired into private life. The Agrarians had already held for years the Home Office, the Defence Ministry, and other key positions, and although their supporter, Dr. Hodža, had recently retained the premiership for them, they were yet a little unwilling to allow the presidency to fall to so pronounced a progressive as Masaryk's obvious successor, Dr. Beneš. The inconsistency of these Czech friends of Herr Henlein was now illustrated by the fact that they toyed with the idea of nominating an exceedingly Germanophobe professor, Dr. Němec,[3] against Dr. Beneš; though this project was abandoned and Dr. Beneš elected by 340 votes out of 450, the only parties which did not vote for him were the small group of Czech Fascists, the nationalist Hungarians, and the followers of Herr Henlein.[4] In January 1936, only a month after this demonstration, the Agrarian Minister of National Defence, M. Machnik, independently, as it seemed, of his Cabinet colleagues, issued an order which was loudly condemned by the Sudeten German population.

[1] See above, Chapter XIII, section (iii), p. 164.
[2] I have seen Agrarian election posters of the kind, but was unable to make copies at the time.
[3] For one example of Professor Němec' attitude to the Sudeten Germans see a speech of his about the enemy being at the gates of Prague, 'for the nationally mixed territory is as near as that', reported in *Večer*, June 3rd, 1936.
[4] These groups all gave in blank ballot papers.

The Machnik Decree (January 28th, 1936) required that any firm which wished to be eligible for orders from the Ministry of Defence should not only employ workmen in the national proportions of the locality, but that its clerical staff should be composed along the same lines. The necessary changes were to be completed within two years at the most. Further, foreign clerks were to be replaced by people of 'Czechoslovak nationality' in these firms, and they were to employ no one who belonged to a political party hostile to the State. Though a case could be made out for this decree—it was not unreasonable that the War Office should not wish to depend upon foreign, almost certainly Reich German, clerks in any way—it created a Sudeten German uproar. The Henleinists assumed that the decree was aimed at them and they were indignant that, after all Herr Henlein's declarations of loyalty, they should be, as they presumed, described as a party hostile to the State, though M. Machnik never made it clear that he was referring to any party in particular.[1] As for the factory hands, it has already been seen that it was the admitted policy of the Czechoslovak authorities to adapt the national proportions to those in the neighbourhood. In two respects, however, the Machnik Decree was open to very serious criticism. If by 'Czechoslovak nationality' the Minister wished to exclude loyal Sudeten Germans or Hungarians from replacing foreign clerks this was anti-minority discrimination. And if Vitkovice (Witkowitz) or the First Brno Machine Factory (*Erste Brünner Maschinen-Fabrik*) were to be disqualified for Defence Ministry jobs until their black-coated staff had acquired local national proportions, great harshness would be involved. At Vitkovice about half the clerical staff was still German though the local German minority was under 20 per cent., while the *Erste Brünner Maschinen-Fabrik* employed about 92 per cent. Czech workmen with about 70 per cent. German clerks and technicians, with the local ratio at just about 80 : 20 Czechs to Germans. As a matter of fact, though the Sudeten German Party appealed to Geneva against the Machnik Decree, it had been more or less repudiated by the Prime Minister before then. The practice of the Defence Ministry continued to be fairly chauvinistic, and yet one cannot entirely ignore the point that if any Government office had a right to be chary of dealing with members of minorities which seemed to have a great deal to do with a hostile foreign state, that office was undoubtedly the Ministry of Defence.

Signs of Germany's disapprobation were multiplying indeed in the winter of Dr. Beneš's election to the presidency, and it seemed as if the Berlin Ministry of Propaganda were determined to cut

---

[1] Indeed the decree had been provisionally drafted some two years earlier, before the existence of the S.d.P.; its origins are a little obscure.

the Moscow–Prague wire by an adroit exploitation of that hysterical state of the Central European mind which made emotional appeals so much more effectual than a reference to facts. On February 8th, 1936, a map of Czechoslovakia with various new air bases marked on it appeared in *Na Strazhe*,[1] the newspaper which counts as the organ of the Moscow Ministry of Defence; the map was headed '*New (novye)* aerodromes in Czechoslovakia'. Taking up what appeared to be pre-arranged *ballons d'essai* in Hungarian and Polish newspapers, the whole Reich German press vociferously reported that the Russians were audaciously publishing maps entitled '*Our (nashi)* aerodromes in Czechoslovakia', and the Reich German wireless stations filled their listeners with horror of the air offensive which was being planned in their rear by a coalition of the Pan-Slav[2] with the Communist and the Jewish ogre, all encouraged by the kindred elements in France. A Russian Air Force mission visited Prague in July, and Russian officers, like the military representatives of other friendly Powers, were naturally present at the next Czechoslovak manœuvres. But nothing beyond the normal intercourse between recent allies occurred. As for the inference that the Czechoslovak Army and Air Force were being more or less taken over by U.S.S.R. staff officers, they appeared to have been based upon nothing more substantial than the fact that one or two White Russians[3] like Generals Vojcechovský and Mackevič, having entered the Czech legions during the War, had remained in the Czechoslovak Army. The German propaganda campaign against the Czech-Russian Treaty, nevertheless, continued at intervals for many months; at last in 1937 it was tacitly dropped, for if it had served its purpose in Eastern Europe, it had not made very much impression in the west.[4]

Thus the début of Dr. Beneš as President was made in the most difficult and daunting circumstances. The vigorous personality of President Masaryk's successor nevertheless immediately made itself felt. In the first place he was convinced that Czechoslovakia must be militarily prepared for the gravest emergencies and rearmament was pushed on at a tremendous pace. A really remarkable change occurred. Just as the life-long pacifist, Thomas

[1] *Na Strazhe, novye,* and *nashi* are the nearest equivalents to the original Cyrillic.

[2] The Pan-Slav charge was not definitely framed as far as I know, but Communism was inferred to be the kind of wretched creed to which Slavs were likely to succumb.

[3] i.e. *ancien régime* Russians (not inhabitants of White Russia).

[4] It is interesting to see that in Schulthess's *Geschichtskalender* for 1936 (published in Munich in 1937) it is categorically stated on the authority of the pro-Nazi *Wiener Neueste Nachrichten* that on Feb. 5th, 1936, the Government of the U.S.S.R. asked the Prague Government to set up another series of air bases. The Czechoslovak *démenti* is mentioned, but the event is recorded as the Vienna newspaper presented it.

Masaryk, had got into uniform and become his nation's commander-in-chief in the days of the Great War, so now the Czechs, who felt their national existence to be once more at stake, laid aside their anti-militarist traditions. There was a noticeable *rapprochement* between the President, who so much resembled an admirably energetic little schoolmaster, and the Army; for the first time in Czechoslovakia the Army became popular. Smart young officers thronged the streets of Prague; Czech military efficiency was certainly improved; one heard high praise from foreign experts of the Air Force; 'Maginot' lines of fortification began to be constructed along the most vulnerable portions of the frontier, especially across the valley of the Oder. A defence loan launched in June to cover extra military expenses was unexpectedly successful.

In the second place President Beneš was determined that Czechoslovak democracy should, if the day came, be dictatorially equipped against Pan-German dictatorship. In April and May the State Defence Law was discussed in Parliament and carried; it is noteworthy that the S.d.P. voted in its favour. The new law went farther than either the Defence Law of 1923, or than the Enabling Act of 1933, which had, incidentally, been renewed since then, and has remained in force ever since.[1] The State Defence Law, an immense piece of legislation, provided for measures to be taken on the outbreak of war; it also immediately established a permanent Supreme Defence Council nominated by the President. Further, it legalized the declaration of a state of 'defence-preparedness', i.e. of martial law, under various conditions, for instance in districts where events had occurred which seriously menaced the unity of the State or its democratic or republican character. In effect nearly all frontier districts, within an average distance of 25 kilometres from the frontiers themselves, were now militarized.[2] Areas under fortification could be forbidden to the public or at least to the camera, politically unreliable people could be expelled, and foreigners forbidden to set foot inside factories whose products, however remotely, might be related to war. Offences arising out of the application of the State Defence Law were tried by ordinary procedure, the defendants being entitled to the usual language rights. The trials were not, however, open to the public, and the accused were compelled to choose the lawyers to defend them from a Government list; espionage could now, in the worst case, deserve the death penalty.[3]

[1] For the background to this new legislation see Chapter XII, section (i), p. 121.
[2] The frontier zone was defined by a decree of June 24th.
[3] Up to the time of writing the death penalty has only once been inflicted —upon a Czech sergeant named Krejza.

Thirdly, President Beneš began a drive in favour of treating those members of the minorities, and especially those Sudeten Germans who were ready to be loyal to Czechoslovak democracy, with greater generosity than in the past. It was extraordinarily difficult to advocate this, now, when Germany's threats to Czechoslovakia made most Czechs more hostile towards the Sudeten Germans, who, as it seemed to them, were only toying with Henleinism till they could get Hitlerism. Again while the Agrarian leaders looked with friendliness towards Asch (Aš)[1] and even cast glances in the direction of Berlin, the Agrarian rank and file was often heard to say the Sudeten German Party ought to be dissolved. But the President argued that the Czechoslovak State, having first shown itself to be formidable by the State Defence Law, should now strive to show itself to be absolutely just. It was at Reichenberg (Liberec), Gablonz (Jablonec), and Eisenbrod (Železný Brod) on August 19th, 1936, that the President spoke out in favour of equality of rights for the Germans who stood by the State. From that time onwards he has travelled busily into the German districts making speeches in German, twitting (also in German) S.d.P. leaders if they consented to meet him, taking a rest in Karlsbad, and in January 1938, with various Ministers, visiting, at the 'New' German theatre in Prague, the performance of the *Meistersinger* which celebrated the opening of that theatre fifty years before.

There was a clear logicality about the behaviour of President Beneš and he continued to press consistently towards the goal he had in view. But the old pre-War vicious circle seemed still to shackle the efforts of conciliators. In 1934 and the first half of 1935 the moderation of Herr Henlein, if the Czechs had been willing to risk taking him at his word, might conceivably have made him eligible as a new activist leader. By the time of the speech he made at Teplitz-Schönau (Teplice-Šanov) on October 20th, 1935, just one year after that at Böhmisch Leipa (Česká Lípa), the situation had visibly changed. On the one hand he now knew that he had nearly two-thirds of the Sudeten Germans at his back, on the other the relations between Prague and Berlin had hardened on account, not only of the Czech-Russian Treaty of Mutual Guarantee, but also because German rearmament was making the German Government feel stronger every day. The Teplitz speech was a clear step away from the moderation of the previous year; it culminated in attacking a foreign policy, which in Herr Henlein's view, hindered the realization of 'a natural policy of Central European solidarity'. Germany, he said, should not always be condemned on account of the military power which was hers again, but should also be honoured as the home of Herder and Goethe, friends of the Czechs.

[1] Herr Henlein's home and headquarters.

We Sudeten Germans [he said] cannot avoid a feeling of bitterness that our state still lives in a relationship of tension towards just the state of that people to which, through descent and culture, we belong. . . . If we speak these things out frankly, we do so in full consciousness of our destiny, to provide natural bridges and natural arbiters between the German and the Czech people and so to make a decisive contribution to Europe's peace.

The old problem of the Slav-German cross-roads was still unsolved. If the Sudeten Germans could not fully accept this State unless it were allied with Germany, they were in just the same position as the Czechs who had clamoured against the German alliance in old Austrian days when Dr. Kramář pressed for a Petersburg-Vienna *rapprochement*.[1] To the Czechs of 1935 a German alliance spelt the surrender of the very character of the State they had so eagerly set up in 1918, for the Germany which now wooed them with menacing frowns was offended if anti-Nazi caricatures were seen at an exhibition of drawings at the Mánes Picture Gallery.[2] To accept her alliance would mean to accept her ideology and to deny their own soul—for she would certainly wish to forbid all anti-dictatorial public utterances. It was lamentable that Czech legislation was cutting down the rights of those who did not accept the ideology of the State, but an extreme Sudeten German had more hope of clemency in Czechoslovakia than a Socialist or Clerical or pacifist in Germany, though not even a racial difference divided these last from their persecutors. Knowing fairly well what system of government was now established in Germany, it was with a good deal of bitterness that many Czechs read Herr Henlein's Teplitz speech in October 1935, for while he demanded an alliance with Germany, he was able in Czechoslovakia to declare: 'He who yet dares to speak an open and free word and to call things by their true name, is never an enemy to the State.'

President Beneš had wished to be firm, and then just, even generous, but his efforts seemed, at first, to be largely self-frustrating. Czechoslovakia's brisk rearmament plans, the new fortifications, and the Defence Law further embittered the position between Sudeten Germans and Czechs. For they caused unemployment to diminish very rapidly in heavy industry at Plzeň (Pilsen), around Prague, and in the Ostrava (Ostrau) region where the workers were Czech by an overwhelming majority. Not only did the Defence Ministry more than ever give its tenders to Czechoslovak and not Sudeten German firms because it then felt safer against German espionage, but it also encouraged factories of any possibly military importance to be built in the Slovakian interior. This, again, meant

[1] See above, Chapter VI.
[2] See German diplomatic protest, April 12th, 1934. Similar protests have been recorded since then.

work rather for Slovaks than Sudeten Germans, but it was strategically axiomatic; after all the Czechoslovaks knew that a German attack might rob them of Bohemia altogether, and throw them back on to Moravia and Slovakia.

The effects of the State Defence Law in all frontier districts were bound to be exceedingly disagreeable for the local population. The names of Henleinist lawyers very seldom appeared on the Government lists and they were therefore unable to defend in Defence Law cases. Czech State police officials multiplied. As the ideological rift between Czech and Sudeten German was widened by one event after another, Abyssinia, Spain, and so on, the Czechs felt less and less able to count on the loyalty of the German population, and the more they tried to secure themselves by sending their own people into the *Randgebieten* the more hostile the Germans became. Endless misunderstandings arose. Some zealous *Národní jednota* man would denounce a Sudeten German, perhaps because he always listened in to the German wireless or perhaps only because the Czech had misunderstood some German remark, and the Sudeten German might then be labelled as unreliable. If the latter kept an inn, his licence might be cancelled or the next time he wished to visit his cousins just across the frontier his passport would be withdrawn. At the frontier anything with a swastika on it, especially any newspaper or anything resembling a pamphlet, might be confiscated. The expanded gendarmerie had to be hastily equipped, and the newer recruits often knew very little German. The local authorities were given wide powers of discretion because it would have been physically impossible to refer all the little disputes that arose to Prague, so that the Sudeten Germans now found themselves complaining that too little was decided at the centre, not, as they had previously complained, too much.

It could not perhaps be helped that people who were innocent and people who were guilty under the Defence Laws suffered together, and that it sometimes took weeks or even months to sort them out. To my own considerable surprise I have been frankly informed by Henleinists that Sudeten German youths often took money from Reich German military authorities to do what spying they could; the Czechs could not let that sort of thing, however amateur, go disregarded. In the earlier years of National Socialism, groups of Reich German Nazis had frequently carried out piratical raids into Czechoslovak territory in order to kidnap or murder some political enemy—there was the famous case of Professor Lessing, and many another. The German railway and customs officials in Eger (Cheb) were known by the Czechs to have the closest relations with the Reich German Secret Police,[1]

[1] Cf. *Manchester Guardian*, Oct. 26th, 1937.

and there was plenty of evidence of collaboration with Sudeten German young men.

The possibility, however, that the Czechs and Sudeten Germans should understand one another's difficulties seemed doomed to diminish. Political life continued to be dominated by an alarming emotional tension, and ideological issues hardened. In the winter of 1935–6 Dr. Patscheider, the schoolmaster of Troppau (Opava), who had been arrested in 1933, was tried at Moravian Ostrava (Mährisch Ostrau) with Dr. Lehmann of Reichenberg and a number of other people associated with the *Bereitschaft* and their newspaper, the *Weg*.[1] They were accused of having united against the Republic, at least since the beginning of 1931, in connexion with a foreign Power or with foreign financial or military factors. The trial lasted from December 9th, 1935, to March 24th, 1936, and the chief accused were found guilty and condemned to two or three years' imprisonment, dating, of course, from the time of their arrest. To the Sudeten Germans the whole thing seemed to be a piece of Czech and Jewish vindictiveness, for the chief judge in the case was a Jew. Dr. Neuwirth, who defended Dr. Patscheider, contended that all his Greater Silesian and Greater German plans were merely cultural and purely romantic, and that since the censor had only twice interfered with the *Weg* it could not be of serious danger to the State. To the Czechs, however, the merely cultural plea seemed a poor excuse since Herr Rosenberg had identified the political and cultural in one *Weltanschauung* which it was un-German not to hold. Further, it was clear that the defendants had been in direct touch with the *Volksbund für das Deutschtum im Auslande*, with Dr. von Loesch and other Reich German organizations, and that they had received money from some of them. The authorities had found a command to revolt drafted by some of the defendants to their followers, and though it appears to have been no more than a draft, few States in Central Europe—especially after 1933—would have felt able to ignore it, the less since the defendant Lamatsch could never explain himself clearly as to whether he had used the word *Reich*, in his letters, to mean the Czechoslovak Republic or the German Reich. Whether these people were dangerous or not to Czechoslovakia would depend upon the use to which Reich Germans would put them. The Patscheider affair hardened the conviction of the Czechs that nationalistic Sudeten Germans, whether they talked about *das Völkische* or *das Bündische*, or, as the Patscheider people did, about *eine stammliche Erfassung* (roughly = a tribal structure), were untrue to Czechoslovakia. The Henleinists, as a matter of fact, had long been embarrassed by the frankly Pan-German talk of the

[1] See above, Chapter XII, section (iv).

Bereitschaft people; they even referred to them as protected by the Czechs in order to discredit the loyalty of the Sudeten German party and declared on one occasion[1] that such people should be denounced to the nearest policeman. From this some people inferred, with how little justification it is impossible to know, that the Patscheider group had been denounced by what they would refer to as their own kith and kin.

The conviction of many Czechoslovaks that the Sudeten Germans, other than the Socialists, Farmers' Party, and Clericals, were nothing but Pan-Germans and Fascists was deepened by Sudeten German reactions to the Reich German wireless all through the winter of 1935–6. Extremist Nazi newspapers from Germany could be fairly effectually forbidden, but it was impossible to silence the loud voices of the Leipzig and Breslau wireless stations. The Czechs had themselves to blame that there was until 1938 no broadcasting in German in the Czechoslovak Republic, and the Reich German wireless, as every one knows, was superbly organized and provided the Germans of Bohemia and Moravia with delightful music, their favourite folk-songs, and so on. The Henleinist and more extreme nationalists soon took all their views about international politics from Nazi Germany. They allowed their blood to run cold over the 'alliance' with Russia and the poisonous cultural influences which it was exuding among them. In the Abyssinian affair they accepted the cynical attitude of Berlin towards the League of Nations and the view that Italy was right to take what she could. 'And then Konrad Henlein wishes us to believe that he is neither Fascist nor Nazi', said the Czechs, who remained whole-heartedly on the side of the League. Indeed, the vindication of its ability to impede aggression might become a matter of life and death to Czechoslovakia; never had the Czechoslovaks had more reason to be faithful to Geneva. As the months passed, however, the force of events appeared to justify the Italian invasion of Abyssinia and the German remilitarization of the Rhineland, and the followers of Herr Henlein, though they appealed to the League against the Machnik Order, were fortified in their adherence to the methods and the force-ideology of Rome and Berlin.

The Patscheider trial had drawn attention to the flow of Reich German funds in a Sudeten German direction. The election campaign of 1935 had been organized by the Henleinists on a scale which was difficult to explain if only Sudeten German resources had been available, and Herr Henlein's journeys abroad, which began to acquire significance with his visits to London in July and December 1935, were known by the Czechoslovak

[1] See *Sudetendeutsche Presse-Briefe*, Dec. 1935.

National Bank to be financed from abroad.[1] The *Gleichschaltung* of Germany meant that all the Pan-German organizations of the Weimar period were gradually captured by the Nazi party. The *Auslandsinstitut* in Stuttgart and the *Deutsche Akademie* in Munich[2] immediately identified themselves with National Socialism; the former had always depended on the party for money. The V.D.A., while willing to change its name from *Verein* to *Volksbund für das Deutschtum im Auslande*, resisted complete Nazi assimilation for some time; indeed, it was only with the resignation of Dr. Steinacher in 1937 that its *Gleichschaltung* became complete, nor was Dr. von Loesch absolutely *persona grata* with the new régime. Meanwhile Herr von Bohle established his *Auslandsorganisation* of the National Socialist Party, which has now been absorbed by the German Foreign Office; this only concerned itself with Reich German citizens, but it meant that the Reich Germans at Eger (Cheb), or such who, in diminishing numbers, were technical experts with Schichts or some other Sudeten German or even Czech concern, were in future organized to be 'bearers'[3] of the Nazi idea. The Nazis had imposed upon their compatriots and co-racialists obligations which were incompatible with respect for private life as understood in democratic countries,[4] and it was often very hard upon Sudeten German individuals that some circulation of funds, which would previously have had no public significance, now involved them in political implications. Thus if a Sudeten German now received something from the V.D.A. he was identifying himself with an unfriendly State as he never had before; it appears to have been mostly through the V.D.A. or Stuttgart that Reich German money was transmitted to Germans in Czechoslovakia. The availability of propagandistic funds, in spite of Germany's financial difficulties, was very remarkable. I remember a profoundly anti-Nazi Sudeten German, whose integrity is as indisputable as human integrity can be, saying to me that he knew perfectly well that, although he had exposed himself as completely anti-Hitlerist, if he wrote to Berlin for money to

[1] Czechoslovak nationals were only able to take 1,000 Kč a month out of the country without a special permit from the National Bank. Herr Henlein has never at any time applied for more than this figure (less than £7 since autumn 1936 and about £7 10s. from Feb. 1934), and it has always been evident that it could not possibly cover his expenses when travelling abroad.

[2] The *Deutsche Akademie*, like the Stuttgart *Auslandsinstitut*, is propagandistic and not to be confused with the small, academic *Süd-Ost Institut* which is attached to the University at Munich.

[3] = 'Träger'. Cf. the Weigel case (section (ii) below). The *Sudetendeutsches Heimatbund* now became more active in Germany, and from 1934 the *Bund Deutscher Osten* worked against the Czechs rather than the Poles. See above Chapter XII, section (ii).

[4] The National Socialists' refusal to accept the claims of the individual to privacy was related to their determination to make the world Jew-conscious, and was, of course, in accordance with their totalitarian beliefs.

do pro-German propaganda he would be generously equipped, all currency regulations notwithstanding.

It is easy to see that while the Sudeten Germans in 1936 increasingly regarded themselves as grossly oppressed by an alien régime which did lip-service only to the ideas of liberty and equality, the Czechs increasingly felt them to be nothing but masked Fascists in the pay of Berlin. In each case suspicion did much to create what it suspected. In June 1936 the fluidity of the period since 1933 may be said to have ended. Until this time Herr Henlein, though decreasingly, had maintained the Böhmisch Leipa contention that he was no Nazi, and his movement had occasionally been criticized by the *Völkischer Beobachter* and the out-and-out Nazi press in the Reich. He was now impelled away from moderation, not merely by the State Defence Law and by international developments, but also by divisions among his own followers. Herr Krebs and Herr Jung were safely in Germany, but their old D.N.S.A.P. collaborator, Herr Kasper, was still in Czechoslovakia; indeed, his influence among working-people was so great that it had been felt to be necessary to appoint him as *Arbeiterführer* in the S.d.P. Further, Herr Haider and what had remained[1] of the *Volkssport* trial defendants had now been free for some time, and their popularity in student circles was considerable; Herr Haider had a following, too, in his native country in Southern Bohemia, where, as in Gablonz (Jablonec) and Silesia, the Nazi idea had had strength before the War. Herren Kasper and Haider and their friends were frank outspoken National Socialists, with at least a thirty years' tradition behind them. They were delighted with everything which had happened in Germany since 1933, and they objected to Henleinist qualifications. Herr Kasper considered the S.d.P. leaders to be 'unsound' in the matter of race, since they accepted the Spann point of view that 'blood' need not be the sole criterion, i.e. that a converted Jew might conceivably become a good German patriot.[2] Herr Kasper objected, too, to the Spann ideology of Herr Rutha and Dr. Brand partly because he thought it tainted with clericalism and largely because of the *ständisch* caste distinctions which it envisaged between the working-people and other social groups; the *Stände* were to be ruled by a special *Staatsstand* of trained political leaders.[3] The old Nazi group

---

[1] After one death in prison and one flight.

[2] Actually the Henleinists, if not 'whole-hoggers', went very far in the anti-Semitic direction, and in the *Turnverband* and most other German nationalist societies in the Historic Provinces the 'Aryan-paragraph' had always been in force. See above, Chapter VII, p. 54.

[3] See above, Chapter XII, section (iv), p. 137. It was interesting to observe how from 1936 onwards the S.d.P. leaders were increasingly anxious to repudiate their association with Professor Spann. They also protested rather too much as to the insignificance of the Nazi opposition.

had various personal differences with the *Kameradschaftsbund*, who, though they had ostensibly dissolved their own organization in 1933, still held all the key positions in the *Sudetendeutsche Partei* and the closely related *Turnverband*. Herr Kasper and his friends were all for Herr Henlein's main idea of Sudeten German unity, for which they were willing to make considerable sacrifices. They had therefore joined the party when not refused admission,[1] but as old fighters, and even sufferers, in the cause they felt they had a claim to some further representation in its highest positions. They also criticized Herr Henlein and his intimate associates as too willing to talk about compromise and too unwilling to bring it temporarily about. It was obviously of first-rate importance to the Sudeten German Party to keep up its appearance of unity. While Herr Henlein resisted any serious change in party personnel, he was unable to prevent the arraignment of perhaps his most trusted lieutenant, Dr. Walter Brand, before a 'Court of Honour'. This was the more significant since Dr. Brand was the man who had advocated a stern hand in suppressing the 'Rebels,[2] his designation for the Kasper wing. Subsequently the 'Court of Honour' found Dr. Brand guilty of dishonourable behaviour[3] and cited a number of examples of what it condemned as intrigues.

Herr Henlein now felt compelled to go farther than this and to make real concessions to the Kasper-Haider point of view; this was, after all, the point of view of the Reich, and of the Reich, it has been seen, he was not financially independent. Indeed evidence is believed to exist of an agreement on May 27th, 1936,[4] between certain Reich German representatives and members of the Sudeten German Party for the *Gleichschaltung* of the Sudeten German press. Whether this agreement was actually made or not, the leading daily paper of the Henleinists, *Die Zeit*, from this time onwards echoed the Reich German press, especially in its international judgements, with astonishing exactness, and the weekly *Rundschau* was not very different, while smaller provincial publications often only differed from the *Zeit* by their more scurrilous tone.

It was in these circumstances that Konrad Henlein delivered his speech at Eger on June 21st, 1936, on the occasion of his re-

---

[1] As in the case of Herr Haider.

[2] See *Die Rundschau*, May 29th, 1936.

[3] Quite precisely he was said to have negotiated behind people's backs.

[4] A series of letters, alleged to have been exchanged between Henleinists and their friends in Germany and Austria, have come into the hands of people in Prague who have made them the basis of a study of Henleinism called *Jejich Boj* (Ihr Kampf) by J. Fischer, V. Patzak, and V. Perth. I have seen a photograph of the alleged letter of May 27th, 1936, and of others in the series, and can only say that they have the appearance of being genuine, are believed to be so by serious people, and have never been categorically repudiated. The authors of *Jejich Boj* are all people of academic standing.

election as leader of his party in the absence of the Kasper people. The speech began with a call for discipline from the old soldier and drill-teacher to insubordinate youth, and followed up Herr Henlein's travels with an appeal to the Great Powers guarantors of the Minority Treaty. He also struck a more militant note in the demands of his party as he framed them now.

We cannot [he said] content ourselves with the nationality law as it stands, because it vouchsafes protection only to individuals, not to whole racial groups. Every people and its responsible leaders must be acknow- ledged to be solely responsible for the adjustment of their own national status.[1]

The Eger speech, though of the greatest significance, scarcely achieved its objects. The anti-Henlein rebels forced Dr. Brand into temporary exile, but their criticism in no way abated. On the other hand, the Premier, Dr. Hodža,[2] interpreted the speech as something of an affront, making it impossible to continue cer- tain preliminary conversations which had been initiated on behalf of his Cabinet with Henleinist representatives;[3] Dr. Hodža also complained that Herr Henlein seemed to prefer to air his grievances abroad rather than to attempt to solve the Sudeten German ques- tion with the Czechoslovaks at home. From this time onwards the Prime Minister felt it impossible to discuss the Sudeten German question except with the Activist parties, among which the German Clericals were now once more ranged with the appointment in July of Herr Zajiček as Minister without portfolio. The Kasper-Haider opposition welcomed the more definitely Nazi tone of the S.d.P. leader's Eger speech, but they still complained that the party was dominated by the old *Kameradschaftsbund* clique, and into the bargain they took the opportunity to condemn the break with Dr. Hodža, for they declared that the Beneš-Hodža willingness to negotiate should be used by more than merely the Activists who could do little but accept such offers as the Czechoslovaks would make. While the opposition to Henlein, often referred to as the *Aufbruch* circle on account of its periodical of that name, should not be neglected nor ignored, it would be misleading to suggest that most rank-and-file S.d.P. people were made aware of it as yet.[4] Nor did the noticeable increase of work among the Sudeten Germans in the summer of 1936 do anything very much to shake the enthusiasm of the ordinary S.d.P. comrade.

[1] *Regelung der volklichen Belange.* See *Konrad Henlein spricht.*
[2] Speech in the Senate, July 2nd, 1936.
[3] It was not until Sept. 1937 that Herr Henlein was received by Dr. Hodža and explained away the Eger speech.
[4] See below, section (ii), pp. 265, 268. The events of February and March 1938, as such events are liable to do, apparently swept away in a common enthusiasm the personal antagonisms which had by that time become more conspicuous.

With the Eger speech Konrad Henlein had burnt his boats. He had demanded more than the protection of the individual citizen, and, in doing so, more than Czechoslovak law or the Minority Treaty claimed to provide. He pleaded, of course, that it was only by protection for the racial group as a whole that the individual could be effectively defended, that the German official so frequently appointed in non-German-speaking territory was lost to his people. This claim that the individual only lived as part of his *Volk* was a definite break with the insistence upon the rights of the individual at Böhmisch Leipa (Česka Lípa) in October 1934, and, pointing as it did towards the autonomy claim of 1937, put an end to ideological compromise. The *Völkischer Beobachter* had loudly complained[1] of the iniquity of the sentiment when M. Karel Čapek wrote, in *Lidové Noviny*, 'We do not wish to Czechify the Sudeten Germans, but we must make them into true Czechoslovaks.' By this he quite clearly meant that while one should provide them with education in their own language and literature, one must demand of them that they accept the political principles which form the basis of the State, just as the United States, for example, demands from Germans who live there as its citizens that they accept the principles of the American constitution. But now Herr Henlein had broken with the Western idea of nationality which involves a quota of common political principles but is independent of race, and had gone right over to the National Socialist conception. This was summed up a little later by the Sudeten German National Socialist *émigré*, Dr. Karl Viererbl, in Herr Alfred Rosenberg's official organ, the *Völkischer Beobachter*, when he wrote 'National Socialism is plainly the German point of view. To persecute and fight against the National Socialist state of mind implies outright oppression of German belief.'[2] At Eger Herr Henlein had exclaimed, 'We would rather be hated with Germany than derive any advantage from the hate against Germany.' If the individual lived only as part of his *Volk* and if the Sudeten Germans were to be so clearly associated with the Reich, then both the Czechs and they themselves were bound to feel that the Sudeten Germans were acknowledging the leadership, not of Herr Henlein, but of Herr Hitler, the *Führer* of the whole German race.

(ii) *From June 1936 to March 1938: the Agreement of February 18th, 1937*

The accuracy with which the pattern of Czech-Sudeten German relations reflects that of international relations became almost more evident during 1936. In July of that year the world began to tremble

---

[1] Jan. 4th, 1935.   [2] July 6th, 1937.

with the disaster of the Spanish Civil War, and ideological frontiers hardened again. Czechoslovak opinion divided, as uncontrolled opinion was bound to divide, and the Agrarian paper
Venkov and other papers on the Czechoslovak Right were for the
insurgents. Czech opinion, on the whole, however, favoured the
Madrid Government, and did so increasingly with the expanding
activity of German and Italian legionaries on behalf of General
Franco. The Sudeten Germans, other than Activists, followed
the lead of the *Zeit* and accepted blood-curdling accounts of the
excesses of the Reds from the Reich German press, while they
felt convinced that, on the Franco side, there were to be found
nothing but order and heroism. It took me some time to accustom
myself to the frequent reiteration among the Henleinists I met of
the question, 'Why does your Mr. Eden support those Reds in
Spain?'

Simultaneously with the outbreak of the war in Spain the League
of Nations had virtually surrendered on the Danzig question, and
the Agreement of July 11th, 1936, between Germany and Austria
had been reached. This was generally interpreted to mean that
Germany had abandoned coercion—together with the boycott of
holidays in Austria—in favour of peaceful penetration. Whether
Austria's independence was now more or less threatened was
disputed between the most competent judges, but at any rate any
violent move from Germany—if it should take place—was now
generally expected to be directed against Czechoslovakia and
Czechoslovakia alone, the more since the German-Lithuanian
quarrel of 1935 appeared to be temporarily liquidated. In effect
it became the darling theme of the *Schwarze Korps*[1] and of extremist party circles in the Reich to plan a second Spain in Czechoslovakia. Such a project was seriously contemplated at least until
Easter 1937, and it is believed by very responsible authorities on
the question that in November 1936 the possibility of a 'lightning
war'[2] against Czechoslovakia was discussed in the highest places
in Germany. Important Reichswehr chiefs are said to have opposed any interruption of the process of rearmament, and to have
backed up their arguments more and more by the indecisive
development of events in Spain; they are also believed to have
been held back by the danger of Russian intervention.

The 'second Spain' idea was, of course, quite another matter
from frank invasion. It involved an internal rising in Czechoslovakia after which it would become impossible to hold back
volunteers from Germany, as from Hungary and Poland, from
coming to the aid of the insurgents. The multi-racial character
of the Czechoslovak State would give rebellion variety and choice;

[1] The chief S.S. weekly in Berlin.   [2] = *Blitzkrieg*.

though Dr. Hodža was one of themselves, even the Slovaks were by no means fully reconciled to the State—one heard of Slovak autonomist meetings where demonstrators had shouted for a Hitler-Horthy-Hlinka front. This sort of thing was probably Magyar in origin, and the plan which came to be favoured was that of a Hungarian revolt in Southern Slovakia. Rumours were briskly circulated, wherever it was hoped that they would bear fruit, to the effect that the Magyars could bear Bolshevization no longer. Sensational accounts of Communist activity in Czecho-slovakia now appeared in the pro-Nazi Hungarian press, for instance in an article in *Magyarság* on January 6th, 1937, which was reported at length in the *Völkischer Beobachter* on the following day. The senior members of the Czechoslovak General Staff, it there appeared, were observing with the greatest concern and fear how the whole Czechoslovak army was being systematically re-organized so as to constitute an outpost of the Comintern in Europe rather than to defend the Czechoslovak State. 'Hundred-weights' of Communist propaganda, 'thousands of telegrams and newspapers' were being distributed; industry was so much in Moscow's grip that employees were engaged not because they were competent but because they belonged to the Communist Party. All this activity was said to be particularly vigorous in the minority areas where at least 1,500 Soviet agents were at work. Just what we and the whole German press have always said, concluded the *Völkischer Beobachter*.

These flights of journalistic imagination appear to have lacked all foundation in fact. The grievances of the Hungarian minority were real. As a peasant population in the main, their problems contrasted sharply with those of the Sudeten Germans, but they were worse off with regard to language rights, and their press was more severely censored. Whereas I never remember a station in the predominantly Sudeten German districts which failed to display its name in both Czech and German, the Magyars, until quite recently at any rate,[1] were treated to nothing but the Slovak place-names. In the mainly German districts the guards on the trains varied from charming correctness in calling out the names of the stations in both languages to a gruff insistence upon Czech alone. I remember no predominantly German place where the post office or other public buildings lacked German inscriptions. In the case of Brno, where the Germans are still just entitled to the official use of their language but the population is 80 per cent. Czech, the station and streets ignore German rights, and if

[1] I only know, from personal experience, that this was true up to the autumn of 1937, but I have been assured that steps towards an improvement have already been taken; Dr. Hodža also made this assurance in his speech of Nov. 17th, 1937. See below.

one asks questions the Czechs shrug their shoulders, and say after all it is not worth putting up the German names now when every one knows that 1940 will put an end to the German 20 per cent.

If the Magyar minority is worse off in the treatment of its language, of Communist pressure upon the Hungarians there have been no signs. On the contrary the police are noticeably harsher in their treatment of Communists in Slovakia than in Bohemia, while the worst persecutors of the Magyars are often new and very nationalistic Slovak officials.[1]

In the atmosphere created by hostile press alarums and excursions in the countries around Czechoslovakia, and with a very real fear of something far worse to come, it was not easy to press Czech and Slovak officials to behave more generously towards their German or Hungarian fellow citizens, so many of whom readily accepted the peculiar legend of the annexation of the country by the Soviet régime. On the one hand, however, in spite of the diversity of their political descent, President Beneš and Prime Minister Hodža arrived at a solid working alliance not always welcome to the Right Wing of the Agrarian Party. On the other, certain younger members of the German Activist parties pressed as hard as they could for some really visible concessions to soothe the minorities; among the so-called Young Activists, the Social Democrat, Herr Wenzel Jaksch, and the German Agrarian, Herr Gustav Hacker, were the most prominent. They drafted their demands in a memorandum which they presented to Dr. Hodža at the end of January 1937. Three weeks later, on February 18th, an Agreement based on these demands was published. In effect this amounted to a Government guarantee that the existing rights of the minorities should be equitably enforced in future and that certain abuses arising out of the period of economic depression should be stopped. For example it was stated that:

The Government will subsidize public works and buildings to a uniform degree for all the districts of the State according to their needs, and it guarantees that everywhere, including, naturally, the areas inhabited by the Germans, work will be given to the local employers and workmen. The central administration which distributes contracts is charged also to exercise a severe control over all the officials subordinated to it so that this principle of economic equity shall be fully respected. . . . The Government, in carrying out measures of social welfare and hygiene, will consider, not only the population figures, but also the scale of unemployment in the various regions.

With regard to the Language Law situation, one small but acute grievance was met in that the Government undertook in future automatically to attach a gratis translation (into the minority lan-

[1] See Macartney, *Hungary and Her Successors*.

guage) of official correspondence with minority communes; hitherto the latter had been forced to do the translating for themselves. The Government also indicated that language tests would in future become less severe.

Now the Agreement of February 18th, 1937, was in reality a very modest affair, but the Czechs felt compelled to take up the challenge of the times and therefore attempted to over-emphasize it propagandistically; although, for obvious prestige reasons, they insisted that Czechoslovakia had nothing for which to blame herself in the past, yet at the same time they declared that a new day of equitable administration had dawned. It was clear the February plan could not undo the effects of the Defence Law, nor make those Sudeten Germans who accepted the theory of the new unity of all Germans under one leader eligible for State employment in Czechoslovakia. The more the 'blood community' of all Germans was talked about, the less was it possible for the Czechoslovak authorities to give them positions of responsibility in the army or the police—indeed activist Sudeten Germans preferred that the police should be Czech and thus outside the circle of Sudeten German recriminations. The State was not in a position to create many new posts, though there was some room for expansion of the railway personnel; even in the railway and postal services, the elaborate espionage activities which had grown up all over Central Europe, and especially in Prague, since 1933, made it essential to be able to rely upon each member of the staff. And unless it were possible to dismiss the Czechs and Slovaks, it was in any case bound to take years before the national proportions in the service of the State could be mathematically adjusted.

What, then, was the value of the February Agreement? I believe that it had a certain psychological value which should neither be exaggerated nor denied. It meant that the most important people in Czechoslovakia intended in future to resist and punish the sabotaging of minority rights by minor officials who were under the influence of the *Národní jednotas*,[1] or *Nebenregierungen*,[2] as the Germans called them. This sabotage had made the worst hole in Czechoslovak armour, and, as Dr. Beneš often points out, the President of Czechoslovakia is no Stalin or Hitler, he cannot so easily dispose of unwelcome resistance. But from this time onwards Czechoslovak officials were repeatedly reprimanded, even on several occasions dismissed, by Dr. Hodža, if he had proof that they were unlawfully causing obstruction at the expense of Germans or Hungarians who were loyal to the State. The rest of the Cabinet varied in the warmth of its reception of the Beneš-Hodža

---

[1] See above, Chapters VII, X, p. 95, XII, section (i), pp. 122 and 125, XIII, (ii), p. 148, XV, section (i), XV, section (viii), p. 221, note 1, XVI (ii), p. 244, &c.

[2] = parallel governments.

drive, and there is no doubt that chauvinist sabotage, sometimes based, like Sudeten German anti-State activities, upon a most genuine devotion to a man's supposed duty, continued. But the important thing was that a corner had been turned.

The February Agreement had been timed with a view to its synchronization with economic recovery. Since the beginning of 1936 employment had increased fairly steadily, though, thanks to rationalization, it lagged behind production. The second small devaluation in the autumn of that year had satisfactory results, purchasing power at home was rising, and a number of new commercial agreements, though not sensational in what they achieved, were all to the good. From early in 1937 the employment situation improved more quickly. Everywhere, though sometimes with the greatest reluctance, it had to be admitted that recovery was bringing very noticeable benefits. Even the Gablonz exporters and the Karlsbad china firms themselves allowed that they were employing 10 to 20 per cent. more people than a year before, though their inclination was certainly to under-estimate the improvement. In the textile industries the improvement, though very uneven, was considerable; Warnsdorf (Varnsdorf) stockings (mostly made by Kunnerts) prospered, but above all the fabric glove industry of Asch (Aš) flourished tremendously, partly because East European Jewish merchants were boycotting Reich German fabric gloves.[1] Between the end of October 1936 and the end of February 1937 the process by which Czech, diminished more quickly than Sudeten German, unemployment was reversed. Of course this sort of statement can scarcely be precise, since every district is a little mixed, and the rival race authorities dispute proportions and criteria. According to the *Deutscher Hauptverband der Industrie* in the Czechoslovak Republic, if the number of unemployed in the Czech districts where the German population is not above 20 per cent. is taken as the standard and called 100, then the following are the figures for the strongly German (i.e. 80–100 per cent. of the population) and mixed (20–80 per cent. German) districts.

	1936			1937	
	October	November	December	January	February
80–100 per cent. German	379	312	257	243	237
20–80 per cent. German	219	185	167	156	154[2]

[1] Whereas in the good year 1929 only 45 million Kč worth of these gloves were exported, already in 1936 112 million Kč worth were exported. (Figures supplied by the Chamber of Commerce at Eger; the devaluation of the Kč slightly diminishes the real increase, but on the other hand the fall in prices has to be considered.)

[2] *Mitteilungen des Deutschen Hauptverbandes der Industrie in der Tschechoslowakischen Republik*, June 24th, 1937.

Though these calculations certainly did not minimize the trouble among the Sudeten Germans, the Czechoslovak authorities allowed themselves to indulge in an unrestrained optimism and claimed that unemployment among the Sudeten Germans would soon be no greater than among the Czechs.[1]

The reaction of Konrad Henlein and his party, as could only be expected, was to reject the February Agreement out of hand. In a speech at Aussig (Ústí) on February 28th the whole thing was bitterly condemned by the S.d.P. Führer; it involved only empty promises, he declared, made to people who could in no way claim to represent the Sudeten German people. Following up his Eger speech, Herr Henlein now explicitly claimed that no Czech offer could be considered unless it involved complete Sudeten German autonomy. Not only was the Sudeten Germans' 'proud and free' membership of the great German *Kulturgemeinschaft* underlined, but two ambiguous threats of some interest were uttered: (i) the Czechs must make good all the wrong they had done the Sudeten Germans since 1918, clearly a very elastic demand; and (ii) the Czechs must not drive them to desperation. This warning seemed to link up with all the foreign talk about minority insurrections and to relate to the 'Second Spain' plans. It became a very potent weapon of propaganda, especially in impressing representatives of the democratic and war-fearing nations, for it confused the urgency of Czechoslovakia's minority problems with the state of tension between the Republic and the Reich.

In the Aussig (Ústí) speech Herr Henlein had taken up the reproach that he always rejected all practical solutions proposed while offering none of his own, by notifying that the S.d.P. was preparing some important Bills to lay before Parliament. These were actually brought before the Chamber on April 27th, 1937. They comprised proposals[2] that:

1. All the members of each nationality in the State are to be enrolled in a national organization which is to constitute a legal personality, which is to direct all aspects of their life, and which can found compulsory social, economic or cultural groups. The Senators and Deputies of each national organization shall elect a 'Speaker' (*Sprecher*) and a deputy Speaker for six years; neither of these officials may be members of the Chamber or Senate; the Speaker is to be the official representative of his nationality in the State, and the guardian of its rights.

[1] See *Hospodářská politika*, March 20th, 1937.
[2] Summarized in the *Sudetendeutsche Presse-Briefe* of April 27th, 1937—full text to be obtained from S.d.P. head-quarters, Prague. For discussion of the proposals see *The Central European Observer*, June 25th, 1937. Also Dr. E. Swoboda, *Die Gesetzesanträge der S.d.P.* and *Warum Volksschutzgesetze* (Leipzig, 1937).

2 and 3. The State is to guarantee compensation for the infraction of minority rights by the officials it employs.

4. Any one who in any way entices any one else into (*a*) declaring themselves of a nationality other than their own, or (*b*) leaving an organization which uses their own language or entering an organization which does not, or any one who causes any one to use a language other than their own in dealing with State officials or representatives of self-governing institutions where this is not required by the law, is to be punished with imprisonment for anything from a fortnight to six months; if an official should behave so the penalty is to be twice as great. Other measures proposed here to protect the nationalities involve similar punishment of any one causing others to sell, bequeath or let landed property or factories, shops or other concerns, which had belonged to the same nationality for at least thirty years, to a member or members of a different nationality. Any employer who dismisses an employee on account of his nationality or engages an employee of a different nationality for a job which has been in the hands of one particular nationality for at least twenty years is also to be liable to imprisonment for anything from a fortnight to six months.

5. Every citizen over the age of 18 has the right and duty to be enrolled, as a member of the nationality into which he was born, in a national register (*Kataster*).[1] Once registered no one is to be able to change their nationality. Special courts and commissions to keep the national registers are to be set up. As soon as the new registration has occurred, it is to replace the census list as the last word on each person's nationality.

6. In addition to the highest courts and the Senate, Chamber and Ruthenian Diet, the national organizations (see 1) are to have the right to appeal to the special Court of Appeal (*Verfassungsgericht*) which can decide whether any law is an infringement of the constitution.

These very interesting proposals, it was claimed by their authors, were intended to strengthen the existing constitution, and with regard to No. 3 it was declared to be unworthy of the Republic that the Imperial decree of March 14th, 1806, should still prevent officials from being answerable for their actions before the civil courts. Now while there was a strong case for a modification of Czechoslovak *droit administratif*, it was not an easy moment for such a change to come about; the suggestion, moreover, involved a demand that the Prague Government, alone among continental régimes, should accept the insular principles of a sheltered Great Britain. The proposals, further, advocated measures which were bound to prevent any kind of symbiosis from occurring in Czechoslovakia. If the centralist tendencies of the legislation of the Republic had hitherto been too great, it was now proposed to

---

[1] Here a great many detailed instructions about parents' decisions for children, &c., follow.

erect barriers between its nationalities such as do not normally exist between the citizens of different sovereign States. Apart from the endless disputes, which would arise *en route*, it would be difficult to prohibit by law that a Slovak should sell land to a Ruthene where he was free to sell it to a Swede: in Switzerland, of which the Sudeten Germans so frequently reminded the Czechs, nothing of the kind was in force, but, of course, the S.d.P. conception was directly descended from the old Defence Society tradition.

At the very same time as they laid such emphasis upon territorialism, the S.d.P. Bills went back to the old personal principle which had formed the basis of the Moravian Compromise in 1905;[1] in combining the two principles, the *Anträge* were reminiscent of the Lodgman proposals of 1917.[2] Since the new Pan-Germanism transcended frontiers, the personal had temporarily triumphed over the territorial principle. The new conception of Sudeten German unity within Pan-German unity meant that it was more important to save every German soul in Brno (Brünn) or Olomouc (Olmütz) than to establish the territorial integrity of Northern Bohemia. Many of the young people, and some of the older, looked forward to a future German dominion throughout Central Europe, whether they envisaged it along Spann or purely Nazi lines, and they saw their mission in preparing for this in the Historic Provinces, the connecting bridge, as Dr. Patscheider and his friends had said, for the reconstruction of the future.

The first of the six *Anträge* was the most controversial of all. In 1934 Herr Henlein[3] had ridiculed the idea of a Sudeten German Parliament, but it was evident that here was a proposal for the totalitarian organization of each racial group within the State; compulsory membership of these *völkisch* communities was demanded, and their subjection to a dictatorial and extra-parliamentary leader, who, instead of a *Führer*, would be known as a *Sprecher*. The nationalist German parties had always condemned parliamentarism and inveighed against the—as they claimed—corrupting consequences of a party system. What the S.d.P. now suggested would reduce parliamentary life to something subordinate, and, at a time when many Czechs believed that theirs was a mission to save European democracy before the oncoming totalitarian tide, it was only to be expected that the Czechoslovak Parliament consistently postponed the discussion of the Henleinist proposals. I have been informed in responsible S.d.P. circles that the autonomy they now envisage would retain for the State as a whole an economic

[1] See above, Chapter VII.
[2] See above, Chapter IX, p. 81; also *Die Junge Front*, June 1937.
[3] In the Böhmisch-Leipa speech.

and juridical unity, together with a unity of the direction of foreign relations. It will be observed that the economic unity they suggest would in fact mean only a customs union, since land and industry are to be fenced off from one another according to their national ownership, while juridical unity would mainly involve the judicial relationship between the nationalities of the State. The Sudeten Germans pointed sarcastically to the steps taken by the Czechoslovak authorities during 1937 towards the realization of autonomy for the 800,000 inhabitants of backward Ruthenia,[1] while they themselves cried out for autonomy in vain.

During the early months of 1937 the Czechoslovak Government, in deference to the general situation and the Agrarian point of view, explored the possibility of an understanding with Germany on the German-Polish model. The Czechs were aware that the Agreement between Germany and Poland had by no means put an end to minority difficulties between the two nations, but it was clear that if Germany only moderated her tone towards Czechoslovakia, the S.d.P. would be considerably weakened. During the period of the most exuberant press outbursts, relations between Czechoslovakia and the Reich remained diplomatically correct, thanks partly to the calm attitude maintained by the Czechoslovak Legation in Berlin. Meanwhile the Czechoslovak Foreign Minister, Dr. Krofta, made it clear that Prague regarded her treaty with Moscow as a purely business arrangement with no ideological implications whatever; at the same time it was indicated that Czechoslovakia could not drop the Russian connexion at the dictation of Berlin.

In her own interest, it was believed by some people, Germany, if she did not mean to attack the Czechoslovaks, must come to some kind of terms with them. Although both Austria and Hungary, at about this time, had shown signs of wishing to draw nearer to Czechoslovakia as a Small-Power gesture against too much Great-Power domination, the meeting of Dr. von Schuschnigg, the Austrian Chancellor, with Signor Mussolini at Venice in March 1937 revealed such Germanophile tendencies in Italian policy that Germany found it feasible to persist in her rather intransigent course. Dr. von Schuschnigg returned home and bravely intimated his intention of taking a line of his own, but the position of Czechoslovakia remained one of considerable isolation, the more since German influence was steadily increasing in Roumania and Yugoslavia. The beginnings of Stalin's offensive against all whom he branded as enemies to the State reduced the diplomatic value of the Soviet alliance and was held to have injured the morale of Russia's fighting forces. When the horror of Guernica occurred

[1] The 1936 figure was 798,813 according to the official statistics.

and the Basques were destroyed by the Spanish Nationalists and their anti-democratic auxiliaries from abroad, it was significant that M. Peroutka implied in *Lidové Noviny*[1] that the Czechs, too, must be prepared to face such assaults and to be defended by no one but themselves.

During June it appeared that Germany was determined to force Czechoslovakia to surrender, i.e. externally to abandon the Russian alliance and internally to give way to Henleinist demands, even to take Henleinists into the Cabinet, perhaps. The aerodromes and Bolshevization stories were more or less dropped, and the German press concentrated on the firmer ground of minority grievances. At the same time, while the *Frankfurter Zeitung*, taking advantage of the difficulties of France, appealed to serious world opinion along the lines that Czechoslovakia impeded better Franco-German relations, a new sensation was launched for the benefit of the susceptible masses. On June 18th, 1937, the *Völkischer Beobachter* published the statement of a Reich German, by name Bruno Weigel, who claimed to have been tortured by the Czechoslovak police in the previous November. Weigel was a chemist who had worked in a Czech gas-mask factory until he was accused of espionage and arrested; he had been released on May 20th and had returned to Germany. Tremendous polemics in the Nazi press and on the wireless indicated that the medieval savagery of the Hussites had now combined with the frightfulness of Bolshevism. 'Such barbarity cannot be settled by mere diplomatic excuses', wrote the *Deutsche Allgemeine Zeitung*, and Czechoslovakia asked herself whether a German attack was to be launched in the guise of a punitive expedition. To what extent Weigel had been actually maltreated it is, of course, impossible to say; the Czechoslovak Government naturally denied the Reich German allegations and hinted at the ample evidence it possessed of Reich German police maltreatment of Czechoslovak citizens. It was generally felt that the Weigel case was at any rate a convenient adjunct at the time of the more diplomatic offensive of the *Frankfurter Zeitung* which was often regarded as the mouthpiece of the *Wilhelmstrasse*.

Though the Weigel case ceased to trouble the international scene surprisingly soon, within the Republic reactions to the incident were characteristic and disagreeable. The Czechs were indignant at criticisms from the country whose concentration camps had become so notorious, while the nationalist Sudeten Germans immediately accepted the story from Berlin. I happened, towards the end of June, to be in and around Tròppau (Opava), where the proximity of the Oder valley and of the great heavy industries of the Ostrava district make Czechoslovakia particularly vulnerable.

[1] See Editorial, June 20th, 1937.

One had a feeling of the acutest tension. In Troppau itself a Sudeten German who disapproved of Hitler and of Henlein told me there were so many Germans under arrest that he usually referred to the police head-quarters as *Das Deutsche Haus*. While I could hear of no serious charge against the behaviour of any of the authorities in Troppau, the police in Moravian Ostrava (Mährisch Ostrau) had an unenviable reputation, especially in their treatment of prisoners from Hlučin (Hultschin).[1] It is true that since 1936 police methods had deliberately been allowed to become more rough. 'The Czechs', as an extremely objective French friend once said to me, 'could not go on as they had, after all the Nazi kidnapping raids across the frontier. Why, they were beginning to feel that the President would be kidnapped from the Hradschin next.' On the other hand, I have never had convincing evidence to suggest that the Czechoslovak police authorities have so much to their discredit as the police authorities of any of the neighbouring countries.[2]

While the international background provided every obstacle to the improvement of the relations between Czechs and Sudeten Germans after February 18th, 1937, economic developments soon became unkind. In the early spring unemployment in the Sudeten German districts continued to decrease and this combined with the February Agreement to make a good impression. The Socialists and Clericals were hopeful as they observed waverers returning to their meetings in spite of the local pressure exerted by the S.d.P. which now renewed its efforts to brand Activism as the shameful thing. Impartial observers believed that the Social Democrats had really made a recovery since 1935, and in various shop-steward elections they slightly improved their position.[3] In August 1936 the President had specifically rejected Sudeten German autonomy, and Dr. Hodža now re-emphasized the veto in answer to the Aussig speech and the six S.d.P. Bills.[4] He was anxious, however,

[1] See above, Chapter XV, section (xi).
[2] With the possible exception of Austria while that State still existed. Naturally the Czech State police or gendarmerie, like railway guards, vary. I remember some disagreeable gendarmes; on the other hand, I once travelled in a bus from Reichenberg (Liberec) to Gablonz (Jablonec) with a gendarme who grinned so amiably all the way that racial differences seemed to thaw as the journey proceeded. And I shall never forget a gendarme at Troppau who came to my hotel to inquire about my birth-place or something he had not been able to read. As soon as the business was done he asked anxiously whether he might ask me quite a different question. Almost with tears in his voice he went on to say (in fairly good German), '*What* do the English think of us? The Germans, you know, abuse us all the time, but *what* do the English think?' He appeared to be simple and conscientious; I do not believe the question was a histrionic performance.
[3] Except at Schicht's Chemical Works, where the S.d.P. had a success.
[4] Though the S.d.P. Bills had not proposed territorial autonomy, it was implicit in many Sudeten German demands and complaints. Dr. Hodža pointed out that any plan of the kind would involve the abandonment of some 700,000 Czechs.

that municipal autonomy should be fully restored in spite of the tension in the frontier districts, and had indicated, soon after the February Agreement, that municipal elections would be held in the autumn in a number of districts, particularly Sudeten German ones.

From about June 1937 the economic recovery had hung fire. The general uncertainty and anxiety, which were to make themselves so unpleasantly felt on the world money markets in the autumn, impeded progress. For the Czechoslovak textile industry one or two circumstances were particularly unfavourable, for example, Polish exporters now received a premium which encouraged them to pour worsted yarns into Czechoslovakia. The importance of this competition can be gauged by the fact that, whereas during the whole of 1936 Poland exported to Czechoslovakia only 18,000 kg. of these yarns, between January 1st and July 31st, 1937, this figure had risen to 195,000 kg., involving the employment of some thousand spinners. Thus the number of textile workers working at unhappy Neudek (Nejdek), for example, fell between mid-August and mid-September from about 3,600 to about 2,500. In January 1937, 81 per cent. of the worsted yarn spinners were working a 40- to 48-hour week, but by the end of September only 44 per cent. were employed for 20 to 30 hours a week.[1] For various reasons employment in textiles fell at Teplitz-Schönau (Teplice-Šanov), Warnsdorf (Varnsdorf),[2] Zwittau (Svitavy), Freudenthal (Bruntál). Thus the economic gains of the early months of the year were diminished, and because it was they who had lost financial solidity and who depended upon international relations, the Sudeten Germans, as they were every time bound to do, again suffered more than the Czech working-people who worked to a much larger extent for the consumer at home.

It would be misleading to suggest that a slight setback had undone a very definite economic improvement since 1935. It would be misleading, too, to suggest that the February Agreement itself was not causing some improvement. A number of Germans were given State jobs, and above all a change in the behaviour of the Czech authorities became evident. One heard of Czech tax collectors who were behaving less bureaucratically to Germans; one heard of more State contracts going to German firms although the German tenders usually remained more expensive. The Czech banks had been making various concessions for some time—the Karlsbad *Kurhäuser*, for instance, were allowed a moratorium—while the State refunded the turn-over tax to the exporters of glass and porcelain. But everything went very slowly, sometimes

[1] Figures supplied by the Union of Textile-Workers.
[2] Warnsdorf had shown a very marked improvement in the spring (1937).

more slowly or more half-heartedly than it need. In the case of a new police station at Karlsbad the design and the work were shared between local people and people from Prague so that no one was very much pleased. Perhaps the greatest need the State could satisfy was to guarantee credit for industrial concerns which were prevented by lack of it from starting work again now that the biggest depression was over. A rule had been made that if a textile mill had been idle for more than eighteen months, it required official permission to reopen it. It was hoped in this way to prevent unsound ventures, but what frequently happened was that the Sudeten German textile employers themselves sent in objections to prevent the rehabilitation of a competitor. Thus technical difficulties were exploited from both sides. The most striking feature of the situation was that the achievements of the February Agreement, such as they were, received no publicity during the summer. One might be days in a Sudeten German town before one extracted from some competent quarter a fairly impressive list of Sudeten German firms which had recently secured official contracts. For there was a boycott from both sides. The more chauvinist Czechs preferred not to know, indeed some people said that it was better they should not, while the S.d.P. had an obvious interest in branding the February Agreement as a farce. With the approach of the municipal elections these tactics grew in importance. The prospect of these elections had also envenomed what had become a standing quarrel since 1933. For the S.d.P.[1] had all along done what it could to adapt Nazi technique to its own *soi-disant* legality. At meetings Herr Henlein's followers addressed him as 'Mein Führer' and the younger people turned up in a self-imposed uniform of white shirts, black breeches, and black riding-boots which were a clear finger-post pointing to S.S. uniforms in the Reich. There were constant squabbles about it, since the police authorities sometimes insisted upon the removal of the boots and even the shirts. While the demeanour of the S.d.P. youth was unmistakably provocative, the Henleiners replied if the *Sokol* people might wear their shirts and their boots and say the Czech equivalent of 'Heil', why not the Sudeten Germans.[2]

On September 14th Masaryk died and political activity halted for a moment. The emotion of the Czech and Slovak people was profound. But *Die Zeit* in its leading article on September 14th declared him to have been the great opponent of the Sudeten Germans, with what justification it is difficult to understand. It

[1] See Chapter XIV.
[2] The *Sokol* uniform with the falcon feather in the peasant cap makes a much less military impression upon the passing observer. When all else failed, the S.d.P. wore cornflowers (the old pre-War Pan-German emblem) and white stockings like the Nazis in Austria.

was interesting to see that *Der Aufbruch*,[1] on the other hand, frankly honoured him as the great patriot he was, not as an enemy to any other people. Yet in spite of the President's obvious desire to include all the nationalities in the funeral obsequies, they inevitably became the occasion of a great legionary rally which, like the Zborov[2] celebration in July, was repellent to the more nationalist Germans. The S.d.P. deputies returned from the Nazi Party Congress at Nürnberg[3] to take part in the funeral procession.

By October the communal election campaign was taken up in earnest, for the voting was to take place in November.[4] On October 6th Herr Rutha, who had long been not only one of Herr Henlein's closest collaborators but in addition his special envoy to Geneva, the Minority Congresses, &c., was arrested on account of serious homosexual charges; at the same time Herr Walter Rohn, the editor of the S.d.P. review *Volk und Führung*[5] and a number of young people were also arrested. The whole affair intensified the bitterness felt between the Henlein ex-*Kameradschaftsbund* leaders, such as Herr Henlein himself, Herren Frank and Kundt and Dr. Neuwirth, who, after capturing the *Turnverband*, had created the S.d.P., and the Kasper-Haider opposition. The opposition had always condemned the influence of men like Herr Rutha in the K.B. and the S.d.P. and among the youths of the *Turnverband*, and the vacillating behaviour of Herr Henlein, in the days which followed Herr Rutha's arrest, gave them further ground for attacks upon the S.d.P. leadership as incompetent. At Rodisfort (Radošov) near Karlsbad early in the autumn[6] there had been a big demonstration of young people in favour of Herr Haider, whose influence was evident in the *Bund der Deutschen*, and was now obviously growing in the *Kulturverband* as well as the *Turnverband*. Meanwhile many working-people were ready to listen to Herr Kasper's criticism of Herr Henlein's industrialist friends, and even of Herr Henlein's own luxuries such as the large Horch car which had been presented to him by industrialists in the Reich. There was certainly a tendency for German working-men to turn away from the S.d.P., and the less politically minded found themselves rather uncertain as to their choice between the activist Social Democrats

---

[1] *Der Aufbruch*, Oct. 1st, 1937.
[2] See above, Chapter VIII, pp. 77–8.
[3] Held from Sept. 6th to 13th.
[4] Early in 1938 Monsieur E. Pezet, vice-president of the foreign committee of the French Chamber of Deputies, stated himself to be in possession of evidence that on Sept. 8th, 1937, the Nazi headquarters in Munich provided the S.d.P. with 960,000 Kč, and on Oct. 16th another 1,088,000 Kč, all to be used in the communal election campaign. See *Prager Presse*, Feb. 2nd, 1938.
[5] This had succeeded *Die Junge Front*, the old *Kameradschaftsbund* review which had now changed hands. (*Volk und Führung* = People and Leadership.)
[6] See *Der Aufbruch*, Oct. 1st, 1937.

and Herr Kasper's racial socialism. The struggle between the two nationalist Sudeten German camps continued unabated to the end of the year. The Henleinists made efforts to assert their authority and expelled Herr Kasper from the S.d.P. and Herr Haider and many of his friends from the *Turnverband*, while pressing others of their sympathizers to resign from positions in the *Kulturverband*.

The Nazi opposition was in a very difficult position. Its members were determined to resist what they continued to regard as clique leadership, but they were anxious not to create an open breach which should reveal to the world that Sudeten German unity was unreal after all. They continued, therefore, to condemn themselves to a policy of passive resistance for a time. They were also handicapped by the curious circumstance that while they were the champions of a pure National Socialism—egalitarian and anti-clerical—such as that which prevailed in the Reich, the Reich German authorities, as in the case of the German minorities in Roumania and Yugoslavia, preferred to support the more conservative element against Hitlerist Germany's most enthusiastic supporters. Berlin's point of view was, no doubt, that the Henleinists were less likely to alarm foreign opinion, and that, since it was essential to emphasize the unity of the Sudeten Germans, the ex-K.B. machinery of the Henleinists was the most convenient apparatus to use. In September both Herren Kundt and Frank and Herr Kasper had attended the Party Congress at Nürnberg, and though the first two were said to have been disappointed by their reception, it was evident that Reich German funds would only be available for the as yet dominant political group of Germans in Czechoslovakia.

In the middle of October a fresh crisis in Reich German-Czechoslovak relations was brought about, this time directly by a Sudeten German affair. On October 17th a great many Henleinist leaders were collected in Teplitz-Schönau (Teplice-Šanov) for political consultations. As Herr Henlein was leaving the house of his friend and collaborator, Dr. Zippelius, a popular demonstration took place there in the Teplitz market-place. Now public meetings in the open, in view of the imminence of the elections, had been forbidden, and the police proceeded to disperse the crowd, and, in the course of doing so, they arrested Herr Karl Hermann Frank, took him to the police station, but released him upon the establishment of his identity, since as a deputy he was entitled to immunity. Sudeten German accounts of the affair described the police as having behaved with fearful brutality in the midst of a spontaneous demonstration from the Sudeten German people. Czech commentators thought 'spontaneous' to be a peculiar adjective in view of the fact that the only people who are known to have skirmished with the police were, besides Herr Frank, the two deputies, Herr Kundt and Dr. Köllner, also protected by parliamentary immunity. I have heard from a chance German eyewitness that the crowd in the market-place was not so large as to have aroused his curiosity—he was crossing the square and did not give the matter a thought at the time. On the other hand, it is probable that the police were nervous and possible that they behaved roughly; they did not hesitate to recognize the deputies' immunity when established, an immunity which is unknown in the rest of Central or Eastern Europe.

With its habitual promptness the Reich German press launched another tremendous offensive, in which the *Völkischer Beobachter*,[1] as ever, took the lead in an outburst signed Dr. K. V. (Karl Viererbl).[2]

At the cradle of the Czech State [he wrote] lies and hatred, murder and terror stood as sponsors. They have never forsaken the brief course of its life. . . . In Siberia during the War Czech deserters led by a crook began to murder and plunder unarmed German prisoners and a defenceless population. When these gangsters, honoured as heroes to-day, were brought back to their home . . . they continued their blood-thirsty handiwork.

The article referred back to the Weigel affair, and asked what must the thousands[3] of imprisoned Sudeten Germans be enduring from the Czech police, if the latter openly behaved as it had at Teplitz. It proceeded to lay the final blame upon the Prague Government which educated its servants *zum Hass gegen das Deutschtum*.

The Sudeten Germans must know [Dr. K. V. wrote] that the whole German Volk stands behind them. . . . The parvenu political behaviour of the Czechs, whose aggressiveness no doubt pleases Moscow and is therefore indulged in, makes them into the perpetual disturbers of peace in Central Europe, the bearers of the sole responsibility for the tension in this area. In Prague they had better observe that the days of German impotence are over, and that we regard the attitude to our *Volksgruppen* abroad, which have always shown themselves to be an orderly element, as the attitude taken up towards ourselves.

---

[1] Oct. 19th—no edition on Oct. 18th, because a Monday.

[2] A Sudeten German *émigré*—see above, p. 223.

[3] According to information supplied by the Czechoslovak Foreign Office, the number of people against whom trial was pending for offences against the Defence of the Republic Act of 1923 (see above, Chapter XII, section (i), p. 121) at the end of the year 1937 was 2,732. Of these 1,331 were Sudeten Germans, 591 Czechs or Slovaks, 575 Magyars, 164 Ruthenians, 9 Poles, while the nationality of the remaining 62 was either not yet ascertained or something other (e.g. Jewish). By far the majority of people under arrest or already sentenced are accused of breaking the 1923 Act; the State Defence Law of 1936 has undoubtedly led to far fewer sentences, though the actual figures appear not to be available. (The minorities always claim that the official figures are an under-estimate.) 1,235 Germans were freed by the Easter amnesty in 1938.

It was scarcely a month since Masaryk's funeral, the Czecho-slovaks remarked, and it was in this fashion that the semi-official organ of Germany attacked his State; many of them felt that it would be difficult ever to forgive the opening words of that article.

On October 20th the *Völkischer Beobachter* followed up the Dr. K. V. article with the publication of an open letter from Herr Henlein[1] to President Beneš with the sub-heading 'Czech Cheka methods endanger the Peace of Europe'. This letter had been sent from Leitmeritz (Litoměřice) on October 18th. It also declared that any further delay in the granting of autonomy to the Sudeten Germans would have catastrophic results, and declared the President to be responsible for the menace to European peace. It was interesting, too, that Herr Henlein informed Dr. Beneš that on his visit to London a few days before he had found understanding for his demands in responsible places. It was an alarming week. The German Foreign Office refused to accept the Czechoslovak protest against the German press campaign. Meanwhile the Czechoslovak authorities cancelled the municipal elections. Here was a test moment if the population was really on the point of revolt. But nothing happened. And in January 1938 the writer had the impression that Herr Henlein's position had become rather weaker than stronger. Though Herr Rutha's suicide[2] had disposed of a part of the problem, dissensions among the oppositional Sudeten Germans were multiplying. The sales of the *Aufbruch* were increasing, while a pamphlet called *Was ist der K.B.*, which came out in January 1938 to expose the *Kameradschaftsbund* from the *Aufbruch* point of view, sold out two editions in a very short time. At last on February 11th, 1938, one week after the German Nazi Party triumph of February 4th over reactionary opposition, the Sudeten German Nazis announced an open breach with the S.d.P.[3] and launched a new 'German Socialist' party upon its career. This was one day before the Agreement of Berchtesgaden, and Austrian events now seemed suddenly to heal the Henlein-*Aufbruch* breach. With what permanence their mutual satisfaction at the destruction of the Schuschnigg régime was to bring the two nationalistic Sudeten German groups together, only the future could reveal.

[1] Also published in the *Berliner Tageblatt* and other papers.
[2] Some Germans spoke of foul play, but, in the face of conclusive evidence, this charge against the Czechoslovak authorities was tacitly dropped.
[3] See *Der Aufbruch* of Feb. 16th, 1938, for the German Socialists' appeal to the public (in the name of the old Nazi leader Hans Knirsch) signed by Dr. Jonak, Herr Brehm, and twelve others. At the same time the *Aufbruch* drew attention to the curious claim of Herr K. H. Frank, in a speech of Dec. 8th, 1937, that Herr Henlein's Böhmisch Leipa speech of Oct. 1934 (cf. Chapter XIV) had laid down lines for a movement thoroughly permeated with National Socialism. The *Aufbruch* of Feb. 16th also announced a breach with Herr Haider on account of charges against him which had now been substantiated.

The distribution of official positions, of State contracts and subsidies, among the Sudeten German population had in the meantime
made, if modest, yet some substantial progress, and at last, in the
Prime Minister's speech in Parliament on November 17th, received
a belated publicity. Dr. Hodža was able to announce that well
above 22·32 per cent. of the total sums invested in the country had
actually been invested in the predominantly German districts in
the last year or so, and that the proportion was increasing. The
Ministry of Posts, for example, in 1936 had spent 32 per cent. of
its outlay on new buildings in Bohemia in the mainly German
country and in 1937 43 per cent.; for Moravia-Silesia the figures
were 32 per cent. and 41 per cent. respectively. The Ministry of
Public Works had also kept above the 22·32 per cent. figure.[1]
State subsidies to the German University, technical high schools,
&c., and to German theatres were now more than restored to their
full proportions;[2] indeed State expenditure per German student
appears now to be definitely above that per Czechoslovak student.[3]

The question of State officials was a more difficult one. Before
February 1937 the proportion of Germans employed by the various
Ministries of State had fallen very low; old officials had—though
by no means always—remained, but new ones had virtually never
been German. Indeed, one of the most emphatic complaints of the
Henleinists had all along been that the Sudeten Germans were
short of 40,000 officials.[4] While the proportion of Germans employed by the Ministry of Justice, of Posts, and of Health had been
about 11 per cent., in the Foreign Office it had touched a low
record of under 1·5 per cent. Only the Ministry of Education, if
teachers were included in the calculation, had been able to show
the percentage of about 21. The most serious difficulty was and
is the lack of Germans who speak adequate Czech. But there were
other difficulties besides. Official jobs in Czechoslovakia, as in all
the Succession States and many other continental countries, were
very poorly paid, and until the slump many Germans would not
have thought of applying for anything so unprofitable. Since the
days when Lodgman had declared it the duty of all Sudetendeutschen to be traitors,[5] their loyalty had been questionable, and
since the triumph of Hitler, it has been seen that this doubtful

---

[1] The varying Czech-German proportions in different regions make these
figures very difficult to estimate with any exactitude.
[2] See Chapter XV. They had fallen too low during the bad slump years.
[3] At the German University—if 100 is taken as the average—a student
costs the State 113·9 and at the Czechoslovak Universities 96·4; at the German
polytechnics 106·7 and at the Czechoslovak ones 97·4.
[4] See above, Chapter XII. The diagrams nos. 33 and 34 in *Die Tschechoslowakei im Spiegel der Statistik* show clearly that, while the number of German
officials had been reduced, that of Czechoslovak officials had only increased very
slightly.   [5] In Parliament in 1922. See H. Klepetař, *Seit 1918*, p. 175.

loyalty was shaken as it never had been before. Many Sudeten Germans were out to boycott the February Agreement by whose failure alone they were likely to profit; indeed, the Party definitely discouraged its members from applying for posts, and the Activists had difficulty in offering enough eligible people. On the Czechoslovak side the convention was allowed for some time to survive that legionaries—who were all Czechs or Slovaks—should receive half of all the jobs that fell vacant; thus only the remaining half was eligible for proportional distribution. By the end of 1937, strangely enough, there were still legionaries waiting for post office jobs.

Dr. Hodža in November was able to indicate a noticeable change with regard to the proportional appointment of Germans, and official policy continued slowly but steadily to improve. Between February 18th and November 30th, 1937, about 1,100 Germans had received official positions, and the Foreign Office, official Statistical Bureau, and Ministry of Posts had done something to make amends for the past to the German minority. While the 1,100 only comprised some 12·5 per cent. of all the appointments made during this period, it should be considered that the enrolment of the gendarmerie overweighted the Czechoslovaks on the list. What was almost more important than the number of actual installations was a very marked change in policy—so that, for instance, it was promised that legionary privileges should be partially waived —and obstacles to the promotion of Sudeten German officials ceased to operate. I remember cases of German postal officials who in October 1937 were still complaining of the perpetual promotion of their Czech juniors over their heads, and who in January 1938 had been promoted for the first time for twelve years.

On February 12th, 1938, the German Chancellor imposed the Berchtesgaden Agreement upon the Austrian Federal Chancellor and insisted upon the inclusion in Dr. von Schuschnigg's Cabinet of the Nationalist, Dr. Seyss-Inquart. This led directly to the annexation of Austria by Germany on March 13th. The position of Czechoslovakia had thereby become a great deal more critical, and the Czechoslovak Cabinet, while still questioning the meaning and fittingness of Henleinist claims, prepared to put the February Agreement into practice by decree instead of waiting to apply it as opportunity offered. Already in January the Government had been contemplating, also, the application of proportions which should take into consideration the larger German minority in Bohemia as compared with that in Moravia-Silesia, and in March they drew public attention to this aim.

The German annexation of Austria was bound to have profound repercussions among the Sudeten Germans, the more since the pro-Nazi movement in Austria had been led by men like Dr.

Seyss-Inquart and Dr. Jury, who were Sudeten Germans them-selves and had been associated with the *Kameradschaftsbund*. It was significant that the force of events had brought these men, who had not originally accepted National Socialism any more than Herr Henlein himself before 1936, to call in the Reich German troops into Austria. The same tremendous National Socialist *élan* now seemed to sweep away the quarrel between Herr Henlein and Herr Kasper, and brought the Sudeten German Agrarians and Clericals over to the side of the S.d.P. While the German Activist parties had always felt critical towards Czechoslovak policy, the news from annihilated Austria, inducing, as no doubt it did, either racialistic fervour or the fear of the concentration camp, now impelled them to join the Henleinist opposition.

CHAPTER XVII

IN CONCLUSION

MANY centuries of struggle lie behind the Czech-German problem in the Historic Provinces. Since 1848 it has been a frankly critical question; in the last ninety years, the circumstances have obviously changed, but the problem has remained the same one. Indeed, the conflict between the Czechs and the Sudeten Germans had become the very condition of pre-War Austrian life; before 1914 the Germans obstructed in the Diet and boycotted the Town Council meetings at Prague where to-day they appear in Parliament and Town Hall. On the other hand, for all the Pan-Slav–Pan-German talk there was never a time when the Czech-German problem constituted a serious international danger; it was the Southern Slav question which led to the outbreak of war.

It is not difficult to understand the mistakes which have been made by Czechoslovakia since 1918; often it is difficult to see how they could have been avoided. However much they prefer to deny it, the Czechoslovaks have inherited a tremendous amount from pre-War Cis-Leithania, a mixture of dilatoriness with respect for the letter of the law, which together constitute, I suppose, what one means by 'bureaucratic'. Czechoslovakia, again, is the heir to an Austrian respect for lawfulness itself and a certain tolerance and fairness, curiously combined with the shaken, yet surviving and recently revivified, traditions of the Habsburg police and censorship. It is really remarkable to find that Sudeten Germans who have consistently preached treason against the Republic in many cases live free and unmolested in its midst; no dictatorship would allow such a thing. The Czechoslovaks have thus inherited a great deal from old Austria-Hungary without its German-Magyar ruling class. This latter circumstance has left them without a very serviceable finesse and a *savoir faire* which did something in the old days to smooth out national quarrels. But in return the Czechoslovak Republic has been liberated from that static feudalism which petrified the Habsburg Monarchy so that some of its most promising reforms proved ineffectual. And if the ideas of Masaryk have been faultily put into practice, a beginning has most definitely been made; he himself was the first to emphasize the need for time. There is, moreover, in spite of the *Schlamperei* tradition, an efficiency, a determination, and a vitality about the Czechs which promise well for the future, if external violence should not distort normal expectation. As for the devotion of the Czechs to democracy as opposed to dictatorship, it is none the less real because, like Polish, and indeed most other democrats on the Continent, they sometimes hesitate to accept the claim to full citizens' rights of non-Czechoslovak minorities whose attitude towards the State is negative. While the policy of the oppositional democratic parties in Poland or Roumania towards their minorities is, on the whole, more liberal than that of the Warsaw or Bucarest régime, in Czechoslovakia the régime leads the way.

Although from the earliest days of the Republic its leaders had rather vaguely claimed 'a certain special position for the Czecho-Slovak language and element',[1] it is not easy to feel quite certain that the liberty of the individual subject is curtailed nowadays on account of his belonging to a minority. A German citizen of Czechoslovakia who accepts the political principles of the State is no more aware of the police or the censorship than a Czech; in any court of law he will be just as well looked after. When he ceases to regard himself as an individual and becomes active as a member of a racial group which pays extensive homage to a neighbouring and—is it too much to say?—unfriendly State, he becomes suspect in the eyes of the State authorities and is sub-jected to annoyance, interference, and severity. If he lives in a frontier district—and he usually does—he will also be subjected, especially since 1936, to sundry restrictions imposed by the mili-tary authorities. If he feels a profound racialistic enthusiasm and scorns an individualistic acceptance of the rule of a polyglot State, then the situation is thoroughly exasperating for him, as it fre-quently was for a Czech with Pan-Slav, or even Czecho-Slovak, enthusiasms in old Austria. The fact that 591 Czechoslovaks were recently under arrest for offences against the Defence Law of 1923 at a time when 1,331 Sudeten Germans were in the same predica-ment[2] makes it plain that, while the Germans are much more likely to break the law as it stands, the law nevertheless is enforced against a substantial number of 'the Czecho-Slovak element' in spite of its 'special position'. The execution of Sergeant Krejza[3] points to the same conclusion. Since the further question of access to official posts has already been dealt with fairly fully,[4] it need only be repeated here that while there had undoubtedly been discrimina-tion in the past, the prospects for a Sudeten German who was reasonably familiar with the Czech language had improved to a noticeable extent before the German annexation of Austria had created a new situation in the spring of 1938.

---

[1] See above, Chapter X, Note of May 20th, 1919.
[2] See above, Chapter XVI (ii), p. 267, note 3.
[3] See Chapter XVI (i), p. 241, note 3.
[4] See Chapter XVI (ii), p. 269.

The Czechoslovaks resent the emphasis laid since 1935 upon the grievances of the Sudeten Germans and their elevation to the rank of an international question of the greatest prominence. As the Czechs point out, the democratic Czechoslovak Republic has given its minorities more equitable treatment and greater opportunities to express their views and win consideration for them than the political system in Italy, Germany, Poland, or elsewhere allows. In spite of flaws in Czechoslovak administration in the minority regions, it would be difficult for any one with any real knowledge of general minority conditions in Central and Eastern Europe to question this. One has only to consider the Germans, Slovenes, and Croats in Italy, the Ukrainians and Germans in Poland, the Poles and Lusatian Slavs[1] in Germany, the Germans and Slovaks in Hungary, the Germans and Hungarians in Yugoslavia and Roumania, and the Jews in Germany, Poland, Hungary, and Roumania, to be certain that the Czech contention is justified. If conditions in mixed and 'language-frontier' districts in Czechoslovakia are distasteful to the Sudeten German inhabitants, their life in the main German areas is, from some points of view, strikingly independent and complete; it should not be forgotten that, in spite of its questioned loyalty, the S.d.P. itself has provided many elected representatives in towns like Brno (Brünn) where elections fell due in the first few years after 1933.[2] And even if the Sudeten Germans are sometimes compelled to accept nominated officials, even if political meetings are sometimes forbidden, even if frontier zones are militarized, they retain, nevertheless, a degree of personal freedom which would be unthinkable in contemporary Germany. They are able to criticize, to combine, to complain, and to disagree, in the press, in Parliament, and abroad. It has been seen, further, that the determination of President Beneš to guarantee their full equality of status has begun to bear fruit. Recent events in Austria have inflamed the old intransigence on both sides, Czech and German, the belief, conscious or subconscious, that one must either devour or be devoured.[3] Apart from disturbances from across the frontiers, there has often, however, been a higher degree of desire for sensible co-operation than the excited cries of the post-1933 period lead the casual visitor to suppose; and practical circumstances might always help to crystallize the co-operative impulses into a driving force.

[1] See above, Chapter X, p. 89.
[2] The Brno elections were in 1935; 19 Germans were elected in a Town Council of 90; of the 19, 13 belonged to the S.d.P.
[3] I came across a minor but typical illustration of the intransigent tradition in a small Bohemian town with a Czech minority of about 25 per cent.; to the amusement of the Germans who told me about it, the Czech minority had decided, since the municipal fire brigade consisted only of Germans, to start a second fire brigade of their own.

There are three alternatives to the policy of Beneš and of February 18th, 1937:

1. *The transformation of Czechoslovakia into a federation of its component nationalities.* This, incidentally, would bear little resemblance to Switzerland, where several of the quasi-autonomous cantons are linguistically mixed. The first difficulty here would be to draw the boundaries, for if there are areas which are overwhelmingly German, it has been seen that the language-frontier districts are indescribably mixed. Admirers of the Kremsier (Kroměříž) Constitution[1] are apt to forget that the subsequent flow of Czech miners to the lignite area and other results of industrialization have made the proposals of 1849 no longer applicable to-day. Territorially it is clear that the Sudeten Germans are most unfortunately scattered from the point of view of providing them with administrative unity within the frontiers of Czechoslovakia. As for the personal or *Kataster* principle advocated in the six propositions of the S.d.P.,[2] this is to be linked with a compulsory organization which would destroy the rights of minorities, Socialist or National Socialist, within the German national group; they would be more helpless than the Sudeten Germans in the Czechoslovak Parliament. Further, if a federal system is to function at all, whether it be a territorial or a personal federalism, it must have some common political assumptions as in Switzerland, the United States, or even in the U.S.S.R.; it is impossible to visualize a successful federalization of Czechoslovakia, even if the psychology of peace could be restored, so long as its German group be dominated by people who hold the political tenets of Prague in contempt. On March 16th, 1938, the S.d.P. leader, Herr Enhuber, made a speech in the Senate at Prague in which he demanded with a new fervour the transformation of Czechoslovakia on the Swiss model. He seemed to forget that this demand is inconsistent with his party's six propositions, and he seemed to ignore the fact that, if the French and German Swiss were to develop hostile political ideologies, the Swiss Constitution might operate no better than that of the Czechoslovak Republic. In the circumstances of to-day it is felt, both by Czechoslovaks and by the democratic Sudeten Germans who remain, that a federalized Czechoslovakia, if federal boundaries were somehow arbitrarily drawn, would be the helpless prey of any powerful and unscrupulous neighbour—no one decentralizes when war is in sight. The S.d.P. advocates also a Swiss foreign policy for Czechoslovakia—its neutralization, that is to say, and the abandonment of the treaty with Russia. To most Czechoslovaks, however, to drop the Russian treaty would be to give up

[1] See Chapter III above.
[2] See Chapter XVI (ii).

their last guarantee against Pan-German control, and—as they believe—to commit national suicide.

2. *A Sudeten German–Reich German Anschluss with the union of Southern Bohemia and Southern Moravia with that part of Germany which was Austria.* Such a solution would present the same impossible problem of discovering a frontier. Whatever line were determined, minorities would be left on the wrong side of it, and there is little reason to suppose that in the new circumstances they would receive any consideration. Totalitarian States by definition have no place for dissidents or minorities; the suppression of the Lusatian Slav newspapers and any other rights these Slavs had retained in Germany in 1937 provides confirmation of this. It is, moreover, generally agreed that the independence of the Czechs would be strategically annulled if this type of *Anschluss* were effected.[1] What is of greater importance from the Sudeten German point of view is that small-scale Sudeten German industry would be catastrophically hit by large-scale Reich German competition,[2] and a long period of intense misery would be inevitable before the essential readjustments could be made.[3] The Sudeten German textile industry could scarcely escape ruin, and manufactured goods, such as the gloves of Asch, would be tremendously hit; or again Reich German (Bemberg) stockings would kill Kunnert's stocking factories at Warnsdorf. Nor is it likely that Bohemian china could survive Reich German competition. While cotton production would be crippled, the Reich could absorb more woollens, but these, on the other hand, are important rather to Czech workers in Brno than to the Sudeten German population.

It should perhaps here be observed that on escaping from official S.d.P. declarations for foreign consumption, it has for years been interesting to observe how many of its members have quite frankly been waiting with eagerness for an *Anschluss*. Even those who are aware of the rigours of Reich German dictatorship are often so much imbued with racialism that they regard union with Germany as the only desirable solution. One member of the Party remarked to me, 'Even if the Devil were ruling Germany, we would rather be part of it.'

If among the non-political and activistically inclined Sudeten Germans the advantages of the frontier between Germany and the Historic Provinces are fully appreciated, among whole-hog National

---

[1] See above, Chapter X.

[2] It has been seen (Chapter IX) that Sudeten German industrialists were opposed to an *Anschluss* with Germany in 1919. It is only since the slump that their losses have induced many of them to shut their eyes to the objections they had until then entertained.

[3] Unless for political reasons the German Government should provide special facilities for Sudeten German industry.

Socialists an *Anschluss* would be nothing but a transitional step towards the third alternative:

3. *The old project of a German Mittel-Europa.* It has been interesting sometimes during the last two or three years to hear rapturous Sudeten German prophecies of a new German invasion of Bohemia with the old 1866 strategy and a victory à la König-grätz,[1] which, this time, shall lead to the reunion instead of the division of the Germans; by reunion, however, it seems to be assumed that the Historic Provinces will be reincorporated with Austria, and will, as Spann and Patscheider circles have urged, constitute the heart of a new German Empire. On the public platform at home or abroad, Henleinist leaders have emphasized the appalling results of a war, above all for the Sudeten German population, yet in the Sudeten German towns and villages near the frontier a German invasion has long been discussed with little anxiety. It is noteworthy that, whereas until recently the answer to any question as to how the Sudeten Germans would react to a German-Czech war was that they would undoubtedly do their duty, since early in 1937 even responsible leaders have laid frank emphasis upon the call of German blood.

A German *Mittel-Europa* has come very much nearer to realization since February and March of 1938. There is, of course, a strong case to be made for this programme, which, should it be fully realized, would bring unity of control, the proverbially efficient organization of the Germans, and the abolition of tariff barriers. As Naumann had conceived it, *Mittel-Europa* was to constitute a great economic and military unity within whose frontiers a complete autonomy in national, linguistic, and educational affairs should be constitutionally guaranteed. Even in this extraordinarily attractive shape, it cannot be ignored that the plan would have brought about precisely that German hegemony to prevent which we fought the Great War from 1914 to 1918. To-day the profoundly liberal conception of a Naumann would be distorted out of recognition by a subjective point of view which condemns the principles of tolerance out of hand; Naumann, himself Prussian, warned his countrymen that not the Reich Germans, but the Austrians, were versed in the problems of Danubian mediation; in 1938, however, Reich Germans are policing the streets of Vienna and the specific qualities of the Austrian are apparently to be lost. *Mittel-Europa* to-day might even involve the compulsory use of the German language for official purposes and the expulsion of non-Germans from key positions in the territories absorbed, as the chauvinist Germans of pre-War Austria

[1] See Chapter IV. The entry of the Reich German troops into Austria in March 1938 has now, of course, partially reversed the settlement of 1866.

demanded; it will certainly bring the suppression of political criticism and anti-Nazi opinion of every kind. Many people believe that Czechoslovakia will now be coerced, as Austria has been, into taking her place in the new *Mittel-Europa*; this may be brought about directly, or again if the Czechoslovaks should be sufficiently isolated as to be forced to accept—at Berlin's instigation—the Henleinists into the Government coalition[1] and therewith, of course, to drop the treaty with Russia. In practice the immediate result would be the paralysis of all non-Nazi political activity and the ejection of the Czech Left and Left Centre from the Czecho-slovak Cabinet. Indeed, since this would place the large Czech working-class[2] in opposition to the régime, the old class-race cleavage between Germans and Czechs in Bohemia and Moravia might become more rigidly demarcated than ever before. It is sometimes forgotten that German National Socialism, like the Pan-Germanism of Schönerer and Karl Hermann Wolf from which it is directly descended, preaches a hierarchy of races and there-with indicates that Germans should rule over Slavs.[3] Further, it appears to claim the self-appointed task of interfering wherever it chooses to descry disorder dangerous to itself. The Reich German attitude towards Czechoslovakia to-day may be summed up in the words of the Sudeten German, Herr Jung: 'The Czechs have shown the world once before at the time of the Hussite wars that chaos is in no way alien to them, and that they are ready to spread this chaos in the world',[4] and it has been seen that the Russian Treaty of 1935 has been used in order to justify this contention to-day. In Habsburg days the non-German races of Central and Southern Europe could hope to capture the monarchy, but nowa-days they have very little prospect of resisting the expansive energy of Germany, unless with Russian support, and when one of them turns towards Russia, the Germans at once feel the menace to become intolerable.[5] Not only must Russia, in the German view, be kept out of Europe, but as the German Chancellor has implied in *Mein Kampf*, German eastern expansion has territorial claims to present to Russia. This conflict of interest appears to induce both Berlin and Moscow to lay extraordinary emphasis upon

[1] On Jan. 1st, 1938, the Right Wing Agrarian leader, M. Beran, published a statement which implied approval of a plan of this kind, but he did not appear to have much support even from the Agrarian Party, and he has abandoned the suggestion since then.
[2] The Czech peasants would be unlikely to support Agrarian leaders who accepted the dictation of Berlin, while the industrial workers would be bitterly hostile.
[3] This is generally taught in German schools to-day. Cf. instructions issued by the Reich Ministry of the Interior in 1933 and subsequently, also *National-sozialistische Erziehung*, no. 47, Nov. 21st, 1936, &c., &c.
[4] R. Jung, *Die Tschechen* (Berlin, 1937). See also Chapter XII, (iv), p. 135.
[5] Cf. Plener's words quoted in Chapter VIII, p. 73.

ideological differences, when to the western observer they seem to be inspired by so many kindred conceptions.

The more one examines the Czech-German problem the more evident it becomes that there is no very clear distinction to be made between the cession of the mainly German territories of Czechoslovakia to Germany and the complete domination of Central Europe—Czech-speaking territory included—by the Germans. In 1919, in their third *Mémoire* presented to the Peace Conference, the Czechs provided illustration of this point *à propos* the economic question. They pointed out that since the Sudeten German territories were economically knit with the Czech interior of Bohemia, if Germany possessed the former she would inevitably covet and absorb or frankly seize the latter.[1]

Les Allemands [Mémoire 3 continued] se sont, pendant la guerre, suffisamment fait [*sic*] connaître, pour qu'il soit possible de juger de la tournure fatale que prendraient les événements, si l'on fournissait aux Allemands l'occasion de s'emparer d'un pays aussi important que la Bohême.

Only by taking the whole of Bohemia could Germany easily safeguard the provisioning of the Sudeten German *Randgebiete*, at any rate until she is more completely mistress of Balkan food supplies.

Czechoslovakia's fear of the economic stranglehold and the consequent political dependence to which a Greater Germany can subject her was aroused at the time of the Austro-German Customs Union project in 1931, and, with Herr Hitler's annexation of Austria in March 1938, is more than ever alive to-day. By excluding Czechoslovak coal and manufactures from Austria, or by cutting Czechoslovakia's commercial communications (via Hamburg, &c.) with the rest of the world, Germany can immensely impoverish the Republic and intensify Sudeten German distress; by merely threatening to do so, she wields a powerful weapon against Prague. The anxiety of the Czechs can also be explained by recalling the tremendous power not merely of Austrian German, but also of Reich German, capital in the Historic Provinces prior to 1914. There has already been occasion to refer to the German capital in the Plzeň (Pilsen) breweries[2] and elsewhere. In fact a whole array of Reich German concerns had branches and capital in the Sudeten lands,[3] the German General Electricity Company of Berlin, for example, or the German-Austrian Mining Company, the Dux Porcelain Works, &c.; for several Reich German concerns, Saxony and Bohemia formed one area of activity. With the fall of Habsburg and Hohenzollern and the rise

---

[1] See Chapter X, pp. 90–1.   [2] See Chapter XI, section (v).
[3] See the Foreign Office Handbook, *Bohemia and Moravia*, published in Jan. 1919, pp. 101–3.

of the Czechoslovak Republic, Czech and other non-German capital was able to take over Škoda's and the breweries of Plzeň and to push its way into this concern and that; gradually the *Živnostenská Banka* came to control a network of industries; all the time, nevertheless, a considerable sum of Reich German capital has remained invested in Czechoslovakia. The Czechs believe that their political independence could never have been fully realized while Austrian and Reich German capital dictated to Bohemian and Moravian industry. The Czechs fear above all that German-Austrian-Balkan tariff union policy, which was so eagerly demanded by the nationalist German parties of Habsburg Austria,[1] and which, they believe, will lead to a German political domination of Central and South-Eastern Europe exactly as the tariff policy of the Prussians before Bismarck led to the Prussianization of pre-War Germany.

The policy of Germany to-day would appear to be in sympathy, not with Naumann, but with many of the Pan-German *Mittel-Europa* demands which were most specifically framed during the Great War, especially at the time of the *Osterbegehrschaft* in 1916.[2] It would certainly be impossible, in practice, for any programme of this kind to remain purely economic in its effects. The German Chancellor's speech on February 20th, 1938, emphatically condemned the Bismarckian decisions of 1866;[3] was there perhaps a tacit claim here, the Czechs must have asked themselves, not merely to post-War Austria but to all that was previously included in the Austria which belonged to the German Confederation of 1815? For was not Masaryk right? To-day it is still a question of whether some 3 million Germans shall be without their own State or whether 10 million Czechs and Slovaks shall be swallowed up in an alien political community;[4] no other alternative seems practically real in view of the extraordinary intricacies of the racial position in the Historic Provinces. Thus, unless modern Pan-Germanism be regarded with indifference or approbation, it would appear that for Czechoslovakia to continue within her Peace Treaty frontiers and to pursue the conciliatory policy which President Beneš has sponsored may remain the least unsatisfactory programme that can be found.[5] The present position in the Republic

---

[1] See Chapter VIII, p. 76.   [2] Ibid.
[3] See Chapter IV, p. 32.   [4] See Chapter IX, p. 80.
[5] The question should here be raised whether the 20 per cent. test for the granting of minority rights is always satisfactory. Where the unit is a big one, as in Prague, a German population (about 50,000 people) larger than that of the whole inner town of Reichenberg (about 40,000 inhabitants) or Karlsbad (about 24,000 inhabitants) is left without the 20 per cent. rights. If Brno loses these rights in 1940, some 60,000 Germans, the largest compact German group in the Republic, will have no legal claim to State schools, though on the analogy of Prague or of Budějovice (where the Germans are only 14 per cent.), they will not in practice be left without a reasonable number of them.

has been represented for some time as an inherent danger to European peace, but the Teplitz incident of October 1937[1] may be counted among the arguments which run counter to this claim. Until at least the end of 1937 there was reason to believe that arms concealed by would-be rebels in Sudeten German territory amounted to a negligible quantity, though, as the *Manchester Guardian* has reported, there have long been depots of arms just across the Reich German frontier. Between October 1937 and February 1938, their own divisions[2] and the growth of a certain disillusionment, after the unending rumours that 'Hitler will come' which had circulated with varying intensity since 1933, had reduced the more extreme Sudeten German hopes a little. But with Herr Hitler's intervention in Austrian affairs in February and the annexation of Austria by Germany in March 1938, Sudeten German expectations rose above any level they had hitherto reached. It is, of course, perfectly natural that the Germans in the Reich should feel an interest in the welfare of the *Auslandsdeutschen*, and especially in that of the Sudeten Germans who live closest to them. Though in pre-War days, and even after the War, many Reich Germans scarcely knew of its existence,[3] the publicity recently devoted to the Sudeten German question, and the Pan-German message of the Third Reich, will make it impossible for the Reich Germans to forget the Bohemian and Moravian Germans again, and bitter indignation has been created in Germany by tendentious accounts of conditions in Czechoslovakia.

Whether the activism of the Sudeten German Government parties or the negativism of the rest of the Sudeten German groups has been more useful to the Sudeten German population was, until recently, a point of some interest, though it threatens now to become purely academic. In the period since 1933 which appears to be ending in 1938, one gained the impression that the less picturesque efforts of the Activists more often led to solid results than spectacular demonstrations from the older Nationalist, or the younger Sudeten German, parties, though there was, of course, a certain interplay of forces. I remember hearing of a good many instances of which the following is typical. At Friedberg (Frymburk) in Southern Bohemia a German school was to be closed. The S.d.P. got up a great campaign of protest, and, as frequently happened, the attitude of the Czechs stiffened; an Activist politician then intervened and the school was allowed to remain.

If the Sudeten German problem be regarded, as it certainly could

---

[1] See Chapter XVI (ii), p. 266.   [2] See Chapter XVI (ii).
[3] Sudeten Germans visiting Germany in the twenties were often asked how it came about that they spoke German so well.

be until this year, as the economic problem of the rehabilitation of a distressed area within the frontiers of the Czechoslovak Republic, it is clear that financial guarantees and other necessities of the kind were more likely to come from the Czechoslovak ministries as the result of direct Activist negotiation than in answer to threats and international appeals. If the Czechoslovak authorities have often seemed slow and unwilling, one or two explanatory considerations should perhaps be recalled. One circumstance which has complicated the German-Czech situation within the Czechoslovak Republic has been the attitude of the Sudeten German industrialists, bankers, and savings bank investors, who have bitterly resented the most timely help from Czech banks. In 1934 the Czechoslovak régime founded a Rediscount Bank with Government funds in order to provide credits where they were most needed. In January 1936, for example, 30·53 per cent. of the credit it was providing at the time was placed at the disposal of Sudeten German co-operative and savings banks, and on the average the German share has been between 25 and 30 per cent., i.e. well above the German population percentage. Many Sudeten German savings have been rescued by the action of the Czechs in expanding the Central Bank of the Czech Savings Banks so as to take over 80 per cent. of the capital of the *Zentralbank der deutschen Sparkassen* which collapsed in 1932.[1] Czechoslovak banks, with substantial help from the State, have rescued the smaller insurance policies held by many Sudeten Germans which appeared to be lost when the Vienna Phoenix Insurance Company broke down in 1936. All these things seem generous in Czechoslovak eyes. The Sudeten Germans cannot, however, forgive the sacrifice of their economic independence which these actions have involved. Indeed their attitude has been one of the most serious obstacles to the welding together of the new State; at the same time, it is in the tradition of the race-conscious inhabitants of old Austria, and entirely comparable with the attitude of the Czechs towards the Austrian German and Reich German capital from whose pre-War control they were so eager to escape, and with their attitude towards a German *Mittel-Europa* of the future. From the economic point of view one obvious requirement in the Historic Provinces is a minimum wage. The Czechs, whose birth-rate has fallen (as their standard of living has risen) well below that of the more primitive Slovaks and far below that of the Ruthenes, have been aware for some time that they themselves will be increasingly subjected to the inroads of cheap labour from the east before the various birth-rates more or less stabilize. But legislation should be able to facilitate the process of adjustment.

[1] See Chapter XIII, section (iii), p. 167.

To consider the history of the Czech-German struggle in Bohemia and Moravia-Silesia is, however, to realize that the problem is more than one of economic distress. Contemporary evidence confirms the evidence of history. It is, for instance, worthy of notice that in Eger, where even the great slump of 1929–35 could not shake economic stability nor induce any really serious distress, Sudeten German intransigence has always been most conspicuous and anti-Czech feeling at boiling-point. On the contrary, in a place overtaken by overwhelming economic disaster like Rothau,[1] it has been seen that the German population has continued to support an Activist Party against the Sudeten German racialists.

In the circumstances of Europe to-day the problem of the Historic Provinces cannot be satisfactorily solved. A wise Government can greatly reduce friction, but, whatever the Government, friction there will be, so long as a racialistic nationalism is regarded as an absolute standard of good. Some common political principle which different races can respect is the cement which is needed to repair the Czech-German structure. The humanism of Thomas Masaryk might gradually have created the necessary cohesion, and the Historic Provinces, by reconciling German with Slav, might have pointed the way towards a genuine solution of the problem of Central Europe.

[1] See Chapter XIII, section (iii), pp. 175 *et seq.*

BIBLIOGRAPHY

It would be almost impossible to mention all the newspapers and pamphlets which it has been necessary to consult in writing this book; I am therefore not attempting to make a list of them. Direct references are given in the footnotes.

Of the vast quantities of propagandistic publications which have been sponsored by the Czechoslovak Government on the one side and Herr Henlein's Sudeten German Party (S.d.P.) on the other, it has not seemed worth while to mention more than the most important, since the attitude taken up is usually so far from objectivity. Monsieur Chmelǎr's *The German Problem in Czechoslovakia* and Monsieur Sobota's *Das tschechoslovakische Nationalitätenrecht* are, however, too valuable to omit, and Herr Henlein's speeches in *Konrad Henlein spricht* deserve to be studied. R. Jung's *Die Tschechen* should be read as symptomatic; I cannot recollect so virulent an attack by a Czech upon the Germans.

(i) Official Publications

Austria-Hungary
Stenographische Protokolle über die Sitzungen des Hauses der Abgeordneten des Reichsrates.
Process Georg Ritter von Schönerer—Neues Wiener Tageblatt. Vienna, 1888.

Czechoslovakia
Administrační Zpráva obce . . . Prahy za rok 1896 &c. (Archives of the City of Prague.)
Statistische Jahrbücher der ČSR
Zprávy státního úřadu statistického Republiky Československé (Mitteilungen der Čechoslovakischen Republik).

Germany
Auswärtiges Amt: Die grosse Politik der europäischen Kabinette, 1871–1914. Berlin, 1922–7.

Great Britain
Department of Overseas Trade: Reports on Economic Conditions in Czechoslovakia.
Foreign Office:
Bohemia and Moravia. (Peace Handbooks, issued by the Historical Section of the Foreign Office, No. 4.) London, 1919.
British Documents on the Origins of the War, 1898–1914. Edited by G. P. Gooch and Harold Temperley. 12 vols. London, 1926–38.

(ii) Other Books

(a) *Books and periodicals dealing with the period up to and including the Peace Conference*

Bauer (Otto): Die Nationalitätenfrage und die Sozialdemokratie. Vienna, 1907.
Beneš (Eduard): Světová válka a naše revoluce. Prague, 1927. (German translation: Die Aufstand der Nationen, Berlin, 1928.)
Bretholz (Professor Bertold): Geschichte Böhmens und Mährens bis zum Aussterben der Přemysliden. 4 vols. Reichenberg, 1921–5.
Cajthaml (F.): Obrázky z 'Deutschböhmen' (Sketches from German Bohemia). Prague, 1923.

Čechische Revue: Published in Prague by Dr. Arnošt Kraus. 1907–12.
CHARMATZ (R.): Oesterreichs innere Geschichte. 2 vols. Leipzig, 1911.
DENIS (Ernest): La Bohême depuis la Montagne Blanche. 2 vols. Paris, 1903.
DÜRICH (J.): V českých službách. 1921.
EISENMANN (L.): Le compromis austro-hongrois. Paris, 1904.
FISCHEL (Alfred): Oesterreichisches Sprachenrecht. Brünn, 1910.
—— Der Panslawismus bis zum Weltkrieg. Stuttgart, 1919.
GRÜNBERG (Carl): Die Bauernbefreiung und die Auflösung des gutsherr-lich-bauerlichen Verhältnisses in Böhmen, und Mähren und Schlesien. 2 vols. Leipzig, 1894.
HÖFLER (Konstantin): Geschichtsschreiber der hussitischen Bewegung.
HUGELMANN (Karl Gottfried), *ed.*: Das Nationalitätenrecht des alten Oesterreichs. Vienna, 1934.
JESSER (Dr. Franz): Das Wesen des nationalen Kampfes in den Sudetenländern. Vienna, 1912.
KERNER (R. J.): Bohemia in the Eighteenth Century. New York, 1932.
KRAMÁŘ (Dr. Karel): Poznámky o české politicě. Prague, 1906.
—— Pět přednašek o zahraničné politicě. Prague, 1922.
KROFTA (K.): Das Deutschtum in der tschechoslowakischen Ge-schichte. Prague, 1936.
LÁNYI (P. Geist): Das Nationalitätenproblem auf den Reichstag zu Kremsier.
MASARYK (T. G.): Palackýs Idee des böhmischen Volkes. Prague, 1898.
—— Světová revoluce. Prague, 1925 (German translation: Die Welt-Revolution, Berlin 1927).
MILLER (David Hunter): My Diary at the Conference of Paris. 21 vols. Privately published, 1924–6.
MOLISCH (Paul): Geschichte der deutsch-nationalen Bewegung in Oesterreich. Jena, 1926.
—— Die sudetendeutsche Freiheitsbewegung in den Jahren 1918–19. Vienna, 1932.
NAUMANN (F.): Mittel-Europa. Berlin, 1915.
NICOLSON (Harold): Peacemaking 1919. London, 1933.
ODLOŽILIK (O.): Wyclif's Influence upon Central and Eastern Europe. (In *Slavonic Review*, vol. vii, No. 21, March 1929.)
PALACKÝ (František): Dějiny Národu Českého w Čechách a w Morawě dle původních pramenů wyprawuje. Prague, 1848–76.
—— Gedenkblätter. Prague, 1874.
—— Geschichte von Böhmen. Prague, 1836–67.
—— Oesterreichs Staatsidee. Prague, 1866.
—— Památník na oslavu stých narozenín Františka Palackého. Prague, 1898.
—— Spisy drobné. Prague, 1898–1903.
PEKAŘ (J.): Smysl Českých Dějin. Prague, 1936.
PEROUTKA (Ferdinand): Budování státu. Prague, 1933.
PFITZNER (J.): Sudetendeutsche Geschichte. Reichenberg, 1937.
PROKEŠ (Jaroslav): Histoire tchécoslovaque. Prague, 1927.
PLENER (Ernst von): Reden von 1873–1911. Ed. by Hans Patzauer. Stuttgart and Leipzig, 1911.
RÁDL (Emanuel): Der Kampf zwischen Tschechen und Deutschen. Reichenberg, 1928.
RASCHHOFER (Hermann), *ed.*: Die tschechoslowakischen Denkschriften für die Friedenskonferenz von Paris, 1919–20. Berlin, 1937.

RAUCHBERG (Heinrich): Der nationale Besitzstand in Böhmen. Leipzig, 1905.

REDLICH (Joseph): Das österreichische Staats- und Reichsproblem. Leipzig, 1920–6.

RENNER (Dr. Karl), under pseudonym R. Springer: Grundlagen- und Entwicklungsziele der öst-ungarischen Monarchie. Vienna and Leipzig, 1906.

SIEGHART (Rudolf): Die letzten Jahrzehnte einer Grossmacht. Berlin, 1932.

SPINA (Dr. Franz): Article in Deutsche Arbeit, 1910, vol. vii, pp. 433–9.

STRAUSS (E.): Die Entstehung der Tschechoslowakischen Republik. Prague, 1934.

TEMPERLEY (H. W. V.) ed.: A History of the Peace Conference of Paris. 6 vols. London, 1920–4.

WINTER (Max): Zwischen Iser und Neisse.

—— Die Blutsauger des Böhmerwaldes.

WOLF (Karl Hermann): Editorial and other articles, and reports of speeches, in Ostdeutsche Rundschau, 1890 to 1908.

WOSTRY (Professor): Das Kolonisationsproblem. 1922.

—— Article in Mitteilungen des Vereines für Geschichte der Deutschen in Böhmen, Heft 3–4, 1915.

—— 'Die Heimatländer der Sudetendeutschen zwischen Ost und West" (in Zeitschrift für sudetendeutsche Geschichte, May 1937).

WICHTL (Dr. Friedrich): Dr. Karl Kramarsch der Anstifter des Weltkrieges. Vienna, 1918.

ZAP (K. F.): Českomoravská Kronika. Prague, 1862. Revised version 1892.

ZEMMRICH (Dr. J.): Sprachgrenze und Deutschtum in Böhmen. Brunswick, 1902.

(b) Books dealing with the post-Peace Conference period

ČAKRT (J.): Rašin als Währungsreformer. Mährish Ostrau, 1926.

CHMELAŘ (Josef): The German Problem in Czechoslovakia. Prague, 1936.

CZECHOSLOVAK NATIONAL BANK: Ten Years of the Czechoslovak National Bank. By various authors. (German version: Zehn Jahre Čechoslovakische Nationalbank). Prague, 1937.

DEUTSCHER HAUPTVERBAND DER INDUSTRIE: Mitteilungen des Deutschen Hauptverbandes der Industrie in der Tschechoslowakischen Republik. Published weekly at Teplitz-Schönau.

—— Tätigkeitsberichte. Published annually.

—— Warum verträgt die Industrie der Tschechoslowakei keine Erhöhung der Erzeugungskosten? 1930.

Deutsches Wirtschaftsbuch für die Tschechoslowakei. Annual, 1933.

FISCHER (Josef), PATZAK (Václav), PERTH (Vincenc): Jejich Boj (Ihr Kampf). Prague, 1937.

FREISSLER (R.): Vom Zerfall Österreichs bis zum tschechoslowakischen Staate. Berlin, 1921.

Germany and Czechoslovakia. Articles by an active and responsible Czechoslovak Statesman (reprinted from the Prager Presse). ['Orbis' publication.] Prague, 1937.

HASSINGER (H.): Die Tschechoslowakei. Vienna, 1935.

HENLEIN (Konrad): Konrad Henlein spricht. Karlsbad, 1937.

JUNG (R.): Die Tschechen. Berlin, 1937.

KLEPETAŘ (Dr. H.): Seit 1918. Mährisch Ostrau, 1937.

KREBS (Hans): Kampf in Böhmen. Berlin, 1936.
LÖWY (Dr. Julius): Die Joachimsthaler Bergkrankheit. Extrait des Comptes-Rendus de la IVe Réunion de la Commission Internationale des Maladies professionnelles. (Lyon, 3–6 avril 1929.)
LÜPKE (Studienleiter Helmut): Lecture at the National Socialist History Teachers' Conference, Bremen, 1935.
MACARTNEY (C. A.): Hungary and her Successors. London, 1937.
MOULTON (Harold G.) and PASVOLSKY (L.): World War Debt Settlements. New York, 1926.
Nationality Policy in Czechoslovakia. ['Orbis' publication.] Prague, 1938. (Especially the Prime Minister's Speech of November 17th, 1937.)
NEČAS (Jaromir): Economic and Social Problems in German Bohemia (in Slavonic Review, vol. xv, No. 45, April 1937, pp. 599–611).
PETERS (Gustav): Der neue Herr von Böhmen. Berlin, 1927.
PFITZNER (J.): Sudetendeutsche Einheitsbewegung. Karlsbad, 1937.
RAŠIN (Alois): Finančí a hospodářská politika československá do Korce v. 1921. Prague, 1922.
RIST (Charles): La Déflation en pratique. Paris, 1927.
SETON-WATSON (R. W.): President Masaryk in Exile (in Slavonic Review, vol. iii, No. 9, March 1925).
SINGULE (Hans): Der Staat Masaryks. Berlin, 1937.
SOBOTA (Emil): Das tschechoslowakische Nationalitätenrecht. Prague, 1931.
SPANN (Othmar): Der wahre Staat. Leipzig, 1923.
—— Vom Wesen des Volkstums. Jena, 1931.
TEXTOR (L. E.): Land Reform in Czechoslovakia. London, 1923.
VEREIN DER WOLLINDUSTRIELLEN MÄHRENS IN BRÜNN: Berichte. Published anually at Brünn.
VONDRACEK (F. J.): Foreign Policy of Czechoslovakia, 1918–1935. New York, 1937.
Was ist der KB? Published by the Aufbruch Press. Prague, 1938.
WHEELER-BENNETT (John W.) and LATIMER (Hugh): Information on the Reparations Settlement. London, 1930.
WINKLER (Erwin): Die Tschechoslowakei im Spiegel der Statistik. Karlsbad, 1937.
WINTER (E. K.): Arbeiterschaft und Staat. Vienna, 1934.

INDEX